SAP PRESS e-books

Print or e-book, Kindle or iPad, workplace or airplane: Choose where and how to read your SAP PRESS books! You can now get all our titles as e-books, too:

- ▸ By download and online access
- ▸ For all popular devices
- ▸ And, of course, DRM-free

Convinced? Then go to **www.sap-press.com** and get your e-book today.

Implementing SAP® BW on SAP HANA®

Palekar, Patel, Shiralkar
SAP BW 7.4—Practical Guide (3rd Edition)
2015, approx. 860 pp., hardcover
ISBN 978-1-4932-1191-3

Jesper Christensen, Joe Darlak
SAP BW: Administration and Performance Optimization
2014, 652 pages, hardcover
ISBN 978-1-59229-853-2

Richard Bremer, Lars Breddemann
SAP HANA Administration
2014, 722 pages, hardcover
ISBN 978-1-59229-952-2

Haun, Hickman, Loden, Wells
Implementing SAP HANA (2nd Edition)
2015, 860 pages, hardcover
ISBN 978-1-4932-1176-0

Matthias Merz, Torben Hügens, Steve Blum

Implementing SAP® BW on SAP HANA®

Bonn • Boston

Editor Sarah Frazier
Acquisitions Editor Kelly Grace Weaver
German Edition Editor Kerstin Billen
Translation Lemoine International, Inc., Salt Lake City, UT
Copyeditor Miranda Martin
Cover Design Graham Geary
Photo Credit Shutterstock.com/1412488/© Neil Wigmore
Layout Design Vera Brauner
Production Kelly O'Callaghan
Typesetting SatzPro, Krefeld (Germany)
Printed and bound in the United States of America, on paper from sustainable sources

ISBN 978-1-4932-1003-9
© 2015 by Rheinwerk Publishing, Inc., Boston (MA)
1st edition 2015
1st German edition published 2015 by Rheinwerk Verlag, Bonn, Germany

Library of Congress Cataloging-in-Publication Data
Merz, Matthias, 1974-
Implementing SAP BW on SAP HANA / Matthias Merz, Torben Hugens, Steve Blum. --
1st edition.
pages cm
Includes index.
ISBN 978-1-4932-1003-9 (print : alk. paper) -- ISBN 1-4932-1003-3 (print : alk. paper) --
ISBN 978-1-4932-1004-6 (ebook) -- ISBN 978-1-4932-1005-3 (print and ebook : alk. paper)
1. SAP Business information warehouse. 2. SAP HANA (Electronic resource) 3. Data warehousing.
4. Database management. 5. Business enterprises--Data processing. I. Hugens, Torben. II. Title.
HF5548.4.B875M47 2015
005.74--dc23
2015004936

Contents at a Glance

Dear Reader,

SAP needs few words when it comes to SAP HANA: simplify, accelerate, innovate. The simplicity and speed offered by SAP HANA is changing the landscape of legacy SAP solutions like SAP BW, the classic SAP tool that you know and love.

It is with this in mind that we now present to you this first edition, *Implementing SAP BW on SAP HANA*. Focusing on the manual migration options for an existing SAP BW system and the new installation of an SAP BW system on SAP HANA, this book delivers full descriptions and step-by-step instructions on the pre- and post-migration steps involved during the transition. Guided by experts Dr. Matthias Merz, Dr. Torben Hügens, and Steve Blum, you'll get real-world experience and tips from their own migrations to lead you through your SAP BW on SAP HANA project. With this resource, you'll be able to not only successfully implement SAP BW on SAP HANA, but master administration, data modeling, and reporting tasks as well.

What did you think about *Implementing SAP BW on SAP HANA*? Your comments and suggestions are the most useful tools to help us make our books the best they can be. We encourage you to visit our website at *www.sap-press.com* and share your feedback.

Thank you for purchasing a book from SAP PRESS!

Sarah Frazier
Editor, SAP PRESS

Rheinwerk Publishing
Boston, MA

sarahf@rheinwerk-publishing.com
www.sap-press.com

Contents

Introduction

Enterprises have successfully deployed SAP Business Warehouse (SAP BW) to analyze their business data for many years. However, it is not possible to always implement today's requirements with regard to flexibility, real-time capability, and efficient handling of mass data in SAP BW. *SAP HANA* is a powerful technology that presents efficient solutions for central problems, such as low performance or long runtimes.

SAP BW on SAP HANA

SAP BW, powered by SAP HANA now combines the comprehensive functions of SAP BW with the major speed benefits of SAP HANA. SAP BW on SAP HANA enables you to implement reporting scenarios that have hardly been considered possible until now. For example, it allows high performance reporting based on very detailed mass data without having to compress the data in SAP BW in advance. However, some SAP customers still have reservations about this relatively young technology. Among other things, the focus is on the following questions: Can SAP BW on SAP HANA already be used in production? Is it possible that problems occur because SAP BW on SAP HANA is used? What are the new data modeling options? What are the changes in the administration? How is reporting affected? What must be considered when migrating from SAP BW to SAP BW on SAP HANA? What is the future of SAP BW reporting?

Goal of this Book

This book provides insight into SAP BW on SAP HANA and helps you answer your individual questions. For this purpose, it first explains the basic principles of SAP HANA and describes its technology and architecture. Based on this, it provides information on the steps that are necessary for the implementation and migration of an SAP BW system to SAP

BW on SAP HANA. It also shows how the usage of SAP BW on SAP HANA affects data modeling, administration, and reporting.

The current releases of SAP HANA and SAP BW provide interesting innovations, such as new InfoProvider types and the consumption of data models from SAP HANA. Most of these functions, however, can be used only if you migrate your SAP BW system to SAP HANA.

Target Audience

This book is aimed at implementation and process consultants, as well as SAP customers who plan to migrate to SAP BW on SAP HANA and want to acquire detailed knowledge about the various migration options and their implementation. IT and project leads can use this book to correctly categorize the specific elements of an SAP BW on SAP HANA migration. This book is also useful for decision makers who must speak in favor or against an implementation of SAP BW on SAP HANA and therefore should have the corresponding technical knowledge. Finally, this book makes the migration to SAP BW on SAP HANA easier for all SAP BW users and SAP BW administrators and introduces numerous innovations, particularly with regard to modeling and administration.

Structure of the Book

This book is divided into nine chapters. The following summarizes the individual chapters for better orientation:

Chapter 1, Introduction to SAP BW on SAP HANA, introduces SAP BW on SAP HANA and describes the differences between this and other scenarios. It addresses the latest challenges in the data warehouse area and discusses the reasons for an SAP BW on SAP HANA migration. In addition, it deals with the technical principles that lead to the high performance of SAP HANA.

Chapter 2 , SAP HANA Architecture, provides you with an overview of the structure and interaction of the software and hardware components that are delivered as the SAP HANA appliance. It conveys a fundamental understanding of database functionality in the background. Furthermore, it describes how hardware can be upgraded and provided in scale-up or scale-out scenarios. This chapter also explains the special features in the operating systems supported by SAP HANA.

Chapter 3, Migration and Implementation of SAP BW on SAP HANA, focuses on how you can set up your own SAP BW on SAP HANA system. Among other things, it introduces the different migration scenarios and explains how you implement a new installation of SAP BW on SAP HANA. In addition, the implementation of SAP BW on SAP HANA and the migration of an existing SAP BW system is also explained step-by-step. For this purpose, the technical requirements, the preparation steps, the actual migration tasks, and the postprocessing steps are outlined in detail.

Chapter 4, Migration Tips and Tricks, discusses how you can avoid pitfalls on your way to implement your own SAP BW on SAP HANA system. It provides numerous tips based on experiences from real-life projects and explains how you ideally implement a proof of concept and what you should consider when going live in production.

Chapter 5, Data Modeling in SAP BW on SAP HANA, describes the changes and innovations of SAP BW data modeling when you use SAP HANA. First, it details the optimized concepts, the new functions, and their effects on ABAP implementations. It then details the development and modeling environment in SAP HANA Studio, SAP HANA-optimized InfoCubes, the simplification of process chains, the changed data warehouse Layered Scalable Architecture (LSA++), the concept of non-active data, the consumption of SAP HANA data models in SAP BW, and the advantages of the Planning Application Kit.

Chapter 6, Administration with SAP HANA Studio, introduces the central administration tool: SAP HANA Studio. The most important tasks in SAP HANA Studio (administration, user and authorization management, monitoring, and database configuration) are illustrated with screenshots.

Chapter 7, Reporting with SAP BW on SAP HANA, addresses the latest reporting trends and the application cases that can be covered with the reporting process. In addition, this chapter describes the SAP Business-Objects BI platform with its various client tools and the access options to your SAP BW on SAP HANA system or to SAP HANA views.

Chapter 8, Nearline Storage for SAP BW on SAP HANA, discusses the archiving process for SAP BW data using Nearline Storage (NLS). It explains how the connection to your SAP BW on SAP HANA system works and how you can archive SAP BW data. In this context, you will learn how to access the archived data from reporting without having to re-import them to the SAP BW system.

Finally, **Chapter 9, Outlook: The Future of SAP BW Reporting**, tries to answer the question of the future of SAP BW reporting. This chapter introduces the reporting options of SAP HANA Live and explains which reasons speak for the usage of an SAP BW system or SAP BW on HANA system in the future.

Special Icons

To indicate important information and thus make it easier for you to use this book, the following icons are used in the text:

[+] Tip
Boxes marked with this icon give you recommendations in relation to settings or tips from professional experiences.

[!] Caution
Boxes with this icon contain important information about the topic under discussion. This icon also warns you about potential sources of error.

[Ex] Example
This icon indicates detailed examples.

[*] Excursion
This icon refers to additional, advanced information.

[⊕] Internet
This icon is used for boxes that contain recommendations for web sites that provide additional information.

Acknowledgments

Numerous colleagues and friends contributed to the success of this book by providing suggestions, criticism, tips, and recommendations. We would like to sincerely thank our colleagues from the Business Analytics and SAP Basis team at Camelot ITLab GmbH. We also want to thank the following colleagues who were always available for technical discussions about the various topics: Christian Folberth, Holger Stümges, Marcel Stefanski, Stephan Bucher, and Denis Reis. Many thanks go to our manager, Biagio Clemente, and to the Camelot management for always promoting and supporting our plan to write this book. In addition to colleagues and friends, numerous customers provided valuable contributions to discussions.

A very special thank you to all of you!

Finally, we want to thank our three editors at SAP PRESS, Janina Schweitzer, Kerstin Billen, and Sarah Frazier for their great cooperation and pleasant collaboration.

Dr. Matthias Merz
Head of Center of Excellence HANA,
Camelot ITLab GmbH
mam@camelot-itlab.com

Dr. Torben Hügens
Head of Competence Center Reporting and Performance Management,
Camelot ITLab GmbH
thue@camelot-itlab.com

Steve Blum
Consultant, Center of Excellence HANA,
Camelot ITLab GmbH
sblu@camelot-itlab.com

SAP BW on SAP HANA combines the speed benefits of SAP HANA with the comprehensive functions of SAP BW. In particular, reporting and loading processes are accelerated enormously. This chapter introduces you to the basic principles of this innovative product.

1   Introduction to SAP BW on SAP HANA

This chapter introduces you to SAP Business Warehouse (SAP BW) on SAP HANA. First, we'll describe the differences between this system and other SAP HANA scenarios. We'll then explain the differences between the side-by-side approach and the integrated approach. The topic of operational analytics and the latest challenges in the SAP BW environment are also discussed. Based on this, the chapter lists reasons for an SAP BW on SAP HANA migration and answers the question of why SAP HANA results in an acceleration in SAP BW.

1.1   Classifying SAP BW on SAP HANA Implementation Scenarios

SAP HANA is an SAP database technology that is designed for high performance. The SAP HANA's special characteristic is its in-memory approach: all data is stored in the main memory. Processing large data volumes is thus much more efficient than it is with traditional databases that first have to load the data from the secondary memory (hard disk) with significantly longer access times. However, SAP HANA is not only a mere in-memory solution. Traditional databases already have appropriate caching procedures that can also be used to access sections of the dataset very efficiently. SAP HANA provides a new function: the usage of the in-memory technology in combination with additional innovative

Basic principles of SAP HANA

software technologies. This includes column-based data handling, the usage of sophisticated compression and access procedures, and the partitioning of database tables. Section 1.4 discusses this in more detail.

SAP HANA appliance
In addition to these innovative software technologies, the usage of an appropriate hardware platform is one of the unique characteristics of SAP HANA. To synchronize the software and hardware components in an ideal way, you can operate SAP HANA exclusively on certified hardware platforms (*SAP HANA appliance*). This approach ensures that the hardware used has the required resources (main memory, cache size, number of processors, etc.) to process as many tasks as possible in parallel. Currently, only two operating systems (SUSE Linux Enterprise and Red Hat Enterprise Linux) can be used with SAP HANA, which allows for additional fine tuning among software, hardware, and operating system. So when you purchase an SAP HANA appliance, the hardware is delivered with optimized operating system parameters and pre-installed SAP HANA software.

Side-by-side approaches
When SAP HANA was announced in spring 2010 and implemented by selected customers in November of the same year, the first decision-makers already recognized that this technology could eliminate fundamental performance problems within the SAP system landscape. At that time, however, no one was ready to exchange a proven database solution of a very young SAP HANA technology. The risk seemed too high that the business could be affected by possibly immature software. Therefore, side-by-side approaches became popular: SAP HANA was used in parallel, or *side-by-side*, to already-existing systems. The concept of this approach is to continuously replicate the data from a rather slow database to the SAP HANA database and to use SAP HANA for a high performance data analysis. In general, one may distinguish between the data mart and the accelerator approach.

1.1.1 Side-by-Side and Integrated Approaches

Data mart approach
As Figure 1.1 (left side) illustrates with an SAP ERP system, the *data mart approach* continuously replicates the data from any database (often called *AnyDB* in literature) to the SAP HANA database. Specific analysis tools can then directly access this data using new interfaces, such as *SAP*

HANA views (see Section 1.1.2). This includes, for example, SAP BusinessObjects Analysis Edition for Office from the SAP BusinessObjects portfolio. With this approach, the data evaluation is extremely accelerated due to the powerful characteristics of SAP HANA. Chapter 7, Section 7.2.2 describes how you can directly access SAP HANA views using SAP Lumira and SAP BusinessObjects Design Studio and evaluate the data correspondingly.

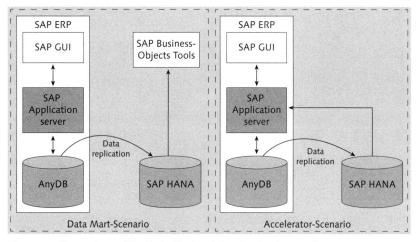

Figure 1.1 Comparison of the Data Mart and Accelerator Approach

On the right side of Figure 1.1, the *accelerator approach* is illustrated. **Accelerator** With this approach, the data is also continuously replicated from a data- **approach** base to the SAP HANA database. Here, however, the focus is not the evaluation of the data using specific tools. Instead, certain transactions in the SAP system are adapted in such a way that they use, not the primary database for read accesses, but SAP HANA. On one hand, this leads to a considerable acceleration of the tasks within SAP GUI. On the other hand, this approach doesn't make it necessary to replace an already-existing database. The disadvantage of this approach is that the data is kept in duplicate and must be updated continuously. Based on the accelerator approach, one of the first solutions marketed was *SAP HANA Profitability Analysis (CO-PA Accelerator)*. This accelerator increases the speed of the profitability analysis within the SAP ERP system in controlling, for example, when using Transaction KE30 (Execute Profitability Report).

<table>
<tr><td>

Integrated
approaches
</td><td>

Today, SAP HANA is a mature product, and instead of side-by-side approaches, *integrated approaches* establish themselves in real life. Compared to the data mart and accelerator approaches, the main difference is that SAP HANA does not run in parallel to an existing database solution; instead, SAP HANA is integrated into the available architecture and replaces the old database. Consequently, data must be neither replicated nor retained redundantly. Based on the example of an existing SAP ERP system, Figure 1.2 illustrates how SAP HANA replaces the old database when the integrated approach is used. Oracle, DB2, MSSQL, or any other database is replaced with SAP HANA within the scope of a technical migration. Due to the performance characteristics of SAP HANA, this exchange already leads to a considerable acceleration in the corresponding applications.
</td></tr>
</table>

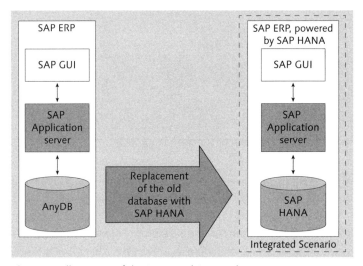

Figure 1.2 Illustration of the Integrated Approach

Code push-down

Also, if the exchange of a database with SAP HANA already leads to a high acceleration in the corresponding applications, the performance potential of this approach is not fully utilized yet. The integrated approaches unfold their potential only when the respective applications are optimized especially for SAP HANA. Up to now, the database layer has been responsible for only providing and storing data. According to the new programming paradigm (see Figure 1.3), mainly performance-intensive processes are moved to the SAP HANA level for acceleration. You can think of moving the programming logic to a lower level of the database. This is also referred to as *code push-down*. The application is then responsible for only the *orchestration* and solely triggers complex calculation operations. The actual calculation takes place directly in SAP HANA at a high speed. Eventually, the application simply consumes the results and forwards them to the presentation layer. The advantage here is that large data volumes do not have to be transferred from the database to the application layer (e.g., an SAP BW application server) first in order to perform calculations there, such as summations. Thanks to the in-memory technology, this or even more complex operations can be performed much more efficiently in the SAP HANA appliance. SAP can therefore successively adapt its own applications to SAP HANA for acceleration.

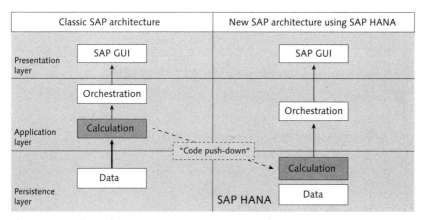

Figure 1.3 Traditional Against New Programming Paradigm

The code push-down principle, however, only works if you use SAP HANA as the primary database (see Section 1.4.5). If you use other databases, for example, to operate an SAP BW system, the application logic is not transferred to the database level. This also applies if the database that is used alternatively leverages an in-memory technology that is similar to SAP HANA. For compatibility reasons, however, it is not necessary to change to SAP HANA. All databases that have been used can still

Code push-down and other databases

be used as usual. Only some new functions (for example, new Info-Providers in SAP BW, such as Open ODS views; see Chapter 5, Section 5.1) or certain products (e.g., SAP Operational Process Intelligence; see *http://help.sap.com/hana-opint*) are exclusively provided for SAP HANA.

SAP BW on SAP HANA

SAP BW on SAP HANA is one of the integrative approaches that combines the functions of SAP BW with the speed benefits of SAP HANA. Thanks to the in-memory technology used in SAP HANA, all SAP BW data is directly stored in the main memory. In contrast to SAP Business Warehouse Accelerator (BWA; see Chapter 3, Section 3.1), reporting is thus accelerated for all SAP BW data. In combination with the other software innovations, such as column-based data handling, you no longer have to implement preaggregations for complex detailed analyses. The time effort for transformation and load processes in SAP BW is considerably reduced with SAP HANA because the code push-down principle is also applied for SAP BW. For example, the sometimes rather time-consuming process of activating data packages in DataStore Objects (DSO) for the generation of delta records was moved to SAP HANA. Chapter 5 describes further advantages and innovations of SAP BW on SAP HANA.

1.1.2 Operational Analytics

To evaluate operational enterprise data, SAP HANA provides new approaches. It allows for reporting and analyses even if you do not use an SAP BW system. For this purpose, the system creates individual data models (SAP HANA views) within SAP HANA that can be directly accessed by analysis tools. For example, if an SAP ERP system runs on SAP HANA, you can evaluate data directly in SAP Lumira or SAP Analysis Edition for Office using the corresponding SAP HANA views. In addition, if you use SAP BusinessObjects Design Studio, you can also create dashboards that are based directly on SAP HANA views. The advantage is that all data is available for evaluations in real time, and you no longer have to replicate the data to an SAP BW system in a time-consuming process. The disadvantage, however, is that the data from different SAP systems cannot be simply merged or harmonized within the scope of the analysis. For this purpose, an additional SAP BW system is necessary (see Chapter 9, Section 9.2). Nevertheless, it is beneficial to use operational analytics with SAP HANA in selected implementation scenarios.

One weakness first-introduced with operational analytics was that pre-defined data models and reports would go missing, forcing users to create them by hand. Today, default data models for the most important SAP HANA products are provided with *SAP HANA Live*. Analogous to SAP BW content, a virtual data model is now available that combines SAP HANA views in different layers. Depending on your license, you can also adapt or extend the SAP HANA views individually. Chapter 9, Section 9.1 provides more information on SAP HANA Live.

SAP HANA Live

You might ask yourself why data models are necessary in SAP HANA at all. To answer this question, let's take a deeper look. Unfortunately, the data that is supposed to be analyzed is rarely provided in only one table; e.g., master data and the corresponding texts are usually stored separately. If a report is supposed to list material texts in addition to specific material properties, then the various tables must be linked to each other. The relevant key figures are also often provided in specific tables. If you want the system to evaluate these key figures using different characteristics, the integration of further tables is required. The result is a complex structure of tables, also known as a *star schema*, in the SAP BW area. However, you can still link the various tables with each other using the corresponding SQL commands to allow for an evaluation. However, it is more efficient to use the already mentioned SAP HANA views because they are SAP HANA modules (e.g., *OLAP Engine*) optimized to perform calculations at a high speed to retrieve data considerably faster. Chapter 2, Section 2.3.2 provides more information on this.

SAP HANA data models

SAP HANA views are modeled in SAP HANA Studio. This tool is based on Eclipse (see *https://www.eclipse.org*) and is the central development and administration tool. SAP HANA Studio supports users with a graphical modeling view for the creation of SAP HANA views. Like SAP BW objects, the created SAP HANA views must still be activated or deployed at the end of the process. Afterward, they are available in various analysis tools, such as SAP Lumira, SAP Analysis Edition for Office, or SAP BusinessObjects Design Studio. The development and modeling environment of SAP HANA Studio is detailed in Chapter 5, Section 5.2. Chapter 6 discusses the administration options of the SAP HANA database.

SAP HANA Studio

1.2   Current Challenges for SAP BW

After giving you an overview of SAP HANA, this section describes which current challenges in the SAP BW environment convince more and more enterprises to use SAP BW on SAP HANA. This section first analyzes how the general conditions have changed, and then it illustrates the disadvantages of relational databases from the technical perspective. Because of these disadvantages, in the past, data was often kept in various systems, each of which were optimized for a certain purpose. A distributed and redundant data concept, however, poses new business challenges to enterprises. These challenges are described at the end of this section.

1.2.1   Changing Environment

Since the introduction of SAP BW in 1997, the environment of this product has changed significantly. The following three essential aspects are particularly important in this context and are discussed in detail:

▸ Accelerated data growth

▸ Real-time data access

▸ Simple and fast operation

Accelerated data growth

According to IDC studies, the worldwide data volume is doubling about every two years (see *http://www.emc.com/leadership/programs/digitaluniverse.htm*). This trend can also be applied to enterprise data. In this case, SAP assumes that the data volume is doubling every 18 months on average.[1] As the central data warehouse solution, SAP BW in particular is affected. If an appropriate archiving solution is not used, the number of data records of the SAP BW InfoProviders will increase exponentially. This growth usually accelerates continuously because the status of reporting increases in general so that data from many new application areas and regions are transferred to the SAP BW system. This can lead to long response times when analyses are performed or long load times when data is further updated in SAP BW. Here, the often limited scal-

---

1   *http://www.vnsgmagazine.nl/ExecutiveDiner/SAP_BSI_HansKroes.pdf*

ability of the existing IT infrastructure and database solution plays an important role.

However, it will be increasingly important to evaluate data in real time. Some years ago, it was sufficient to consolidate data once a week or once a month and to generate the reports during night processing. Today, the requirements have changed considerably. It is increasingly important to counteract undesirable developments in a targeted manner and at an early stage. In this context, access to real-time data is an important prerequisite. And, due to the introduction of smartphones, the latest key figures must now be available via mobile ad hoc accesses.

Real-time data access

In other applications, SAP BW end users see every day that search processes in giant datasets—for example, Google search processes—take only a few moments. At the same time, various software providers, such as Apple, prove that modern graphical user interfaces can be designed with simple and intuitive views. SAP has already recognized the significance of these aspects some years ago. In 2011, Jim-Hagemann Snabe, one of the two chairmen of SAP SE until 2014, put it aptly when he said that SAP must become "Apple simple and Google fast." SAP HANA contributes to this goal significantly.

Simple and fast operation

1.2.2 Disadvantages of Relational Databases

One of the main tasks of an SAP BW system is the timely provision of data with the goal of being able to evaluate and analyze it efficiently. From the technical perspective, this requires efficient data handling with optimized read operations. In reality, relational databases are often used for this purpose. The data is stored in various, usually row-based tables. In a relational database, the data can be stored largely free of redundancies if certain normalizing rules are considered when modeling data (*http://en.wikipedia.org/wiki/Database_normalization*).

Relational databases

Especially in cases when an SAP BW system is used, the focus is not on redundance-free data management, but on high speed read accesses. The data is stored internally in a denormalized *star schema* or *extended schema* in which one fact table (for key figures) and several dimension tables (for characteristics) form a star-like structure. This layout allows for

Complex and time-consuming load process

a high-performance and dimension-independent evaluation of key figures. Unfortunately, this also requires that the data be retained in various
tables and linked to the corresponding primary and foreign keys. In this
case, a specific logic that splits the data appropriately when it is transferred to the database and stores it in the tables provided for this purpose
is necessary. In SAP BW, the load process (Extract, Transform, Load [
ETL]) controls this, which requires additional time.

Time-consuming
indexing

To access the respective data records efficiently, relational databases use
database indexes. This index structure accelerates the search process and
sorting by certain attributes in the database. But, the creation of these
kinds of indexes is time-consuming. Furthermore, you must update the
index structure after inserting a new data record. The SAP BW system
also uses indexes internally for performance optimization. For example,
an InfoCube may have an index in order to accelerate read accesses.
When new data records are imported to the InfoCube, this index must
also be updated; however, particularly in case of large data amounts, this
may delay the load process. It is faster to delete the index before triggering the load process and then create it anew after completion of the load
process. This is a common procedure for the creation of SAP BW process
chains.

Analytical
operations

In SAP BW, the data analyses often use analytical operations, such as *slic-
ing* (filter restriction using one dimension), *dicing* (filter restriction using
several dimensions), or *drill down* (drilling aggregations down to a
detailed level). These operations are usually directly executed in the SAP
BW system. To perform the necessary calculations, the system must first
retrieve the data from the database. From there, large data amounts are
transferred between the database and the SAP BW application server,
even if only a few data records are shown to the user at the end. It would
be more efficient to already perform this kind of operation at the database level. This could considerably reduce the amount of data transferred and even accelerate the execution of the operations. In addition
to analytical operations, the SAP BW system implements other performance-intensive process steps. These include, for example, the activation of DSO data packages and the execution of planning functions
when the BW Integrated Planning (BW-IP) is used. If you use SAP BW on

SAP HANA, analytical functions and numerous performance-intensive steps are directly executed in SAP HANA, which considerably accelerates these processes (see Section 1.4.5).

So that you can efficiently evaluate large data amounts with relational databases, *materialized views* are provided. Here, the comprehensive initial data is stored persistently and in a compressed way in an additional table. SAP BW works with this concept for the creation of *aggregates* for InfoCubes. The advantage is that the aggregation does not have to be performed at runtime so that the data can be evaluated more quickly. This makes sense particularly if several analysis scenarios are based on the same datasets. The disadvantage of this approach is that the dataset of the materialized views is outdated when the initial data is changed, so data inconsistencies may occur. In this case, you must update the materialized views, which again requires some time. Furthermore, performance problems can occur if the drilldown was changed during the analysis in such a way that the aggregation level changes. You can then no longer use the data of the aggregate and must access the InfoCube directly. If you use SAP BW on SAP HANA, you do not have to provide materialized views.

Materialized views

1.2.3 Distributed Data Retention

Due to the various requirements, various IT systems that partly leverage the same data are often used. Depending on the purpose, these systems are optimized for a certain application case. A parallel operation of operational transactional systems (*OLTP*, Online Transactional Processing) and decision-making systems for the execution of complex data analyses (*OLAP*, Online Analytical Processing) is a common practice. OLTP systems, such as SAP ERP, are generally used for traditional business applications and require high-performance write and update processes. The data amount that is processed in a transaction step is usually small, and the evaluation options are often limited. Here, the data is created mainly in normalized database tables. In contrast, OLAP systems, such as SAP BW, are designed to process various read queries, sometimes with very large data volumes. Write operations take place only within the scope of periodic data updates. To support this scenario, the data is usually stored

OLTP vs. OLAP

in the denormalized *star schema* or *extended star schema*, as described in Section 1.2.2.

OLAP cache and SAP BWA

In reality, further systems are used in addition to OLTP and OLAP systems. This may be the case, for example, when OLAP systems reach their limits due to large datasets or complex evaluations. Certain analysis tasks need more execution time, which makes it difficult to work efficiently. Modern OLAP systems, such as SAP BW, thus have a buffer (*OLAP cache*). Here, calculated results are stored for some time and directly used for acceleration, if required.

However, every new drilldown whose interim result has not been provided in the cache leads to longer execution times. To avoid this problem, there is another solution for SAP BW: *Business Warehouse Accelerator* (BWA). This is an additional hardware solution that, on the basis of an in-memory technology, provides selected data for a particularly fast evaluation. The execution time of complex analyses can therefore be reduced considerably. However, this solution also has a critical disadvantage: two different systems are used simultaneously for data retention, and the data must be synchronized between them correspondingly. Otherwise, evaluation inconsistencies may occur if certain reports use the BWA for performance optimization and others do not. If you use SAP BW on SAP HANA, you no longer need BWA for acceleration; all data is then stored in SAP HANA and thus already provided in the main memory, so all evaluations are immediately accelerated, and redundant data retention is omitted. Consequently, a lot of enterprises decide to use an SAP BW on SAP HANA system. The next section deals with other reasons for migration.

1.3 Reasons for Migrating an SAP BW System to SAP HANA

Let's turn our attention to the reasons for an SAP BW on SAP HANA migration. On one hand, you have the restrictions of SAP BW, but on the other hand, you have the advantages of using SAP BW on SAP HANA.

1.3.1   SAP BW Restrictions

Based on your daily work with SAP BW, you may know some restrictions that the SAP BW system has, and have wished, at least once, for a technology to avoid them. The following are some key restrictions for SAP BW:

- Low performance and long waiting times in reporting
- Considerable time and effort for transformation and load processes
- Redundant data retention and inflexible data modeling
- High administration effort for the SAP BW system and the IT infrastructure

One of the major restrictions of SAP BW is the partially low performance during the execution of reports and analyses. Depending on the amount and complexity of the data, the processing of individual analysis steps in the SAP BW system may take several minutes and thus slow down the processes in the various business departments significantly. In one year, this can amount to numerous hours that employees have to wait. The possible side effects of this include a reduced quality of work.

Low performance and long waiting times

Transformation and load processes also require a lot of time in SAP BW. Consequently, the corresponding processes run at night or on the weekend. This should ensure that the system resources are mainly available for analyses and are not affected by running background processes. The time frames that are available for the transformation and load processes become increasingly smaller: due to the international environment, it is no longer sufficient when a global SAP BW system is available for reporting only between 6 a.m. and 8 p.m. EST. Instead, it becomes more and more necessary to extend these time frames to ensure access from other countries and time zones. If the data from more regions and countries is centrally merged in SAP BW, the data volume also increases. Consequently, it becomes harder to solve this conflict with the existing IT infrastructure.

Transformation and load processes

Section 1.2.3 already described redundant data retention and its consequences for SAP BW. This section addresses the various layers within the SAP BW system (see Chapter 5, Section 5.5). Often, the SAP BW

Data retention and data modeling

system transfers mainly unchanged data from a DSO in the *data propagation layer* to an InfoCube in the *reporting layer* to accelerate the reporting process. Redundant retention of identical data, however, leads to considerably long load times and requires additional memory capacities in the database. If you use SAP BW on SAP HANA, you do not necessarily have to use InfoCubes to accelerate reporting. Even worse, it can be a disadvantage to use InfoCubes in SAP BW without SAP HANA; for example, for data modeling or remodeling. If data has already been imported to an InfoCube, its structures, such as the dimensions, cannot be changed directly because an InfoCube in the database is mapped using numerous tables according to the star schema or extended star schema (see Section 1.2.2). The *remodeling toolbox* (Transaction RSMRT) enables you to adapt the InfoCubes without having to empty data content first. But, this is more complex because you previously have to define the appropriate remodeling rules and schedule a change run later on. For some adaptations, it may even be necessary to edit the InfoCube directly. In this case, the InfoCube data must be deleted first to implement the necessary modifications. Then, the data is re-imported to the InfoCube, and the index is created anew. Both approaches are relatively time consuming and prone to errors in real life. This looks different for SAP BW on SAP HANA. Here, direct remodeling is possible, for example, moving an InfoObject to other dimensions. You then do not have to use specific tools or empty the InfoCube first.

Administration effort

If you use SAP BW without SAP HANA, the administration effort for the SAP BW system, the primary database, and the often-used BWA is quite high. You require several tools for the administration of SAP BW, database, and BWA to, for example, create backups. The administrators must be familiar with all of these tools and trained correspondingly. Additionally, the capacity of the BWA is usually limited. If you want to replicate the data of a new InfoCube to the BWA (*indexing*) and the existing main memory is not sufficient, a manual intervention is required. Loading data in InfoCubes for mere performance reasons can result in significant costs and administration efforts. The duplicate data retention requires additional system resources, and the administrators might have to extend the file system more often—that is, configure hard disks or memory solutions and, if necessary, change the database administration. Furthermore, backups require a larger memory medium and take longer. If you use SAP BW on SAP HANA, you no longer require the BWA, and the administration effort is reduced considerably. This section discusses this in greater detail later on. Because aggregates, indexes, and database statistics are no longer necessary, the administration is easier (see Chapter 5, Section 5.4). For example, the execution of process chains no longer leads to errors with regard to InfoCube indexing. Because the mentioned process steps are omitted and the speed increases significantly with SAP BW on SAP HANA, administrators will be more flexible in the future with regard to the scheduling of load processes at night.

1.3.2 Advantages of SAP BW on SAP HANA

Now that we've discussed the essential restrictions in SAP BW, this section deals with the advantages resulting from the use of SAP BW on SAP HANA. Figure 1.4 illustrates the most central aspects.

Certainly, the most important advantage of SAP BW on SAP HANA is the high speed with which analyses and reports can be performed. This results from the in-memory technology, the numerous software-related innovations, and the optimized hardware (see Section 1.4). For example, in several projects, SAP BW reports were reported as being more than 30 times faster. The execution duration of a report could also be reduced from one minute to less than two seconds, which allows for a considerably more frequent and interactive usage of the reports in SAP BW. This enables you to optimize existing business processes or design completely new process flows. SAP sometimes refers to Yodobashi, a Japanese electronics goods retailer. At this enterprise, the introduction of SAP HANA reduced the calculation of incentive payments for customers from three days to two seconds (see *http://www.news-sap.com/hana-teched-2011-plattner-in-memory*). Yodobashi can now inform its customers anytime about the current value of their credit memos collected in the incentive program, as well as about the new status of the bonus credits after a purchase. SAP BW on SAP HANA therefore not only significantly accelerates reporting, but also allows for the implementation of completely new business processes that would have otherwise been impossible to carry out.

Performance increase for reporting

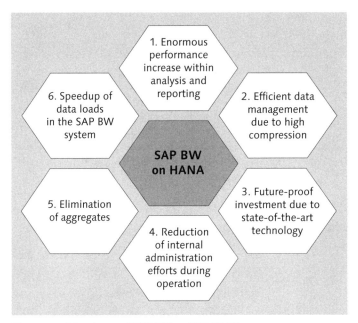

Figure 1.4 Advantages of SAP BW on SAP HANA

Efficient data
retention

In addition to an increase in performance, SAP HANA also makes data retention processes more efficient. Due to the column-based data storage, the memory size of the database is reduced because specific and powerful compression methods are used. Column-based data handling is particularly efficient for SAP BW data because aggregates are often formed on the basis of numerous rows, but only a few columns (see Section 1.4.2). Faster access to data and other performance characteristics of SAP HANA make it possible that SAP BW data no longer has to be provided in denormalized tables. A high reporting performance for SAP BW on SAP HANA is always guaranteed, irrespective of whether the data is provided in a flat DSO table or in an InfoCube. Correspondingly, if you use SAP BW on SAP HANA, you can usually omit InfoCubes (see Chapter 5, Section 5.1) and redundant data retention in SAP BW, such as the storage of data in a DSO and in an InfoCube, in order to accelerate reporting. If you have created data flows that enrich or modify data on its way to the InfoCube, these InfoCubes are still required after a migration to SAP BW on SAP HANA. However, you can convert them into SAP

HANA-optimized InfoCubes (see Chapter 5, Section 5.3), which accelerates the reporting performance considerably and allows for a direct remodeling of InfoCubes.

In the future, SAP HANA will be the basis for further SAP products, and existing products will be increasingly optimized for SAP HANA. It is thus a future-proof solution with a high level of protection on investment. It may be worthwhile to become familiar with this state-of-the-art technology today. Furthermore, there are already products that are exclusively available for SAP HANA, such as Operational Process Intelligence (see *http://help.sap.com/hana-opint*). If it becomes necessary to use these kinds of products in the future, it pays off if you are already acquainted with the technology. SAP BW on SAP HANA is the ideal initial scenario because it was one of the first SAP HANA solutions on the market. The product now is rather mature, so it can be used in production without special risks.

State-of-the-art technology

As already mentioned, you no longer need the BWA for SAP BW on SAP HANA, so the maintenance and monitoring effort for this component is omitted. Administrators must still be introduced to the SAP HANA-specific tools once (see Chapter 6), but a duplicate administration of the two separate memory technologies is no longer necessary. Because the data retention is more efficient and materialized views are no longer required in SAP BW on SAP HANA, the administration effort is further reduced, for example, for the generation of database statistics, the deletion or creation of indexes, or the maintenance of aggregates.

Reduced administration effort

Until now, it was nearly impossible in SAP BW to efficiently perform complex analyses with a large set of detailed data, so the data was often aggregated in the SAP BW data flow, for example, to aggregate data from a daily basis to a monthly basis. This made it possible to execute the respective evaluations in a reasonable time frame because it reduced the required data volume. If you use SAP BW on SAP HANA, you no longer have to aggregate data. Thanks to the efficient data retention, you can create reports in SAP BW on SAP HANA directly on the basis of detailed data (document level). This results in a higher level of detail in reporting and still allows for high-performance evaluations of non-aggregated mass data.

Elimination of aggregations

Accelerated load
processes

Finally, SAP BW on SAP HANA also significantly accelerates the load processes when data is further updated in SAP BW. The code push-down (see Section 1.4.5) moves performance-intensive process steps directly to SAP HANA for efficient processing. In SAP BW, for example, this is the activation of DSO data packages. Because the denormalized *star schema* or *extended star schema* is not used and the data is stored directly in the main memory, the load processes in SAP BW are accelerated. In real life, it has been proven that an SAP BW on SAP HANA migration can also reduce the execution times of the process chains considerably. In one case, for example, the initial execution of a rather comprehensive process chain could be reduced from more than 10 hours to about six hours. For this purpose, the system was migrated to SAP BW on SAP HANA, and the InfoCubes were converted to SAP HANA-optimized InfoCubes (see Chapter 5, Section 5.3). Additional optimizations, such as the use of DSO instead of InfoCubes for reporting, allow for further significant accelerations of the load processes.

Summary

This section discussed the numerous reasons for an SAP BW on SAP HANA migration, made prominent by the current restrictions in SAP BW and the various advantages associated with the use of SAP BW on SAP HANA. In addition to a considerable increase in performance for analysis and reporting, topics such as protection of investment, efficient data retention, reduced administration effort, and acceleration of the load processes play an important role. The advantages of SAP BW on SAP HANA are generally based on the software and hardware innovations of SAP HANA, which are discussed in the following section.

1.4 Basic Technical Principles

Databases, the relational database model, and SQL as the query language date from the 1970s and are based on IBM's R database system. All databases that are largely used today (DB2, Oracle, Microsoft SQL Server, and so on) have the same basic principles. Since the early days of standard software and SAP, the amount of data to be stored in enterprises and the computing power of the processors have increased significantly.

The performance of hard disks has fallen far behind, and even today's SSD hard disks cannot catch up with this performance lead. The system bottleneck and the runtime of database queries consequently depend on the transmission speed between the hard disks and the main memory.

Databases aim to provide data promptly to allow for making business decisions on the basis of this data. The hard disk speed has already not met these latest requirements for a long time. To compensate, only some data has been copied in the form of caches to the main memory, so the access speed is increased considerably for a small amount of data. SAP HANA goes one step further and leverages the in-memory technology. This means that the entire database is provided in the main memory. However, the innovations of SAP HANA should not only be limited to the in-memory aspect. Innovations such as column-based data retention, the insert-only procedure, the partitioning of tables, and the pushdown principle of the SAP systems also contribute to the performance of SAP HANA.

Database speed

The result is a significant speed benefit compared with other databases, which makes previously impossible scenarios feasible for the first time. The technology aims to adapt the runtimes of data analyses to the speed of today's internet search engines in order to also change the usage pattern for standard software.

1.4.1   In-Memory Technology

The concept of in-memory databases is not new. For example, with TM1 (today: Cognos TM1), IBM's portfolio has provided a database that performs processes in the main memory since 1984. At that time, the idea of replacing slow hard disks with memory as the storage medium for data of a database seemed appealing.

Past concepts

In TM1, the amount of data to be processed was limited by the high main memory requirements. The past hardware did not allow for mass data processing in the main memory, so TM1 could not establish itself against other databases. However, SAP took up the idea again and started to develop in-memory databases with TREX in the 1990s, when the price for main memory was already considerably lower. First, TREX served as a search and indexing service, and later on, as the basis for BW

TREX

Accelerator (BWA), which was published as an enhancement of the SAP NetWeaver system in 2005. It does not replace the main database of the SAP BW system but quickly provides selected InfoCubes from the main memory for it.

SAP HANA   Studies conducted under the lead of Hasso Plattner at the Hasso Plattner Institute of the University of Potsdam (HPI) aimed to implement analytical and transactional operations (OLTP and OLAP) in one system on the basis of the same in-memory–based database. Furthermore, the response time was supposed to be reduced considerably to enable completely new application scenarios. This vision was first implemented with the SanssouciDB database and in the SAP HANA product at the Hasso Plattner Institute. Standard business applications, such as SAP CRM or even SAP ERP, can now be operated on a completely main memory–based database. It is provided as an SAP HANA platform that has various interfaces to SAP or external systems in addition to the database. The platform also contains a tool that enables you to directly access the database and its administration: SAP HANA Studio. Furthermore, you can develop native applications on the database, and it provides function libraries for analytical processes, such as forecasts.

To ensure an appropriate hardware performance, SAP HANA is provided only in a package with certified hardware (SAP HANA appliance). Chapter 2, Section 2.1 discusses the hardware in more detail.

Processor and RAM   The ratio between the amount of main memory and the number of processor cores is of particular importance because every main memory area is processed by an assigned processor. A single SAP HANA server (single node) can currently reach a size of up to 4TB main memory and 80 processor cores. By combining several systems, you can create even larger databases (multi node). If these large servers are combined to a multi-node system (*scale-out approach*), huge SAP HANA systems are feasible. In various experiments, system sizes of up to 100TB main memory were checked for performance, so SAP HANA can also be used for extremely large systems.

This size of main memory leads to new hardware problems, which must be solved in collaboration with hardware providers and SAP. Chapter 2, Section 2.1.5 discusses this in more detail.

1.4.2 Column-Based Data Retention and Compression

Despite the price decline over the decades, main memory is still an expensive resource. The data to be stored must thus be compressed in an in-memory database as efficiently as possible. For this purpose, SAP HANA uses a combination of various technologies.

A characteristic feature of SAP HANA is the column-based storage of the most tables. Because data in a column has the same data type and includes similar data (for example, gender, nationality, date), the data compression rate is considerably higher than in the usual row-based databases.

A common technology is *dictionary encoding*. Here, every value that occurs in a column is entered in a dictionary and assigned to an ID, respectively. If the same value occurs several times in the column, memory space is saved by storing only its ID, and not the raw data (see Figure 1.5).

Compression

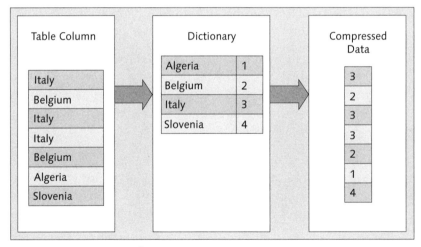

Figure 1.5 Dictionary Encoding

You can use more of the potential of the column-based storage by clustering successive IDs with the same value (*cluster encoding*). For this purpose, you divide the table with IDs into several clusters of the same size. If the ID within such a cluster always has the same value, it is stored only once. Depending on the size of the selected cluster and the structure of

37

the data, you can merge numerous entries of the column. This particularly applies to sorted columns. Figure 1.6 illustrates this using an example with cluster size 3.

Figure 1.6 Cluster Encoding

A similar compression technology does not use clusters but additionally stores the number of successive same values: *run length encoding*.

The compression methods mentioned are only examples of numerous possible measures that enable the most efficient compression. The methods used depend, among other things, on the data type of the column.

Compression rate   The database's compression rates that can be achieved depends largely on its structure and content. SAP says that they have already achieved compression rates of more than 20, so for 100GB of user data, less than 5GB of main memory would be required. Our empirical values show that a ratio of 5:1 to 7:1 is common.

Database tables of SAP systems may contain up to 150 columns. If you want the system to calculate the total of one column—for example, all sales of the last year—the system first has to search every single row in a row-based database for the corresponding column. In column-based databases, the relevant figures are stored successively, anyway, and can thus be read and aggregated considerably faster. In analytical systems, these queries are primary queries, which means that they usually benefit significantly from column-based systems.

Row-based storage   Regardless, SAP HANA can also work with row-based storage of data,
in SAP HANA   which is often used by system tables, such as in statistics.

1.4.3 Insert-Only Procedure

The read and write processes in column-based tables are performed by an SAP HANA component, the *column store*. It consists of the *main storage* and the *delta storage*. In column-oriented tables, write processes are much more complex than in row-based tables. To add a data record in row-based tables, the system must perform a single contiguous write operation because the rows are stored without interruption. If the table is sorted, the system has to sort it again at the end. In a column-based table, in contrast, the data record cannot be stored at once. The system must perform a memory operation for each column, and each column must be sorted again because a different sorting of a column affects the data order in the other columns. The advantage of column-based data retention, however, is the fast data access, particularly to individual columns. For this reason, these tables are also referred to as read-optimized tables.

To avoid this effort, a second row-based, unsorted table is used for new data records. This is the delta storage.

Delta storage

Write operations are performed in this delta storage first. Because the delta storage is in the main memory, all changes to it are stored in a delta log. If data is read, this process takes place in the main storage and in the delta storage. A *delta merge* is performed at regular intervals. Here, the data is transferred from the delta storage to the main storage. If necessary, the system then executes sorting and compression algorithms. The delta logs are emptied during this process. Figure 1.7 illustrates this process.

Delta merge

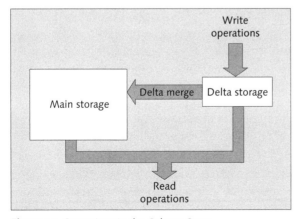

Figure 1.7 Operations in the Column Store

Because the delta merge transfers several changes to the main storage at the same time, the performance bottleneck has less impact than if each change were transferred individually. This compensates for the disadvantages of column-based databases.

1.4.4 Partitioning

Partitioning a database means having the system automatically subdivide tables and their content into several small tables. In general, you distinguish between horizontal and vertical partitioning, that is, a division according to column or row (see Figure 1.8). The users of the database still view a large, contiguous table. SAP HANA leverages this function for column-based tables only. All partitioning methods that are available in SAP HANA are horizontal partitionings.

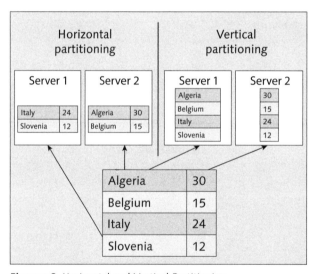

Figure 1.8 Horizontal and Vertical Partitioning

Advantages SAP HANA uses partitioning to avoid various restrictions. For example, only two billion entries can be stored for each table. With partitioning, the entries are distributed across the number of partitions, and a table of more than two billion entries exists only for the database users. The performance of the table access also increases because various operations are performed in parallel without impacting each other. In addition, the delta merges explained in Section 1.4.3 are accelerated because only parts of the table, and not the entire table, must be reorganized.

You obtain the most benefits, however, if you use an SAP HANA cluster in which partitioned tables are distributed across several physical servers. This way, the workload is distributed efficiently across the servers involved.

SAP HANA can work with various partitioning types. They differ by the way in which data records are transferred to particular partitions.

Partitioning types

To distribute the data as equally as possible, you should use the *hash partitioning* method. Here, the system calculates a hash based on one or several columns of the table's primary key. This hash is then used to determine to which partition the corresponding data record is moved, as follows:

▸ **Round-robin partitioning**
Round-robin partitioning distributes data records across all partitions according to their sequence.

▸ **Range partitioning**
With range partitioning, the data records are distributed based on the column of the primary key. This method enables you to define partitions for individual values or value ranges.

▸ **Multi-level partitioning**
You can also combine several partitioning algorithms to allow for an individual distribution of the data. This method is called multi-level partitioning.

The SAP system usually defines for itself how it partitions its tables, but you can also partition the tables manually. Hash partitioning is ideal for tables whose content you don't know, while range partitioning should be used for a distribution on the basis of periods.

1.4.5 Push-Down Principle

The defined goal of SAP HANA is to allow as many calculations as possible to be directly performed in the database, and not by the application system. SAP wants to utilize the fact that the data in SAP HANA is already provided in the main memory for processing and that sufficient processor resources are available. To perform complex calculations at the database level, more and more parts of the application system logic are moved to the database. This is referred to as the *push-down principle* (see Figure 1.3). During the execution, the system checks at specific places whether an SAP HANA database is operated in the minimum required version. If this is the case, a modified program logic is executed that transfers calculations using specific SQL queries or database procedures to the database.

Push-down in SAP BW Because SAP BW has supported SAP HANA as the primary database for several years, the push-down principle is used often. For example, a new Data Transfer Process (DTP) execution module, *SAP HANA Execution*, is available since SAP BW 7.4 SPS 05. Figure 1.9 illustrates the difference between a DTP based on SAP BW on SAP HANA (on the right-hand side) and a DTP in an SAP BW system on another database (on the left-hand side).

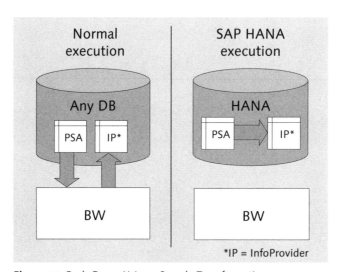

Figure 1.9 Push-Down Using a Sample Transformation

In the SAP HANA execution DTP mode, all calculations of the corresponding transformation are performed within SAP HANA, as well as the transfer from the source tables to the target tables. This concept is particularly useful for transformations because both the source table and the target table are located in the SAP HANA database.

In the database, *Application Function Libraries (AFL)* are used for this purpose. In these libraries, SAP combines selected application functions. These are procedures that are written in C++ and can directly access the SAP HANA resources. Their close connection to the programming code ensures that the performance is higher than that of database procedures that were defined in SQLScript or R.

Application Function Libraries

Currently, there are two Application Function Libraries: *Business Function Library* (BFL), which encapsulates business functions, and *Predictive Analysis Library* (PAL) for forecasts. Their functions are used in SAP products that are based on SAP HANA but can also be utilized in custom procedures or programs. Their usage, however, is not automatically covered by every SAP HANA license.

Since SAP BW 7.4 SPS 05, SAP BW on SAP HANA provides the PAL functions in the new SAP HANA Analysis Processes, for example. They allow for the processing of data using the default functions available in the PAL. You can then store and further use the results in a database table or DSO InfoProvider, for example. This enables SAP BW users to create processes themselves that benefit from the performance of the push-down principle.

1.5   Summary

The usage of SAP HANA has changed over the years: first, the focus was on the implementation of side-by-side approaches to accelerate selected evaluations (data mart approach) or applications (accelerator approach). Today, SAP HANA is implemented almost exclusively on the basis of integrated approaches. The existing database, e.g., in an SAP BW system, is replaced by the SAP HANA database. The SAP BW system then benefits from the unique performance characteristics of the SAP HANA database, which leads to a significant acceleration of reporting and load processes.

Usage of SAP HANA over the course of time

SAP Business Suite,
powered by
SAP HANA Because the usage of SAP HANA as a database for SAP BW systems today achieves excellent results, SAP now wants to focus on the development and usage of SAP HANA for further products, such as SAP Business Suite. *SAP Business Suite, powered by SAP HANA* also transfers and correspondingly accelerates performance-intensive processes to the database using a code push-down. However, it is not yet possible to operate SAP BW and SAP Business Suite on a shared SAP HANA database. SAP still sticks to the vision of Hasso Plattner to develop SAP HANA to a database for the simultaneous operation of OLAP and OLTP applications, but it will surely take some years until this goal is achieved. In the meantime, data must still be transferred between OLTP and OLAP systems. This will change only if both systems can access the same tables. SAP has already taken the first steps into this direction. For example, Operational Data Processing (ODP; see Chapter 5, Section 5.1.1) already enables the data from the source systems to no longer have to be stored in the Persistent Staging Area (PSA). Instead, the required data can be called directly from the source system for further processing in SAP BW. If you also use Open ODS views, redundant data retention in SAP BW can be completely omitted (see Chapter 5, Section 5.1.2).

SAP BW on HANA SAP BW on SAP HANA's success is based on the existing restrictions in SAP BW and the numerous advantages of SAP BW on SAP HANA to overcome these restrictions. The challenges in SAP BW include the criticized performance and long waiting times in reporting. SAP BW on SAP HANA is convincing due to a high performance, which is based on the in-memory approach and column-based data handling. The fact that numerous customers have already experience in the usage of the in-memory technology due to the integration with BWA also contributes to the acceptance of SAP BW on SAP HANA. Overall, SAP BW on SAP HANA has reached a level of maturity that justifies an explicit recommendation of its usage. You can benefit from the additional functions that are available exclusively in the SAP BW on SAP HANA scenario and reduce the complexity of your SAP BW system significantly. Today, SAP BW users have the following complaints:

▶ It takes too long until new scenarios are implemented in SAP BW.

▶ The night processing is too short to load the data.

▶ The execution time of some reports is too long.

SAP BW on SAP HANA has overcome these obstacles.

Nevertheless, the migration and usage of SAP BW on SAP HANA have some pitfalls you should avoid. The following chapters explain how you can avoid possible errors and optimally use SAP BW on SAP HANA. For this purpose, Chapter 2 first introduces the architecture of SAP HANA, and Chapter 3 discusses the implementation of a new SAP BW on SAP HANA system and the migration of an existing one.

Further structure of the book

SAP HANA is delivered as an appliance and is therefore a complete product consisting of server hardware and an operating system. This chapter discusses these individual parts in detail. You learn about their significance, which selection options you have, and what you need to consider.

2   SAP HANA Architecture

Chapter 1, Section 1.4 already described which innovative principles set SAP HANA apart from other databases. Let's now discuss the *architecture*, that is, the interplay of the various components of an SAP HANA system. The term architecture refers to hardware and software in general, and SAP HANA processes in particular.

Section 2.1 discusses the criteria for a certified SAP HANA system. We will explain the terms scale-up and scale-out for upgrading an existing SAP HANA system. Deploying an in-memory database imposes special requirements on data security and main memory management. For this reason, these topics are outlined in separate sections. As an alternative, you will also learn about SAP HANA's cloud options.

Structure of this chapter

Section 2.2 deals with the question of how to enable parallel usage of an SAP HANA server for various purposes. Operating SAP HANA on virtual machines is discussed separately. Finally, we'll discuss some specifics for selecting the operating system.

Within the scope of architecture, you receive a detailed description of SAP HANA's functionality. Chapter 6 and other parts of this book will refer to SAP HANA processes and engines. Their functionality is described in Section 2.3. The index server process is discussed separately because it is the core of SAP HANA and is thus responsible for a multitude of tasks.

Current information While reading, bear in mind that SAP HANA is a fast-developing product: while this book was being written, another operating system was released for productive use in SAP HANA, some details of the main memory management were changed, and live operation of virtual machines was permitted. To keep you up-to-date, reference is made to the corresponding SAP notes whenever possible. If a topic is of particular interest to you, we recommend that you obtain the latest information from these notes.

2.1 Hardware

Like desktop PCs, today's servers follow a flexible hardware concept. Their hardware and software supports the highest possible combination variety of the various hardware components. This becomes clear when you consider the effort that hardware providers, operating system manufacturers, and customers must make to develop, maintain, and install drivers.

Union of software and hardware In the IT world, however, there are some famous counter-examples, for instance, Apple devices; Sony game consoles, Microsoft, or Nintendo; or mini-computers like Raspberry Pi, which are very popular among tinkerers. For these products, the collaboration between hardware and software is as close as possible. The less programming and driver codes must be adapted in the various components, the lower the effort will be for development and execution. Consequently, software projects emerge that feature stunning performance. An application development that strongly focuses on hardware therefore results in better performance.

SAP HANA appliance SAP HANA follows a similar concept. For this purpose, guidelines were created for the hardware and software environment on the servers so that the database operation always takes place in a highly homogeneous environment. This is to ensure high performance and low error-proneness for each appliance. At the moment, only a certified selection of servers and operating systems is supported for productive usage in SAP HANA. The complete product consisting of hardware, operating system, SAP HANA, and all related tools is referred to as an appliance. Customers can therefore choose among predefined packages when purchasing SAP HANA for production purposes. Depending on the scenario, several servers are deployed for scale-out, test and development systems, or high-availability scenarios.

The following discusses the various options of which hardware you can deploy and how to use it.

2.1.1 Certification

Certified hardware is required particularly for the productive usage of SAP HANA. SAP has already certified several servers from most SAP hardware partners for usage with SAP HANA. The certification process checks the hardware components for their performance; this involves the speed of processors, the main memory, and their ratio. For an SAP BW on SAP HANA system, for example, the necessary ratio is 16GB per processor core when using an 8-core processor. Additionally, the speed of the network interface and hard drives is taken into account. At the moment, support is provided for servers with Intel processors only. Servers that have passed this process successfully are listed in the *Product Availability Matrix* (PAM). They are subdivided into servers that are run with SUSE Linux Enterprise Server for SAP Applications or with Red Hat Enterprise Linux. Some of them also support virtualization via VMware vSphere for live operation.

Hardware certification process

The *tailored data center integration* is an alternative. Here, you can individually compile the hardware package, which is usually delivered in an appliance, in cooperation with your hardware partner. You still require a certified server and a certified storage solution. Savings are possible if you already own parts thereof. You may then deploy this hardware for productive usage of SAP HANA. Different from the appliance approach, you must then install and configure the operating system and SAP HANA yourself. The employee responsible requires a certificate for attending a training for SAP HANA installation administrators. This can be a cost-efficient alternative for customers who already have appropriate high-performance hardware. For this purpose, you should first execute the test tool in SAP Note 1943937 (*http://service.sap.com/sap/support/notes/1943937*). This tool checks the components of the server and

Tailored data center integration

provides an initial assessment of its suitability. Here, the network connection and the speed of the storage solution are tested in particular.

2.1.2 Cloud

SAP HANA can be operated in the cloud for both testing and production purposes. Cloud offerings are usually deployed if the emphasis is on a cost-efficient scaling and particularly low IT overhead. A wide variety of offers has emerged in recent years.

Definition
The cloud is one of the latest technology trends. Because this vogue term is often used incorrectly, we want to first explain what a cloud offering actually is. In 2011, the National Institute of Standards and Technology (NIST) provided a definition (see *http://csrc.nist.gov/publications/nist-pubs/800-145/SP800-145.pdf*) that establishes the following characteristics for cloud services:

- The consumer can provision hardware resources automatically without human interaction.
- The service is available in the network (usually via the Internet).
- The provider's virtual and physical resources are assigned to the customers.
- Resources can be adapted and scaled flexibly to customer requirements as needed.
- The load and usage is measured to provide transparency for customers and providers.

Service and channel
In summary, a cloud is an IT service that is provided to multiple customers via a network. Here, you must distinguish which service is offered via which channel. A distinction is usually made among the following three types:

- *Infrastructure as a Service* (ITaaS) provides the customers with their share of hardware that is managed by the provider.
- *Platform as a Service* (PaaS) does not permit direct access to the hardware, but upload and operation of self-developed software. Interaction is made using tools provided by the provider.

▶ *Software as a Service* (SaaS) only permits the usage of an application that is provided and operated by the provider on separate servers and made available via a network, usually the Internet. All SAP offers in the SAP HANA area are assigned to this method.

A distinction is made by the customer range of a cloud service. If it is used by one organization exclusively, it is referred to as a *private cloud*. In this cloud, customers are, for example, departments or individual employees of an enterprise. The provider can be an external company or the enterprise-internal IT department. If, however, the service is available to all organizations, this is referred to as a public cloud. If the provider is an external company, it also assumes liability for failures, maintenance, and operating costs. These are typical reasons for using a cloud solution. The definition of the private cloud applies to several products that already existed before this term was created, starting with simple network drives.

Private cloud/ public cloud

Besides the new SAP HANA-based offers, SAP also provides the cloud-based SAP Business ByDesign or solutions of enterprises like SuccessFactors and Ariba that were acquired by SAP. Enterprises like Amazon offer cloud hosting of "regular" SAP applications within the scope of Amazon Web Services (AWS).

There's a wide variety of cloud offerings for SAP HANA:

Cloud offers

▶ **SAP HANA One/development edition**
Several cloud offers exist with which you can try and test SAP HANA quickly and without hardware expenditure. SAP HANA One is a HANA instance with 60GB that can be used via Amazon Web Services, for example. Currently (April 2015), the price amounts to about $3.50 per hour. You have full control over a virtual machine with a preinstalled SAP HANA database. If you develop your own applications on this virtual machine, you may use it in live operation.

This doesn't apply to other providers of the SAP HANA cloud development edition. They vary in their hardware dimensioning but are often more cost-efficient. These variants are not suited for usage in the SAP BW on SAP HANA environment, but they can give you a first impression of SAP HANA at a reasonable price.

▶ **Trial offers**

Some offers are available for free for a limited period of time. At the moment, trial programs are available for the SAP HANA development edition, SAP BW on SAP HANA, and SAP ERP on SAP HANA. These offers can usually be deployed via the Amazon cloud, which involves some minor costs, depending on the usage duration. But you should still use these inexpensive offers to receive an initial impression of the corresponding solution.

▶ **SAP HANA Infrastructure, DB Services, and App Services**

The SAP HANA Infrastructure Services offer is also provided by Amazon Web Services and includes only the appropriate hardware for operating SAP HANA in the cloud. The license is not included in the price, so you must purchase the SAP HANA license yourself. In exchange, the SAP HANA Cloud Infrastructure systems offer up to 1 TB main memory and support scale-out. If you don't have a license of your own, you can deploy SAP HANA DB Services because they already include a license. SAP HANA App Services additionally provide advanced tools and options for application developers.

▶ **SAP HANA Cloud Platform**

SAP HANA Cloud Platform cannot be used for operating SAP HANA systems. It is intended for developing native SAP HANA applications only. For this purpose, each SAP partner or customer can create a developer account and try the platform for free. For financial reasons, SAP operates the free trial version on servers that several developers access at the same time. As a result, their rights are restricted considerably. In particular, user management, administration, and monitoring cannot be made. Data administration, development of own applications on SAP HANA, and modeling of SAP HANA views is possible without any problems. Thus, the trial version of SAP HANA Cloud Platform is a good and free option to deal with these topics.

▶ **SAP HANA Enterprise Cloud (HEC)**

SAP HANA Enterprise Cloud is intended for productive operation of SAP applications on SAP HANA. It is also the default solution for the cloud operation of SAP BW on SAP HANA. The servers used for this purpose are provided by SAP directly or by selected partners around the world. In this offer, the software is fully managed and maintained for you. A support team is available 24/7, and the data center equipment ensures availability. Consequently, SAP HANA Enterprise Cloud is the first choice for enterprises that want to outsource their IT activities completely.

2.1.3 Scale-Up/Scale-Out

Every database server reaches its storage capacity limits after a while. If you don't want to reorganize your data or utilize a nearline storage solution, then you must upgrade your hardware resources (more information is available in Chapter 8). In the case of SAP HANA, this entails the purchase of additional main memory and further processors, as well as higher requirement of hard disk memory for backups, logs, and data images. Two upgrade methods exist: scale-up and scale-out.

Scale-up means to upgrade the already existing server(s) without increasing their number. For this purpose, the existing servers are upgraded; many certified SAP HANA servers are built on various blades for this reason. A blade includes all typical hardware components and thus presents a work unit. Another board is added for the upgrade to prevent major intervention of the hardware structure. Scale-up is possible only up to the limits that SAP certified for this server. These limits currently amount to 2TB or 4TB main memory and 80 processor cores.

Scale-up

A scale-out scenario is implemented for larger upgrade projects. Here, the existing system is supplemented with additional servers. SAP HANA now runs on several servers in parallel. The server cluster that emerges here includes a master server that assumes coordination and operates some SAP HANA processes alone from then on (for example, XS Engine and statistics server). This master server and the remaining servers distribute the load among themselves. This is achieved, for example, by table partitioning; the partitions are then distributed to the individual servers. Calculations and database accesses are made on different cluster servers, depending on the required data. For this reason, you should distribute the data to the servers using partitioning after you've implemented a scale-out scenario (see Chapter 1, Section 1.4.4). More detailed information on this procedure is available in SAP Note 1908075.

Scale-out

[+] **Optimal Number of SAP HANA Servers**

The basic principle applies that the performance of an individual server out-weighs the performance of several connected servers with the same overall hardware because no communication is required between the connected servers via the network.

When you operate SAP systems, however, it often occurs that several processes compete for the same resources. Deploying an SAP HANA database that is distributed to several servers can therefore result in acceleration. SAP Note 1702409 provides information on this topic, with a focus on SAP BW on SAP HANA.

You should also consider operating one or more servers that allow for continued operation after failure in case of emergency. Servers of the development or test systems are often used for this purpose.

Collective data access

When you operate several servers, they must all have access to data. Logs and data are stored, for example, on a shared network drive or exchanged between servers. These scenarios must be implemented by the hardware partner.

If a server fails, you must take measures to resume operation again. The next section examines this.

2.1.4 High Availability/Data Availability

Power outage results in complete loss of data in the main memory. Because SAP HANA stores this data in the main memory, you must prevent this loss in case of emergency. An initial step is to continuously create save points, logs, and backups, which is discussed in Chapter 6, Section 6.3.2. Additionally, SAP HANA supports various techniques:

▸ **Mirroring**
Mirroring is a parallel operation for identically structured servers whose datasets are synchronized (mirrored) continuously. If the primarily used server fails, the mirror server recognizes this and continues operation smoothly. This is the safest but also the most expensive method. Normally, the mirror server doesn't serve any purpose but incurs considerable costs for hardware procurement and operation. You should also note that the mirror server and the original server are

set up in different locations. Only then can you prevent the two servers from being inoperable for the same reason (flood, power outage, fire, and so on).

▶ **Cold standby**
In an SAP HANA cluster, one of the servers can be used as a cold standby server. This is an inactive server that automatically steps in if another server fails. To continue operation, this server must first reconstruct the data of the failed server's main memory. In contrast to a mirror server, this cannot be done continuously because you don't know in advance which server will fail.

▶ **Auto restart service**
A software error or incorrect configuration of SAP HANA can result in an unplanned cancelation of an SAP HANA process. In this case, SAP HANA will restart the process immediately and restore the original state.

2.1.5   Main Memory Management

The entire main memory is divided into areas that are each managed by a specific processor.

The shared usage of the main memory therefore requires communication between the processors. If you use the *Non-Uniform Memory Access (NUMA) architecture*, one board can comprise up to four processor sockets that are interlinked via interfaces. All processors are linked with one another for optimal performance (see Figure 2.1).

NUMA architecture

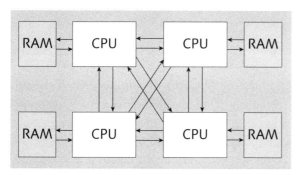

Figure 2.1 NUMA Architecture

For boards with more than four processor sockets, the current design does not permit an interface between all processors. If a processor core wants to access data that is assigned to another processor core, the data must be transported in several steps. On average, access to the main memory features lower performance in this case. So far, such systems often use eight processors in the form of two NUMA architectures that are linked with one another.

Because a lot of time is lost for this type of communication and with an increasing number of processors and sockets, it becomes more and more important in larger systems to reference the calculations for a specific main memory area to the assigned processor.

SAP HANA main memory pool

Typically, memory management is carried out by the operating system. However, the operating system doesn't have any information on the structure and relevance or the dependencies of database tables and their interim results. SAP HANA is supposed to distribute calculations to as many processor cores as possible to keep the processing time as short as possible. For this reason, SAP HANA assumes main memory management completely. To do so, SAP HANA's index server process creates a separate main memory pool when the database is started. During operation, it reserves main memory for program code, database tables, temporary calculations, and other internal processes, such as database statistics. If the reserved memory is no longer required, it remains in the main memory pool and is not returned to the operating system again, as is the case in other applications. If the memory is to be occupied again, SAP HANA can decide which areas are suited here. For this reason, the operating system will report a higher main memory usage that is caused by SAP HANA processes than actually exists.

Figure 2.2 shows a sample structure of the memory pool. The memory for tables is subdivided into column store for column-based tables and row store for row-based tables. Only SAP HANA knows the amount of free memory and its composition; the operating system is informed about only the total amount of main memory that is occupied by the index server.

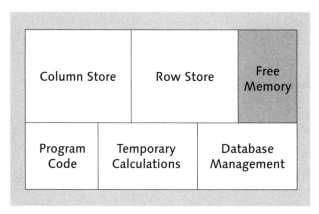

Figure 2.2 Structure of the Main Memory Pool of SAP HANA

The process of memory allocation is continued up to a predefined limit, referred to as *global allocation limit* (see Chapter 6, Section 6.4.1). If more main memory is required beyond this limit, occupied memory must be released again. For this purpose, database tables are "unloaded," in other words, removed from the main memory. Then, they are available only on the hard disk and no longer benefit from the main memory's speed. In this case, SAP HANA tries to unload data that has not been used for a very long time, and it is capable of removing only parts of tables from the main memory. It is also possible to predefine tables that are supposed to be unloaded first in such a case. In an SAP BW system, this primarily concerns data from PSA tables and write-optimized DSOs, which are not used for evaluation or analysis in regular operation (see Chapter 5, Section 5.6). Sufficient dimensioning of hardware ideally prevents the unloading of tables. Exceptions involve activities with a particularly high main memory usage, for example, database updates. This is a typical example for one of the many optimizations that SAP developed in cooperation with various hardware partners.

Global allocation limit

It is easy to identify a main memory shortage; however, it is rather difficult to determine the actual main memory usage of SAP HANA. For this purpose, we'll discuss main memory management in more detail. Figure 2.3 shows some main memory variables that occur in the course of database operation.

Main memory variables

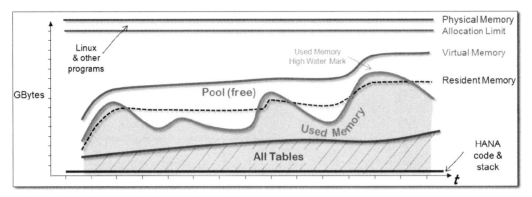

Figure 2.3 Main Memory Variables of SAP HANA Over Time (from "SAP HANA Memory Usage Explained")

If the runtime environment requires main memory from SAP HANA, a request is sent to the operating system and the respective SAP HANA process receives *virtual memory*. This memory has not been assigned to a concrete location in the main memory, but it authorizes SAP HANA to occupy main memory in the further course of the program. If this memory is then physically filled with data, it is referred to as *resident memory*. It is assigned to a main memory area and can then be used by the process. Accordingly, there's a difference between virtual memory and resident memory that results from the reserved main memory that has not yet been utilized.

In SAP HANA, *used memory* refers to the memory that is actually reserved by program code, tables, temporary calculations, and database management (but may not be occupied yet). The difference in the memory reserved by the operating system (virtual memory) is the free memory of the main memory pool. If main memory was reserved and is no longer required, it still remains in the resident memory and is thus part of the pool. The used memory can therefore be greater or less than the resident memory.

The used memory is the decisive variable for main memory usage. It may not exceed the predefined main memory limit.

2.2 Software

The dimensioning of hardware, as well as the database innovations of SAP HANA, live up to their potential particularly when you deploy the software that was developed on this basis. Existing products like SAP BW have been adapted for this purpose. Additionally, an entire product portfolio of native SAP HANA applications arises. Let's now discuss the question of how to operate them jointly.

The original operating concept of SAP HANA included a dedicated (that is, sole) operation of the database on the server. It was not released for productive systems to use several applications on an SAP HANA appliance or several databases on a server. In the meantime, the regulations are considerably more flexible and develop further. For this reason, we can provide only a snapshot that illustrates the additional options that open up and where you can obtain information on the relevant topics.

2.2.1 SAP HANA and Other Applications

If you deploy an SAP HANA database in your enterprise, you can utilize it for different purposes at the same time. SAP refers to this principle as *Multiple Components One Database* (MCOD). However, this principle does not apply to every conceivable combination, which is why SAP publishes a continuously updated whitelist that lists all permitted combinations. You can find details in SAP Note 1661202. Bear in mind, however, that the parallel use of several applications on SAP HANA must be taken into account when you plan the resource requirement. This information is supplemented by SAP Note 1666670, which deals with the question of whether various SAP BW systems may use the same SAP HANA database. At present, this is possible only for test and development systems; for production systems, it is expressly forbidden. Figure 2.4 illustrates these scenarios at the top right and the bottom left.

Multiple Components One Database (MCOD)

Another option is the parallel operation of several SAP HANA databases on the same server. Each installation of SAP software is usually identified with a three-digit SID. For this reason, this scenario is referred to as *multi-SID*. SAP Note 1681092 currently states that multi-SID scenarios

Parallel operation

are permitted only for test and development systems. Figure 2.4 presents this scenario at the top left. The implementation via virtual machines, which is discussed in Section 2.2.2 forms an exception here. Figure 2.4 shows this scenario in action at the bottom right.

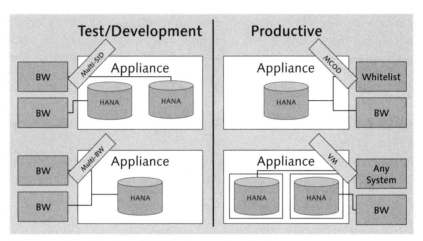

Figure 2.4 Operating Several Applications on One Appliance

Some customers use external products like backup or monitoring software, as well as anti-virus products. They are also subject to restrictions, which are discussed in more detail in SAP Note 1730928.

Figure 2.4 provides a summary of the different scenarios. Note that these conditions may change in the course of time. If you want to examine a specific method in more detail, you should consult the SAP notes that have already been mentioned.

2.2.2   SAP HANA on Virtual Machines

Virtualization A virtualization software divides the available hardware for several systems and programs. As a result, several programs or systems can operate completely independently of one another on the hardware. Virtualization is thus an alternative to the normal operation of several applications or to multi-SID installations in SAP HANA.

There are two completely different approaches for virtualization that we want to discuss for this purpose: hardware virtualization and operating system virtualization.

Hardware Virtualization

In the case of hardware virtualization, a component that is referred to as *hypervisor* or *virtual machine monitor* (VMM) controls and allocates resources. A hypervisor may already be preinstalled, depending on the server. Imagine a hypervisor as some kind of upstream operating system: only the hypervisor can access the hardware and enable system monitoring and administration. After it has been installed, you can use it to define virtual machines that contain their own (guest) operating systems. This ensures completely independent operation of virtual machines.

Hypervisor

In the meantime, the CPU must differentiate among the processes of the various virtual machines. Instead of using the hypervisor for this purpose, AMD and Intel developed special command sets (Pacifica and Vanderpool, respectively) that can be addressed by the guest systems without detours.

This results in an environment with different operating systems that are completely independent. Hardware is accessed directly and with high performance. The best known hypervisors include XEN (Citrix), KVM (Red Hat), and vSphere (VMware).

Benefits

SAP Note 1788665 deals with this topic and is updated on a continued basis. At present, only the usage of VMware vSphere is supported for operating SAP HANA on virtual machines. For this purpose, you must still use a certified SAP HANA server or a server that is verified by SAP HANA tailored data center integration. In this case, however, live operation is supported. If you want to deploy this scenario, you should also refer to SAP Note 1995460. It discusses all restrictions, important documents, and tips that are required for setting up virtual machines. Right now, it must still be decided whether several SAP HANA databases are to be operated on a virtual machine in parallel.

Important SAP notes

Operating System Virtualization

Operating system virtualization follows a different approach. In this case, an operating system that was installed normally provides several of its guest instances that are executed in separate environments (*containers*).

Live operation of SAP HANA in such a container is not supported at present (April, 2015). This scenario can be used for test and development systems, however.

With this method, only one operating system is run that usually simulates an image of the actual hardware. It can be addressed more directly, and the overall overhead can be only 1%. The effort of setting up a container for virtualization is lower that with hardware virtualization.

Container

Containers use their own applications, users, services, and directories, but they can also be inherited by the operating system. Internally, the superordinate operating system groups the container's executed processes. These *kernel control groups* can be monitored and managed with a high level of detail. It is possible, for example, to restrict to concrete main memory areas or CPU cores.

2.2.3 Operating System

The operating system is one part of the SAP HANA appliance. Only SUSE Linux Enterprise Server for SAP Applications has been permitted so far for optimal operation. In the meantime, the selection was extended with Red Hat Enterprise Linux Server for some certified servers. Some special regulations, which are discussed first, apply to the two operating systems.

SUSE Linux Enterprise Server for SAP Applications

In addition to its server operating system, the enterprise SUSE Linux also publishes a version adapted for SAP whose packages are compatible with SAP applications. This version also comprises a proprietary *high-availability extension*, an installation wizard for SAP applications, and support tailored for SAP customers.

Some recommendations exist for operating SAP HANA on this operating system. They are summarized in SAP Note 1944799. It includes the selection of software packages and instructions for maintaining and supporting the operating system.

Red Hat Enterprise Linux Server

Red Hat Enterprise Linux Server is developed by Red Hat and is the leading product for Linux operating systems on servers in the enterprise segment. Red Hat's products are heavily represented on the U.S. market. Because it was released for SAP HANA after the SUSE operating system, the number of SAP HANA appliances that run with Red Hat is still low.

To use SAP HANA on Red Hat, you must first make some adaptations to ensure optimal operation. All necessary steps are summarized in SAP Note 2013638. These steps are not required for SUSE Linux Enterprise Server for SAP Applications because it has already been adapted for operating SAP applications.

Adaptations

General Notes

New versions of the installed software packages are required for both operating systems if SAP HANA is to be deployed as of version 80. You can find a list of the relevant changes in SAP Note 2001528.

Each configuration change to the operating system should first be checked for its impact on the SAP HANA operation. General instructions for configuration changes are available in SAP Note 1730999. A blacklist with prohibited configuration changes is maintained separately in SAP Note 1731000. We recommend that you take these SAP notes seriously because incorrect configuration or non-compatible software packages can result in unpredictable behavior in SAP HANA. Frequently, the causes are no longer known in this circumstance, and the responsible persons search for the error only in the database.

Configuration changes

2.3   Processes

The tasks of SAP HANA are implemented through several processes. You can monitor both the resource utilization and possible error sources of these processes via the operating system or SAP HANA Studio (see Chapter 6, Section 6.3).

Therefore, this section discusses the tasks of these individual processes. You will also learn about the internal functioning of the particularly important index server process:

▶ **Index server**
  The index server is the core of SAP HANA. It contains and processes all data of the database and therefore occupies a considerable amount of the main memory. Calculations are made by different engines depending on their type. An exception is the analysis of text data that is run in the preprocessor process. Section 2.3.1 discusses the functioning of the index server. SAP HANA engines are described in a separate section (see Section 2.3.2).

▶ **Statistics server**
  The statistics server records a huge number of performance and hardware data during an SAP HANA operation. Over time, this allows you to identify weak points or performance peaks (see Chapter 6, Section 6.3). The statistics server's task can be assumed by the name server as of HANA Revision 70 (see Chapter 6, Section 6.4.3).

  In an SAP HANA cluster, the statistics server runs on a host only.

▶ **Name server**
  The name server is required for operating an SAP HANA cluster. It knows all SAP HANA servers and the data they manage.

▶ **Preprocessor server**
  SAP HANA is capable of evaluating texts with regard to language and content. It also includes the analysis of positive or negative sentiments in texts (sentiment analysis). This can be used, for example, for interpreting large amounts of texts from social media. The preprocessor runs this analysis.

▶ **XS engine**
  The Extended Application Services (XS) engine manages and operates

native SAP HANA applications that can be developed in JavaScript (XSJS). SAP utilizes this option, too. Components for the administration and monitoring of SAP HANA are implemented in XS to an increasing extent. Even entire SAP applications—for example, Operational Process Intelligence—are developed and operated in XS. The operation of SAPUI5 applications and the creation of ODATA interfaces for application development also take place in XS.

In an SAP HANA cluster, the XS engine runs on a host only.

2.3.1 Index Server

The index server is the central SAP HANA process. All pure database activities are run on this server. Accordingly, its structure is complex and documented for the public only to some extent. The following, therefore, deals with the tasks of the index server and provides a rough overview of how they are carried out.

Database Accesses

Applications, SAP systems, and technical and human users constantly connect to SAP HANA to run operations. The index server ensures the management of sessions. This particularly concerns the authentication during the logon process and the rights management of existing database connections. Chapter 6, Section 6.2 discusses rights management in more detail. Authentication can also be assumed by external systems (Kerberos, SAML-base identity providers). In this case, the index server ensures the communication with these systems. You can also set up an encrypted communication via HTTPS.

Authentication and rights management

Administration of Database Objects

All tables, SAP HANA views, database views, procedures, development objects, schemas, and other database components are managed by the index server. This means, among other things, that it retains all metadata. Metadata is, for example, the structure, authorizations, names, and descriptions, as well as code to be executed.

Metadata

Managing Stored Data

Row and column store In SAP HANA, you can store data based on a column or row. The technical implementation is performed by the two index server components, row store and column store. The storage of data for restore on the hard disk is also organized by the index server. Chapter 1, Section 1.4.3 describes the functioning of the column store.

Executing SQL Commands

Engines Read and write operations in SAP HANA are usually transferred via SQL. When an SQL statement is received, it is first analyzed and then forwarded to the corresponding component of the index server. Procedures, for example, are processed by a separate component, and special SQL commands of the planning engine are forwarded to the corresponding planning component. These components are referred to as *engines*. They carry out the actual processing of statements. A separate engine, the calculation engine, is also used for calculations in SAP HANA views (see Chapter 5, Section 5.2).

Commands are executed by the SQL engine in several steps. The following describes the SQL and calculation engines in more detail.

2.3.2 SAP HANA Engines

In SAP HANA, the actual execution of data operations takes place in engines. Each calculation type is mapped by a separate engine. The following sections discuss some of these engines providing greater insight into the functionality of SAP HANA.

Calculation Engine

The calculation engine is used, for example, by SQL scripts or calculation views. Chapter 5, Section 5.2 outlines the modeling of calculation views. In calculation views, you can even carry out functions of the calculation engine directly. This can result in faster evaluations if you have sufficient knowledge of the SAP HANA architecture and the engine performance.

Application function libraries are part of the calculation engine. They contain functions written in C++ that the calculation engine can access directly. However, they cannot be developed manually. Popular examples include the predictive analysis library, which comprises functions for developing forecasts, and the business function library, which offers functions for financial calculations.

Application function libraries

The functions of the application function libraries can be deployed via special SQL commands or functions that are predefined by SAP. By means of the predictive analysis library, for example, you can set up your own processes via SAP HANA Analysis Process in an SAP BW on SAP HANA system and then schedule their execution in a process chain (see Figure 2.5). This allows you to utilize the benefits of the calculation engine from the SAP BW system without detailed technical knowledge.

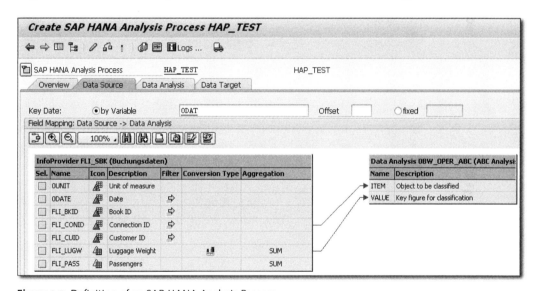

Figure 2.5 Definition of an SAP HANA Analysis Process

SQL Engine

Prior to execution, SQL commands for reading or writing data are formatted by a component that is referred to as an *optimizer*. Here, calculation steps are adapted so that they can be performed with a high level of

Optimizer

performance. This includes the handling of temporary results, merging of data from various tables, or the search within tables.

Additionally, this ensures that parallel reading and writing to the same tables does not lead to deviation, resulting in inconsistencies. The optimized command can then be executed, and the row store and column store of the corresponding tables can be accessed.

[+] **SQL Engine for SAP HANA Calculation Views**

When you model calculation views, they are executed by the SQL engine instead of the calculation engine.

This can result in a considerably faster execution because the SQL engine optimizes command chains more strongly. You must observe some restrictions, however, when you choose the SQL engine. For example, you may not use any analytic views, attribute views, or calculation views with SQL script as the data source. All restrictions that must be observed are available in the SAP HANA modeling guide at *help.sap.com/hana_platform*.

Join Engine

Merging data The only task of the join engine is to merge data from several tables. It is used by attribute views. The calculation engine also provides a method for joins of tables. To understand this necessity, you must be familiar with the resource consumption of the engines. If several engines process the same command, data exchange is necessary between them. Particularly for SAP HANA views, the performance varies greatly if you deploy only one instead of several SAP HANA engines.

OLAP Engine

The OLAP engine is used by analytic views and InfoCubes from the SAP BW system. It is aligned with the architecture of the star schema (see Chapter 1, Section 1.2.2) and is equipped with its own optimizer. A particular benefit of this engine is the fast execution of analytical calculations through parallel implementation of aggregation.

The setup of an SAP BW on SAP HANA system usually takes place when migrating an existing SAP BW system. For this purpose, you must first check the technical requirements and run preparation steps. Further actions are necessary after a migration to ensure smooth operation.

3 Migration and Implementation of SAP BW on SAP HANA

This chapter focuses on how you can set up your own SAP BW on SAP HANA system. Initially, you get to know the various migration and implementation scenarios. The most important scenario, the manual migration of an existing SAP BW system to SAP HANA, takes center stage in this chapter. For this reason, we'll first provide an overview of the technical requirements that must be met for implementing an SAP BW on SAP HANA migration. You will then receive step-by-step information on the preparatory measures, the migration process, and the post-processing activities.

At this point, please note that this book cannot replace trainings on SAP HANA, SAP BW, or administration of SAP NetWeaver systems. This chapter, rather, aims at extending existing knowledge and bringing you up to date.

3.1 Migration and Implementation Scenarios

There are different scenarios that lead to your own SAP BW on SAP HANA system. The simplest case is usually a new installation. For customers who have not used any SAP BW system so far, this may be an interesting approach because a new installation is less elaborate than a migration, which involves time-intensive preparatory and post-processing work. If you can imagine large data volumes before an SAP BW

New installation

implementation and if reporting speed is one of your top priorities, it's worth relying on SAP HANA technology today. It is no longer recommended to implement a new SAP BW system in combination with Business Warehouse Accelerator (BWA; see the box "SAP BW on SAP HANA vs. Business Warehouse Accelerator").

Enterprises that have deployed SAP BW successfully for many years would consider a new installation only in exceptional cases, for example, if another BW system is to be set up in addition to an existing one. Another reason could be that customers want to get rid of any "legacy systems." It's also conceivable to transfer selected data models from a legacy system after the installation of a new SAP BW on SAP HANA system and re-establish the data there. However, the effort for releasing dependencies of different data models is generally high and should not be underestimated.

[+] | **SAP BW on SAP HANA vs. Business Warehouse Accelerator**

SAP BW on SAP HANA and the Business Warehouse Accelerator (BWA) both accelerate the execution of BEx queries at runtime. However, the technical architecture of the two approaches differs considerably. When using BWA, you can deploy two storage technologies (relational database of the SAP BW system and BWA) in parallel for data retention. In the case of SAP BW on SAP HANA, however, you can only use SAP HANA as the primary database system. In this case, all SAP BW data is retained in the main memory, and reporting is accelerated for all data. When you use BWA, in contrast, reporting can be accelerated only for specific data. To do so, you must transfer data of individual InfoProviders explicitly to BWA (*indexing*). In contrast to BWA, the speed of data load processes is also increased with SAP BW on SAP HANA. On one hand, this omits time-intensive steps in the process chains, for example, the generation of indices for InfoCubes. On the other hand, performance-intensive processes, such as activation of DSO requests, are run directly on the SAP HANA database. By deploying SAP HANA and the Planning Application Kit (PAK), you can also considerably speed up the execution of planning functions. Ultimately, the remodeling of InfoCubes in SAP BW on SAP HANA is also significantly easier thanks to the simplified data model.

Migration When you are performing an SAP BW on SAP HANA migration, the primary database of an SAP BW system is replaced by SAP HANA (see Figure 3.1). It is irrelevant here whether the SAP BW system has run on

Oracle, DB2, MS SQL Server, or MaxDB so far. For this reason, this is often referred to as a migration of *AnyDB* to SAP HANA. The previous database is no longer required after the migration is completed and can usually be switched off completely. All data, SAP BW objects, and data models are still available after migration. This is also referred to as a *non-disruptive approach* because the SAP BW system's operation can be continued without major interruptions. The BWA that is potentially used for performance optimization loses its right to exist in an SAP BW on SAP HANA scenario. While BWA optimizes data of only selected Info-Providers for fast reporting, SAP HANA retains all data in the main memory and thus accelerates all reports.

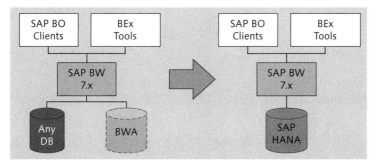

Figure 3.1 High-Level System Architecture Before and After SAP BW on SAP HANA Migration

For an SAP BW system, the database and possibly BWA is replaced with SAP HANA within the scope of a migration. Experience has shown that manual migration (also referred to as the *classic* migration method) is deployed most frequently. The involved tools have proven successful when implementing a *heterogeneous system copy* (system migration including a database or operating system change). Several additional tools and special reports are provided for SAP HANA that must be used before and after the actual migration phase. Preparations, implementation of migration, and concluding measures are discussed in the subsequent sections of this chapter.

Manual migration

An alternative to manual migration is to use the database migration option (DMO), frequently in combination with post copy automation (PCA). DMO allows you to run a system upgrade and a migration to SAP

DMO and PCA migration options

HANA in just one step. This can be particularly useful if the SAP BW system doesn't yet have the required version for implementing a migration (see Section 3.1.3). The basic idea of PCA is to automate the numerous individual steps, particularly for post-processing an SAP BW on SAP HANA migration. This is supposed to ensure, among other things, that all migration steps are executed completely and in the correct sequence.

RDS *Rapid Deployment Solutions* (RDS) are provided optionally to accelerate the implementation of SAP solutions. Section 3.1.4 presents three RDS packages that are relevant for SAP BW on SAP HANA. For example, SAP provides the RDS package Rapid Database Migration of SAP BW to SAP HANA with which you can speed up an SAP BW on SAP HANA migration.

The following sections discuss the previously presented migration scenarios in more detail.

3.1.1 New Installation

New installation and its benefits
A new installation of an SAP BW on SAP HANA system comprises the installation of the SAP BW server and its connection to an already existing SAP HANA database. Here, *SAP BW server* refers to an SAP NetWeaver system (ABAP), which provides all SAP BW features and is configured accordingly. To illustrate the deployment of an SAP NetWeaver system for SAP BW tasks, this is often referred to as an SAP BW system. The benefits of a new installation of an SAP BW on SAP HANA system are that there are no dependencies to already existing systems and that the installation effort is rather low. In contrast to migration, there is hardly any preparatory work required, for example, changeover from reporting authorizations to analysis authorizations, splitting a *dual-stack system* (ABAP/Java split), or implementing cleanup activities (housekeeping).

Transferring old data models
If you want to transfer data models of existing SAP BW systems to a newly installed SAP BW on SAP HANA system, this involves corresponding steps. You must first collect the required SAP BW objects (InfoAreas, InfoObjects, InfoProviders, process chains, BEx queries, and so on) in the source system and then transport them to the new system.

For particularly comprehensive data models, it may also be necessary to distribute objects to several transport requests and import them to the target system in the appropriate sequence. Experience has shown that this can involve a lot of time and effort. Finally, you need to connect the source systems with the new SAP BW on SAP HANA system and initialize and schedule the data load processes. SAP generally advises against transporting objects across different releases. However, SAP Note 1808450 describes that it's generally possible to transport between SAP BW systems that are not based on SAP HANA and SAP BW on SAP HANA systems.

Before you start with the installation of your SAP BW on SAP HANA system, you should first download and familiarize yourself with the current documents and notes (see the "Information Material for New Installations" box). First, read the master guide and the end-to-end implementation roadmap to obtain a sound overview. Then read the installation guide and call the SAP notes that are currently available.

Documentation

Information Material for New Installations
For more information on new installations, please visit the following: ▶ Master Guide—SAP NetWeaver 7.4: *http://service.sap.com/installNW74* ▶ End-to-End Implementation Roadmap SAP NetWeaver BW: *http://service.sap.com/installNW74* ▶ Installation Guide—SAP NetWeaver Application Server ABAP on SAP HANA: *http://service.sap.com/installNW74* 2—INSTALLATION • SAP NETWEAVER SYSTEMS • INSTALLATION: SYSTEMS BASED ON SAP NETWEAVER 7.1 AND HIGHER • SAP HANA DATABASE ▶ SAP Note 789220—Support Package Releases of NetWeaver Installations/Upgrades: *http://service.sap.com/sap/support/notes/789220*

You must define the requirements for your hardware and software using these documents and consider the intended purpose of your system. Additionally, you must plan which software components will be deployed (BI Java, SAP Enterprise Portal, and so on) and whether you will run the installation as a default, distributed, or high-availability system. These

Planning

planning activities hardly differ from those of other SAP systems. But you should consider that dual-stack installations (ABAP and Java Stack with common SID) are no longer supported. You should also note that only the operating systems, SUSE Linux Enterprise (SLES) and Red Hat Enterprise Linux (RHEL), are currently approved for the SAP HANA appliance (see SAP notes 1944799 and 2009879). However, you can still operate the SAP BW application server with another operating system as usual (see SAP Note 1067221). Details on the technical release information are available in the product availability matrix at *http://service.sap.com/pam* • SAP NETWEAVER 7.4 • TECHNICAL RELEASE INFORMATION.

SAP HANA appliance

For the remaining part of this section, we'll assume that you use an SAP HANA appliance with the required hardware equipment. It is usually provided, built, and set to an operational condition by certified hardware partners. Hardware partners are often responsible for the sizing of the SAP HANA system. The term *appliance* should not lead you to consider the system as a *black box*. After the initial setup, you must perform periodic maintenance work (import of updates and patches), and it may be necessary to conduct further configuration measures (for example, setting up a backup). In some circumstances, these tasks are not covered in a support contract with the hardware partner, and they must be fulfilled either internally by the IT department or externally by third parties.

Certified hardware

If no SAP HANA appliance is available to you, you may install the SAP HANA database on non-certified hardware for test purposes (see the "SAP HANA Database without Certified Hardware" box). Note here that you cannot reach the high speed of a real appliance. This approach is not approved by SAP, and problems in subsequent operation cannot be excluded. If you still consider such a test installation, the hardware used should have sufficient memory. If the main memory is too small, the operating system may be required to swap parts of the main memory to the hard disk during runtime. In this case, the deployment of the in-memory SAP HANA database would be inappropriate on this hardware.

SAP HANA Database without Certified Hardware   **[*]**

An SAP HANA database can be installed partially on non-certified hardware for test purposes. In this context, SUSE Linux Enterprise (SLES) or Red Hat Enterprise Linux (RHEL) must be installed as the operating system. Experience has shown that at least 32–64GB main memory should be available for subsequent usage for SAP BW on SAP HANA. Refer to the current installation guide to install the SAP HANA database. It is available at *http://help.sap.com/hana_appliance* under INSTALLATION AND UPGRADE INFORMATION.

If you run the installation using the graphical user interface `hdblcmgui` as described in this guide, the hardware check outputs an error message (see Figure 3.2).

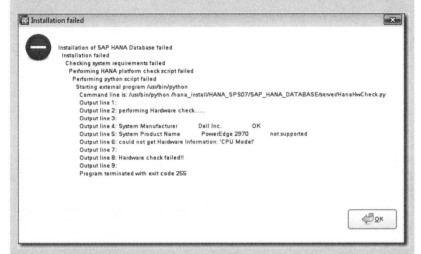

Figure 3.2 Installation Fails Due to Hardware Check

In this case, you can set the `IDSPISPOPD` environment variable before calling the installation as follows:

```
export IDSPISPOPD="1"
```

This instructs the installation routine to skip the usual hardware check. Also, this often enables the installation of the SAP HANA database on a virtual machine. To check whether the environment variable is set correctly, proceed as follows:

```
python
>>> import os
>>> 'IDSPISPOPD' in os.environ.keys()
```

If the environment variable was set correctly, Python returns True as the result. You can leave the environment with exit() or Ctrl + D. If you execute hdblcmgui again, the installation will be successful in most cases (see Figure 3.3).

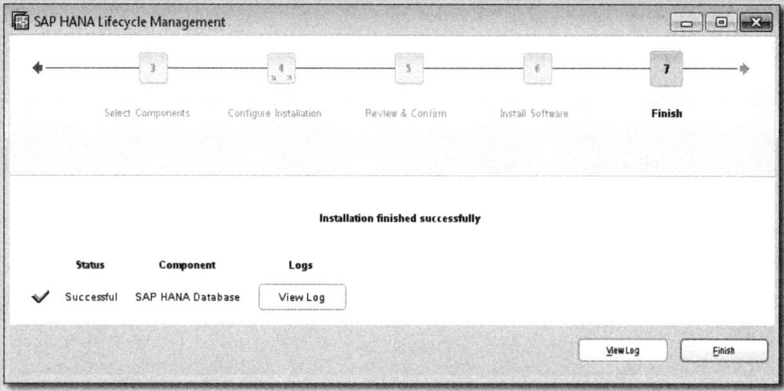

Figure 3.3 Successful Installation after Skipping the Hardware Check

Checking general requirements

If the SAP HANA appliance is ready for operation, you can then prepare the installation of the SAP BW application server. By means of the installation guide (see "Installation Material for New Installations" box), you should check whether the minimum requirements are met for the existing hardware, software, and operating system. Note that the requirements differ depending on the operating system used and that the installation guide is available in operating system-specific versions.

Separate hardware for SAP HANA DB and SAP BW AS ABAP

Up until support package 06 of the SAP HANA platform, it was not permitted to install the SAP BW Application Server ABAP (SAP BW AS ABAP) directly on the SAP HANA appliance. The SAP HANA database (SAP HANA DB) and the SAP BW AS ABAP are operated on separate hardware systems in this approach. To prevent performance problems, it is decisive to have a high transfer rate among all systems. SAP recommends that you set up a dedicated server network communication with 10Gbps (see SAP Note 1514967). The disadvantage of operating SAP HANA DB and SAP BW AS ABAP separately is that another server must be purchased, set up, and maintained on a regular basis in addition to the SAP HANA appliance. The advantage of this approach is, however, that the database and the application server don't compete for common hardware resources.

With the release of support package 07 of the SAP HANA platform, you can now also install and operate the SAP BW AS ABAP on the SAP HANA appliance. This approach is referred to as the *multi-component deployment strategy* (see SAP Note 1953429) and is supposed to enable an installation of an SAP BW on SAP HANA system with optimized resources and costs. Specifically, note that this release also extends to the high-availability setup using the SAP HANA system replication. The advantage of this approach can be found in the low costs because an additional server is omitted. However, SAP BW AS ABAP and SAP HANA DB can only run on one piece of hardware jointly if the system resources are dimensioned accordingly. In such a case, you must ensure that sufficient main memory and CPU power is available on the SAP HANA appliance. To determine the correct sizing requirements of your system, you can use the SAP QuickSizer (*http://service.sap.com/quicksizer*). Additional information is available in SAP Note 1637145 and Section 3.3.3.

Installing SAP BW AS ABAP on the SAP HANA appliance

In earlier versions of SAP BW on SAP HANA, you could not operate SAP BW Application Server Java (SAP BW AS Java) on an SAP HANA database. In initial customer projects, this fact repeatedly led to discontent because it was not possible to switch off the old database, and two different database systems (SAP HANA for SAP BW AS ABAP and another database for SAP BW AS Java) had to be operated as a result. But today, these initial problems are a thing of the past. Now you don't require a separate database to operate the SAP Enterprise Portal (EP) or BI Java. SAP Note 1849151 provides a comprehensive list of all SAP BW components that are released for SAP HANA. Moreover, SAP BW AS Java can now be operated on the same SAP HANA database as SAP BW AS ABAP. You can find this information in the *whitelist* provided in SAP Note 1661202. SAP NW AS Java can now be installed as a Multiple Components One Database (MCOD) installation (see SAP Note 1661202). In an MCOD installation, a second schema is created in the SAP HANA database, which is then used exclusively by SAP BW AS Java.

SAP BW AS Java

Installation media

You can download the media and files required for installing the SAP BW on SAP HANA system as usual from the SAP Service Marketplace (*http://service.sap.com/swdc*) • INSTALLATIONS AND UPGRADES • BROWSE OUR DOWNLOAD CATALOG • SAP NETWEAVER AND COMPLEMENTARY PRODUCTS • SAP NETWEAVER • SAP NETWEAVER 7.4 • INSTALLATION AND UPGRADE). We recommend using the latest respective versions.

Software Provisioning Manager

You can install an SAP BW on SAP HANA system using the Software Provisioning Manager (SWPM). In addition to installations, this tool can also be used for the migration of products based on NW AS ABAP and Java. The SWPM succeeds the product- and version-specific SAP installer (SAPinst) and is part of the *Software Logistics Toolset*, also called SL Toolset. You can download the SWPM via the SL Toolset URL: *http://service.sap.com/sltoolset*. Choose SOFTWARE LOGISTICS TOOLSET 1.0 • SYSTEM PROVISIONING • DOWNLOAD TOOL there. Unpack the *.SAR* file using the command SAPCAR -xvf <file name>. To avoid problems during installation, you should always deploy the latest version of SWPM. For more information, please refer to SAP Note 1680045.

Windows vs. Linux/Unix

Before you start with the installation of your SAP BW on SAP HANA system using SWPM, you should check some operating system settings first. For example, if you plan the installation of NW AS under Windows as a distributed system, you should perform a domain installation. Then, you must ensure that all servers belong to the same domain and the domain user is entered in the group of the local administrators, respectively. In a Windows installation, also make sure that NTFS is used as the file system. To avoid problems during installation, we advise you to switch off the Windows server firewall temporarily. Under Linux/Unix, you should check the used users (root, <SID>adm, sapadm) and groups (sapsys, sapinst) for their correct assignment prior to installation. The necessary information is available in the NW AS installation guide (see previous box). Under Linux/Unix, you should also check the time zones used by the SAP HANA appliance and the future NW AS using the date command. If you determine deviations for the time zones, you should modify them on the NW AS and, only in exceptional cases, the SAP HANA appliance. Further details are available in the SAP HANA Server installation guide.

To execute SWPM, start `sapinst` or `sapinst.exe` with a user that has administrator rights. However, don't use the `<SID>adm` user for this purpose. The most important command line parameters of SWPM are provided in the subsequent box. After startup, the system displays a selection of the applications to be installed, for example, SAP NetWeaver 7.4. Prior to the actual installation, you should run a *prerequisites check* for the respective product (see Figure 3.4).

Installation using SWPM

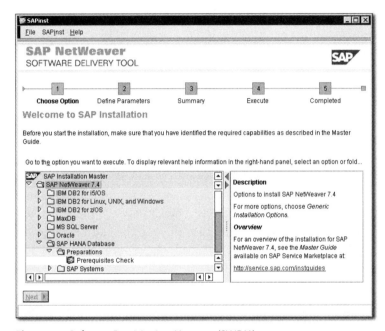

Figure 3.4 Software Provisioning Manager (SWPM)

The prerequisite check allows you to review the system settings and will ensure an accurate operation of the SAP BW AS ABAP. This check determines possible sources of error, for example, a main memory whose volume is dimensioned too low or a swap area that's too little, well in advance. After the prerequisites check is complete, restart SWPM and install the selected product. You no longer require a *Solution Manager key*, which was required for starting an installation. The subsequent steps of the installation process are identical to those that are made within an SAP BW on SAP HANA migration (target system setup). For this reason, we won't discuss them in further detail here, but instead refer you to Section 3.4 and the SAP installation guide.

[+] | **Command-Line Parameter SWPM**

Particularly in the Linux/Unix environment, you often have to decouple graphical display components from the installation process. To do this, you can start the installation on the server without output using ./sapinst -nogui. You can then start the user interface separately via a client PC, as follows: ./sapinstgui -host <server> -port <port>. If you use virtual host names, you should also transfer them to the tool as parameters: ./sapinst SAPINST_USE_HOSTNAME-<virtual server> -nogui. To get an overview of all possible parameters, you can call sapinst.exe -p.

Concluding work

After SAP BW on SAP HANA (NetWeaver AS ABAP based on the SAP HANA database) is installed successfully, you must configure some basic settings, like for other SAP systems. The initial customizing of the SAP BW system basically doesn't differ from the other SAP BW installations. The installation of the license and the import of patches or SAP notes are done as usual on the SAP BW side. However, we recommend checking and, if necessary, correcting any inconsistencies between the DDIC runtime objects and the database tables. For this purpose, use Transaction DBACOCKPIT and the RSDU_TABLE_CONSISTENCY report, as described in Section 3.5.3.

3.1.2 Manual Migration

Migration

A distinction is made between different scenarios when performing migrations in the SAP BW area. Different approaches apply depending on whether you want to migrate a complete system group (SAP BW and source systems), a standalone SAP BW system, or a source system only. Within this chapter, the SAP BW on SAP HANA migration refers to the conversion of a single SAP BW system to SAP HANA (see SAP Note 886102). We assume that the source systems (for example, connected SAP ERP systems) are operated without any changes and that these source systems then provide the new SAP BW on SAP HANA system with data after the migration is complete.

In the SAP NetWeaver environment, the term *migration* is a synonym for making a *heterogeneous system copy*. This scenario is generally used if the operating system or database has to be exchanged for an SAP system. Section 3.4 presents useful documents and sources for the SAP BW on SAP HANA migration (see Section 3.4, "Information Material on SAP BW on SAP HANA Migration"). As the term *system copy* already suggests, the migration is not implemented in the original system directly. Instead, a copy is made of the existing SAP system (original system) that can be executed directly in the new system environment. To do this, all data of the original system is initially exported to the file system. The SAP system is then installed in the new system environment (that is, using another database or a new operating system). The previously exported data of the original system is imported to the new SAP system during this installation process.

Migration through heterogeneous system copy

In the SAP BW on SAP HANA migration, the previously used database of an SAP BW system is exchanged by an SAP HANA database. From a technical point of view, this migration process is based on the described concept of a heterogeneous system copy. For this reason, all data is initially exported from the existing SAP BW system (see Figure 3.5). Then, the SAP BW application server (ABAP) is reinstalled and a database connection is established to the SAP HANA database. The previously exported data is then imported to the "empty" database of the new SAP BW on SAP HANA system. You as the administrator can choose whether you want to install the new SAP BW AS ABAP in a new environment or in the existing one. Provided that you choose the same environment, you may first uninstall the existing SAP BW system. The system ID (SID) and the logical system name can be kept, depending on the migration scenario. After you've completed the migration, the content of the original and the target system should not differ from the SAP BW perspective. However, you will immediately notice the considerably higher performance in the SAP BW on SAP HANA system, for example, when navigating through Transaction RSA1 or in reporting.

SAP BW on SAP HANA migration

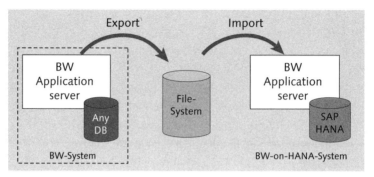

Figure 3.5 Migration via Export and Import

Project and time planning Now that we've roughly outlined the procedure of an SAP BW on SAP HANA migration from the software perspective, let's turn our attention to project and time planning. They should be addressed in good time and with sufficient buffer, particularly with regard to the migration of live SAP BW systems. From the organizational perspective, the required contractual agreements should be concluded with all stakeholders six months prior to the projected migration, at the latest. Different stakeholders may be involved depending on the project's constellation. Table 3.1 shows the participating stakeholders and their typical responsibilities for the common case that the hardware is supervised by external service providers, and external know-how is required to conduct the SAP BW on SAP HANA migration.

Partners Involved	Typical Allocation of Tasks and Responsibilities
SAP or software partner	Licenses
Hardware provider	SAP HANA appliance
Hardware partner	Setup and startup of the SAP HANA appliance, possibly setup of a high-availability solution and/or backup solution
IT consulting partner	Support for planning and implementing the SAP BW on SAP HANA migration and system training for employees
IT outsourcing partner	Preparation of the IT landscape, possibly carrying out homogeneous system copies, and support for the new system landscape after the end of migration

Table 3.1 Typical Tasks and Responsibilities of External Partners

Besides these external partners, you must also consider the availability of internal employees and their know-how and training. New hardware should be delivered and set up approximately two months before the migration of the first SAP BW system. A high-availability solution that is provided optionally should also be set up as soon as possible and accepted with corresponding tests at least on the database side. As soon as the SAP HANA appliance is ready for operation, you can set up the backup and integrate SAP HANA with the existing monitoring system. You should use the remaining time for fine-tuning all stakeholders, as well as running intensive tests of the new database system.

Once the organizational basic conditions have been coordinated, you can turn your attention to the technical details of the migration process. In our understanding, you can divide this process into the following four phases:

Four phases of the SAP BW on SAP HANA migration

1. Check of technical prerequisites

2. Preparation steps

3. Migration implementation

4. Post-processing

At about the same time as the initial project planning, you should already check the technical prerequisites for the SAP BW on SAP HANA migration. If you use, for example, an SAP BW system in version 7.0, you must consider some points in advance. These include, among others, that no migration can be made with dual-stack systems and that the concept of reporting authorizations is no longer supported as of SAP BW 7.3. Particularly the last point repeatedly resulted in some negative surprises in the past. If you fail to convert reporting authorizations to analysis authorizations and if you identify this as a necessary prerequisite for an SAP BW on SAP HANA migration too late, your entire schedule will get mixed up. We therefore recommend checking all technical prerequisites as soon as possible. More information is available in Section 3.2.

Phase 1: Technical prerequisites

If the technical prerequisites for migration are met, you can start with preparation steps. Here, you must first decide whether the preparatory work takes place on the system to be migrated or whether a *homogeneous system copy* is created for this purpose (see Section 3.3.1). If you

Phase 2: Preparation steps

run an SAP BW on SAP HANA migration for the first time, for example, within the scope of a PoC, we strongly advise you to create a homogeneous copy of your SAP BW system. Then, all other preparatory measures don't need to be made on an actively used system and therefore have no negative impact on the running operation if there is an error.

In the next step, you should clean up the SAP BW system to be migrated using cleanup or housekeeping activities (see Section 3.3.2). These activities are particularly important for the future use of SAP HANA because all data is retained in the main memory later on. And this main memory is rather expensive. Accordingly, you should, for example, delete or archive technical tables with log entries of previous years or content of InfoProviders that are no longer used prior to migration. Already, during these cleanup activities, it is vital to check the dimensioning of the SAP HANA appliance's main memory (see Section 3.3.3). SAP provides a special report (/SDF/HANA_BW_SIZING) for this purpose, which you should execute several times in the source system, as required. The sizes determined by the report should correspond to your SAP HANA appliance. As the next step, we recommend executing the checklist tool (ZBW_HANA_CHECKLIST; see Section 3.3.4). This report analyzes whether your system can be used for the migration and subsequent operation under SAP HANA. Detail checks are run for various categories (for instance, database, basis, SAP BW technical content, and so on), and the results are illustrated with traffic lights. Section 3.3 discusses the individual steps for preparing an SAP BW on SAP HANA migration.

Phase 3: Migration When performing the migration, you must first export the dataset of the SAP BW system to be migrated to the file system. To do so, you must prepare the original system and shut it down temporarily during export (see Section 3.4.1). For export, we recommend that you use the option of parallel export/import because this considerably accelerates the migration process. With this option, you can already start with the installation of the new SAP BW AS and the import in parallel instead of waiting for the export to complete. This normally reduces the migration time by several hours. However, you must also ensure that the export and import systems have access to a common directory. Like for the new installation scenario, we recommend running the prerequisite check before setting up the new SAP BW AS (see Section 3.1.1). When you install the target system, the data is imported from the file system (possibly in parallel to the running export) in the *Import ABAP* step.

After you've started the new SAP BW on SAP HANA system, you should make a database backup so that you can start over at this backup point in case of error. Then, your SAP Basis administrator must carry out some activities at the operating system and database level (see Section 3.5.1). Then, you must perform SAP BW-specific activities (see Section 3.5.2): ideally, check the new system for inconsistencies and, if required, take appropriate repair measures (see Section 3.5.3). Finally, some SAP BW on SAP HANA-specific post-processing needs to be done, for example, conversion of InfoCubes to SAP HANA-optimized InfoCubes, which can further accelerate the data loading processes and fully exploit the potential of the SAP BW on SAP HANA system.

After all four phases have been completed, the new SAP BW on SAP HANA system should be ready for operation. Bear in mind that the migration process could be different in your environment. Technical and/or organizational reasons like internal regulations could require you to deviate from the procedure described here. So, discuss the actual process with all parties involved and adapt the working steps to your requirements. Provided that you run a PoC prior to migrating a live SAP BW system, you will determine such deviations at an early stage.

3.1.3 Migration Options: Database Migration Option (DMO) and Post Copy Automation (PCA)

The database migration option (DMO) is a new procedure in which a system upgrade and an SAP HANA migration are carried out in one step or with one tool only. This can be particularly useful if the original system doesn't have the required version for implementing the SAP BW on SAP HANA migration yet (see Section 3.2). DMO is not available as a standalone tool; it is an optional extension of Software Update Manager. Figure 3.6 shows examples for different approaches for upgrading with subsequent HANA migration. At the moment, the start release can be SAP BW 7.00 (or higher), and the target release, SAP BW 7.31 (or higher). In the case of a planned upgrade including a migration to SAP HANA, you would first have to upgrade an SAP BW 7.0 system to

Phase 4: Post-processing

Variant migration process

Database migration option (DMO)

release SAP BW 7.3/7.31 or 7.4 using SUM if you deploy the classic approach without DMO. Only then can you migrate to SAP HANA using SWPM as described in Section 3.1.2. But if you use DMO, it is possible to migrate the SAP BW 7.0 system directly to SAP HANA and version 7.31/7.4. An SAP BW on SAP HANA migration with DMO and target version 7.3 is not provided. In this context, consider the update and upgrade paths supported by DMO, which are available in the PDF attachment of SAP Note 1813548.

Benefits of DMO   The benefits of DMO are obvious. When running a system upgrade and a migration to SAP HANA at the same time, you can considerably reduce the required time and effort. With DMO, for example, you can omit the update of the original system, which is required in some cases. The system downtimes for the SAP BW system are also considerably lower because some steps can be skipped, and only one maintenance window is required (instead of two).

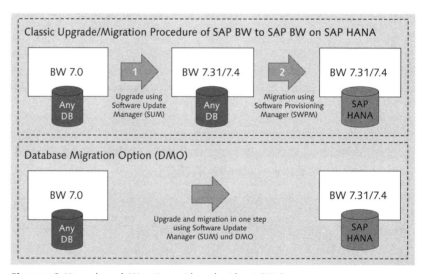

Figure 3.6 Upgrade and Migration with and without DMO

Documentation   The "Information Material on DMO" box provides an overview of the most important information material on DMO. Besides the most critical SAP notes, it also contains a reference to the DMO pages in the SAP Community Network (SCN). Moreover, you can find the official update guide and the link to the "SAP First Guidance," which we want to recommend specifically.

Information Material on DMO

The following resources provide further information on DMO:

▶ SAP Note 1813548—Database Migration Option (DMO) for Software Update Manager:
http://service.sap.com/sap/support/notes/1813548

▶ DMO Page in SCN:
http://scn.sap.com/docs/DOC-49580

▶ Upgrade Guide—Update of SAP Systems Using SUM 1.0 SP10 with DMO:
http://service.sap.com/sltoolset, scroll down, expand the SYSTEM MAINTENANCE area. There, you can find the download link for the upgrade guide.

▶ SAP First Guidance—Migration BW on HANA using the DMO option in SUM:
https://scn.sap.com/docs/DOC-46824

To use DMO, your SAP BW system must have a minimum version. This version is indicated in SAP Note 1813548. At the moment, DMO requires at least an SAP BW 7.0 system with the software components SAP_BASIS Support Package (SP) 17 and SAP_BW SP 19. In addition, you must also deploy a Unicode system. DMO doesn't yet have a function for Unicode conversion; however, it is expected to be available in future versions. With DMO, you can migrate only standalone ABAP systems, which is why a dual-stack split may be required previously. At the moment, the target release with DMO is SAP BW 7.31 or 7.4.

Prerequisites for using DMO

For better understanding, we'll briefly explain the technical background for the interaction of SUM and DMO. For many years, the method of *system switch upgrades* has been used for implementing system upgrades. In this method, a second application server (*shadow instance*) is set up, which is operated in parallel to the existing one. This shadow instance is already created in the version of the future target release and uses independent database tables. During the upgrade, some process steps can thus be moved to the shadow instance. The SAP system is still available to the users, and the system downtime is reduced. The new target system is then completed in a downtime phase toward the end of the migration. This rough approach was slightly adapted for DMO. In DMO,

Technical background

the tables of the shadow instance are now created directly on the SAP HANA appliance. As a result, the database tables are already used in the SAP HANA appliance during the upgrade, and a subsequent SAP BW on SAP HANA migration becomes obsolete.

Executing SUM with DMO You can start the upgrade process, including the migration to SAP HANA, via the web browser because all steps are carried out within the new *SAPUI5* user interface (see Figure 3.7). For this purpose, the SAPHostControl service must run on the server side, and SUM must be registered in the SAP host agent beforehand. For Windows, you can check whether this service is already running using the Task Manager under SERVICES. If required, you can start it from there. SUM is registered in the SAP host agent using a command line call (see the "Registering SUM in the SAP Host Agent" box). You then need to enter the URL *http://<host name>:1128/ lmsl/upgrade/<SID>/doc/gui* in your web browser to start the upgrade and migration process. Log on as the <SID>adm user there.

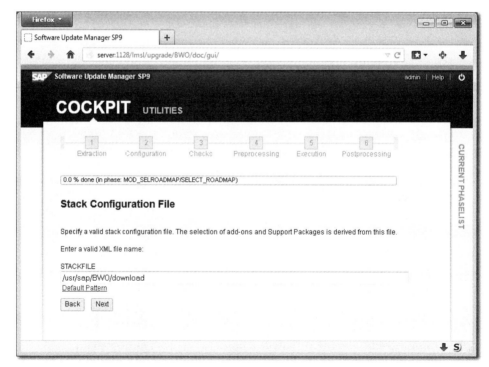

Figure 3.7 New SAPUI5 User Interface of Software Upgrade Manager for DMO

Registering SUM in the SAP Host Agent	[+]

Command-line call under Windows:

```
D:\install\SUM\abap>SUMSTART.BAT confighostagent
```

Screen output:

```
Base Dir: D:\install\SUM\abap
SID: BW0
Modified Base Dir: D:\install\SUM\abap
Registering SUM in SAP Host Agent...
Creation of file C:\Program Files\SAP\hostctrl\exe\
operations.d\sumstart.conf
Registering SUM in SAP Host Agent finished.
```

The subsequent process steps are broadly analogous to the other upgrades. For DMO, however, you must answer some database-specific questions, for example, whether you want to migrate the system to another database during upgrade. You require a migration key if you want to switch to SAP HANA (see SAP Note 317096). In a subsequent dialog box, you must enter the host name, SID, and the system ID of the SAP HANA database. You also need to enter the password for the SYSTEM database user. The associated SAP HANA database client is installed in advance so that the access to SAP HANA works with regard to data during the upgrade. If you use DMO, you must note that it is a rather new solution. Because developments are promoted quickly in the SAP HANA environment, you should carefully read the documents mentioned in the previous box before you upgrade with DMO.

SAP HANA-specific process steps

Like DMO, the use of PCA is optional in an SAP BW on SAP HANA migration. By means of PCA, you can specifically automate extensive post-processing work after a migration. For this purpose, the individual work steps are covered in predefined task lists. These lists are automated to a large extent and handled in the given sequence in the appropriate migration phases. This usually results in higher quality because, with PCA, you can exclude accidental skipping of individual work steps and resulting consequences, for example. Furthermore, PCA is supposed to reduce the number of necessary manual activities, which usually results in less time and resource requirements. PCA also enables you to adapt the predefined task lists (Customizing) or create new custom lists. The

Post copy automation (PCA)

work steps can be performed either as dialog or as background processes and resumed easily in case of error. To get started with the PCA topic, we compiled some documents in the following box.

> **[⊕]** **Information Material on PCA**
>
> The following resources provide further information on PCA:
>
> ▶ SAP Note 1707321—BW System Copy: Post Copy Automation (BW PCA):
> *http://service.sap.com/sap/support/notes/1707321*
>
> ▶ SAP Note 1614266—System Copy: Post-Copy Automation (PCA)/LVM:
> *http://service.sap.com/sap/support/notes/1614266*
>
> ▶ ABAP Post-Copy Automation Installation Guide:
> *http://service.sap.com/instlvm*—SAP NETWEAVER LANDSCAPE VIRTUALIZA-
> TION MANAGEMENT—SAP NETWEAVER LANDSCAPE VIRTUALIZATION MANAGE-
> MENT 2.0
>
> ▶ SAP BW Post-Copy Automation Guide for Enterprise Edition:
> *http://service.sap.com/instlvm*—SAP NETWEAVER LANDSCAPE VIRTUALIZA-
> TION MANAGEMENT—SAP NETWEAVER LANDSCAPE VIRTUALIZATION MANAGE-
> MENT 2.0
>
> ▶ Post Copy Automation (page in SCN):
> *http://scn.sap.com/docs/DOC-43270*
>
> ▶ PCA Troubleshooting Guide:
> *http://wiki.scn.sap.com/wiki/display/TechTSG/%28PCA%29+ABAP+Post-
> Copy+Automation*
>
> ▶ BW PCA FAQ: *https://scn.sap.com/docs/DOC-48779*

Landscape Virtualization Management PCA is an extension of the *SAP Landscape Virtualization Management* (LVM; see SAP Note 1614266). SAP LVM simplifies or automates the configuration, implementation, monitoring, and administration of the SAP system in both physical and virtual environments. From the software perspective, SAP LVM is an add-on to SAP AS Java. Specifically for SAP BW migrations, however, you can also use PCA without SAP LVM. Here, you must note that you still require a license for the enterprise edition of SAP LVM (see SAP Note 1707321). The following section describes the usage of PCA without SAP LVM.

PCA for older system versions If you want to use PCA for older ABAP systems, you must first install PCA there. Stick to the "ABAP Post-Copy Automation Installation Guide" for this purpose. As described in this guide, download the *PCAI<VER-SION>.SAR* file from the SAP Service Marketplace. You can find it under *http://service.sap.com/swdc* • SUPPORT PACKAGES AND PATCHES • BROWSE OUR DOWNLOAD CATALOG • SAP NETWEAVER AND COMPLEMENTARY PRODUCTS • SAP NW LANDSC VIRT MGT ENT • SAP NW LANDSC VIRT MGT ENT 2.0 • COMPRISED SOFTWARE COMPONENT VERSIONS • POST COPY AUTOMATION. Copy the archive file to the application server, and unpack it as *<SID>adm* to a temporary directory. Then, open a console and go to the *PCAI* subdirectory. In this subdirectory, call STARTUP for Linux or UNIX systems, or STARTUP.BAT for Windows. PCA is installed via a Java web start application (*.jnlp* file extension), which goes through the usual installation phases (see Figure 3.8). After successful installation, you must import the required license as described in the "ABAP Post-Copy Automation Installation Guide."

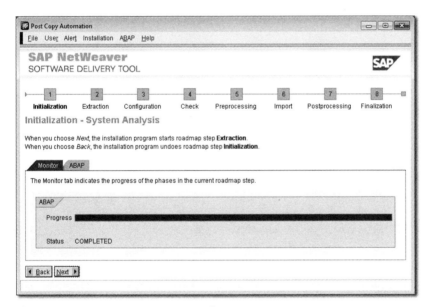

Figure 3.8 "Post Copy Automation" Installation

Whether you use PCA with or without LVM, you must first check that the system to be migrated is up to date and import SAP notes as appropriate. This is necessary because the required functions and system

Note analysis program

91

settings for PCA are delivered in support packages and/or SAP notes. A new note analysis program partially automates this process. Implement this program as described in SAP Note 1614266. For this purpose, create the new report Z_SAP_NOTE_ANALYZER in Transaction SE38, and copy the source code from the attachment of the said SAP Note. Execute the report, and click the LOAD XML FILE button (see Figure 3.9) to load the two XML files successively from SAP notes 1614266 (SAP Basis-specific) and 1707321 (SAP BW-specific).

Figure 3.9 Note Analysis Program for Executing PCA

When you continue now, the conditions defined in the XML files are checked for your system. If required, the background job then loads the missing SAP notes to your system. In this case, you must wait until this process is complete. This download can take more than an hour, depending on the scope and number of required notes. The subsequent analysis checks whether all SAP notes required for PCA have been integrated. The results of the check are displayed in a table (see Figure 3.10), and missing notes can be included via the ACTION column.

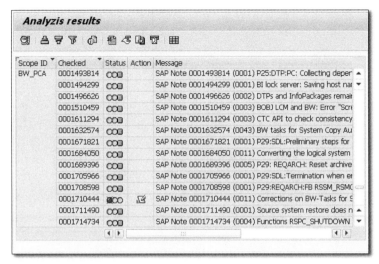

Figure 3.10 Results of the Note Analysis Program (PCA)

As mentioned previously, PCA is based on predefined task lists. They can be processed via the task manager in Transaction STC01. The following two lists are relevant for SAP BW systems, specifically within the scope of an SAP BW on SAP HANA migration:

Task lists

▸ SAP_BW_COPY_INITIAL_PREPARE
  Task list of preparatory measures that are performed in the original system prior to migration (in particular, cloning delta queues)

▸ SAP_BW_BASIS_COPY_INITIAL_CONFIG
  Task list for post-processing in the target system for concluding the migration

At this point, we won't discuss any more available lists (for example, for running a system refresh).

The migration in the SAP environment is based on making a system copy and transferring data from the original system to the target system that is to be newly created (see Section 3.1.2). From a technical point of view, the original system can still be operated after the migration is complete. Within the scope of an SAP BW on SAP HANA migration, for example, it is possible to test the target system that results from the migration before it replaces the original system. From an SAP

Cloning delta queues

BW perspective, however, this parallel operation results in problems when providing data from the source systems. If you use delta-capable DataSources, the changed data records are temporarily stored in a buffer (*delta queue*) in the connected system. A delta queue is always assigned to exactly one SAP BW system and thus cannot provide both the original and target system. Using PCA, it is possible to duplicate the delta queues in the source systems prior to system migration. This allows parallel provision of two SAP BW systems without requiring another delta initialization. This process is often referred to as *cloning delta queues* and can be executed when you process the SAP_BW_COPY_ INITIAL_PREPARE list. Figure 3.11 shows the individual work steps of this task list in Transaction STC01. The HELP option provides references to further detailed information of the respective work steps. Note that there are general restrictions when you clone specific DataSources. For more information, see SAP Note 1932459.

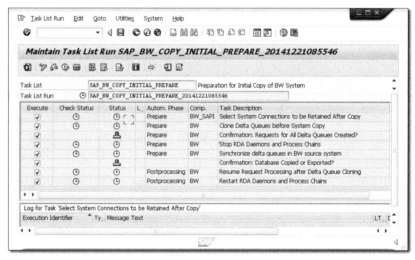

Figure 3.11 Display of the SAP_BW_COPY_INITIAL_PREPARE Task List in Transaction STC01

Post-processing The SAP_BW_BASIS_COPY_INITIAL_CONFIG task list is comprehensive and automates the post-processing after a migration (see Figure 3.12). For this reason, it is run in the target system and involves several cleanup activities.

Figure 3.12 Display of the SAP_BW_BASIS_COPY_INITIAL_CONFIG Task List in Transaction STC01

For example, these cleanup activities delete obsolete spool entries, outdated information in ABAP Basis tables, or background jobs that were copied from the original system. This is followed by the basic activities, among others, for setting up standard jobs, licenses, system profiles, operating types, and conversion of logical system names. Additional SAP BW-specific process steps include, for example, the update of RFC connections, configuration of the ALE/IDoc interface, and reset of the generation indicator for DSO activation programs. Section 3.5 discusses some of these steps in more detail.

Summary   In conclusion, it can be said that PCA facilitates the manual tasks, particularly for migration post-processing, and can increase the quality of the entire process due to automatic processing. Prior to a migration, you can use PCA to clone delta queues, which allows for parallel operation of the two SAP BW systems (original and migrated target system). It must be considered, however, that the setup of PCA causes high effort, particularly for older SAP BW systems. If errors occur during the migration process, they must be solved manually, even if PCA is deployed. Therefore, it strongly depends on the individual case whether PCA can reduce the migration time considerably through task lists and work step automation. From our point of view, DMO is a promising approach because it can considerably reduce the time and effort required for an SAP BW on SAP HANA migration. This applies specifically if the original system doesn't yet have the version that is required for implementing a migration. Because DMO is a rather new technology, time will tell whether it can establish itself.

3.1.4   Rapid Deployment Solutions

Rapid Deployment
Solutions (RDS)
Rapid deployment solutions (RDS) involve quick-start packages that allow for accelerated and low-risk implementation of SAP solutions. RDS packages comprise predefined configurations and content that is aimed at common enterprise processes. As a general rule, RDS doesn't adapt the SAP solution to individual customer requirements. This considerably reduces the complexity, effort, and costs for go-live. On the other hand, enterprise requirements are covered only to a certain extent, which often results in subsequent customer-specific adaptations.

RDS packages usually consist of the following components:

▸ **Software**
  Predefined configurations for SAP solutions

▸ **Content**
  SAP best practices, templates, and tools for accelerated implementation

▸ **Knowledge transfer**
  Guidelines and training materials

▸ **Services**
  Implementation service with clearly defined scope at a fixed price

An introduction to SAP RDS can be found here: *http://www.news-sap.com/* **RDS solutions**
sap-simplifies-cloud-adoption-new-sap-best-practices-packages-successfactors-hcmsuite/. Additionally, more than 150 RDS solutions that are currently available are presented in detail at *http://service.sap.com/rds*. In the context of SAP BW on SAP HANA, the following three RDS packages, which we'll discuss briefly, are particularly interesting:

- Rapid Database Migration of SAP BW to SAP HANA
  (*http://service.sap.com/rds-hana-bwmig*)

- SAP IQ Nearline Storage and Retention Management RDS
  (*https://service.sap.com/rds-nls*)

- SAP Business Intelligence Adoption RDS
  (*https://service.sap.com/rds-bia*)

The Rapid Database Migration of SAP BW to SAP HANA RDS solution **Rapid Database**
supports the database migration of an existing SAP BW system to SAP **Migration (RDS)**
HANA. Like for the other migration options discussed in this book, the existing SAP BW content (data flows and data) is still available at the end of the migration. The RDS package comprises a Step-by-Step Guide (HTML-based interface), via which you coordinate the individual migration phases (Start, Deploy, Run; see Figure 3.13).

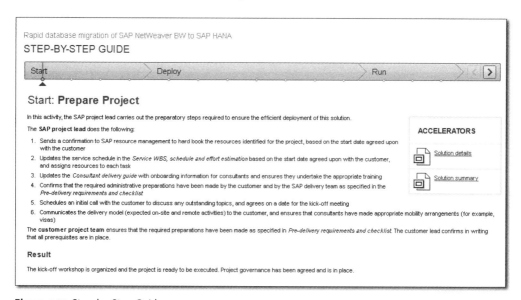

Figure 3.13 Step-by-Step Guide

The respective activities are supported with numerous documents, for example, presentations or questionnaires. The RDS package also contains instructions with detailed work steps for cleaning up an SAP BW system (housekeeping order list). For further information on this RDS solution, refer to the previously mentioned website and SAP Note 1667731.

Nearline Storage (NLS)

The SAP IQ Nearline Storage and Retention Management RDS allows you to connect SAP BW on SAP HANA with a *nearline storage (NLS) system* (see *http://en.wikipedia.org/wiki/Nearline_storage*). This enables you to swap SAP BW data to a secondary storage to reduce the data volume of the SAP HANA database (see also Chapter 8). This approach is particularly suitable for historic data, which is used comparatively rarely in reporting. In contrast to classic archiving via Transaction SARA, the access to archived SAP BW data is still possible when you deploy an NLS system. In other words, BEx queries can access data stored in the NLS system without having to load data back to the SAP BW system.

Advantages and disadvantages of NLS systems

The major advantage of NLS systems is that the main memory requirement for the SAP HANA in-memory database decreases as a result of the lower data volume. If you plan the deployment of an NLS system at an early stage, you may purchase a smaller and more cost-effective SAP HANA appliance or do without an expensive *scale-out solution*. Additionally, you can effectively restrict the data growth through NLS and an appropriate data retention strategy. An NLS system also helps customers to save license costs if the licensing is volume based, which is common for SAP HANA. The disadvantage of such a solution, however, is that the performance is lower for the analysis and reporting of archived data. For this reason, you shouldn't archive all data of the InfoProviders to an NLS system. Another disadvantage is that the operation of an NLS system involves additional costs.

Nearline Storage RDS

According to SAP, the NLS connection can be implemented within 12 weeks by means of the SAP NetWeaver BW Nearline Storage RDS package. From the technical perspective, this requires an SAP BW system with SAP BW 7.3 SP09, or 7.31 SP07 or higher. An SAP Sybase IQ database must also be installed. The RDS package comprises a step-by-step and configuration guide, as well as business process documentation. The quick guide of SAP Note 1887076 provides additional information on the installation of this RDS solution.

While the two previous RDS packages focus on an accelerated implementation of SAP solutions, SAP Business Intelligence Adoption RDS deals primarily with the provision of content. The RDS package includes numerous executable reports or scenarios for SAP BusinessObjects Dashboards, Webi, Crystal Reports, Explorer, Analysis Edition for OLAP, Design Studio, and SAP Lumira. From the technical point of view, these scenarios use, among other things, an SAP BW on SAP HANA system with SAP BW content, the SAP HANA database, and an ERP system. The different scenarios thus cover virtually all integration options of the various SAP solutions. In terms of content, the focus is on CEO analytics, sales, financial, purchasing, manufacturing, and more. In general, large parts of the RDS package can also be used without SAP HANA, but some examples require SAP BW on SAP HANA. For further information on these RDS packages, refer to the above website and SAP Note 1913805.

Business Intelligence Adoption RDS

3.2   Technical Requirements for Migration

To be able to migrate an SAP BW system to SAP HANA, some technical requirements must be met. Initially, the SAP BW system itself must have predefined minimum versions. For this purpose, you must check the versions of support packages and the kernel used, and update them as required. The previous database of the SAP BW system must also be updated before the migration begins. To prevent performance problems later on, it is important to have a high transfer rate between all systems. SAP recommends that you set up a dedicated server network communication with 10Gbps (see SAP Note 1514967).

Technical requirements

You must also check the requirements for the SAP HANA appliance. If some weeks pass between the delivery and the planned SAP BW on SAP HANA migration, the version of the preinstalled SAP HANA database may no longer be up to date. Talk to your hardware partner to ensure that the current database version is implemented on your SAP HANA appliance. Note that there are technical problems when upgrading SAP

SAP HANA appliance requirements

HANA revision 69 to version 70. In this case, don't update to revision 70, but directly to 72 (see SAP Note 1948334). Because further version conflicts cannot be excluded in the future, we advise you to read the corresponding SAP notes carefully before you update or upgrade SAP HANA. In general, you must also update the used SAP HANA client tools (for example, on the application server) after you've updated the SAP HANA database. The size of the SAP HANA appliance is also decisive in addition to the SAP HANA database's version. The hardware must meet the size requirements of your SAP BW system. This topic is discussed in Section 3.3.3. To find out which SAP HANA revision is suited for your specific scenario, you should read SAP Note 2021789 carefully because this note outlines the SAP HANA revision and maintenance strategy. It also informs you whether a *datacenter service point version* already exists for a specific support package stack (SPS) of the SAP HANA database that was verified by SAP for the productive use. When this book was completed, the highest available version of the SAP HANA database was Revision 82 (SPS 08).

Linux kernel and software packages

To avoid potential errors during operation, SAP recommends that you always use the latest kernel package for the SUSE Linux Enterprise (SLES) operating system (see SAP Note 1310037). For the *SLES for SAP Applications* version under SAP HANA, we also recommend that you deploy at least kernel version 2.6.32.19 (see SAP Note 1600929). Use the `cat/proc/version` command to identify the kernel version that is installed on your system. Your hardware partner will usually deal with this topic, but a second look on the system surely can't hurt. Further Linux information is also available in SAP Note 1944799, which contains, among other things, a list of required Linux packages. Recommendations on other operating system settings are provided in SAP notes 1824819 (for SLES 11 SP2) and 1954788 (for SLES 11 SP3). Information on the requirements for operation under Red Hat Enterprise Linux (RHEL) is available in SAP Note 2009879. If you use the SAP HANA database in revision 80 or higher with RHEL 6 or SLES 11, it is mandatory to import additional operating system software packages (GCC 4.7 library). You can find further information on this topic in SAP Notes 2001528 and 2020199.

A manual SAP BW on SAP HANA migration, as is described here, is only supported for SAP BW systems with version 7.3, 7.31, and 7.4, at the moment. So, if you want to migrate an SAP BW 7.0 system to SAP HANA, you must first update this system to a higher release or utilize the DMO migration option, which we discussed previously (see Section 3.1.3). In either case, you should first check which SAP BW authorization concept is used on the system (see the "Checking the BW Authorization Concept Used" box). If you still use the outdated reporting authorizations, you must first migrate to analysis authorizations before you upgrade your system. Also, bear in mind that you can't migrate any dual-stack systems to SAP HANA. If you're still deploying such a system, you must implement an ABAP/Java split prior to the upgrade (see SAP Note 1797362).

SAP BW system requirements

Checking the SAP BW Authorization Concept Used

[+]

If you want to migrate an SAP BW 7.0 system to SAP HANA, you must first implement an upgrade. As of SAP BW 7.3, however, the concept of reporting authorizations (RSR authorization objects) is no longer supported. Therefore, prior to the upgrade, you should determine whether your system already uses analysis authorizations or still deploys reporting authorizations. For this purpose, call Transaction RSCUSTV23 in SAP BW. If the obsolete procedure is still active, as you can see in Figure 3.14, you must change the authorization concept before an upgrade and thus before the SAP BW on SAP HANA migration. Although SAP provides the RSEC_MIGRATION report to support the migration, it is hardly possible to implement a full authorization migration without any manual intervention due to the different concepts.

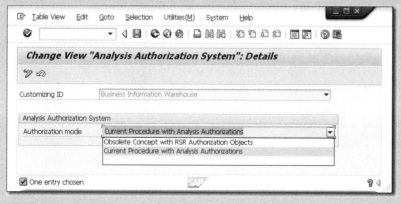

Figure 3.14 Configuration of the SAP BW Authorization Concept

If the SAP BW system (ABAP stack) to be migrated already has version 7.3, 7.31, or 7.4, additional preconditions must be checked. The requirements with regard to the support package stack (SPS), SAP kernel, and HANA database are discussed in SAP Note 1600929. We summarized the information that was valid when this book was written for the various SAP BW system releases.

SAP BW 7.3

To ensure a smooth SAP BW on SAP HANA migration of an SAP BW 7.3 system, you must meet the minimum requirements listed in Table 3.2. An SAP BW 7.3 system under SAP HANA uses SAP kernel 7.20_EXT_REL by default. If you plan the setup of a distributed SAP HANA landscape (*scale-out*), SAP recommends using the 721_EXT kernel because it now includes some performance improvements (see SAP Note 1600929).

Component	Required Version
Support package stack	Minimum SPS 08, SPS 10 recommended
Supported databases	IBM DB2 LUW 9.7 IBM DB2/400 7.1 IBM DB2 for z/OS V9, V10 MaxDB 7.8 MS SQL Server 2008 Oracle 11.2 SAP Sybase ASE 15.7
SAP HANA	Minimum SPS 06 (Revision 69), SPS 08 (Revision 82) recommended
Kernel	720_EXT: PL 300, R3loadctl PL 412 721_EXT: PL 100

Table 3.2 Migration Requirements for an SAP BW 7.3 System

SAP BW 7.31

The minimum requirements listed in Table 3.3 must be considered for an SAP BW 7.31 system. An SAP BW 7.31 system also uses the 7.20_EXT_REL kernel by default, which should be exchanged with the 721_EXT kernel when you set up a *scale-out* architecture.

Component	Required Version
Support package stack	Minimum SP05, SP09 recommended
Supported databases	IBM DB2 LUW 9.7
	IBM DB2/400 7.1
	IBM DB2 for z/OS V9, V10
	MaxDB 7.9
	MS SQL Server 2008
	Oracle 11.2
	SAP Sybase ASE 15.7
SAP HANA	Minimum SPS 06 (Revision 69), SPS 08 (Revision 82) recommended
Kernel	720_EXT: PL 300, R3loadctl PL 412
	721_EXT: PL 100

Table 3.3 Migration Requirements for an SAP BW 7.31 System

To ensure an error-free SAP BW on SAP HANA migration of an SAP BW 7.4 system, you must meet the minimum requirements listed in Table 3.4. If you want to migrate or operate SAP BW 7.40 with a support package status lower than 05, despite the general recommendation, you should use SAP HANA SP06 in revision 69 or the latest maintenance revision available. To utilize all functions of SAP BW on SAP HANA with SP05, you must deploy SAP HANA with SPS 07. Unfortunately, SAP Note 1600929 doesn't provide information about which databases are supported for a migration to SAP HANA below 7.4. We derived the missing information for you from the *product availability matrix* (PAM) and other SAP notes, like SAP Notes 1914052 or 1951491. However, we ask for your understanding that we can't guarantee the correctness of this data.

SAP BW 7.4

Further information on the technical requirements is also available in PAM (*http://service.sap.com/pam*) and in the section "Prerequisites and Implementation Considerations of the End-to-End Implementation Roadmap" (see "Information Material for New Installations" in Section 3.1.1).

Component	Required Version
Support package stack	Minimum SP05
Supported databases	IBM DB2 LUW 10.5
	DB2/400 7.1
	IBM DB2 for z/OS V10/V11
	MaxDB 7.9.008.23
	MS SQL Server 2012 SP1 CU7
	SAP Sybase ASE 15.7.0.122
	Oracle 11.2.0.3
SAP HANA	For SAP BW 7.4 up to SPS 07:
	Minimum SPS 07 (Revision 74),
	SPS 08 (Revision 82) recommended
	For SAP BW 7.4 as of SPS 08:
	SPS 08 (Revision 82 or higher)
Kernel	For SAP BW 7.4 up to SPS 07:
	Minimum PL 41 (741_REL)
	For SAP BW 7.4 as of SPS 08:
	Minimum PL 14 (742_REL)

Table 3.4 Migration Requirements for an SAP BW 7.4 System

3.3 Preparation Steps

Having previously discussed the technical requirements for an SAP BW on SAP HANA migration, let's now turn our attention on the preparation steps. Here, you'll first learn about the backgrounds and benefits of the optional step of creating a copy of the (live) SAP BW system before executing the SAP BW on SAP HANA migration. Then, we'll outline the cleanup activities in SAP BW, which are also referred to as *BW housekeeping activities*. The goal is to reduce the memory size of the current SAP BW database as much as possible to keep the initial main memory requirement of the future SAP BW on SAP HANA system as low as possible. You'll then learn how to derive the size requirements for the operation of an SAP BW system under SAP HANA from your current SAP BW system. We'll also introduce you to the checklist tool with which you can automatically check whether your SAP BW system is suited for migration. Finally, we discuss some more tools that could be useful for an SAP BW on SAP HANA migration.

3.3.1 Creating a Homogenous System Copy

Creating a homogeneous system copy is an optional step in an SAP BW on SAP HANA migration. This step pays off if you deploy the new SAP HANA technology for the first time and haven't gathered any practical experience yet. In this case, you shouldn't start off with the migration of a production landscape. You shouldn't underestimate the risks that essential aspects might not be considered to their full extent due to the high complexity and that the running operation could be obstructed as a result. We therefore recommend that you implement the first migration to SAP HANA with an SAP BW system that is not used in production. If a *BW sandbox* (isolated SAP system) is available, you can use this sandbox for the SAP BW on SAP HANA migration. Then, it could be useful to first run a *system refresh* from the production system to guarantee that the SAP BW data is completely up to date. If no such sandbox system is available yet, you should create an SAP BW system copy from one of your existing systems (at least temporarily).

When does a homogeneous system copy make sense?

If you use your production system as the basis, this provides a decisive benefit: you can perform extensive performance and system analyses without any risk after you've created the system copy and migrated it to SAP HANA—as if you'd migrated the production system directly. For this reason, this scenario is also ideally suited for running a proof of concept, particularly if you want to evaluate the speed benefits based on enterprise-specific production data (see Chapter 4, Section 4.2).

If you decide on a homogeneous SAP BW system copy, you first create a one-to-one copy of the SAP BW (production) system (❶ in Figure 3.15). For this to happen, the previously used database technology, for example, Oracle, DB2, or MS SQL Server, is used. All preparatory measures for the SAP BW on SAP HANA migration, such as cleanup activities or system validation, then take place in the system copy ❷. The prepared SAP BW system copy is then migrated to SAP HANA in the next step ❸. The concluding migration activities are performed on the SAP BW on SAP HANA system ❹.

Technical procedure

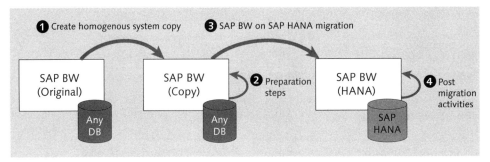

Figure 3.15 Typical Procedure for an SAP BW on SAP HANA Test Migration

Advantages of an SAP BW system copy

Copying an SAP BW production system and running an SAP BW on SAP HANA migration with this system copy results in the following advantages:

▸ No risk for the SAP BW production system in the case of an SAP BW on SAP HANA migration (side-by-side approach).

▸ No downtimes for the production system during the preparatory measures, SAP BW on SAP HANA migration, and post-migration measures.

▸ The system copy contains all data of the production system. There, you can analyze all issues and examine any technical problems that might occur.

▸ All preparatory measures—for example, cleanup activities—can be tested without any risk in the system copy before the same steps are carried out similarly in the production system.

▸ If a PoC is planned with a smaller SAP HANA appliance (for example, lower main memory equipment to save costs), you can clear SAP BW data of InfoProviders that are no longer required individually before migration.

▸ The effort for creating a homogeneous system copy is usually low because customers or IT outsourcing partners are familiar with this process.

Disadvantages of an SAP BW system copy

Creating an SAP BW system copy usually doesn't entail any disadvantages. Here are some aspects that should be considered, though:

▸ You may need to consider additional costs and time due to the upstream copy activities.

▸ You may need to provide additional hardware resources for creating and temporarily operating the SAP BW system copy.

▸ After the migration of the system copy, the SAP BW on SAP HANA instance usually cannot be used for replacing the existing SAP BW production system.

We want to discuss the last item in more detail. After a copy of the SAP BW production system was successfully migrated to SAP HANA and put into operation again, you may ask yourself if this system would also be suitable for replacing the current production system. This is conceivable in theory, but rather problematic in real life. One major reason is that the SAP BW production system and its clone were operated separately for a specific amount of time. During this time, new data is frequently loaded to the production system, and data flows and reports are updated. The gap between the production system and the copy grows with each transport that is imported to the production system. If local changes are permitted in the production system—for example, creation or adaptation of local BEx queries—you have to spend a great effort to transfer these changes to the SAP BW on SAP HANA system. Also, if the delta queues on the SAP BW system were not cloned when the copy activities started, you often must reconstruct most of the data (see also the marginal note "Cloning Delta Queues" in Section 3.1.3). The effort for removing these system differences is usually very high and error prone. In general, it's more useful, faster, and safer to subsequently carry out the migration of the SAP BW production system using the newly acquired knowledge.

Creating a standalone SAP BW system copy is comparatively easy from a technical point of view because neither the database type nor the underlying operating system changes. For this reason, this is also referred to as a *homogeneous* system copy. The data of the source system doesn't need to be exported to a file system first. Instead, the data can be copied directly using database-specific tools. They considerably simplify this process because the database-specific copy methods usually run very fast and without any errors. SWPM, which was presented previously (see the marginal note "Software Provisioning Manager" in Section 3.1.1), is deployed to make a homogeneous system copy. Make sure that you select the HOMOGENEOUS SYSTEM COPY option instead of the standard

Creating a system copy

system copy method (see Figure 3.16). All subsequent steps for creating a system copy are as usual.

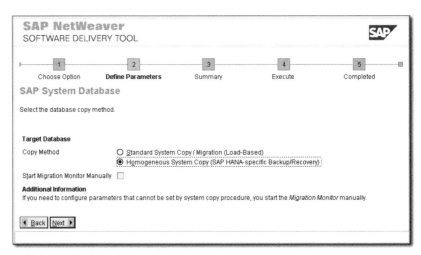

Figure 3.16 Homogeneous System Copy with SWPM

Summary From our point of view, you should always create a homogeneous system copy if you want to migrate an SAP BW system to SAP HANA for test purposes, which is often the case, for example, for PoC (see Chapter 4, Section 4.2). The additional effort is acceptable, and the advantages usually outweigh the disadvantages. You can thus test critical system activities—for example, data cleansing and repair actions—without any risks before you carry out the same steps for the migration of the SAP BW production system.

3.3.2 Cleanup Activities (SAP BW Housekeeping)

Why should you carry out cleanup activities? The size of the original system is an important aspect for the SAP BW on SAP HANA migration. Experience has shown that the amount of data that is undesired or no longer required increases continuously over the years. On one hand, this includes basic data, such as system statistics, log entries, or temporary objects. On the other hand, it also involves SAP BW data: for example, if obsolete InfoProviders still contain datasets or if change log tables feature extensive change histories, which are no longer required for the delta update. All of this data increases the costs of data retention, extends the system downtimes in case of maintenance, and reduces the performance of the SAP BW system. SAP therefore recommends scheduling regular *BW housekeeping activities* for data cleansing (see the "Important Housekeeping Principles for Keeping Your SAP NetWeaver BW in Good Shape" set of slides at *http://scn.sap.com/docs/DOC-13132*).

Unfortunately, the significance of data cleansing is not always recognized to the required extent. In real life, corresponding activities occasionally miss out. Cleanup and reorganization processes are also often omitted when creating new SAP BW applications. Users may create process chains that load data properly to the SAP BW system, but they don't provide for periodic deletion operations for cleansing the *Persistent Staging Area* (PSA). If the relevant PSA data packages are not deleted manually every now and then, this inevitably leads to a continuously growing memory requirement. In an SAP BW on SAP HANA migration, all data of the original system is transferred completely and then retained in the main memory. If no sufficient data cleansing takes place beforehand, you must also provide a larger main memory. This could result in higher costs for purchasing expensive hardware due to the larger main memory equipment. You may also have additional license costs if the licensing is coupled with the main memory utilization, which is common for SAP HANA. So you should reduce the size of the original system through targeted cleanup activities prior to an SAP BW on SAP HANA migration. The relevant steps will be discussed in detail in the following. Section 3.3.3 presents a tool with which you can identify the memory size requirements of your future SAP BW on SAP HANA system. It can be useful to run this tool multiple times to monitor the effectiveness of your cleanup activities over time.

Next, we'll detail the cleanup activities you can carry out in SAP BW systems prior to an SAP BW on SAP HANA migration. Although this applies to the entire book, we want to explicitly point out once again that we generally cannot assume any liability for possible errors and their results, careful examination notwithstanding. Any steps that are executed by you or third-parties are always at your own risk.

Disclaimer

Preferably, start with the planning of the SAP BW system cleanup as early as possible. On the one hand, users often underestimate the organizational effort, for example, if approvals must be obtained for deleting data in an SAP BW system (see the marginal note "Cleanup Activities" in Chapter 4, Section 4.1). On the other hand, many of the cleanup activities discussed here can be started in advance, independently of the SAP BW on SAP HANA migration. However, it can be useful to repeat some of these steps immediately before the migration begins. After all, the SAP BW system continues to operate, which is why new, undesired data can accumulate. Once you've carried out the cleanup activities in your SAP BW system yourself, you can judge for yourself which steps are worth repeating. For further background information, refer to the SAP documents and sources that are compiled in the "Information Material on SAP BW Cleanup Activities" box.

[⊕] **Information Material on SAP BW Cleanup Activities**

The following provide further information on SAP BW cleanup activities:

▸ Set of slides: Important Housekeeping Principles for Keeping Your SAP NetWeaver BW in Good Shape:
http://scn.sap.com/docs/DOC-13132

▸ Set of slides: Periodic Jobs and Tasks in SAP BW:
http://scn.sap.com/docs/DOC-11516

▸ SAP First Guidance document—BW Housekeeping and BW-PCA:
http://scn.sap.com/docs/DOC-46433

▸ Creating the SAP BW Housekeeping Task List:
http://scn.sap.com/docs/DOC-46240

▸ SCN Overview Page for SAP BW Cleanup Activities:
http://scn.sap.com/docs/DOC-7856#section16

▸ Data Management Guide:
http://service.sap.com/dvm • ADDITIONAL INFORMATION • DATA VOLUME MANAGEMENT • DATA MANAGEMENT GUIDE 6.6

▸ SAP Note 1829728—Task List for BW Housekeeping:
http://service.sap.com/sap/support/notes/1829728

▸ SAP Note 706478—Measures Against Fast Growing Basis Tables:
http://service.sap.com/sap/support/notes/706478

The subsequent subsections are structured as follows. We'll first present the BW housekeeping task list, which you can use to automate some cleanup activities. Then, you learn about the steps that you must carry out for cleaning up your SAP BW system. These steps are subdivided into SAP Basis and SAP BW activities.

Overview of the subsequent procedure

BW Housekeeping Task List

SAP provides a BW housekeeping task list to support regular SAP BW maintenance. If you already deploy an SAP BW system with minimum version SAP BW 7.30 with SPS 10, SAP BW 7.31 with SPS 08, or SAP BW 7.40 with SPS 06, you can use this list directly. Otherwise, you must execute the pre- and post-processing steps that are more or less elaborate, depending on your system's version. These steps are described in SAP Note 1829728. If your system doesn't have the minimum version mentioned previously and you must therefore implement the task list, you should first check whether your SAP BW system meets all preconditions. To do so, use the note analysis program, which was already described in the context of the DMO and PCA migration options (see Section 3.1.3). After you've loaded the two XML files (Basis- and SAP BW-specific provisions), the program's view changes (see Figure 3.9 and Figure 3.17).

Implementation of the BW housekeeping task list

Select the BW HOUSEKEEPING TASKS AND TASK LISTS option in this context. All SAP notes that are required for implementing the task list are loaded to the SAP BW system. Then, deploy the note analysis program again to check which notes must be imported. The program displays the results in a table (see Figure 3.10), and you can trigger the required implementation by navigating to the ACTION column. Ensure that you import SAP Note 1589145 for executing task lists, as well as the associated extensions (see SAP Note 1829728) to your system. The BW housekeeping task list is then implemented as described in SAP Note 1829728. If required for your version, import the appending source code ZNOTE_ 1829728_PRE.TXT to your system and execute it. After you've implemented SAP Note 1829728 in Transaction SNOTE, you must possibly import the ZNOTE_1829728_POST report to your system and execute it, too. Subsequently, the BW housekeeping task list is available for initial usage.

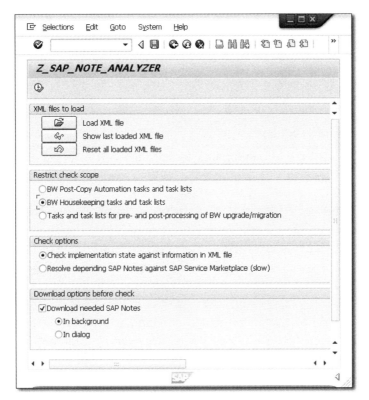

Figure 3.17 Note Analysis Program for the BW Housekeeping Task List

Using the BW housekeeping task list The BW housekeeping task list defines various tasks that relate to cleanup activities and SAP BW system maintenance. You can view and execute the SAP_BW_HOUSEKEEPING task list using Transaction STC01. Choose the BW housekeeping task list, and click GENERATE TASK LIST RUN F8. Figure 3.18 shows the list with its various tasks. They are each assigned to a specific phase (REPAIR, CLEANUP, or POSTPROCESSING). By clicking the checkbox in the first column (EXECUTE), you can plan a task for execution. If required, you can select the 📝 icon (EXECUTE PARAMETER) to provide further information. In the DELETE BW STATISTICAL DATA step, for example, you can thus define a period that specifies that statistical data of a specific period is to be deleted.

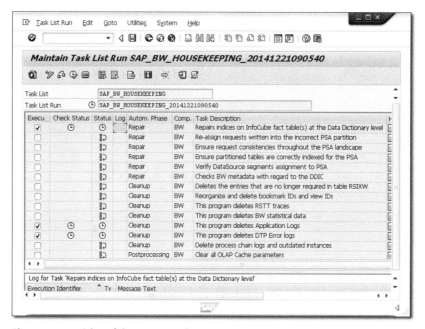

Figure 3.18 Display of the BW Housekeeping Task List in Transaction STC01

Weighing the Deletion of Statistical Data	**[+]**

Prior to running the cleanup activities, consider how you want to deal with the statistical data in the SAP BW system and whether you can delete the content of the corresponding InfoProviders (technical name 0tct_xxx) or statistical tables (RSDDSTAT*). In most cases, statistical data occupy a lot of memory space and are no longer required afterwards. But if you want to use this data to run before and after evaluations following the SAP BW on SAP HANA migration, you should only delete data outside the time to be considered. Select a longer period of time if you're unsure. You can also delete the statistical data itself later, in the SAP BW on SAP HANA system.

The BW housekeeping task list comprises, among others, steps for correcting inconsistencies, for example, related to fact tables of InfoCubes, partitioning of PSA tables, and SAP BW metadata. Moreover, the task list also includes cleanup activities, for example, for deleting logs, statistical data, and the OLAP cache. Table 3.5 provides an overview of the individual tasks. For readers who are interested in the technical background, we've included the respective ABAP reports that are called internally by

Overview of BW housekeeping tasks

the task manager to process a specific task. You obtain a good overview of the tasks that are already covered in the BW housekeeping task list and which steps may still be missing.

Task	Description	Internal ABAP Report
01	Correct indices of InfoCube fact tables	SAP_INFOCUBE_ INDEXES_REPAIR
02	Correct partition assignment of PSA requests	SAP_PSA_PARTNO_ CORRECT
03	Correct inconsistencies of PSA tables	RSAR_PSA_CLEANUP_ DIRECTORY or RSAR_PSA_CLEANUP_ DIRECTORY_MS
04	Correct indexing of partitioned tables	RSAR_PSA_PARTITION_ CHECK
05	Correct DataSource segment assignment to PSA	RSAR_PSA_NEWDS_ MAPPING_CHECK
06	Check inactive BW objects	RSUPGRCHECK
07	Delete data from Table RSIX-WWW (preliminary calculations of web reporting components)	RSRA_CLUSTER_ TABLE_REORG
08	Delete or reorganize bookmark IDs and view IDs	RSRD_BOOKMARK_ REORGANISATION
09	Delete logs of the RS trace tool (RSTT)	RSTT_TRACE_DELETE
10	Delete BW statistical data	RSDDSTAT_DATA_ DELETE
11	Delete application logs	SBAL_DELETE
12	Delete DTP error logs	RSO_DTP_ERROR_ LOG_DELETE_UI
13	Delete process chain logs and outdated instances	RSPC_INSTANCE_ CLEANUP
14	Delete OLAP cache	RSR_CACHE_FULL_ RESET

Table 3.5 Overview of Work Steps of the BW Housekeeping Task List

Executing the task list at regular intervals

SAP provided the BW housekeeping task list primarily to automate recurring routine tasks in SAP BW. Accordingly, you should schedule this task list regularly, for example, on a monthly basis. If you haven't scheduled this list yet, you should execute it at least once before the SAP BW on SAP HANA migration. Provided that your SAP BW system still uses an older release and you don't want to or can't implement the task manager or the task list in advance, you should perform the tasks listed in Table 3.5 manually. But before you call one of the previously mentioned ABAP reports manually in your system, you should get detailed information on the relevant step. Use the information material compiled in the previous box to obtain this information.

Basis Activities

Before you run an SAP BW on SAP HANA migration, you should generally check which SAP Basis tables are particularly large in your system (for example, larger than 100 MB) and carry out cleanup activities, if possible. To identify particularly large tables, you can deploy database-specific tools or use Transaction DBACOCKPIT in the SAP BW system. In the DBA Cockpit, you can find, for example, a list of the largest database tables for an Oracle database under SPACE • SEGMENTS • OVERVIEW • TOP SIZES. For the SAP HANA database, you can also find comparable information in the DBA Cockpit under SYSTEM INFORMATION • SIZE TABLES.

Cleaning up SAP Basis tables

You can also use the SMIGR_BIG_ROW_STORE_TABS ABAP report (see SAP Note 1634681), which identifies all row-based tables for SAP BW 7.4 systems from the *Data Dictionary* (DDIC) and analyzes them accordingly. Under SAP BW 7.3, however, the report additionally requires access to the *rowstorelist.txt* file, which is attached to SAP Note 1659383, for example. Call the report using Transaction SE38. Then, define a minimum size (for example, 100 MB) to identify the largest tables, and click EXECUTE. Your SAP NetWeaver or database administrator surely knows more options to find large tables in your SAP BW system. You should then carry out the cleanup measures that are described in SAP Note 706478 for the identified tables. You can find more information on cleaning up system-specific tables in the "Data Management Guide" (see "Information Material on SAP BW Cleanup Activities" box in this section).

The following now details the general cleanup activities in the SAP Basis area. Besides the activities described here, some older SAP documents

General cleanup activities in the SAP Basis area

may contain additional steps. Today, these are usually covered by the BW housekeeping task list and therefore don't have to be executed manually. These steps include, for example, the deletion of outdated application logs via Transaction SLG2, which is carried out by the task list indirectly via the `SBAL_DELETE` report (see Table 3.5, Task 11). Table 3.6 provides an overview of cleanup activities.

No.	Activity	Transaction or Report
1	Clean up log records for table changes	SCU3, RSTBPDEL
2	TemSe reorganization	SP12, RSPO1041
3	Delete old background jobs	RSBTCDEL2
4	Delete "abandoned" job logs	RSTS0024
5	Reorganize SAP Office documents	RSBCS_REORG

Table 3.6 Cleanup Activities in the SAP Basis Area

Step 1: Clean Up Log Records for Table Changes

Cleaning up log records

First, check whether the table logging is activated in your SAP BW system by calling Transaction SCU3. If you receive the error message "Table logging currently not active in your system," you can skip this cleanup activity. Otherwise, you should check via Transaction DB02, for example, the current size of Table `DBTABLOG` (log records for table changes) and whether it makes sense to run this cleanup measure. Follow SAP Note 41300 to delete or archive entries of the table logging. In Transaction SCU3, choose EDIT • LOGS • DELETE from the menu to start the `RSTB-PDEL` deletion report. Then, specify a time and select the tables for which you want to delete the logs. Also use the SAP Notes 434902 and 732470 to check whether the table logging is activated unnecessarily for some tables, and deactivate it.

Step 2: TemSe Reorganization

Cleaning up TemSe

The temporary sequential (TemSe) file is used as the storage system for storing spool requests or job logs of the background processing, for example. The relevant data can be stored in both the file system and the database. Reorganize the TemSe prior to an SAP BW on SAP HANA migration as defined in SAP Note 48400, TemSe and Spool Reorganization. In this context, run a consistency check (Transaction SP12 • TEMSE DATA STORAGE • CONSISTENCY CHECK). Then, select the inconsistencies to be deleted, and choose DELETE SELECTION. You can also utilize the RSPO1041 report to delete outdated spool requests. Note, however, that the RSPO0041 report that used to be deployed frequently is outdated now and should no longer be used (see SAP Note 130978).

Step 3: Delete Old Background Jobs

To delete old background jobs, call the RSBTCDEL2 report. In the lower area, a checkmark is set by default for TEST RUN. Deactivate this checkmark for deleting jobs. To receive more details during report execution, click the ⓘ icon or refer to SAP Note 784969.

Deleting background jobs

Step 4: Delete "Abandoned" Job Logs

It may occur under certain circumstances that job logs still remain in the SAP system even though the associated job has already been deleted. You can delete these "abandoned" job logs using the RSTS0024 report. SAP Note 666290 provides more detailed information.

Deleting job logs

Step 5: Reorganize SAP Office Documents

You can reorganize the data that accumulates when using SAP Office documents using the RSBCS_REORG report. Note here that you must implement the correction of SAP Note 1003894 in older systems. This should no longer be required for SAP BW 7.3 and 7.4 systems. You will find more details in SAP Note 966854.

Reorganizing SAP Office documents

SAP BW Activities

To clean up data in SAP BW, we recommend that you generally check whether you can delete or archive SAP BW data that is no longer required. Particularly when you perform a PoC (see Chapter 4, Section 4.2), it is usually possible to delete content of unused InfoProviders in advance, provided that you previously created a homogeneous system copy (see Section 3.3.1). You must also decide whether InfoProviders with redundant data—for example, DSOs at a lower level of the LSA architecture (see Chapter 5, Section 5.5)—can be emptied prior to the

SAP BW on SAP HANA migration. You can also consider the deletion of master data that is no longer required for data cleansing (see SAP Note 1370848). Some older documents still indicate that aggregates must also be emptied before an SAP BW on SAP HANA migration. However, it is no longer required to run this measure because aggregates are not exported during a migration to SAP HANA (see SAP Note 1644396). Real-life experience has shown that you obtain the best results when cleaning up PSA tables and change logs. Table 3.7 provides an overview of SAP BW cleanup activities, which are discussed in more detail next.

No.	Activity	Transaction or Report
6	Clean up Persistent Staging Area (PSA)	RSPC
7	Clean up change logs	RSPC
8	Compress InfoCubes	RSA1
9	Delete temporary SAP tables	SAP_DROP_TMPTABLES
10	Delete outdated messages, parameters, and temporary DTP data	RSBATCH_DEL_MSG_PARM_DTPTEMP
11	Delete DTP error stacks	RSB_ANALYZE_ERROR-LOG, RSBM_ERRORLOG_DELETE
12	Archiving of BW objects	SARA

Table 3.7 Cleanup Activities in the SAP BW Area

Step 6: Clean Up Persistent Staging Area (PSA)

Cleaning up PSA Before an SAP BW on SAP HANA migration, you should delete PSA tables whose data has already been loaded to other InfoProviders. You can generally delete PSA entries by creating a process chain with the process type DELETE REQUESTS FROM PSA and executing it in Transaction RSPC. If you want to find out which PSA tables should be deleted in your system, you can use the SAP HANA sizing report, which is presented in Section 3.3.3. Another option is described in the SAP Document "SAP BW—PSA/Change Log Deletion Governance," which describes the implementation of an ABAP report (ZBW_IDENTIFY_PSA; see *http://scn.sap.com/docs/DOC-12012*). Use Table RSTSODS to identify the assignment between DataSource and PSA. If you also determine PSA inconsistencies, read SAP Note 1150724, which describes the usage of corresponding correction programs. You can also delete the PSA error logs using the RSSM_ERRORLOG_CLEANUP report (see SAP Note 706478).

Step 7: Clean Up Change Logs

The change log data is also stored in the PSA tables. For all DSOs to which many requests have been loaded, you should delete the change log before an SAP BW on SAP HANA migration, provided that you don't require the relevant information for the delta update or an initialization. For this purpose, you can create a process chain as described in step 06, which now requires the DELETE REQUESTS FROM CHANGE LOG process type.

Cleaning up change logs

Step 8: Compress InfoCubes

To reduce the size of InfoCubes, you should compress them. Particularly consider those InfoCubes that have a high number of entries in the F tables. You can utilize the SAP_INFOCUBE_DESIGNS report to check the number of entries in InfoCubes. If you use an Oracle database, you can also run the SAP_DROP_EMPTY_FPARTITIONS report with the SHOW option (see SAP notes 430486 and 590370). Call the ADMINISTRATION function in Transaction RSA1 for the relevant InfoCubes, and go to the COMPRESS tab. Enter the appropriate request ID, and click on RELEASE.

Compressing Info-Cubes

Step 9: Clear Temporary SAP Tables

With the SAP_DROP_TMPTABLES report, you can delete temporary SAP BW objects from tables whose technical name starts with /BI0/0. However, it is not checked at runtime whether the corresponding SAP BW objects are still being used. This can result in terminations when queries, Info-Cube compressions, or data extractions are executed, provided that the relevant SAP BW activities run at the same time as the report. For more information about this report, see SAP Note 1139396. Details on the affected tables are available in SAP Note 449891.

Clearing SAP tables

Step 10: Delete Outdated Messages, Parameters, and Temporary DTP Data

The entries of Table RSBATCHDATA, which contains SAP BW runtime data, can be deleted using the RSBATCH_DEL_MSG_PARM_DTPTEMP report. Call this report directly via SE38, and enter the following parameters:

Deleting outdated system data

- ▶ DEL_MSG = 3
- ▶ DEL_PAR = 3
- ▶ DEL_DTP = x

The first two parameters define the number of days after which messages (DEL_MSG) or parameters (DEL_PAR) can be deleted (three days, respectively, in this case). Unfortunately, the exact functioning of the last parameter (DEL_DTP) is not documented sufficiently and must be set to delete table entries successfully. For more information, refer to SAP Notes 1338943 and 1511501.

Step 11: Delete DTP Error Stacks

Deleting DTP error stacks

First, run the RSB_ANALYZE_ERRORLOG report to display the DTP error stacks for your system. This allows you to check the error situation of the respective DTP and correct it as required. SAP provides the RSBM_ERRORLOG_DELETE report for deleting DTP error stacks. In this context, also refer to SAP Note 1938158, which recommends creating an index and running the report multiple times to optimize performance.

Step 12: Archive SAP BW Objects

Archiving SAP BW objects

By means of the classic archiving method (Transaction SARA), you can swap various SAP BW objects permanently from SAP BW and thus reduce the system size. However, the data is then no longer accessible. If you must access archived data later on, you first must reimport them to the SAP BW system. Table 3.8 provides an overview of archiving objects that are usually suited for archiving prior to an SAP BW on SAP HANA migration.

Archiving Object	Description
IDOC	Archiving of *Intermediate Documents* (IDocs); see SAP Note 1572522 for more information. Then, use SAP Note 505608 to check whether a reorganization of IDoc links can be carried out using the RSRLDREL report.
BWREQARCH	Archiving of request administrative data.

Table 3.8 Selected Archiving Objects of Transaction SARA

Archiving Object	Description
RSECPROT	Archiving of authorization logs. You can also use Transaction RSECADMIN to delete data (see SAP Note 1592528).
RSEC_CHLOG	Archiving of change records for analysis authorizations (see SAP Note 706478).

Table 3.8 Selected Archiving Objects of Transaction SARA (Cont.)

Other BW Housekeeping Activities

The presented activities certainly enabled you to clean up a large amount of tables and thus considerably reduce the target size of your SAP BW on SAP HANA system. If required, you can also perform additional cleanup activities in SAP BW. The "SAP First Guidance" document provides an overview of additional activities (see Section 3.3.2, "Information on SAP BW Cleanup Activities"). In section 1.1.4.1, "Additional Housekeeping Tasks," of the "SAP First Guidance" document also lists options for correcting inconsistencies in SAP BW. These include, for example, Transaction RSSGPCLA, via which you can delete programs that are already generated but outdated, or the ANALYZE_RSZ_TABLES report for removing inconsistencies. If you want to run the last-named ABAP report in repair mode, you should deploy least SAP BW 7.3 with SP 11 or import the relevant patches. After you've completed the cleanup activities in SAP BW, you can then identify the size requirements for the SAP BW on SAP HANA system.

Additional activities

3.3.3 Identifying and Checking Sizing Requirements

The relevant sizing requirements of an SAP HANA appliance are often identified by the participating hardware partner within the scope of a *hardware sizing*. In the SAP environment, the term *sizing* refers to the determination of system resources required for smooth operation of an SAP system and the necessary selection of the appropriate system architecture. In this process, the focus is on identifying the technical key figures, such as CPU performance or number, main memory equipment, hard disk capacity, or network bandwidth. The following now presents some general aspects for identifying the size requirements of SAP

Hardware sizing

HANA. You'll then learn about the sizing report for SAP BW on SAP HANA. We compiled an overview of the essential SAP documents relevant for this section in the "Information Material for Identifying SAP HANA Size Requirements" box.

[⊕] **Information Material for Identifying SAP HANA Size Requirements**

The following provide further information on identifying SAP HANA size requirements:

▶ General introduction to SAP sizing ("Right-Sizing Your Hardware"):
http://scn.sap.com/docs/DOC-8296

▶ SAP HANA Server Installation and Update Guide:
http://help.sap.com/hana/SAP_HANA_Server_Installation_Guide_en.pdf

▶ SAP Note 1514966—SAP HANA 1.0: Sizing SAP In-Memory Database. The attachment includes the general "SAP HANA In-Memory Database Sizing Guideline":
http://service.sap.com/sap/support/notes/1514966

▶ SAP Note 1637145—SAP BW on HANA: Sizing for SAP HANA. The attachment includes the special "SAP BW on HANA Sizing Guideline":
http://service.sap.com/sap/support/notes/1637145

▶ SAP Note 736976—Sizing Report for BW on HANA: The attachment includes the documentation for the "SAP BW on HANA Sizing Report":
http://service.sap.com/sap/support/notes/1736976

▶ SAP Note 1702409—HANA DB: Optimal Number of Scale-out Nodes for SAP BW on SAP HANA:
http://service.sap.com/sap/support/notes/1702409

Compression factor   The database size to be expected for SAP BW on SAP HANA can be derived from the size of the previous SAP BW system (*footprint*). Thanks to new compression procedures and a column-based data handling, SAP HANA's SAP BW data occupies considerably less memory space. In real life, however, the size savings vary highly. The *compression factor* (i.e., the size of the original database, divided by the size of the SAP HANA database after import) often ranges between 5 and 7. The effectiveness of compression ultimately depends on which original database is used and whether this database already uses compression procedures. In general, you shouldn't attach too much importance to the compression factor, but instead identify the size requirements of your SAP BW system using the sizing report.

The target size of the SAP HANA database directly influences the main memory equipment of the SAP HANA appliance because SAP BW on SAP HANA retains virtually all data in the main memory. However, the overall requirement for the main memory doesn't just involve the requirements for data retention. For example, some parts of the main memory must be reserved for temporary objects and for calculations at runtime. Various services of the SAP HANA database and the operating system also require their own main memory spaces, respectively. For technical reasons, SAP HANA can't allocate the entire main memory. Instead, you can reserve only 90% of the initial 64GB and 97% of the other memory areas of SAP HANA. More information is available in the PDF document *HANA_Memory_Usage_v2.pdf*, which you can download at *www.saphana.com/docs/DOC-2299*. If further applications (for instance, an SAP BW application server) are to be operated on the same hardware platform in addition to the SAP HANA database, their main memory requirement must also be taken into account. The "Simplified Calculation of the Main Memory Requirement" box illustrates an example for better understanding.

Main memory requirement

Simplified Calculation of the Main Memory Requirement [Ex]

An SAP BW system whose database size is 2TB is supposed to be migrated to SAP HANA, and the compression factor is 4 in this case. The SAP BW data of the original system is retained mainly on the hard disk, and only smaller data areas are loaded to the main memory at runtime. After the SAP BW on SAP HANA migration is complete, virtually all data is retained in the main memory. Due to the compression factor of 4, we can assume, in simplified terms, that the SAP BW data will occupy approximately 512GB of main memory. Also, the SAP HANA operation requires approximately 50GB main memory (services and caches). If we also assume that an additional 100GB must be reserved for temporary calculations, the overall requirement for the main memory amounts to 512GB + 50GB + 100GB = 662GB in this example. Because, as described previously, only parts of the available main memory can be allocated, an SAP HANA appliance with 1TB of main memory must be acquired.

Some facts were simplified in this example to ensure better understanding. We ignored, for example, that aggregates and database indices are no longer required for SAP HANA and that the data volume is reduced accordingly, compared with the original system. Also, SAP HANA can

Premises

compress column-based data more effectively than row-based data. To estimate the size requirements of the main memory correctly, the calculation would also have to consider the ratio of column-based and row-based data with the respective compression factors. The estimation of the main memory requirement should also take into account the expected data growth of the coming years. If you plan the deployment of an NLS system (see the marginal note "Nearline Storage" in Section 3.1.4), the data archiving strategies must be included in the evaluation of the main memory requirement.

Scale-up vs. scale-out approach

For larger SAP BW systems, it is possible that the maximum permissible main memory equipment of an SAP HANA appliance is not sufficient to map all SAP BW data in the main memory. If it is not possible to *scale-up* the memory because the maximum has already been reached, the data must be distributed across various instances (*scale-out*). An overview of the two approaches is available in Chapter 2, Section 2.1.3. In this case, SAP HANA must be installed as a distributed database that consists of multiple servers, also referred to as scale-out nodes (see Figure 3.19).

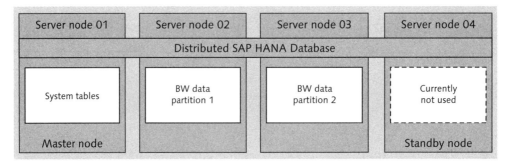

Figure 3.19 Schematic Structure of a Distributed SAP HANA Database with Four Server Nodes

The purpose of the *master node* is basically to cover the workload of the SAP BW application server and retain the row-based system tables in the main memory. The other nodes (*slave nodes*) process the master and transaction data, which is stored on a column basis under SAP HANA. If more than two slave nodes are used, SAP HANA can partition the SAP BW data and distribute it to the various servers. The data load time is reduced because of the parallel accesses, and the reporting speed is increased. It is also possible to add further nodes to the distributed SAP HANA database later on. However, this results in additional work because the data must be repartitioned and distributed across all nodes. *Standby nodes* allow you to implement high-availability scenarios and take over the task of another server node in case of failure.

If memory bottlenecks arise at runtime, the data can temporarily be displaced from the main memory. In this case, specially labeled data is removed preferentially from the main memory (see Chapter 5, Section 5.6). In SAP BW, this primarily involves data that is retained in write-optimized DSO and in PSA tables and is not used regularly for data loading processes or reporting. If you still need to access displaced data at runtime, this data is reloaded from the hard disk to the main memory. In this case, the system loads the smallest possible amount of data, for example, a specific partition of a column. The outlined mechanism is fully automated and requires no manual interventions.

Handling memory bottlenecks

All other system resources that must be identified for a smooth operation of SAP BW on SAP HANA can be derived from the main memory. This includes, for example, the hard disk capacity, which must have a size of at least 60GB plus four times the size of the main memory (see *SAP HANA Server Installation and Update Guide*, page 14–15). Note, however, that the backup data is not saved on the same medium, and additional capacities must be provided for backups. A user-dependent CPU dimensioning, which is common for an SAP system, is not planned, either. Instead, a fixed ratio of main memory and number of CPUs was specified for SAP BW on SAP HANA (see the PDF document *SAP_BW_on_HANA_Sizing_V1_6.pdf* in the attachment of SAP Note 1637145). This means that, for example, one core must be available for 16GB main memory (if you use a CPU with 8 cores). Every certified SAP HANA appliance already observes these specifications and provides additional system resources that are sufficient in relation to the main memory.

Further system resources

Sizing Report for SAP BW on SAP HANA

It has become clear that it is a core task for the SAP BW on SAP HANA migration to identify main memory requirements. This task is often assumed by the hardware partner, but it can also be useful to identify or

Identifying size requirements yourself

check the sizing requirements yourself. Fortunately, you don't have to calculate the main memory requirement yourself. Instead, you can use the sizing report provided by SAP for this task. You should no longer use the database-specific scripts of SAP Note 1637145. The sizing report is already integrated with newer SAP BW systems. For older systems, this report can be implemented manually. All necessary information on this topic is available in SAP Note 1736976. You should read this note carefully before running the sizing report note and, if required, import its corrections to your SAP BW system. Remember that you require at least SP 08 for the component ST-PI 2008_1_700 to import the relevant corrections. If you don't run any SAP BW system yet and require an initial sizing, you must use the SAP QuickSizer instead of the sizing report (*http://service.sap.com/quicksizer*).

Starting the sizing report Call the sizing report using Transaction SE38. Enter the technical name /SDF/HANA_BW_SIZING, and click EXECUTE F8. The initial screen opens (see Figure 3.20), where you can enter basic parameters for calculating the SAP HANA database size.

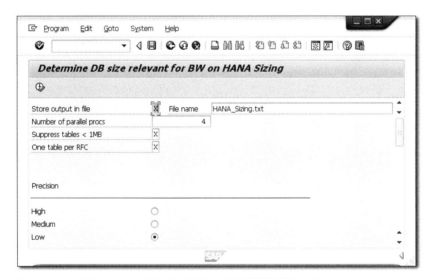

Figure 3.20 Initial Screen of the SAP BW on SAP HANA Sizing Report

Initially, specify a file name (for example, "HANA_Sizing.txt"), under which the report saves the results. If you want to call the sizing report several times—for example, to monitor the impact of your cleanup activities on your forecast database size—you should enter a separate name for each call. Otherwise, you overwrite the results of the previous call. You can also specify here how many CPUs are used for calculation. The higher the number, the faster you get a result. Pay special attention to production systems, and don't set the value too high; otherwise, this could decrease the system's performance.

The sizing report's output lists all tables that were used for the calculation. You can suppress smaller tables using the SUPPRESS TABLES < 1MB option. Moreover, you can run the report with three levels of precision. The more precise the result should be, the longer the runtime will take. Real-life experience has shown that the differences are sometimes rather low and that it makes sense to run the report more often with the lowest level of precision.

The sizing report also provides the option to include only specific Info-Providers in the sizing calculation. You can include the expected data growth for identifying the memory sizes. For this purpose, you specify the number of years and either a percentage or fixed data growth. Ultimately, you can also indicate whether write-optimized DSOs are to be taken into account for calculating the main memory. According to the concept of non-active data, the content of write-optimized DSOs is not retained permanently in the main memory. For this reason, their size is usually not relevant for the main memory calculation (see Chapter 5, Section 5.6).

Additional options of the sizing report

The primary task of the sizing report is to calculate the future database size under SAP HANA and to identify the future main memory requirement. To do so, it comprehensively analyzes the current SAP BW system, specifically the underlying database. Only row-based tables are available in the database prior to an SAP BW on SAP HANA migration. To identify the size of the subsequent SAP BW on SAP HANA system, however, the sizing report must take into account at runtime whether row-based or column-based tables are created in the future. As you can see in Figure 3.21, the identified memory consumption is output separately for rows and columns under the SUMMARY section. Let's now discuss this present sizing report output in more detail. The analyzed SAP

Evaluating the output of the sizing report

BW system currently includes 60.5GB of data, which will be available in row-based tables later on (for example, system tables). The share of SAP BW data that will be retained on a column basis is considerably higher. Their size amounts to 727.1GB in this system. The sizing report further breaks down the SAP BW data and indicates how much memory space is required for the various SAP BW objects (InfoCubes, DSO, change log, and PSA). This information can be particularly useful when you carry out cleanup activities (see Section 3.3.2). The sizing report helps you to easily identify the scope of change log files in the SAP BW system and whether targeted cleanup activities would pay off.

```
SUMMARY
=======


ABAP Size Row Store:            60.5  GB.  No. of tables:    1869

ABAP Size Column Store:        727.1  GB.  No. of tables:   42561
  Thereof:
          InfoCubes    389.7 GB                              1114
          Std. DSO      51.4 GB                              1564
        Change logs    130.0 GB                               493
          w/o DSO       16.0 GB                                58
              PSA      105.1 GB                              1493
        Master Data      8.5 GB                             10039
    Customer Tables      0.4 GB                                73
        Aggregates:  (not counted)                           1597

TOTAL:                                                      44893
```

Figure 3.21 Sizing Report Output (Part 1)

Sizing details   In the Sizing Details section (see Figure 3.22), you can view how the current memory usage will impact your future SAP BW on SAP HANA system. As a result of excellent compression within SAP BW or SAP HANA, which we've already discussed, the memory usage reduces to 41GB for row-based data and 129GB for SAP BW data under SAP HANA. Additionally, 50GB of memory is reserved exclusively for caches and services. In total, 220GB main memory is required for the analyzed SAP BW system, as is indicated in the DATA [GB] column. Some additional memory is required for temporary calculations, which is taken into account in the TOTAL [GB] INCL. DYN. column. The minimum main memory requirement for the SAP BW on SAP HANA system, therefore, is 390GB.

```
SIZING DETAILS
==============

(For 512 GB node)      data [GB]      total [GB]
                                       incl. dyn.
 Row Store                   41               82
 Column Store               129              258
 Caches / Services           50               50
                      _____
 TOTAL (All Servers)        220              390


SYSTEM INFORMATION
==================

 Report version :            1.8.9
 Execution date and time:    16.06.2014  09:30:01
 Runtime:                    01:24:07
 Parallel degree:            3 (s)
 Precision settings:         L
 Consider non-active data:   NO
 Use system subset:          NO
 RDBMS:                      ███████
 Operating System:           Windows NT
 hostname:                   ███████
 SID:                        ████
 Release:                    SAP_BW  740   SP0006
```

Figure 3.22 Sizing Report Output (Part 2)

The other details of the sizing report output indicate how many server nodes and which type thereof you require for implementation (see Figure 3.23). For the given example, you can see that the minimum size required (390GB) can be attained with a server node of 512GB, as well as a server node of 1TB.

```
MINIMUM SIZING RECOMMENDATION - CURRENT
==========================================

                           Phys. memory per node:    512 GB    1024 GB

Memory Requirement (Minimum Total):                   390 GB    390 GB
Disk Space Requirement - data (Minimum Total):        390 GB    390 GB
Disk Space Requirement - logs (Minimum Total):        390 GB    390 GB
Number of Nodes incl. master  (Minimum Total):          1         1

NOTE:
- Please carefully read documentation attached to SAP NOTE 1736976
  for a detailed description of the sizing procedure and its results!
- Disk space requirement calculation no longer includes space for backups
  dumps, etc. This space has to be provided on additional disk volumes. The
  guidance for sizing these additional requirements is described within the
  documentation attached to SAP Note 1736976.
```

Figure 3.23 Sizing Report Output (Part 3)

In the case of a larger SAP BW system, the sizing report output comprises detailed information for the sizing of the master node and the other server nodes. Figure 3.24 provides another output of the sizing report for better understanding. In this example, the SAP BW on SAP HANA system can be implemented either with three server nodes with 512GB each or as a separate SAP HANA appliance with 1TB. The SIZING DETAILS for the distributed SAP HANA database system (scale-out) must be read as follows: 149GB of main memory must be provided for the master node, which retains system tables for the most part. However, 800GB of memory is required for managing SAP BW data. If server nodes with 512GB each are available, this data must be distributed to two additional servers. For the scale-up approach, the simplified calculation is as follows: 700GB for SAP BW data + 99GB for system data + 50GB for caches and services results in 849GB, which is within the scope of the allowable memory space of a 1TB server.

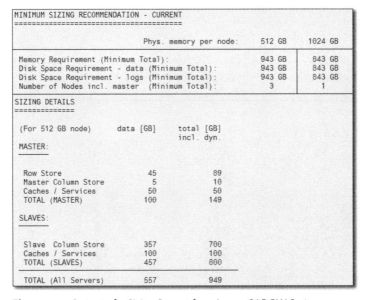

Figure 3.24 Output of a Sizing Report for a Larger SAP BW System

Summary For smaller SAP BW systems or sandbox systems, you can now determine for yourself the necessary sizing requirements for your future SAP BW on SAP HANA system. Due to the complexity, we recommend consulting experts with extensive experience with larger systems and the implementation of a distributed SAP HANA database. This task is often assumed by the hardware partner, anyway, but it is still helpful if you understand the interdependencies and can verify the relevant sizing recommendations of third parties.

Moreover, the sizing report is also suited for monitoring your BW housekeeping activities. You can, for example, execute the report before and after a specific cleanup activity to assess its effectiveness. It is also helpful that the report lists all tables that were analyzed. These are sorted by size, and the PSA or change log tables with many entries can be easily identified, thanks to the labeling (P) or (C). Finally, you should run the sizing report shortly before the SAP BW on SAP HANA migration to make sure that the SAP BW system's data volume is within the defined scope and that the system resources of the SAP HANA appliance meet the size requirements.

Reopening the Sizing Report Output [+]

The result of the sizing report is saved in the *DIR_HOME* directory (for example, *D:\usr\sap\<SID>\DVBMGS00\work*) in the SAP BW system by default. Even if you don't have direct access to the directory level of the server, you can open the output file via the SAP GUI. To do so, call Transaction AL11 (see Figure 3.25), and double-click DIR_HOME.

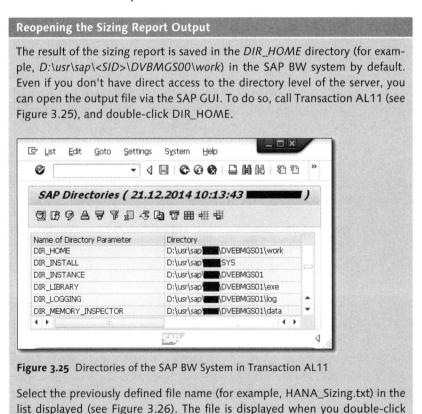

Figure 3.25 Directories of the SAP BW System in Transaction AL11

Select the previously defined file name (for example, HANA_Sizing.txt) in the list displayed (see Figure 3.26). The file is displayed when you double-click this row. You can also transfer this file to your local computer via the menu option LIST • SAVE/SEND • FILE.

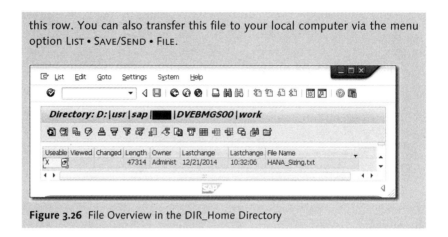

Figure 3.26 File Overview in the DIR_Home Directory

3.3.4 Preliminary System Validation

Checklist tool

If you followed our recommendations from the previous sections, you've already cleaned up your SAP BW system successfully and thus were able to reduce the target size of the future SAP BW on SAP HANA system considerably. Additionally, you aligned the sizing requirements of your SAP BW system with the resource equipment of your SAP HANA appliance. The next step now involves the system validation to ensure a smooth SAP BW on SAP HANA migration. For this purpose, SAP provides the *checklist tool*, which you should use before the migration. It automatically checks the prerequisites for an SAP BW on SAP HANA migration and aligns the properties of your SAP BW system with the best practice guidelines for smooth operation.

Installation

The checklist tool is attached to SAP Note 1729988 (see *http://service.sap.com/sap/support/notes/1729988*). The attachment includes the *SAP_BW_HANA_Checklist_<version>.zip* archive file for the ABAP source code of the tool, an overview presentation, and a more comprehensive how-to guide. To install the checklist tool, call Transaction SE38 to create the new ZBW_HANA_CHECKLIST ABAP report as an executable program in your development system. Copy the source code from the archive file (*ZBW_HANA_CHECKLIST.abap* for SAP BW 7.x systems and *ZBW_HANA_CHECKLIST_3X.abap* for older SAP BW 3.x systems) to the ABAP Editor. Save and activate the report. Before you execute it, you should check whether the necessary prerequisites are met in your SAP

BW system. For SAP BW 7.x systems, the ST-PI component must have version 2008_1_700 or higher. For SAP BW 3.x systems, the same component must have version 2005_1_640 as the minimum. You can check this in your SAP BW system by calling SYSTEM • STATUS and clicking on the 🔲 icon to display the component information. SAP recommends using the current version available for the SAP host agent (see SAP Note 1031096). Otherwise, some operating system information cannot be evaluated and thus is not included in system validation.

Now, call the checklist tool in your sandbox or development system, and check the correct functioning of the tool. If your SAP BW system is based on an older version (for example, 7.00 or 7.01), errors may occur at runtime or when activating the checklist tool. In this case, some necessary software components may be missing in your SAP BW system. The how-to guide of SAP Note 1729988 describes how to proceed in this case. Follow these recommendations to comment out the relevant areas in the source code. You can then reactivate the report. You should be able to identify the relevant sections in the source code easily because the blocks are each marked with *** BEGIN and *** END. You can undo these modifications after a system update. Once you've ensured in the development system that the ABAP report is working properly, transport it to the SAP BW system that you want to migrate to SAP HANA. To execute the checklist tool, log on to this SAP BW system and start the report via Transaction SE38.

Checking and transporting the report

After execution, the initial screen shown in Figure 3.27 is displayed. Under the CHECKS tab, you can select the categories in which checks are to be made. At the moment, more than 250 different checks can be run automatically in the following categories:

Selecting categories

▶ GENERAL CHECKS

▶ DATABASE

▶ SAP BASIS

▶ CORRECTIONS (for SAP Basis, SAP BW, and add-ons)

▶ BW DATA WAREHOUSE MANAGEMENT

▶ BW OLAP PROCESSOR

▶ BW PLANNING PROCESSOR

- ▶ BW Enhanced Infrastructure
- ▶ BW System
- ▶ BW Technical Content
- ▶ Customer objects
- ▶ Checks for the Post Copy Automation tool (PCA)

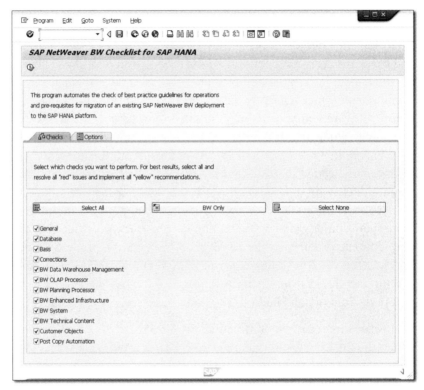

Figure 3.27 Initial Screen of the Checklist Tool

You can choose the required categories using the Select All, BW Only, and Select None buttons. In principle, nothing speaks against running all checks. In real life, however, it may be possible that you as the user don't have the necessary authorizations for all categories. In this case, the report must be executed by several persons with different selections. It is advisable to restrict the categories if you try to troubleshoot a specific error and the check of all categories would take too long.

After you've selected your categories, locate the OPTIONS tab. There, you can define whether you also want to execute long-running checks (INCLUDE LONG-RUNNING CHECKS). If you use DMO (see Section 3.1.3), you should make the relevant selection here. You can also specify that the logs generated will be saved (SAVE LOG). In this case, the program saves the results in the application log under the `MIGRATION` sub-object of the `RSD` object (see Transaction SLG1). Provided that you use SAP BW 7.3 or SAP BW 7.31 as the original system, you can also specify whether the checks are to be made for the same system version or you intend to deploy SAP BW on SAP HANA in version 7.4 later on. After you've made your selection, you can click EXECUTE ⊕ or press F8 to start the report.

Options

After the checklist tool is executed, you probably receive an output with a very large number of warnings and error messages (see Figure 3.28). For the SAP BW system in our example, 45 errors are found and are marked with a circle traffic light icon.

Output and trouble-shooting

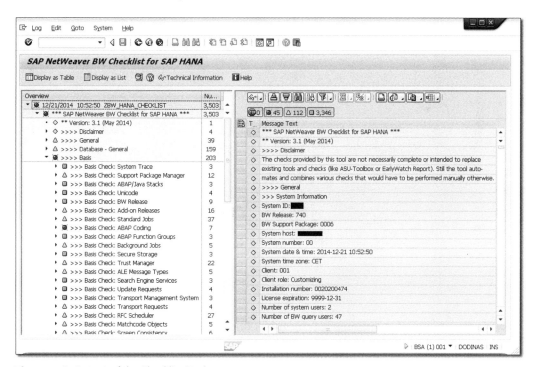

Figure 3.28 Output of the Checklist Tool

SAP explicitly recommends that you troubleshoot all errors before you start the migration to SAP HANA. Sometimes correcting these errors may be somewhat more comprehensive, so you should transport the ABAP report to the relevant SAP BW system at an early stage to estimate the correction effort already some months prior to the scheduled migration. Some of these problems, such as inactive InfoObjects, can be solved quickly; others, however, may be more elaborate if SAP notes and/or support packages must be imported. Go through the individual errors, and delegate the troubleshooting to the responsible persons in you enterprise. Only if all errors marked with circle traffic light icons are corrected in the SAP BW system can you be sure that no undesired side effects will occur during the migration to SAP HANA.

Once all errors have been remedied, you can turn your attention on the warnings (triangle icons). Remove as many of them as possible. Here, we recommend that you make at least those updates that involve interfaces of SAP HANA or the migration tools. For more information on possible errors, refer to the how-to guide that is attached to SAP Note 1729988. There, you can find additional information on the respective checks in the individual categories and references to other SAP notes.

Check routines for SAP BW on SAP HANA

Also note that the checklist tool comprises check routines for SAP BW on SAP HANA systems. Once you've successfully migrated your SAP BW system to SAP HANA, you should rerun the ABAP report. You may receive further errors and warnings, which you should also correct to ensure smooth operation.

[+] **Saving the Results Locally in HTML format**

HTML is a suitable target format to transfer the results to your computer. In this format, you can view the report's output, including icons, on other computers or mobile devices, as well (see Figure 3.29).

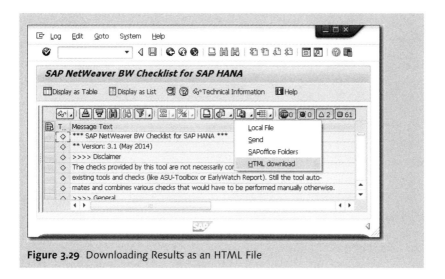

Figure 3.29 Downloading Results as an HTML File

3.3.5 Additional Tools

We'll now present some additional tools that provide useful information within the scope of an SAP BW on SAP HANA migration. A good overview of these tools and the currently available versions is available under *http://scn.sap.com/docs/DOC-40984*. The overview of this website also includes the tools already discussed here, for instance, the sizing report (see Section 3.3.3) or the checklist tool (see the previous section). The following sections describe the *ABAP Routine Analyzer*, *BW Transformation Finder*, and *BW Migration Cockpit*.

The ABAP Routine Analyzer enables you to analyze the performance of ABAP routines that are used in data flows. Here, you can detect all ABAP statements that should be optimized for operation under SAP HANA. To install the tool, download the attachment of SAP Note 1847431. The *SAP_BW_ABAP_Analyzer_<version>.zip* archive file includes the source code that you must transfer to your SAP BW system. Create ABAP Report ZBW_ABAP_ANALYZER in Transaction SE38, and copy the source code accordingly. Save and activate the report. Click EXECUTE ⏺ (or press F8) to navigate to the initial screen of the tool (see Figure 3.30).

ABAP Routine Analyzer

137

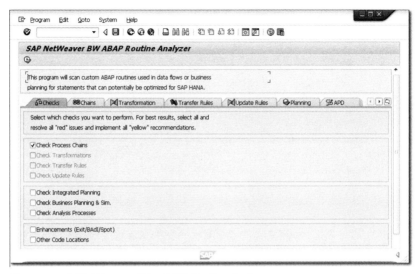

Figure 3.30 Initial Screen of the ABAP Routine Analyzer

Identifying problematic ABAP statements In the default setting, you can examine the process chains in your SAP BW system. To do so, you can set the relevant filter criteria or select the desired process chains on the CHAINS tab. It is also possible to analyze individual transformations, planning functions, or analysis processes instead of entire process chains. Based on your selection, the tool then determines whether it is useful to optimize the relevant ABAP statements for SAP HANA. In Figure 3.31, for example, a potential problem was identified for the considered transformation because a direct database access to another DSO is done using the SELECT SINGLE statement within a characteristic routine. In this case, the logic should be implemented with internal tables for performance reasons, or it should at least be replaced with the default function READ FROM DATASTORE. You can find further information on the ABAP Routine Analyzer in the associated documentation, that is, the how-to guide and the overview presentation that are attached to SAP Note 1847431.

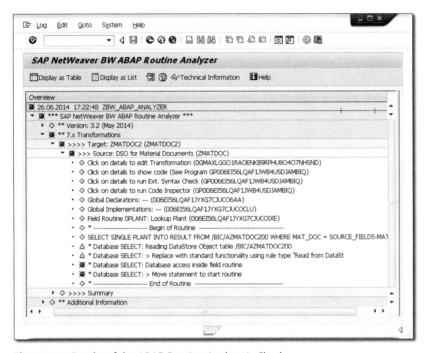

Figure 3.31 Results of the ABAP Routine Analyzer's Check

The second tool to be considered involves the BW Transformation Finder. It enables you to search for transformations in SAP BW systems using your own search criteria. For example, you can determine that the tool should find only transformations with a currency conversion or characteristic routine. You can also specify which traffic light icons (green, yellow, or red) are assigned to the respective criteria in the output. To install the Transformation Finder, download the attachment of SAP Note 1908367. In this case too, the archive file (*SAP_BW_Transform_Finder_<version>.zip*) contains the source code, which you must copy to your SAP BW system. Create ABAP report ZBW_TRANSFORM_FINDER in Transaction SE38, and copy the source code accordingly. Save and activate the report. Then, click EXECUTE to view the initial screen of the tool ⊕ (see Figure 3.32).

BW Transformation Finder

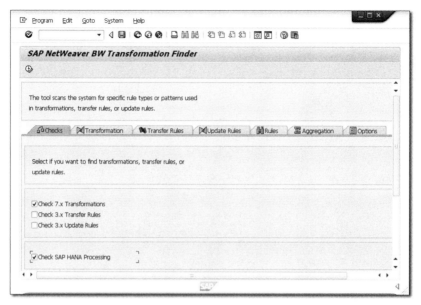

Figure 3.32 Initial Screen of the BW Transformation Finder

Usage options of
the BW Transforma-
tion Finder

You can use the BW Transformation Finder, for example, to identify all InfoProviders that can be omitted in principle under SAP HANA. Here, all InfoCubes that obtain data from a DSO come into consideration without further modification. Under SAP BW on SAP HANA, you can achieve equivalent reporting speed if the BEx queries are based on a DSO. Using this tool, you can find such InfoProviders indirectly via the corresponding transformations. For these, you can then decide whether you keep them unchanged or want to remove them from your SAP BW system. Consider this carefully before you delete an InfoProvider; ideally, you can exchange the InfoProvider with the DSO in the relevant MultiProvider. But if you built your reporting directly on an InfoCube, you should transfer the existing BEx queries to the appropriate DSO using Transaction RSZC.

Application for SAP
BW on SAP HANA

Once you've successfully migrated your SAP BW system to SAP HANA using at least version SAP BW 7.4, it is worthwhile to execute the Transformation Finder again. Use the CHECK SAP HANA PROCESSING option, which is available on the CHECKS tab under SAP HANA, to display whether a transformation can be run on the SAP HANA database (see the section "Code Push-Down in Transformations" in Chapter 5, Section 5.1.2). In this case, the transformation or associated DTP can be executed with considerably higher speed. Let's consider the result of the example in Figure 3.33, in which two transformations have been analyzed. The first transformation for InfoSource 0PA_AS_2 cannot be executed directly in SAP HANA because it contains an ABAP routine. The execution of the transformation for InfoSource 0PA_AS_3, however, can be moved directly to the SAP HANA database. In this case, you can adapt the associated DTP after the SAP BW on SAP HANA migration and select the SAP HANA EXECUTION there.

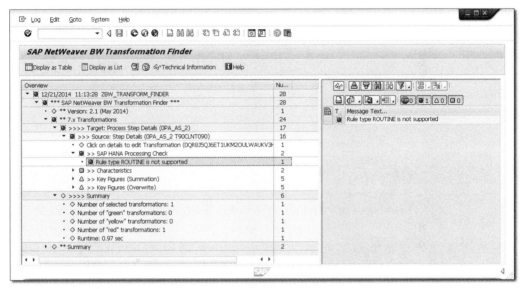

Figure 3.33 Results of the BW Transformation Finder Check after Migration to SAP HANA

The last tool to be presented here is called BW Migration Cockpit. It combines various tools to make the SAP BW on SAP HANA migration more user friendly. Like the other tools, you must first install the cockpit in your SAP BW system. To do so, download the attachment of SAP Note 1909597. The source code that you must copy to your SAP BW system is available in the attached archive file (*SAP_BW_Migration_Cockpit_<version>.zip*). Create ABAP report ZBW_HANA_MIGRATION_COCKPIT in Transaction SE38, and copy the source code accordingly. Save and activate the

BW Migration Cockpit

report. Choose EXECUTE 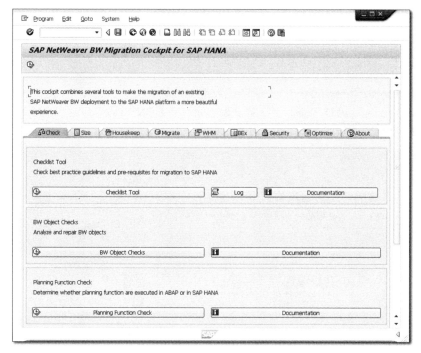 to navigate to the initial screen of the BW Migration Cockpit (see Figure 3.34).

Figure 3.34 Initial Screen of the BW Migration Cockpit

The most critical tools that are referenced from the BW Migration Cockpit have already been presented or will be presented later on. The BW Migration Cockpit provides only very few new features, which is why we won't discuss this tool in further detail here. More detailed information is available in the overview presentation that is attached to SAP Note 1909597.

3.4   SAP BW on SAP HANA Migration

Having looked at the preparation steps of a migration, this section now looks at the actual SAP BW on SAP HANA migration. As was already outlined in Section 3.1, the following sections focus on a manual migration (classic migration method) due in part because this is the method that is most frequently used in real life. The "Information Material on SAP BW on SAP HANA Migration" box lists useful documents and sources on this topic.

Information Material on SAP BW on SAP HANA Migration

The following provides further information on SAP BW on SAP HANA migration:

▶ Website on system copy and migration in SCN:
  http://scn.sap.com/docs/DOC-8324

▶ Best Practice Guide—Classic Migration of SAP NetWeaver AS ABAP to SAP HANA:
  http://scn.sap.com/docs/DOC-47657

▶ Heterogeneous ABAP System Copy—Technical Overview:
  http://scn.sap.com/docs/DOC-34258

▶ System Copy and Migration Guides:
  http://service.sap.com/sltoolset—SOFTWARE LOGISTICS TOOLSET 1.0—DOCU-MENTATION—SYSTEM PROVISIONING—SYSTEM COPY: SYSTEMS BASED ON SAP NETWEAVER <RELEASE>—<PLATFORM>

▶ Additional Information for the SAP BW on SAP HANA Migration under BW 7.3:
  http://scn.sap.com/docs/DOC-12262

▶ Additional Information for Scale-out Scenarios:
  http://scn.sap.com/docs/DOC-39682

▶ SAP Note1600929: Information on SAP BW on SAP HANA:
  https://service.sap.com/sap/support/notes/1600929

▶ Implementation—BW on HANA Export/Import:
  https://scn.sap.com/docs/DOC-41588

▶ SAP Note 886102—Copy of the System Landscape for SAP NetWeaver BW:
  https://service.sap.com/sap/support/notes/886102

▶ SAP Note 1775293—Migration/System Copy to HANA Using the Current SWPM:
  https://service.sap.com/sap/support/notes/1775293

Next, as an example, we'll describe the SAP BW on SAP HANA migration using an SAP BW 7.4 system (ABAP stack) based on Oracle 11.2. In this scenario, the SAP BW application server is operated on separate

Scenario

hardware under Windows 2008 R2. A certified SAP HANA appliance is available for migration (single-node system). The migration is done using the SWPM (see the marginal note "Software Provisioning Manager" in Section 3.1.1) with the latest version available (see Section 3.2). All preparation activities that must be carried out in advance (see Section 3.3) have already been made. Because the system to be migrated is a sandbox system already, the optional step for creating a homogeneous system copy has been skipped here. Furthermore, we assume that the system ID (SID) of the SAP BW system remains unchanged during the SAP BW on SAP HANA migration.

Procedure of the SAP BW on SAP HANA migration As shown in Figure 3.35, the migration of the SAP BW system starts with the export of all data. To do so, we start the SWMP and connect it with the present SAP BW application server ❶. Using this application server, the SWPM accesses the database and exports all data to the file system ❷. The SWPM is then started in the target environment to build the new SAP BW on SAP HANA system. Initially, a new SAP BW application server that uses SAP HANA as the primary database is installed ❸. The SWPM is then used to import the previously exported data to the new SAP BW on SAP HANA system ❹.

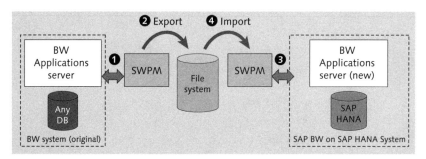

Figure 3.35 Schematic Procedure of the SAP BW on SAP HANA Migration

Considering current SAP documents When you carry out the migration, it is vital that you consider the current migration guidelines and SAP notes. If you identify any differences, you should follow the SAP documents in case of doubt. These are updated continually and adapted to the current available software versions.

3.4.1 Export Preparations

Before you can export the current state of the SAP BW system, you must first take some preparation steps. These activities ensure that the SAP BW system is in a consistent state in order to avoid possible data losses during the export phase. The following lists the most essential steps. Version-dependent guides and SAP notes, however, also include some supplementary steps. Depending on your system version, you should use the documents that are provided in the "Information Material on SAP BW on SAP HANA Migration" box to determine whether you must schedule additional steps.

Step 1: Lock Users

To successfully export the SAP BW system in a consistent state, you must temporarily stop the operations in SAP BW. To do so, all users must be locked temporarily from the system. Here, it is important that you exclude the administrators that are involved in the migration, emergency users, and the DDIC user from the locks. Use Transaction SU01 to lock individual users in SAP BW and Transaction SU10 to lock multiple users at the same time. First, choose all users for which no system lock has been set yet. To do so, click the LOGON DATA button in Transaction SU10, and choose the USERS WITHOUT LOCKS ONLY option under SELECTION BY LOCKS. Initially, select all users, and then remove the previously described administration users from the selection. Save this list so that you can undo the lock process later on without releasing IDs that have been locked before. Then, click the LOCK icon 🔒. Before you continue, check whether any users are still logged on to the system using Transaction SM04. Proceed with the subsequent steps after all users have logged off from the SAP BW system.

Locking users

Step 2: Stop the Process Chains

In the next step, you must stop the internal processing operations in the SAP BW system. For this purpose, you must temporarily stop the process chains and the processes of the *Real-Time Data Acquisition* (also referred to as RDA daemons) using the `RS_SYSTEM_SHUTDOWN` report in Transaction SE38 (see Figure 3.36). Choose SHUT DOWN PROCESSES, and

Stopping the process chains

select the PROCESS CHAINS and DAEMONS options. Then, click EXECUTE ⊕ or press [F8].

Figure 3.36 Stopping the Process Chains

Step 3: Clear Delta Queues

Clearing delta queues

To lower the risk of a possible data loss, SAP advises you to clear the delta queues of connected source systems prior to the export and transferring existing entries to the SAP BW system. To do so, log on to the connected source systems and start Transaction RSA7. Check in the displayed table whether it lists DataSources for your SAP BW system that have a value greater than zero in the TOTAL column. In this case, you should run the corresponding InfoPackage in your SAP BW system for the relevant DataSource to transfer the data to the SAP BW system. If technical connection problems occur, the background users that are required for this operation may already be locked. Unlock them temporarily for the data transfer. Provided that you've created delta queues in the SAP BW system, this data should also be retrieved from the connected systems.

Step 4: Stop Job Processing

Stopping the background processing

You must also temporarily stop the background processing so that the data in the SAP BW system remains unchanged during the export. This step also ensures that the jobs are not executed uncontrolled in the future SAP BW on SAP HANA system after the migration work is done.

For this purpose, call Transaction SE38 in the SAP BW system, and start the BTCTRNS1 report for stopping the background processing. Note that this report doesn't require any further entries and thus starts immediately. After successful execution of the report, you receive an output as shown in Figure 3.37.

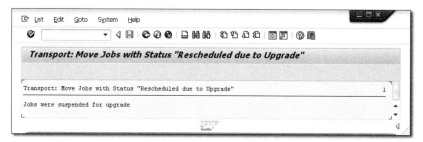

Figure 3.37 Stopping the Background Processing

Step 5: Clear Temporary SAP Tables

Even if you've already cleared the temporary SAP BW tables within the scope of the cleanup activities, you should now rerun this step after all activities are discontinued in the SAP BW system. As described in step 9 in Section 3.3.2, call the SAP_DROP_TMPTABLES report for this purpose.

Clearing SAP tables

Step 6: Update Table DBDIFF

Table DBDIFF contains information about deviations between the corresponding objects of the Data Dictionary (DDIC) and the database. This table records, for example, if objects in DDIC have another type than in the database. All differences that are not recorded correctly in this table prior to running the export can result in technical problems later on. For this reason, you should call the SAP_UPDATE_DBDIFF report in Transaction SE38 to update these entries.

Updating Table DBDIFF

Step 7: Export Native Database Objects

The SMIGR_CREATE_DDL ABAP report generates SQL statements that you can use to transfer native database objects of the current SAP BW system to the SAP BW on SAP HANA system. The report creates several SQL scripts that are all listed in the SQLFiles.LST file. All files generated by

Exporting database objects

the report are imported later on, when you create the target environment and the database objects are reconstructed in the SAP HANA database. But before you execute this report, you should check whether all important corrections and enhancements have been imported to your system. For this purpose, carefully read SAP Note 1921023. Then, execute the ABAP report in Transaction SE38. As illustrated in Figure 3.38, choose SAP HANA DATABASE as the target database. Enter the appropriate path on the SAP BW application server under INSTALLATION DIRECTORY.

Figure 3.38 Exporting Native Database Objects

If you operate this application server under UNIX or Linux, make sure that the SAP BW system has the required authorizations for writing to this directory. Observe SAP Note 2022386 if the files generated are too large. In some circumstances, problems may occur relating to the Java memory requirement when you execute the Software Provisioning Manager.

The TABLE CLASSIFICATION and ESTIMATED TABLE SIZE options are selected by default when you call the report, although these options are required only for distributed SAP HANA databases. For more information, please refer to SAP Note 1921023. Under SAP BW 7.3 and 7.31, the report includes the additional option ROWSTORE LIST. If you select this option, the report generates the rowstorelist.txt file, which includes all SAP tables that are to be created with row basis under SAP HANA. In this case, you no longer require the RowStore list from SAP Note 1659383 (see SAP Note 1815547). This file is required later on for creating the target environment for SAP BW 7.3x systems. For SAP BW 7.4 systems, however, this list is no longer needed. So, if you run the SMIGR_CREATE_DDL report in an SAP BW 7.4 system, this option is not provided.

Export settings

You don't have to select the SUITE ON HANA option for an SAP BW on SAP HANA migration. This option is used for migrating SAP Business Suite systems only. It generates, among other things, the HDB_TABLE_CLASSIFICATION.TXT file that contains information on the classification of tables for the distribution and partitioning in a distributed SAP HANA database. In this context, you must note, however, that the *scale-out* option is not generally released for SAP Business Suite systems yet (see SAP Note 1825774).

Step 8: Check the DDIC Password

Before you continue with the export phase, you should check the DDIC password in the SAP BW system as the last step. To do so, log on to Client 000 as the DDIC user. You must enter this password later on to complete the migration. If you can't determine the password, you must reset it before the export.

Checking the DDIC password

3.4.2 Export Phase

After you've prepared the SAP BW system appropriately, you can now start the export activities. In the standard case, you first export the SAP BW system. Once this export is completed successfully, the export files are made available to the target system as the basis for the new SAP BW application server. Due to the sequential execution of the export and import phases, the SAP BW on SAP HANA migration takes comparatively long. For this reason, we'll use the option for parallel export and import. This allows you to start the import in parallel to the export, which considerably reduces the overall duration of the SAP BW on SAP HANA migration. However, in this case, you must save the export files in a directory that you can access from the target environment. To create the necessary directory structures, you must call the SWPM in the environment of the SAP BW original system using the EXPORT PREPARATION option.

Starting the Export Preparation phase Section 3.1.1 already described how to call the SWPM. For your SAP BW original system, start `sapinst` or `sapinst.exe` with a user that has administrator rights. However, don't use the `<SID>adm` user for this purpose. Select your system version and the currently used database from the overview. Choose SYSTEM COPY • SOURCE SYSTEM • BASED ON AS ABAP TOWARDS SAP HANA DB • EXPORT PREPARATION, and click NEXT (see Figure 3.39).

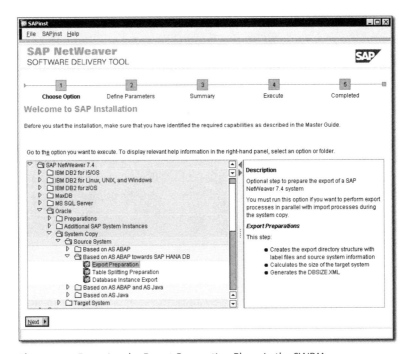

Figure 3.39 Executing the Export Preparation Phase in the SWPM

In the next dialog window, enter the path to the profile directory (for example, *D:\usr\sap\<SID>\SYS\profile*) and the password of the <SID>adm user. Then, check the SID and the server name, and click NEXT. You must now enter the export directory. Don't use a network directory for this purpose; instead, use a local directory like *D:\Export\DB* in our example (see Figure 3.40). This enables you to prevent possible inconsistencies during file export. If you want to use this option for parallel export and import, you must add a network share to this directory. Only then can you access this directory and the export files contained therein from the target system during the export run.

Directories

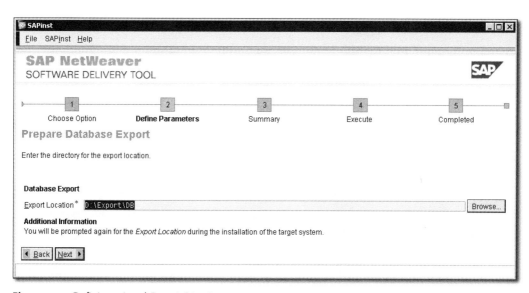

Figure 3.40 Defining a Local Export Directory

In the next step, choose SAP HANA DATABASE as the future database for the target system. Then, recheck all of your entries before you start the execution. The SWPM creates the export directories as illustrated in Figure 3.41. Most of the directories are empty at this point. Only the LABEL.ASC files and another configuration file are stored for labeling in the ABAP subdirectory. The current SWPM session is completed after the export directory structure has been created successfully.

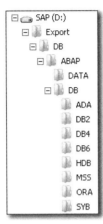

Figure 3.41 Generated Export Directories

Starting the
Database Instance
Export phase

Restart the SWPM as the next step. Like before, select your system version and the database version. Then, select System Copy • Source System • Based on AS ABAP towards SAP HANA DB • Database Instance Export. The next dialog windows are identical to those of the Export Preparation phase. Enter the path to the profile directory and the password of the `<SID>adm` user. Then, check the system entries. Subsequently, choose the export directory you've just created (for example, *D:\Export\DB*). This step asks you whether the SAP BW system is to be stopped manually later on. If you activate this option, you'll have better control over the subsequent processes.

In the next dialog window, you must enter the directory that you've used for the execution of the `SMIGR_CREATE_DDL` ABAP report for exporting native database objects (see step 7 in Section 3.4.1). In our example, the path is *D:\Export\SMIGR*. If you now click on Next, an input screen opens, as shown in Figure 3.42.

Here, you must select SAP HANA Database as the target database again. With the Split STR-Files option, you can specify whether the STR files, which are structures that contain the definition of tables, indices, or views, for example, into various smaller data packages during the export process. You should not select the Start Migration Monitor

MANUALLY option because if you do, the system doesn't automatically start the migration monitor (*MIGMON*), which controls or optimizes the parallel load processes, among other things.

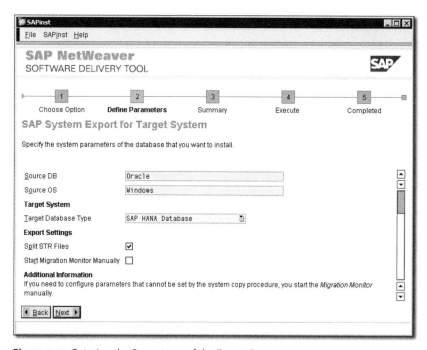

Figure 3.42 Entering the Parameters of the Target System

In some circumstances, the next view contains a warning, as shown in Figure 3.43. Two files are not found in our example (HDB_TABLE_CLASSIFICATION.TXT and rowstorelist.txt). The first file is required only if you use a distributed SAP HANA database, so you can ignore this warning if you operate a single SAP HANA instance only (see SAP Note 1921023). For SAP BW 7.4 systems, you can also ignore the second warning relating to the rowstorelist.txt file (see step 7 in Section 3.4.1). Provided that no other problems exist, you can choose CONTINUE and click NEXT to skip the warning.

Skipping the warning

153

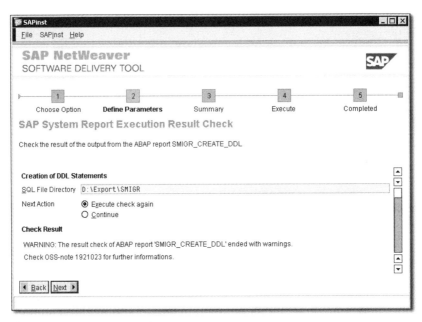

Figure 3.43 Warning During Export

Export options In the next dialog window, choose the NEW EXPORT FROM SCRATCH option to start a new export run. You are then prompted to select which method the R3szchk tool should use to identify the size of the original database. The database-independent option USE DATA DICTIONARY INFORMATION is selected by default here. In our projects, however, we've had good experiences with the second option, USE DATABASE-SPECIFIC IMPLEMENTATION. This option may be less precise because it uses internal statistics data and is not always up to date, but the execution is considerably faster. In one case, the R3szchk run was reduced from 90 minutes to just 10 minutes. After you've clicked NEXT again, an input screen opens, which provides options for splitting files. If you additionally called the SPLITTING TABLE PREPARATION export phase beforehand, you should specify the generated file here. We omitted this option in our example. In our opinion, however, you should increase the number of the largest tables to at least 50, as illustrated in Figure 3.44. In this case, the 50 largest tables are split into separate data packages respectively, which in turn allows for accelerated parallel processing.

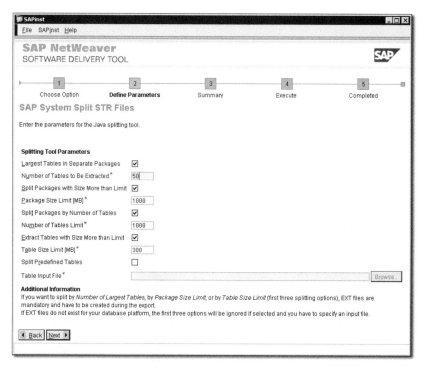

Figure 3.44 Parameters for Splitting Files

You must enter general export parameters in the next input screen (see Figure 3.45). Depending on the hardware used, you must first specify the system-internal byte representation. A general distinction is made between *little-endian* and *big-endian systems*. SAP Note 552464 provides a general introduction to this topic. Your participating hardware partner can inform you whether your system is little-endian or big-endian. Also define the number of processes that should run in parallel during the export later on. In this context, SAP recommends scheduling two or three parallel R3load processes for each CPU. If you want to use the option for parallel export and import, as we suggest, you must specify this at this point. Select the checkbox for PERFORM PARALLEL EXPORT AND IMPORT, then click NEXT.

Export parameters

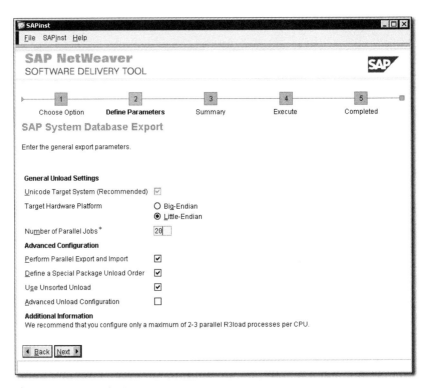

Figure 3.45 Export Settings

Export sequence
In the next window, you must define the export sequence. Simply use the default setting Size. In this case, the export is carried out sorted by size, starting with the smaller packages. The package size then increases gradually. The number of parallel processes that you've defined previously (in our example, 20, which is entered in the Number of Parallel Jobs field in Figure 3.45) must now be split into two groups. Unless good reasons exist, we recommend keeping the default values.

Click Next again, and the next input screen opens. There, you must specify how export data is transferred to the target system. We've selected Use Network Share because we made the export directory available to the target system via a network share. In the next step, you define a directory for the communication exchange in which status files are exchanged between the two systems. In our example, we created the new directory *D:\Export\MIGMON* for this purpose. You should create this directory locally on the SAP BW application server and make it available to the target system via a network share (see Figure 3.46). Check your entries once again.

Figure 3.46 Defining the Communication Directory

Next, you start the export run. It stops after a while, and the notification from Figure 3.47 is displayed. To continue, you must shut down the SAP BW system and then click the OK button.

Starting the export

Figure 3.47 Notification for Shutting Down the SAP BW System

Don't Start the SAP BW Original System Again	**[!]**

While the export is running (see Figure 3.48), you can already continue with the import preparations. Ideally, however, you shouldn't start the SAP BW original system again. If you still need to do so, you must ensure that no data is loaded from the connected source systems.

Figure 3.48 Running the Export

If delta records are called otherwise—for example, after the export run is complete—these data records are missing in the SAP BW on SAP HANA system later on, which may result in inconsistencies. In this case, you can resolve these inconsistencies only through new initialization and reconstruction of data.

[+] | **Predicting the Runtime**

By means of the UMG_R3LOAD_RUNTIME_PREDICTION report, you can determine the approximate runtime of the export. Information on using this report is available in the application's help when you click the **H** icon. For more information, you can also refer to SAP Note 857081.

3.4.3   Import Preparations

Checking the storage space
Only a few activities are required for the import preparations. First, you should check the size of your file system so that sufficient storage space is available for the target environment. Because you normally deploy a certified SAP HANA appliance, this condition should be met automatically.

Before you start the import phase, you must set the log mode of the SAP HANA database in such a way that the log files are overwritten during import. Otherwise, it may happen that the log files' storage medium reaches its capacity limit, and crashes occur during migration. It is also important to reset the log mode to the original value after the import run is complete. Note that the log files can be generated again only after a backup of the database is made (see Chapter 6, Section 6.4).

Defining the log mode of the SAP HANA DB

To deactivate the generation of log files, open SAP HANA Studio and double-click your SAP HANA system. Go to the CONFIGURATION tab in the ADMINISTRATION perspective. Enter the search term "Log_mode" in the filter box, or expand the tree GLOBAL.INI • PERSISTENCE. An input window opens if you double-click LOG_MODE. For SYSTEM, set the log mode parameter to OVERWRITE, and then click SAVE. As soon as the OVERWRITE value is active (see Figure 3.49), the SAP HANA database overwrites the log files (redo logs) periodically and doesn't wait for backups. For this reason, a *point-in-time recovery* is no longer possible then, so don't use this setting in production systems. The backup mechanism continues in the background, unaffected by this change. It copies the log segments to the intended medium (basepath_logbackup parameter) every 15 minutes by default (log_backup_timeout_s parameter). You should also temporarily stop this process during an SAP BW on SAP HANA migration. To do so, choose the ENABLE_AUTO_LOG_BACKUP parameter under GLOBAL.INI • PERSISTENCE in the same view, and set it to NO. SAVE this change.

Deactivating the log generation

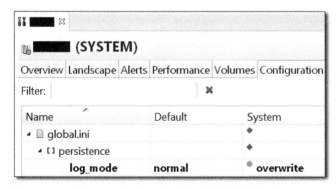

Figure 3.49 Changing the Log Mode in SAP HANA Studio

Setting up system users

If you deploy Windows as the operating system for your future application server, you must decide whether the Windows system users are to be created locally or as members of a domain. If you want to use the option for parallel import and export, it can be useful to create this user directly in the domain. Depending on the system configuration, this simplifies the access to the export directory, which was created locally on the original system. The general rule applies to all operating systems that the access to export data must always be ensured for the <SID>adm user during the import run. If you are unsure about the correct configuration, consult your responsible network expert. You can start with the import if the log mode was set correctly and the remote access to the export directory is possible.

3.4.4   Import Phase

Checking the access to the network drive

Provided that you opted for the parallel export and import option, you can now already start with the import phase, even though the export is still running. Before you start the SWPM again for your target environment, you should check once again that you can access the existing export directory. For our example, we will access this directory via the network using \\<server name>\directory. You don't have to assign a separate drive letter to the directory because the SWPM can't use this letter directly. If you receive an error message when you try to access the remote directory, this could be caused by the firewall settings. If you deploy Windows Server 2008, you may need to temporarily lower the security level of the USER ACCOUNT CONTROL (UAC) function.

Starting the SWPM for import

Now, start the SWPM on the target server, and choose your SAP BW version and SAP HANA DATABASE as the target database. Then, select SYSTEM COPY • TARGET SYSTEM • STANDARD SYSTEM • BASED ON AS ABAP • STANDARD SYSTEM, and click NEXT (see Figure 3.50).

You must specify in the next step whether you prefer the TYPICAL or CUSTOM installation method. We recommend selecting CUSTOM here because you are then provided with considerably more configuration options. You don't have to use them all and can take over the default settings unchanged. Specify the SID of your SAP BW system next.

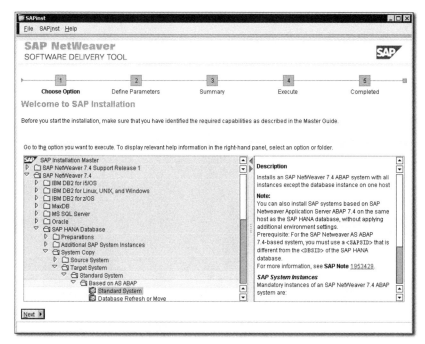

Figure 3.50 Calling the SWPM for Creating the Target Environment

If you carry out an SAP BW on SAP HANA migration and want to replace your original SAP BW system, we recommend entering its SID here. For the sake of simplicity, we will restrict our explanation to this case in this book. If you want to change the SID, you must schedule additional activities subsequently, for example, the call of Transaction BDLS for implementing the logical system names (see SAP Note 886102). Next, enter the path to the SAP kernel, and specify an administrator password.

Because the database is supposed to be changed during the migration, you must choose the default copy method for running a heterogeneous system copy. You should not choose the START MIGRATION MONITOR MANUALLY option: you want the migration monitor (MIGMON) to start automatically. Next, enter the connection parameters to your SAP HANA database. These include the database ID (DBSID), the server name, the instance number, and the password. Click NEXT until an input screen is displayed in which you must enter the path to the SAP HANA Client. Make sure that the versions of the client and database match (see

Database information

Section 3.2). Next, you must specify the path to the export files. Enter the network patch directly. For our example, the path is *server name*\ *Export\db\abap* (see Figure 3.51). You can usually keep the default settings in the other input screens. If specific details, such as the SAP schema, of your original system don't comply with the standard, you must change the input screens accordingly.

Figure 3.51 Access to the Remote Export Directory

Ignoring warning messages

If you received warning messages already when executing the SMIGR_ CREATE_DDL report, they will also be displayed during the configuration of the import run in the SWPM (see "Step 7: Export Native Database Objects" in Section 3.4.1). Provided that the files are available with the file extension *.sql*, you can ignore the displayed warning messages that inform you that the two files rowstorelist.txt and HDB_TABLE_CLASSI-FICATION.TXT are missing. For this purpose, select the CONTINUE option under NEXT ACTION (see Figure 3.52), and click on NEXT. The next step prompts you to provide the HdbLandscapeReorgParameters.SQL file and enter the corresponding path. This file is attached to SAP Note 1900822. However, you need to download it only if you deploy a distributed database. If you use a single SAP HANA instance, as in our example, you can choose the DO NOT USE A PARAMETER FILE option and skip this item, too.

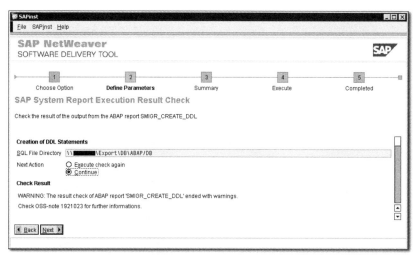

Figure 3.52 Skipping Warning Messages

In the next input screen, you must provide import-specific information (see Figure 3.53).

Migration key

Figure 3.53 Defining the Database Import Parameters

Analogous to the export, you must also define the number of parallel processes with which the import is carried out. SAP recommends using two or three parallel processes for each CPU. Then, you must enter a *migration key*, which is required for transferring encrypted data during migration. You must request this key specifically for your system via the website *http://service.sap.com/migrationkey*. If you want to use the option for parallel export and import, as suggested, you must set the checkmark for PERFORM PARALLEL EXPORT AND IMPORT.

Specifying the communication directory

You must specify the communication directory in the next input screen. The exporting and importing SWPM instances exchange critical control information via this directory (see Figure 3.54). In the original system, we specified the *d:\Export\MIGMON* path for our example. Accordingly, the path must be entered with the corresponding server prefix in the target system, for example, "\\<server name>\Export\MIGMON."

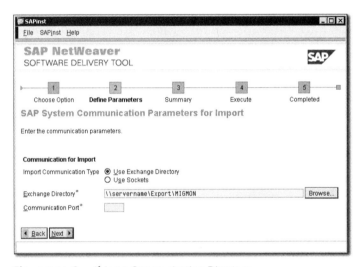

Figure 3.54 Specifying a Communication Directory

Instance number

Next, assign a new instance number for the SAP system. The instance number is a two-digit figure that uniquely identifies SAP components on a computer. In this context, you must assign an instance number for the primary application server (PAS) and the *ABAP SAP Central Services* instance (ASCS). Further information on PAS and ASCS instances is available in the document under *http://scn.sap.com/docs/DOC-42518*.

Moreover, you can decide if the installation routine should include an interruption before the new SAP BW on SAP HANA system is started. We omitted this option for our example. Now, you must enter the password of the DDIC user from Client 000. During the preparation activities, we already indicated that you would require this password (see "Step 8: Check the DDIC Password" in Section 3.4.1).

DDIC password

Finally, all selected parameters are displayed in an overview. Check them carefully, and correct any possible errors. When you click NEXT, the system starts with the installation of the SAP BW on SAP HANA system (see Figure 3.55). You must analyze the log files if problems occur during installation or import. The corresponding directory is usually displayed in the error message. An occasional problem is that the <SID>adm user of the SAP BW application server has no access rights for the export files, and import therefore aborts.

Checking your entries

Figure 3.55 Executing the Installation Procedure

For parallel export and import, you can now trace the activities on both systems at the same time. While the export is still running on the SAP BW original system (see Figure 3.55), the existing data packages are

Parallel export and import

already imported on the SAP BW on SAP HANA target system. In Figure 3.54, you can follow this in the footer. In our example, there are 30 parallel imports (RUNNING), 79 packages are available for import (WAITING), and 27 are already completed (COMPLETED). The number of available packages will gradually increase until the export run is completed successfully in the original system. Once the import phase is also completed successfully, you've already mastered the biggest obstacle of migration. Now, start with the post-processing, which is discussed in Section 3.5.

In case of error
If you encounter an error during the import run that you can't remedy despite intensive analysis, you should open an SAP customer message. For this purpose, log on to the SAP Service Marketplace with your user (*S-User*), and choose HELP & SUPPORT • PRODUCT ERROR. The processing time for troubleshooting depends on the priority. To accelerate this process, you should enter a very meaningful test, open the system connections already at this point, and select the correct application component. Consider our remarks in the "Creating an SAP Customer Message in Case of a Problem" box.

[+] **Creating an SAP Customer Message in Case of a Problem**

If an error situation that you can't correct occurs during the SAP BW on SAP HANA migration, you can create an SAP customer message. SAP Note 752505 provides basic information on this procedure. It describes which information and log file should be provided to SAP. Create a customer message for the relevant SAP BW system, and open the system connections. Select one of the following application components, and ideally document your problem with screenshots:

▶ BC-INS-MIG-TLA: For concrete problems with a specific migration tool
▶ BC-INS-MIG: For general problems during the SAP BW on SAP HANA migration
▶ BC-DB-HDB-INS: For database-specific problems with SAP HANA

3.5 Post-Migration Steps

Post-processing
After you've successfully completed the SAP BW on SAP HANA migration using the SWPM, you must finish with some post-processing work. Like in every SAP BW system migration, this also involves several activities in

the SAP Basis area, such as setup of the transport landscape, maintenance of operation modes, or adaptation of the RFC server group. The Basis activities that arise after the SAP BW on SAP HANA migration don't really differ from the activities that you perform after the migration of SAP BW systems with a regular database. For this reason, we'll discuss them only briefly and primarily present new activities specifically required for SAP BW on SAP HANA.

3.5.1 General Post-Processing

Before you start with the SAP BW-specific post-processing, we recommend taking the following steps immediately after the SAP BW on SAP HANA migration.

Step 1: Switch on Log Mode and Run Backup

Before you execute any other steps, we strongly advise you to reset the database's log mode and create a backup. To do so, open SAP HANA Studio, and go to the CONFIGURATION tab in the ADMINISTRATION perspective (see Section 3.4.3). Expand the GLOBAL.INI • PERSISTENCE tree. An input window opens if you double-click LOG_MODE. Set the log mode parameter of SYSTEM back to NORMAL. You must also reset the value for ENABLE_AUTO_LOG_BACKUP to YES. Note that the database doesn't generate any log files until a backup has been created. In the standard case, you open the backup dialog for this purpose by right-clicking your SAP HANA system in the system tree. Select BACKUP AND RECOVERY • BACK UP SYSTEM from the menu. If another backup method is configured for your system, you should use this method instead of the default method.

Resetting the log mode and running a backup

Step 2: Activities at Operating System and Database Level

Then, your responsible SAP Basis administrator should carry out some activities at the operating-system level of the new SAP BW application server. These include, among others, the adaptation of the instance and default profile; connection of external software components, such as job scheduler or monitoring solutions; and the integration of application-specific network directories, such as NFS mounts. Moreover, some database tables must be cleared after the migration. An overview of these

Settings in the operating system and database

activities is available in the respective migration guide (see Section 3.4, "Information Material on SAP BW on SAP HANA Migration").

Step 3: Basis Activities in the SAP BW System

SAP Basis activities in SAP BW

As mentioned initially, we want to outline the general SAP Basis activities only briefly. Because the individual steps are discussed in detail in the migration guide, we provide an only overview in Table 3.9. This table does not claim to be exhaustive, and changes are possible for new versions.

Activity	Transaction
Perform installation check	SM28 or SICK
Import system profiles	RZ10
Maintain operation types	RZ04, SM63
Check logon groups	SMLG
Set up spool server	SPAD, SP12
Import SAP license	SLICENSE
Maintain security settings	STRUST, SECSTORE
Adapt RFC server groups	RZ12
Adapt RFC connection	SMQR, SM58, SM59
Maintain partner profiles	WE20, WE21
Set up transport system	STMS
Check external commands	SM69
Maintain DBA Planning Calendar	DB13

Table 3.9 Overview of Most Critical SAP Basis Activities

Step 4: Execute the Post-Migration Report

Executing the post-migration report

Call Transaction SE38, and enter the program name RS_BW_POST_MIGRA-TION. This program is generally used to carry out database-specific adaptations after a heterogeneous system copy. A separate variant (SAP& POSTMGRHDB) is available for the changeover to SAP HANA, which you should use. Start the report in the background by clicking the WITH

VARIANT button and selecting said variant. Provided that you want to run the report directly, ensure that the checkmark is set for the CREATE CALC VIEWS CUBES/INFOOBJECTS field. Otherwise, the system doesn't create the logical indices, and queries may not be executable (see SAP Note 1695112). This report's runtime is long and sometimes requires more than an hour, depending on the system size and version.

3.5.2 SAP BW-Specific Post-Processing

Next, you must carry out the SAP BW-specific post-processing activities in your new SAP BW on SAP HANA system.

Step 5: Restore Myself System and SAP BW Source Systems

Due to the locking of all users in the original system and creation of a system copy, the users are also automatically locked in the SAP BW on SAP HANA system. You should unlock the technical system users again if you haven't done so yet. Make absolutely sure that no SAP BW end users are released at this point. Then, check in the MODELING • SOURCE SYSTEMS view of Transaction RSA1 whether you can access the SAP BW Myself system. To do so, expand the tree of SAP BW systems, and right-click your SAP BW system. Then, click CHECK in the displayed menu. If you receive an error message, you must analyze and troubleshoot it. In many cases, it is sufficient to execute the RESTORE menu item. Then, also CHECK and RESTORE the connected source systems. Here, you may need to enter the passwords of the relevant background users. For this reason, you should preferably carry out these steps together with the administrator that is responsible for the respective systems.

Restoring Myself system and SAP BW source systems

Step 6: Adapt BI Lock Server

If you use BW Integrated Planning (BW-IP), you may need to adapt the configuration for the lock server (*BI enqueue server*) using the transaction for the BI lock server. If, for example, the name of the SAP BW application server has changed, you must correct it here. If you also use the SHARED OBJECTS MEMORY option for managing the lock table, you may receive an error message at runtime. Then, you should switch the administration of SHARED OBJECT MEMORY OF A SERVER to the LOCK

Adapting the BI lock server

SERVER option, which is available on the LOCK TABLE tab of Transaction RSPLSE. For more information, please refer to SAP Note 1594606.

3.5.3 Identifying and Remedying Inconsistencies

The following describes how to identify possible inconsistencies in the SAP BW system and remedy them before the SAP BW system is released.

Step 7: Check PSA

Checking PSA

With the `RSAR_PSA_NEWDS_MAPPING_CHECK` report, you can check for all DataSources whether the respective PSA is obsolete or inactive. For this purpose, execute the report without the repair option in Transaction SE38. If the report identifies inconsistencies, you should execute it again with the repair option. Note that you must reestablish the source system connections and release the defined technical users before executing the report.

Step 8: Check SAP BW System for Inactive Objects

Checking the SAP BW system for inactive objects

You can optionally run the `RSUPGRCHECK` report to ensure that all InfoObjects, DSOs, and InfoCubes are activated correctly after the SAP BW on SAP HANA migration. Start this report in Transaction SE38, and set the checkmark for DISPLAY LOG (see Figure 3.56). This report also has a long runtime and possibly aborts in dialog mode. Then, you must execute the report in the background. In this case, however, you don't receive any direct output on the screen, nor will you find any log in the relevant job log. The output of this report is available in the RSUPGRCHECK.<SID> file of the DIR_PUT directory or its *tmp* subdirectory. If the *DIR_PUT* directory points to an invalid location or is not available in Transaction AL11, you must change this accordingly before the report run. If you receive warning messages for this report in the SAP BW on SAP HANA system, you can ignore them if they have already been displayed in the original system prior to migration. Otherwise, you should check the error carefully and observe the "Activation of Inactive SAP BW Objects" box.

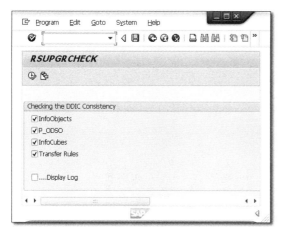

Figure 3.56 Checking the SAP BW System for Inactive Objects

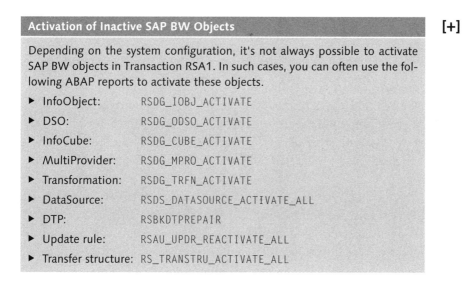

Activation of Inactive SAP BW Objects   **[+]**

Depending on the system configuration, it's not always possible to activate
SAP BW objects in Transaction RSA1. In such cases, you can often use the following ABAP reports to activate these objects.

- InfoObject: `RSDG_IOBJ_ACTIVATE`
- DSO: `RSDG_ODSO_ACTIVATE`
- InfoCube: `RSDG_CUBE_ACTIVATE`
- MultiProvider: `RSDG_MPRO_ACTIVATE`
- Transformation: `RSDG_TRFN_ACTIVATE`
- DataSource: `RSDS_DATASOURCE_ACTIVATE_ALL`
- DTP: `RSBKDTPREPAIR`
- Update rule: `RSAU_UPDR_REACTIVATE_ALL`
- Transfer structure: `RS_TRANSTRU_ACTIVATE_ALL`

Step 9: Correct Inconsistencies of Tables

You can check and correct the inconsistencies of tables exclusively for
SAP BW on SAP HANA systems using the `RSDU_TABLE_CONSISTENCY`
report. The first run identifies the inconsistencies. To do so, start the
report in Transaction SE38, and choose STORE ISSUES. Then, set the
checkmark for all available consistency checks, as illustrated in Figure
3.57, and execute the report.

Correcting
inconsistencies
of tables

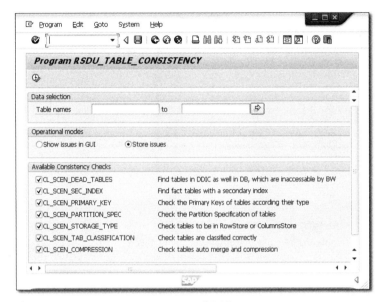

Figure 3.57 Correcting Inconsistencies of Tables

After the report is executed successfully, the system displays an overview with the check results. Now, click Back ([F3]) to return to the input screen. Choose the Repair option, and then click Show. The system displays a list with error categories. Double-click the first row that has a red traffic light icon. The objects in question are now displayed. Select those objects that are marked with the REPAIRABLE status, and click Save ([Ctrl] + [S]). Click Back ([F3]) to return to the overview. Double-click the next row, and follow the same steps as before. After you've selected all repairable objects and saved your selection, you can execute the report with the previously selected Repair option.

Step 10: Remedy SAP BW Inconsistencies

Remedying SAP BW inconsistencies

After an SAP BW on SAP HANA migration, it may be necessary to remedy SAP BW-specific inconsistencies, for example, in connection with BEx queries. For several years, SAP has provided the ANALYZE_RSZ_ TABLES report with which you can run consistency checks for the most critical database tables and identify inconsistencies in query definitions, for example. You can run the report for a pure error analysis at any time without any risks. However, the repair mode has sometimes caused problems. In a concrete case, the report unintentionally deleted query elements (variables and references) due to a bug, although these elements were still used actively in the SAP BW system. As a result, large parts of the reports no longer worked. The error has been fixed by SAP in the meantime. Considering this example, we advise you to first check the proper functioning of the report in a test system. Moreover, we recommend using the report or the respective repair procedures as of version SAP BW 7.3/7.31 with SPS 11, and 7.4 with SPS 06 only. See also SAP Note 1930178.

Step 11: Resolve DDIC Inconsistencies

By means of the RUTMSJOB report, you can correct inconsistencies in the Data Dictionary (DDIC). After you've executed this report, select all check options and execute them immediately. Several testing jobs that require more time for execution are thus scheduled in your system. You can retrieve the current status at any time using the JOB OVERVIEW button. After all jobs have been completed successfully, you can view the results by clicking the RESULTS button. The system can automatically run cleanup activities for some checks.

Resolving DDIC inconsistencies

Step 12: Check MultiProviders

You can delete or rebuild the metadata runtime by means of the RSR_MULTIPROV_CHECK report. Start the report via Transaction SE38, and choose ALL MULTIPROVIDERS. This resets the shared memory buffer of all MultiProviders. See also SAP Note 1626753.

Checking MultiProviders

Step 13: Execute Consistency Checks Using the DBA Cockpit

Call the DBA Cockpit in in your SAP BW system using Transaction DBACOCKPIT. On the left side, select DIAGNOSTICS for your SAP BW system, and double-click MISSING TABLES AND INDEXES. Then, click REFRESH ($\boxed{\text{Shift}}$ + $\boxed{\text{F4}}$). The system displays the results of the consistency checks. Figure 3.58, for example, indicates a missing primary index in

Consistency checks using the DBA Cockpit

the database. You can correct these inconsistencies by clicking the 🖹 icon in the ACTION column. If you receive general errors when running the DBA Cockpit, please refer to SAP Note 1640741.

Figure 3.58 Running Consistency Checks Using DBACOCKPIT

3.5.4 SAP BW on SAP HANA-Specific Post-Processing

After you've carried out the general and SAP BW-specific post-processing and, ideally, corrected all inconsistencies, you must now walk through some more activities that need to be performed once in your SAP BW on SAP HANA system.

Step 14: Deactivate Password Change for System Users

In the default configuration, the system prompts you at regular intervals to change the passwords of SAP HANA users. Although this makes sense from the security point of view, this can also cause problems for system users because their passwords are often stored in other systems, or jobs are scheduled for them. If such a password changes and you don't modify the environment accordingly, this may affect the operating procedure. So, you should deactivate the periodic password change for selected users. For security reasons, you must consider this carefully. You can deactivate the password change with the following statement:
`alter user SAP<SID> disable password lifetime`.

Deactivating the password change for system users

Step 15: Adapt Privileges

As specified in SAP Note 1897236, check whether the database user SAP<SID> has `Select` privileges for accessing the _SYS_REPO and _SYS_BIC schemas. You can use the following SQL command for this purpose: `SELECT GRANTEE, GRANTOR, OBJECT_TYPE, SCHEMA_NAME, PRIVILEGE, IS_GRANTABLE, IS_VALID FROM SYS.GRANTED_PRIVILEGES WHERE GRANTEE = 'SAP<SID>'`. If the privileges are missing for the said schemas, you must add them to the SAP<SID> user. Log on as the SYSTEM user, and expand the tree below your SAP HANA system in SAP HANA Studio. Go to SECURITY • USERS, and double-click SAP<SID>. As illustrated in Figure 3.59, choose the OBJECT PRIVILEGES tab. Use the ➕ icon to add _SYS_REPO and _SYS_BIC, and set the checkmark for READ, respectively, on the right side of the window. Then, click on the ⊕ icon (DEPLOY).

Adapting privileges

You no longer need to assign the `Select` privileges to the user for Tables TABLE_PLACEMENT and SCHEMAVERSION because the TABLE_REDISTRIBUTION role encapsulates the required rights and is assigned automatically by the SWPM (see SAP Note 1908075). Chapter 6, Section 6.2 provides more information on privileges in SAP HANA.

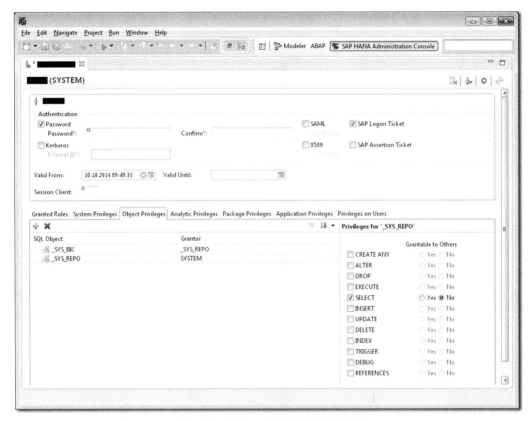

Figure 3.59 Adapting Privileges in SAP HANA Studio

Step 16: Conversion of InfoCubes in SAP HANA-Optimized InfoCubes

Converting
InfoCubes

To reach the full performance potential in SAP BW, you should convert the existing InfoProviders to SAP HANA-optimized InfoCubes after the SAP BW on SAP HANA migration. Conversion is done for selected or all InfoCubes in Transaction RSMIGRHANADB. Chapter 4, Section 4.3 provides a detailed description that also discusses the problem of outdated FactViews. This topic is also discussed from the modeling perspective in Chapter 5, Section 5.3.

Step 17: Activation of the Planning Application Kit (PAK)

By activating the *Planning Application Kit* (PAK), you can considerably increase the speed when using BW Integrated Planning (BW-IP) because numerous planning functions are executed directly through code pushdown in the SAP HANA database. The PAK activation, however, usually requires a separate license. Chapter 5, Section 5.8 discusses this topic in greater detail.

Activating the Planning Application Kit

3.5.5 Concluding Activities

Now, it is time to set the SAP BW on SAP HANA system to an operational condition again. To do so, call the BTCTRNS2 report to start the batch job execution again. Now, also plan process chains using the RS_SYSTEM_SHUTDOWN report. Also, implicitly import the patches required for SAP BW on SAP HANA. Chapter 4, Section 4.1 describes how to identify the SAP notes that are relevant for your system. You can then release the locked users again using Transaction SU01 or SU10. Make sure that you don't release too many users accidentally. Before you inform them about the successful completion of the migration, you should first check whether some data flows and reports are working properly. Also, remember that the end users must log on to the new SAP BW application server to access the SAP BW on SAP HANA system and that the corresponding configuration data must be adapted in the SAP GUI.

Concluding measures

Provided that you also deploy a BW Application Server Java, you must additionally ensure that the Java system uses the new SAP BW on SAP HANA application server. Depending on your configuration, you must also adapt the UME configuration and update certificates as required. You can use the "SAP BI Diagnostics & Support Desk Tool" to check your system configuration (see SAP Note 937697).

BW Application Server Java

This chapter provided an overview of the various migration scenarios and discussed the four phases of the SAP BW on SAP HANA migration in detail. After checking the technical prerequisites, you learned about the preparation steps, such as cleanup activities. This was followed by a comprehensive description of the manual SAP BW on SAP HANA migration with the option for parallel export and import. Finally, we discussed the required postprocessing steps after the migration. You now

Summary

have an extensive overview and understanding of the SAP BW on SAP HANA migration. Chapter 4 provides practical examples so that you can achieve maximum benefits. Chapter 5 then details the benefits that an SAP BW user can achieve in an SAP BW on SAP HANA system.

On the way to your own SAP BW on SAP HANA system, there are numerous pitfalls you should avoid. This chapter provides valuable tips that help you implement SAP BW on SAP HANA.

4   Migration Tips and Tricks

Now that we've discussed the migration of an existing SAP BW system to SAP HANA in Chapter 3, this chapter provides numerous useful tips for implementation in real life. For this purpose, it gives general recommendations (Section 4.1) before analyzing the situation in a proof of concept (Section 4.2) and for an SAP BW on SAP HANA migration of a system landscape (Section 4.3).

4.1   General Recommendations

Hardly any other SAP area develops as quickly as the SAP BW on SAP HANA environment. This becomes apparent in the short intervals in which new SAP HANA support packages are released. Each package contributes to continuous improvement of functions, stability, and speed. It is therefore obvious that you should use only the latest software versions. The commonly-held principle of always keeping the version of SAP components one version below the currently available version should not be applied to SAP BW on SAP HANA. If you want to use new SAP BW functions, such as Open ODS Views (see Chapter 5, Section 5.1), new CompositeProviders (see Chapter 5, Section 5.7), or SAP BW modeling tools (see Chapter 5, Section 5.2), you must implement the latest SAP notes via Transaction SNOTE. In addition, you should keep in mind that certain SAP HANA revisions have been specially verified for production (*datacenter service point version*). To determine which SAP HANA revision meets this requirement, read SAP Note 2021789, which defines whether a data center service point version is already available

Using the latest software versions

for specific Support Package Stacks (SPS) of the SAP HANA database. If so, you should, if possible, use this version (or higher versions of the same SPS) in production. The following URL provides release notes with the latest information on new SAP HANA revision: *http://help.sap.com/ hana/Whats_New_SAP_HANA_Platform_Release_Notes _en.pdf*.

HANA Cookbook   In addition to the version of the software used, the version of the documentation should also be the latest version. The *HANA Cookbook* for BW, for example, is not up-to-date for all topics. Among other things, it contains guidelines for the migration of an SAP BW system to SAP HANA (*https://cookbook.experiencesaphana.com/*; see Figure 4.1).

Figure 4.1 Parts of the SAP BW on SAP HANA Cookbook No Longer Up-to-Date

You can also use the HANA Cookbook as an introduction and as a reference for basic concepts. More information on the migration process is included in Chapter 3. Furthermore, you should read the available documents of the SAP First Guidance Collection for SAP BW on SAP HANA, which you can find at *http://scn.sap.com/docs/DOC-28467*. These are up to date and refer to the currently available software versions. According to our information, SAP also plans to update the HANA Cookbook by integrating the content of the documents of the SAP First Guidance Collection. However, we don't know when this revised version will be available.

To determine whether your SAP BW on SAP HANA system is up to date, you should check the versions of the most important software components. Ideally, you will begin with the SAP HANA database; the easiest way to determine its version is to use SAP HANA Studio (see Chapter 6, Section 6.1) or SAP GUI via SYSTEM • STATUS • DATABASE DATA (see Figure 4.2). Compare the version determined (in our example: 1.00.72) to the version that is currently available in the SAP Software Download Center. To do so, go to *http://service.sap.com/swdc* and select SUPPORT PACKAGES AND PATCHES • A - Z INDEX • H • SAP HANA PLATFORM EDITION • SAP HANA PLATFORM EDIT. 1.0 • ENTRY BY COMPONENT • HANA DATABASE • SAP HANA DATABASE 1.00 • LINUX ON X86_64 64 BIT.

Checking the
SAP HANA revision
used

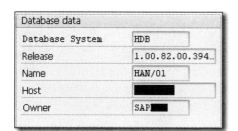

Figure 4.2 Determining the Version of the SAP HANA Database

Next, check the version of the SAP HANA client. The client is used by the SAP BW system—that is, by the ABAP work processes—to establish the connection to the SAP HANA database. For smooth operation, it is thus critical that the SAP HANA client and the SAP HANA database have the same version status. The `hdbinst.exe` tool enables you to have application servers with Windows display the version of the SAP HANA client, including its installation path (see Figure 4.3).

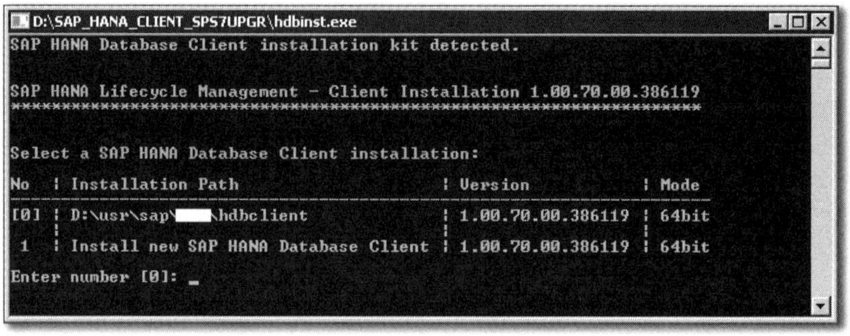

Figure 4.3 Determining the Version of the SAP HANA Client

SAP HANA Studio

SAP HANA Studio should ideally also have the same version as the SAP HANA database. However, if you want to have access to several databases with various versions, SAP HANA Studio should have the version of the highest SAP HANA database revision. Within SAP HANA Studio, you determine the version used via HELP • ABOUT SAP HANA STUDIO. For more information, see Chapter 6.

Basic software components (Kernel, DBSL, and so on)

Because the integration of application server and database is very high with SAP BW on SAP HANA (see Chapter 1, Section 1.4.5), you should also import the latest Support Package Stack (SPS) to the SAP BW application server. In addition, you should keep the basic software components—such as kernel, dispatcher and work process (disp+work), R3 programs (R3ldctl, R3load, R3szchk, and so on), and the *Database Shared Library* (DBSL)—up-to-date. To check the versions of the SAP kernel and DBSL, you can call SAP GUI SYSTEM • STATUS • MORE KERNEL INFORMATION • . The KERNEL INFORMATION item provides you with information on the latest kernel version and database information with information on the version of the DBSL (see Figure 4.4). Alternatively, you can determine the version at the operating system level by executing disp+work.exe -V on the SAP BW server for Windows. Here, you obtain a list with kernel information and the already implemented patches. For the most recent information on the available DBSL patches for SAP HANA, see SAP Note 1600066.

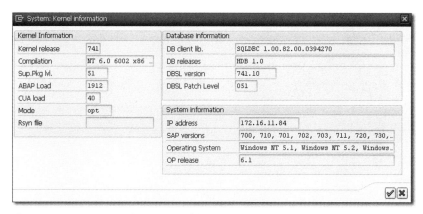

Figure 4.4 Determining the Version of the Kernel and DBSL

If you want to migrate to SAP BW on SAP HANA using the SWPM (see the marginal note "Software Provisioning Manager" in Chapter 3, Section 3.1.1), you should use the latest SWPM version available. Depending on the system status, it may also be necessary to update the existing SAP BW system before migrating to SAP HANA. Critical preliminary corrections here help avoid unexpected complications during the migration. This includes, in particular, the corrections listed in SAP Note 1921023 for the `SMIGR_CREATE_DDL` report, which is described in detail in Chapter 3, Section 3.3.5.

You should follow the general SAP recommendation to also import critical patches to the SAP BW on SAP HANA system after the completion of the migration. For a better overview, Excel lists are provided that contain detailed information on which SAP notes are relevant for your system. You obtain the respective Excel overview as follows:

Implementing critical SAP notes

- SAP Note 1846493 for SAP BW on SAP HANA 7.3x systems

- SAP Note 1949273 for SAP BW on SAP HANA 7.4 systems

Figure 4.5 shows an excerpt of the Excel list for SAP BW on SAP HANA 7.4 systems. By setting a filter, you can filter for the support package stack that you deploy. The MANUAL ACTIVITIES column additionally indicates whether you have to take preparation and post-processing measures manually when implementing notes.

SAP Notes for BW on HANA 7.40											
How to use this spreadsheet This spreadsheet contains a list of SAP Notes that are relevant for BW on HANA installations on 7.40 Support Package 5 (or higher). It is not a complete list of all relevant SAP Notes and it is not mandatory to apply them. The list is intended as a good starting point if you are searching for SAP Notes that should be applied on top of the aforementioned Support Packages. You can filter the list by application "areas" and you should restrict it according to the release and Support Package of your system to filter out irrelevant SAP Notes.											
							The SAP Note is relevant if your system is on...				
Area	Note Component	Note Number	Note Description	Entered in this list on	Manual Activities	Note # with UDC rep.	7.40 SP 05	7.40 SP 06	7.40 SP 07	7.40 SP 08	7.40 SP 09
IObj Master Data Maintenance	BW-WHM-DBA-MD	2033623	InfoObject Master Data Maintenance - Sammelkorrekturen #7	19.08.2014	no		yes	yes	yes	yes	
BW Modeling Tools	BW-MT	2055414	BW Modeling Tools - Sammelhinweis SP08 5/1	22.08.2014	no		yes	yes	yes	yes	
Archivierung	BW-WHM-DST-ARC	2039479	Probleme in der Massenpflege von Datenarchivierungsprozessen	25.08.2014	no						
BW HANA Smart Data Access	BW-BEX-OT-DBIF	2033728	BW HANA SDA: Korrekturen in SP9 für BW 7.40	25.08.2014	Yes	2046253				yes	
HANA Model Generation	BW-WHM-MTD-HMOD	2069062	External SAP HANA view for CompositeProvider: keyfigure values are multiplicated	19.09.2014	no		yes	yes	yes	yes	
HANA Model Generation	BW-WHM-MTD-HMOD	2068357	External SAP HANA view: corrections for SAPKW74009	26.09.2014	Yes		yes	yes	yes	yes	
Archivierung	BW-WHM-DST-ARC	2075032	Zurückgeladene archivierte Daten erzeugen falsche Bestandskennzahlen	09.10.2014	no		no	no	no	yes	yes
HANA Analysis Process and HANA T	BW-WHM-DST-HAP / BW-W	2067912	SAP HANA transformations and analysis processes: SAP Notes for SAP NetWeaver 7.40 with Support Package 8 or 9	30.10.2014	no		no	no	no	yes	yes
In-memory Planning	HAN-DB-ENG-PLE	1957136	1957136 - Revision 71 Enhancements for Planning Functions	17.11.2014	no		yes	yes	yes	yes	yes
In-memory Planning	HAN-DB-ENG-PLE	2009666	Revision 74 Enhancements for Planning Functions	17.11.2014	no		yes	yes	yes	yes	yes
In-memory Planning	HAN-DB-ENG-PLE	2056075	Planning : new check 'ALL_IN_FILTER'	17.11.2014	no		yes	yes	yes	yes	yes
In-memory Planning	BW-PLA-IP	2642470	BW-IP (PAK): Problems when you connect SAP HANA data sources (DSO planning)	17.11.2014	no		yes	yes	yes	yes	yes
In-memory Planning	HAN-DB-ENG-PLE	2074556	Revision 84 Enhancements for Planning Functions	17.11.2014	no		yes	yes	yes	yes	yes
Planning	BW-WHM-DBA-COPR	2072212	HCPR: CompositeProvider corrections for Release 7.40, part 9	17.11.2014	no		no	no	no	yes	yes
In-memory Planning	BW-PLA-IP-PF	2052750	HDB: 'Distribute with Reference Data' in Revision 74 to 83	17.11.2014	no		yes	yes	yes	yes	yes
In-memory Planning	BW-PLA-IP-PF	2089157	HANA: Verteilen mit Referenzdaten	17.11.2014	no		yes	yes	yes	yes	yes
In-memory Planning	BW-PLA-IP	2094791	Dump "S_CHECK_MIN_REVISION_74-01-"	17.11.2014	no		yes	yes	yes	yes	yes
In-memory Planning	BW-PLA-IP	2085284	Analyse Tools für Fehlermeldungen im PAK	17.11.2014	no		yes	yes	yes	yes	yes
In-memory Planning	BW-PLA-IP-PF	2072136	SAP HANA: FOREACH var IN SELECTION	17.11.2014	no		yes	yes	yes	yes	yes

Figure 4.5 Excel List with Critical SAP Notes for SAP BW on SAP HANA 7.40 Systems from SAP Note 1949273

Here is a tip for how you can search for new SAP BW on SAP HANA notes that may not be included in the Excel lists yet. To do so, run a search with a restriction to selected software components. Go to *http://service.sap.com/notes* and select RESTRICT BY SOFTWARE COMPONENTS (ONLY EXPERTS) as the search option, as illustrated in Figure 4.6. Here, enter SAP_BW as the software component, and enter your release number (for example, 740). By clicking the magnifying glass (FROM SUPPORT PACKAGE), select the available support package to restrict the number of notes to those that are relevant for your system status. Don't forget to specify an appropriate search string, such as "HANA", before clicking SEARCH. This may lead to different results. If you then view the notes found, don't get confused by the respective short text. Sometimes, specific system versions, such as "NW 7.30," are listed, but this does not mean that such a note can be implemented only to an SAP BW 7.3 system. In some cases, you can also implement it to an SAP BW 7.4 systems. For example, SAP Note 1953984 (HDB: Development of tool classes for NW 7.30 SP12) can also be implemented in an SAP BW 7.4 system as of SPS 06.

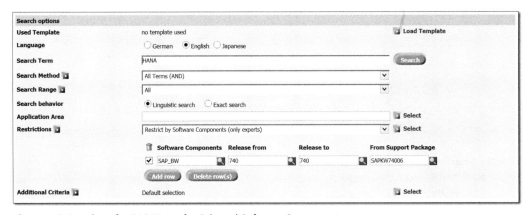

Figure 4.6 Searching for SAP Notes for Selected Software Components

In addition to ensuring that the software used must be up-to-date, you must also make detailed preparations to be able to use SAP BW on SAP HANA successfully. So, make yourself familiar with this topic at an early stage and, if possible, attend the corresponding training lessons. To migrate to SAP BW on SAP HANA, especially the employees from the SAP NetWeaver/Basis and Business Warehouse departments must cooperate closely because a lot of measures must be adapted or taken in collaboration. It makes sense to involve at least one person from each respective team in the training process. You should also obtain support from an experienced expert or consulting firm, particularly for SAP BW on SAP HANA migrations in production.

Trainings

Internet Information Sources for SAP BW on SAP HANA   [⊕]

The number of operated SAP BW on SAP HANA systems has grown considerably in the last months and, consequently, so has the number of publications on the Internet. From our point of view, you should take a look at the numerous SAP HANA-specific blogs, such as the following:

▶ SAP BW Powered by SAP HANA, SAP Community Network:
  http://scn.sap.com/community/netweaver-bw-hana

▶ SAP BW Powered by SAP HANA—Some Points to Remember for Database Migration to HANA:
  http://scn.sap.com/community/netweaver-bw-hana/blog/2013/08/29/ sap-bw-powered-by-sap-hana-some-points-to-remember-for-database- migration-to-hana

▶ The SAP Hana Reference for NetWeaver Basis Administrators: *http://scn.sap.com/community/hana-in-memory/blog/2013/05/27/andy-silvey--sap-hana-command-line-tools-and-sql-reference-examples-for-netweaver-basis-administrators*

▶ 10 Golden Rules for SAP BW on HANA Migrations: *http://scn.sap.com/community/hana-in-memory/blog/2014/02/16/10-golden-rules-for-sap-SAP BW on SAP HANA-migrations*

System landscape and technical details

Before migrating to SAP BW on SAP HANA, you should define the exact details of the future system landscape. In the migration phase, avoid technical or architecture-related changes, as well as the implementation of new functions that are not directly linked to the migration to SAP HANA. Before migrating to SAP BW on SAP HANA, test for all servers involved whether the names are correctly broken down in the *Domain Name System* (DNS). Sometimes, only the breakdown from server name to IP address is tested. However, you should also explicitly check the reversed case—that is, verify whether the IP addresses are correctly assigned to the server names. Only if the name breakdown functions correctly in both directions does the system not encounter network-specific error messages during the implementation and future operations.

Cleanup activities

Address the *cleanup activities* topic (see Chapter 3, Section 3.3.2) at an early stage. Because SAP HANA stores all data mainly in the main memory (for details, see Chapter 5, Section 5.6) and the available space in the main memory is limited, you should take your time to focus on this aspect. In addition to considering the effort for planning and implementing these steps, you should keep in mind that you may require authorizations to delete data in production systems. Depending on the rules that apply in your enterprise, it may be necessary to obtain the approvals or signatures of various contact persons. Experience has shown that these persons find it hard to assess which data can be deleted permanently. The archiving of obsolete SAP BW data is thus an alternative to its deletion. By means of the classic archiving method (Transaction SARA), you can reduce the data volume in SAP BW and simultaneously avoid possible authorization problems. The data is then archived in the file system and can be reimported to the SAP BW system anytime. But before using this archiving method in production, you should test it carefully to ensure that the reimport works properly in your system. If you use the SARA archiving for data cleansing, you must copy the generated archiving files to the new SAP BW system after the successful SAP BW on SAP HANA migration. Only then can you reimport the previously archived data to the SAP BW on SAP HANA system.

Experience has shown that the SAP BW on SAP HANA migration of a production system sometimes leads to other error messages than the migration of a development system of the same system landscape. If these errors occur during a go-live weekend for the first time, for example, they may delay the defined schedule. If you created a homogeneous system copy of your SAP BW (production) system as recommended (see Chapter 3, Section 3.3.1), you can use this SAP BW system for a migration test first. Your hardware should be ready for this some weeks before the scheduled SAP BW on SAP HANA migration because the SAP HANA database is generally ready for operation when you implement the SAP HANA appliance. In addition to the system validation (see Chapter 3, Section 3.3.4) and cleanup activities (see Chapter 3, Section 3.3.2), this phase is ideal for the import and export runs for testing purposes (see Chapter 3, Section 3.4). During these tests, you may omit some of the preparatory and post-processing measures. The goal here is to detect possible migration errors at an early stage, and not to create an SAP BW on SAP HANA system that can be used right away.

Testing the migration in advance

Before starting with the migration tests, you should generate a backup of the initial (that is, "empty") SAP HANA database. This enables you to reset the database to the initial status any time without having to use SQL commands, such as `drop schema`. At last, you want to operate your production system and not the SAP BW test system in the SAP HANA appliance. Therefore, you must delete the database content of the SAP BW test system from the SAP HANA database after having completed all tests. For this purpose, you can simply use the previously created database backup.

Creating a backup of an "empty" database

If the system displays error messages during the migration test—for example, when the database is imported (see Chapter 3, Section 3.4.4)— you should try to identify the reasons for their occurrence. If necessary, terminate the test run and solve the problem on the source system. After

Testing parts of the migration repeatedly

that, you can reset the SAP HANA database by reimporting the previously created database backup. Then, restart the data export and import. You can repeat this procedure as often as required until all problems are solved. Finally, you should carefully perform all steps that helped solve the problem in your production system. The reason is that the SAP BW test system is based on a copy of the production system, and the same errors probably also occur during the SAP BW on SAP HANA migration if no adaptations are made. This iterative approach enables you to determine and solve potential errors at an early stage. Furthermore, the migration test allows for verifying the scheduled phases of the SAP BW on SAP HANA migration and, if necessary, optimizing them.

4.2 Proof of Concept

Advantages of a proof of concept

A *Proof of Concept* (PoC) generally serves to prove the feasibility of a certain concept (*http://en.wikipedia.org/wiki/Proof_of_concept*). In addition, a PoC helps answer open questions, reduce possible risks, and increase acceptance among all persons involved. In an SAP BW environment, a PoC is often implemented to demonstrate that all customer-specific requirements for the live operation of SAP BW on SAP HANA can be met to the full extent. In particular, it is analyzed whether the data flows and reports still function without errors after the migration to SAP BW on SAP HANA. You can also quantify exactly the increase in speed with SAP HANA on the basis of your data, SAP BW models, and reports. A PoC can also be used to further examine the new in-memory technology with regard to its suitability for your specific purposes. The following box summarizes the advantages of a PoC for SAP BW on SAP HANA.

[+]

Advantages of a Proof of Concept for SAP BW on SAP HANA

The following are some advantages to the PoC:

▶ Checking data flows and reports for their error-free functionality

▶ Minimizing risks for the future implementation of SAP BW on SAP HANA and excluding misinvestments

▶ Quantifying performance benefits on the basis of your specific data, data models, and reports to evaluate costs and benefit aspects

▶ Checking the ability to be integrated of SAP BW on SAP HANA into your IT infrastructure

▶ Acquiring or deepening expert knowledge

▶ If you involve the employees at an early stage, the migration usually enjoys greater acceptance and is actively supported

If you're never implemented an SAP BW on SAP HANA migration in your enterprise or environment before, you should use a PoC. Like the introduction of the production system, it also requires careful project planning. In addition to hardware, license, and budget issues, you must also take into account the availability of employees and their level of knowledge. It can also be helpful to involve an experienced consultancy team to avoid forgetting critical project planning steps and ensure that the defined schedule is realistic.

Among other things, the implementation of a PoC for SAP BW on SAP HANA involves costs for licenses, the working time of your employees, new hardware, and external consulting services, if required. With regard to license costs, you should contact SAP directly. If you want to evaluate SAP BW on SAP HANA for only a few weeks, these costs should not make up a very large proportion. The time effort of your employees, and thus the corresponding proportion of the costs, can constitute a significant part of the PoC. But, this buildup of expertise will pay off later on, during the go-live of SAP BW on SAP HANA, because the training costs will be rather low and potential errors won't be made that often. If you want to involve external consultants in your PoC, you should make sure that knowledge is transferred and the focus is not only on planning and implementation aspects. Experience has shown that the coaching approach is ideal when the employees perform the work steps themselves after having received the respective training.

Costs

The hardware costs often make up a critical proportion of the PoC. Here, it makes sense to check at an early stage whether you plan to replace an existing server soon. Under certain conditions, the SAP HANA appliance can replace this server after the completion of the PoC and, consequently, be used for something else. Therefore, the hardware costs can be split between the PoC and the other project, which theoretically leads

Hardware

to a reduction of the PoC costs. If it is also sufficient to test only the most important data models and reports in the PoC, you may procure "smaller" and less expensive hardware. In this case, you must necessarily create a homogeneous system copy of your SAP BW production system. In this SAP BW test system, you can delete the data of all InfoProviders that are not critical for the PoC. This reduces the data volume and thus the main memory requirement on the SAP BW on SAP HANA system.

It is hard to generally answer the question of whether it is possible to move the PoC to the cloud to further reduce the costs. SAP provides *SAP HANA Enterprise Cloud* (HEC) for the live operation of SAP BW on SAP HANA (see *http://www.saphana.com/community/about-hana/cloud-options*), but due to cost reasons and the time-limited deployment, it is hardly suited to be used in the PoC. Alternatively, SAP also provides a 30-day trial offer for the usage of SAP BW on SAP HANA and SAP BusinessObjects BI in the Amazon cloud (for more information, see *http://marketplace.saphana.com/p/3954*). This environment enables you to gather practical experience with SAP BW on SAP HANA and run basic tests. However, because the SAP BW system is provided with preinstalled functions, it is probably possible to use your specific SAP BW models and data in this environment only to a limited extent.

Selecting SAP BW scenarios Within the scope of the PoC, you must first select SAP BW scenarios that you then test respectively. You should select particularly those data flows and reports that are business critical or used frequently. After the migration to SAP BW on SAP HANA, you must check whether those elements still function without errors. In addition, you should select reports for the test that currently have performance problems. Normally, you already know where the reason for the problems lies from the feedback of the user departments. For example, if BEx queries have a runtime of several minutes, they can be used to compare the performance of your SAP BW production system and SAP BW on SAP HANA. To obtain a comprehensive overview, it makes sense to consider load processes in addition to reports. Here, you can basically select solely SAP BW internal processes. Load processes from the source system to SAP BW can be ignored to a large extent. Often, the source system is the limiting factor here, which is why the use of SAP HANA won't result in increased performance. In particular, for further data updates, the runtimes will be considerably shorter for updates between PSA and the various InfoProviders, for example. The PoC also allows you to determine the speed benefits in detail and whether they open new time windows for process chains. Consider which other SAP BW activities are critical with regard to performance aspects. For example, if you often use the SELECTIVE DELETION for InfoProviders for a large set of data records, it makes sense to also test these activities. If you use SAP BW Integrated Planning (BW-IP), you should include some of your planning applications in the PoC. It may also be useful to evaluate the Planning Application Kit (see Chapter 5, Section 5.8).

For the selected scenarios, you first check in the SAP BW on SAP HANA system whether the data flows and reports still function without errors. For this purpose, use the experiences you have gained, for example, within the scope of a system upgrade. It is also helpful to involve the users of the user departments in your tests because they should usually quickly notice if some reports cannot be called correctly, for example.

Checking functions for error-free operation

If the selected data flows and reports run without errors in the SAP BW on SAP HANA system, the next thing is to define the execution time of reports and process chains. Determine exactly which reports must be called in which sequence and which navigation steps are supposed to be performed. Then, perform these steps in both the SAP BW production system and the SAP BW on SAP HANA system. Here, you must consider that SAP BW uses an internal cache (OLAP cache) for performance optimization. When measuring the time, you should thus ensure that this cache is emptied first; otherwise, your measurements can be falsified. However, empty the OLAP cache in an SAP BW production system only after consultation because the execution time of all SAP BW reports will increase significantly afterward. For this purpose, call Transaction RSRT in the SAP BW system, select CACHE MONITOR • DELETE, and confirm the confirmation prompt with YES.

Determining the execution time

To determine the runtimes, you don't have to sit in front of the server with a stopwatch. Instead, you can refer to the PROCESS CHAIN MAINTENANCE (Transaction RSPC) to obtain the respective times. For reports, the SAP BW system also provides a function for runtime determination.

Here, you don't call your BEx query on the web or via Excel, but in Transaction RSRT of the SAP BW system. In the so-called *Query Monitor*, enter the technical name of the query and click EXECUTE + DEBUG. In the next dialog box (DEBUG OPTIONS), select the DISPLAY STATISTICS DATA option in the GENERAL EXECUTION OPTIONS category. In older SAP BW versions, this option is provided in the OTHER category. As an alternative to completely emptying the SAP BW cache, you can also select the DO NOT USE CACHE option (see Figure 4.7).

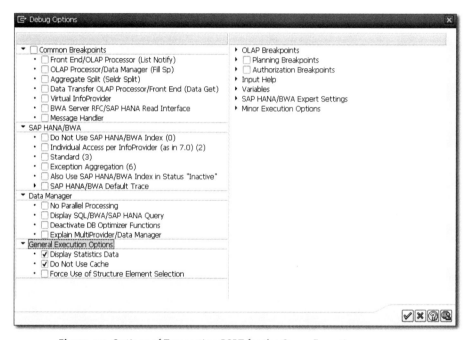

Figure 4.7 Options of Transaction RSRT for the Query Execution

After the execution, the system first displays the query results. If you click the BACK icon 🔄, the system displays the statistics data for the previously executed query (see Figure 4.8). Here, you can view the steps performed (EVENT TEXT column) and the number of data records processed (COUNTER column). The execution time of the individual steps is listed in the DURATION column in seconds, and the column total enables you to determine the total runtime of the query.

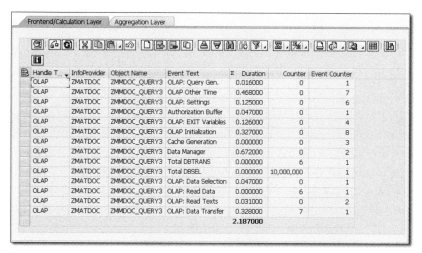

Figure 4.8 Statistics Data for Determining the Runtime of a Query

After obtaining the results for SAP BW and SAP BW on SAP HANA, you can now compare the values of the two systems. Determine for each user department by which factor the execution of SAP BW reports and process chains have been accelerated. This allows you to derive how much time you can save by using SAP BW on SAP HANA in the future. You can also perform a monetary analysis for these time savings, which form an essential basis for the investment decision within the scope of the cost/benefit analysis. The identified runtimes also enable you to determine whether certain processes can now be executed more often. For example, if it is possible to run complex simulations more frequently or import data for more up-to-date reporting to SAP BW more often, this usually results in benefits for the business. This should also be considered within the scope of the cost/benefit analysis of the SAP BW on SAP HANA implementation.

Analysis

Some enterprises additionally use the PoC phase to evaluate possible alternatives to SAP BW on SAP HANA. This includes, for example, hardware upgrades of the existing SAP BW system for performance optimization. The integration of faster hardware components, more main memory, and SSD hard disks is sufficient to noticeably increase the system performance. However, experience has shown that there are usually worlds between SAP BW on SAP HANA and the possible alternatives

Alternatives

with regard to performance. Once you have worked with an SAP BW on SAP HANA system and experienced the increase in speed for your specific SAP BW data, data models, and reports will hardly ever want to go back to less performance.

Evaluating further requirements

Within the scope of the PoC, it makes sense to verify further requirements in addition to checking the functionality and performing runtime measurements. Among other things, this includes the integration of the SAP BW on SAP HANA system into your infrastructure, for example, with regard to *monitoring* or *scheduling*. You can also check security mechanisms, such as database authorizations, user management, or audit options, in the PoC. Perhaps you can already include database-specific encryption methods in the tests. For more information on single sign-on and data volume encryption, read the SAP HANA Security Guide at *http://help.sap.com/hana_appliance* under SECURITY INFORMATION • SAP HANA SECURITY GUIDE.

Managing new technologies

The database and system administrators involved should acquire the knowledge of how to work with SAP HANA Studio and the SAP HANA database (see Chapter 6) during the PoC phase. At the end of the PoC, they should be particularly familiar with the monitoring functions, updates of SAP HANA-specific software components, and the configuration and usage of the backup and recovery solution. If you use a *scale-out solution* (that is, an SAP HANA database deploys several server nodes) or a high-availability architecture, the corresponding hardware partner usually also provides support via knowledge transfer, as required. A deep knowledge of the new technologies is an essential requirement for reacting to possible problems appropriately during production.

Summary

At the end of the PoC, you should know whether your data models and reports work without errors with SAP BW on SAP HANA. At this time, you can usually precisely evaluate which costs a rollout will incur. Furthermore, you also know which concrete speed benefits SAP BW on SAP HANA provides for your data, data models, and reports. If you have also analyzed all benefits with regard to costs, the decision makers have all critical information to speak in favor of or against the implementation of SAP BW on SAP HANA.

4.3   Migration of an SAP BW System Landscape

When actually rolling out SAP BW on SAP HANA, the main goals are different than during the PoC phase. When you migrate an entire system landscape, the focus is on implementing the migration smoothly, continuing to run operations largely unaffected by this, and minimizing possible downtimes to a. It is not sufficient to verify the general functionality of SAP BW on SAP HANA by means of selected examples. Instead, all data models and reports must work 100% correctly after completion of the migration.

Migration of an SAP BW system landscape

Because it is hardly possible to migrate a multilevel SAP BW system landscape at once, you must take several steps. Like other system conversions, this process also includes some pitfalls, which you should avoid. Basically, you should have gathered comprehensive experience with SAP BW on SAP HANA before beginning with the migration work. If you have already implemented a PoC, you already have the required theoretical and practical knowledge. If the PoC phase dates back several months, you should inform yourself about possible innovations in the SAP BW on SAP HANA environment. If you haven't been involved in the PoC and have mainly theoretical knowledge, you should first gain practical knowledge, for example, by migrating an *SAP BW sandbox*.

Procedure

When converting a multilevel system landscape, you should first migrate the development system. Here, do not perform further system adaptations. If possible, you should also avoid upgrading your SAP BW system shortly before you start with the actual SAP BW on SAP HANA migration. If the period between the upgrade and the migration to SAP BW on SAP HANA is too short, you may not notice possible errors and problems at first. If you detect them after the completion of the SAP BW on SAP HANA migration, you may not be able to determine the exact cause, which makes it more difficult to find a solution. In one case, for example, the execution of BEx queries with exception aggregations led to numerous problems in the SAP BW on SAP HANA system. First, it was assumed that this was caused by the SAP HANA migration. Only at a later stage was it detected that the problems had already occurred after the upgrade. Because only queries without exception aggregations had been tested before the migration to SAP BW on SAP HANA, this error

Development system

was identified that late. Therefore, it is important not to include too many processes in the SAP BW on SAP HANA migration and to schedule sufficient time for testing after the migration of the development system.

In the context of an SAP BW on SAP HANA migration, some SAP presentations sometimes address a non-disruptive DB migration (see "Technical considerations when migrating an existing NetWeaver BW system to run on SAP HANA," at *http://scn.sap.com/docs/DOC-30245*). According to this resource, all data models, reports, and load processes are supposed to work immediately, without errors, after a migration to SAP BW on SAP HANA. You should not implicitly trust this statement. In some cases, an SAP BW on SAP HANA migration does lead to problems. For example, problems may occur if native SQL commands are used in the ABAP source code of a start routine or a *FactView* are accessed directly. Because the second case is not very obvious, it is described in more detail in the following.

SAP BW 3.0 already created a FactView for every InfoCube. This Fact-View allowed for access to the merged dataset of E and F fact tables (see SAP Note 561961). FactViews have the `/BIC/V<InfoCube>F` technical name and, according to SAP Note 1766419, they are used in the context of *open hub scenarios* or for *export DataSources*. When converting Info-Cubes into *SAP HANA-optimized* InfoCubes (see Chapter 5, Section 5.3) via Transaction RSMIGRHANADB (see Figure 4.9), you must take into account that the FactViews are no longer required due to the simplified SAP BW on SAP HANA data models. When you convert standard Info-Cubes into SAP HANA-optimized InfoCubes, the system automatically deletes the FactViews, and you can no longer create them with the `RSDU_INFOCUBE_FACTVIEW_CREATE` function module. The absence of these views may have serious impact if a FactView is directly accessed by the customer-specific programming logic. For example, if the logic accesses a FactView that is no longer available in a start routine, the *Data Transfer Process* (DTP) is canceled, and the system displays the error message, "The `/BIC/V<InfoCube>F` category is not available." Even though the use of FactViews in the customer-specific programming logic is not really good programming style, it is sometimes done in real life. Correspondingly, you should convert not only selected InfoCubes, but all InfoCubes into SAP HANA-optimized InfoCubes in the development system. This enables you to determine possible problems caused by missing Fact-Views already in the development system so that you have enough time to solve them.

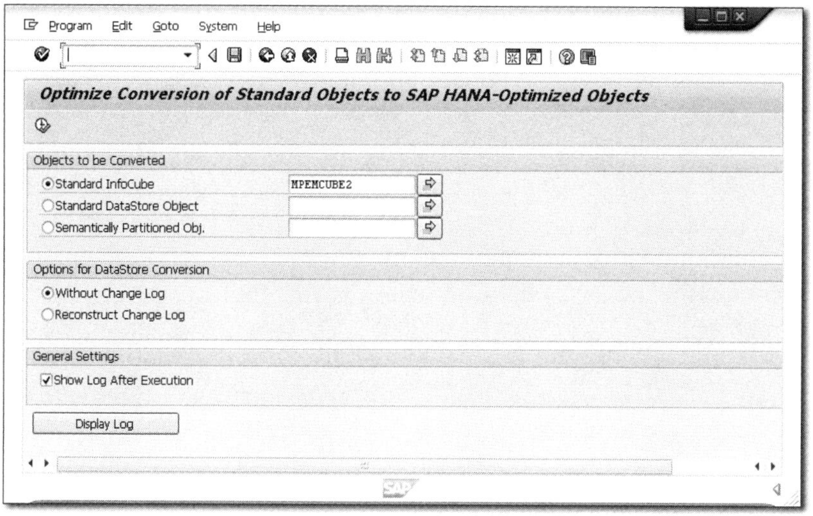

Figure 4.9 InfoCube Conversion Optimized for SAP HANA

In the context of the InfoCube conversion, please also keep in mind that you must previously compress inventory InfoCubes via the *Marker Update* (for more details, refer to Section 9 of the SAP First Guidance document "Inventory InfoCubes," at *http://scn.sap.com/docs/DOC-28525*).

In some cases, the conversion of InfoCubes to SAP HANA-optimized InfoCubes can result in an error message and a termination, for example, if the E fact tables of the InfoCubes have not been partitioned correctly. Then, you should first try to solve the actual problem before restarting the conversion run for the InfoCube involved. For incorrectly partitioned E fact tables, SAP Note 1695778 provides a solution that is usually successful. In such cases, you should use the RSDU_TABLE_CONSISTENCY report to solve the problem. For this purpose, perform the report with the following settings (see Figure 4.10) in the background:

Incorrect partitioning of InfoCubes

▸ OPERATIONAL MODES: STORE ISSUES

▸ AVAILABLE CONSISTENCY CHECKS:

▸ CL_SCEN_PRIMARY_KEY

▸ CL_SCEN_PARTITION_SPEC

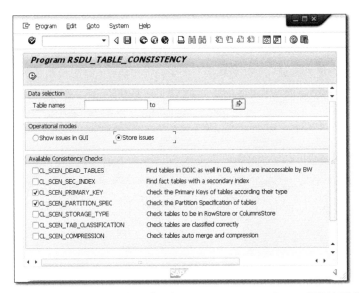

Figure 4.10 Correcting the InfoCube Partitioning Using Report RSDU_TABLE_CONSISTENCY

For more information on the execution of this report, see Chapter 3, Section 3.5.3.

Locks in the InfoProvider migration

If you then trigger the conversion run for the respective InfoCube again, it is usually performed successfully, without any error messages. In some cases, there are still problems due to incorrectly defined locks after the error correction because an internal table logs the current status of the InfoCube conversion. So, if the conversion run is canceled without correcting the status, the status may be wrong. In the case of a new conversion run, this incorrect status of the InfoCube is read from the table that keeps the application from performing a new conversion. Figure 4.11 illustrates the effects of such a lock for the sample conversion of the MPEMCUBE1 InfoCube. In particular, the message text "Lock NOT deleted for: Migration of InfoProvider" demonstrates the problem. Only if the lock is reset in the system can a conversion run for the respective InfoCube be successful. Here, you should create a customer message, and not change the internal control tables yourself.

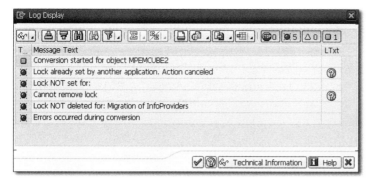

Figure 4.11 A Lock Preventing the InfoCube Conversion

Although we recommend not manipulating the internal control tables, you can still view their content. It is particularly useful to take a look at the following tables:

Analyzing locks

▸ RSDRI_HDB_CNV (Status Table for InfoCube Conversion)

▸ RSMIGROBJ (Lock Entries for Object Migration)

Table RSDRI_HDB_CNV enables you to determine the status of the Info-Cube conversion. For this purpose, the respective values of the STATUS and COMMAND columns are critical. Value 01 for STATUS indicates that the conversion is still in the initial phase, while value 99 and the entry _ FINALIZE for COMMAND specify that the InfoCube conversion has been successful. The corresponding lock entries are maintained in Table RSMIGROBJ. With this table, you can determine whether your InfoCube is affected by a lock. For this purpose, simply check whether the OBJECT column contains the technical name of your InfoCube. If the problem can be solved with the lock entries, the InfoCubes are converted successfully (see Figure 4.12).

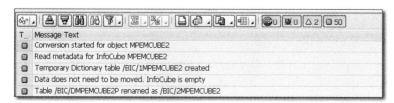

Figure 4.12 Successful InfoCube Conversion

Testing the transports

If all InfoCubes in the development system have been converted successfully, you should test your data flows thoroughly. If you have to adapt any elements, you shouldn't transfer the changes immediately. The transport of objects between the development system and the quality assurance system may lead to problems because the two SAP BW systems use different databases. SAP recommends using the same database platforms within a transport landscape. However, it is generally possible to transport objects between SAP BW on SAP HANA systems and SAP BW systems that are not based on SAP HANA, without errors (see SAP Note 1808450). Nevertheless, you should avoid transports in this phase, if possible, or at least minimize the number of transports and quantity of transferred objects. It is additionally critical that a combined transport landscape be operated for a short period only, for example, until the next SAP BW system can be migrated to SAP HANA.

Quality assurance system

If the SAP BW on SAP HANA migration of the development system did not lead to serious or unsolved problems, the next step is the migration of the quality assurance system (Q system). The procedure is analogous to that for the development system; however, you should consider that the Q system often stores larger data volumes. This can considerably increase the time and effort for the migration, particularly for the export and import phase. You should therefore temporarily deactivate the log mode of the database for the import phase or activate the overwrite mode. Otherwise, the database generates very large log files when importing the data. In one project, this led to further problems. In this case, an SAP HANA appliance with flash storage technology was used for fast log file storage. Because this medium has only a limited size, the log files are regularly transferred to another medium. The SAP HANA database and the flash memory, however, were so fast when importing the data that the process for storing the logs was too slow, and the flash memory reached its capacity limit. This resulted in follow-up errors, and in the end, the log mode had to be deactivated and the import process repeated. However, remember to immediately activate the log mode after the completion of the data import and perform an additional database backup.

You should also take into account long data export and import times for the migration of the production system. In contrast to the Q system, however, the downtimes must usually be considerably shorter, so a particularly useful method is to export and import data in parallel (see Chapter 3, Section 3.4, SAP BW on SAP HANA) in addition to the *table splitting* optimization method. Here, the import phase is already triggered in parallel with the export, and the system transfers data even though the export has not yet been completed. This optimization method contributes to almost halving the migration time.

Production system

Within the scope of the *SAP OS/DB migration check* (see *http://service.sap.com/osdbmigration*), SAP provides customers with support for an SAP system migration if they want to change the operating system and/or the database. In the context of an SAP BW on SAP HANA migration, SAP defines that this *migration check* is generally mandatory when migrating a production system. Only if you use this service offer does SAP support your migration. The *migration check* comprises two sessions that are executed via remote access. In the analysis phase, the technical and organizational requirements for the migration are checked in the source system. This is supposed to contribute to identifying possible problems at an early stage and minimizing potential risks. The analysis phase usually takes place four to six weeks before the system migration. You are provided with a questionnaire in advance that is supposed to help determine whether the planned migration scenario is realistic and can be implemented from the technical perspective. After the analysis session, you'll receive a detailed report that includes concrete recommended actions, such as the modification of SAP HANA parameters. Some weeks after the completion of the migration, a second session (verification session) takes place to check or ensure that the system works properly in the new environment. Please note that you can utilize the migration check for an SAP BW on SAP HANA migration only if the respective SAP system is properly registered with SAP—that is, by specifying the installation number specified in the maintenance contract.

SAP OS/DB migration check

You may still encounter pitfalls after the migration. The change to SAP HANA also results in a change of the data types used by the database. For example, the SAP-internal data type for a character string (CHAR) is

Different data types of the databases

mapped to `VARCHAR2` in an Oracle database and to `NVARCHAR` in SAP HANA. The migration to SAP HANA includes a conversion of all SAP tables to the new HANA data types. As far as we know, this usually does not lead to any problems. This applies in particular if you use only SAP-specific programs and functions to access the data from the database. But if you have also used database-technical functions, programs, or SQL commands (for example, to export tables) the situation changes. Experience has shown that the export processes of a database table may differ before and after the SAP HANA migration, but in this concrete case, the cause was not the different data types, but the initial values of the individual database fields (the "The Initial Value of the Database Field" box contains more information on these terms). Before we discuss this problem in detail, the following section first illustrates the consequences of an SAP BW on SAP HANA migration for the database.

[*]

The Initial Value of the Database Field

The initial value specifies with which value a database field is defined. This will be explained based on an example of a date field.

In SAP HANA, an SAP date field is created with the `NVARCHAR` data type and a length of 8 (see Figure 4.13). In the field with a dimension of eight characters, you can define any date in the year/month/day format: for example, `20141231` for 12/31/2014. If an SAP application reads this field, the SAP interface displays the date as usual. But, what happens if the date field is still empty? In this case, the database returns the initial value. For a date, this is always `00000000`. SAP applications often display this value as 00/00/0000.

Name	SQL Data Type	Dimension	Key	Not Null	Default
Date	NVARCHAR	8		X	00000000

Figure 4.13 Illustration of a Date Field in SAP HANA

Effects of the SAP BW on SAP HANA migration to database tables

Let's take a look at an example that demonstrates the changes to the database tables when you migrate to SAP BW on SAP HANA. For this purpose, we created a standard DSO (see Figure 4.14) in an SAP BW system (not based on SAP HANA). The following analyzes the table of this DSO before and after the migration to SAP BW on SAP HANA and points out the differences.

The successful creation of a DSO in the SAP BW system includes the creation of several database tables for data retention at a later stage. For the ZMATDOC DSO described above, this is Table /BIC/AZMATDOC00 for active data, for example. You can use Transaction SE11 to view the structure of this table (see Figure 4.15). In addition to the field description, you can view the data type (in the SAP system) and the maximum length. In a classic SAP BW system, this table structure is identical to that in an SAP BW on SAP HANA system. The individual SAP data types (e.g., CHAR), however, are mapped differently in the respective databases, as already described.

DataStore Object	Techn. name / value	Data type	Length
▼ 🗐 DSO for Material Documents	ZMATDOC		
▶ 🔩 Object Information			
▶ 🗐 Settings			
▼ ⚷ Key fields			
• 📇 Material Document	0MAT_DOC	CHAR	010
▼ 🖿 Data Fields			
• 📇 Material	0MATERIAL	CHAR	018
• 📇 Plant	0PLANT	CHAR	004
• 📇 Posting Date in the Document	0OI_BUDAT	DATS	008
• 📇 Movement type (inventory management)	0OI_BWART	CHAR	003
• 📇 Quantity	0QUANTITY	QUAN	009
• 📇 Unit of measure	0UNIT	UNIT	003
▶ 🗀 Navigation Attributes			
▶ 🗀 Indexes			

Figure 4.14 Sample DSO

Dictionary: Display Table

⇐ ⇒ ⍋ ⍟ ⍦ ⍤ ! ⍦ ⍦ ⍦ ▢ ▤ ▦ ▦ ▦ Technical Settings Indexes... Append Structure...

Transparent Table	/BIC/AZMATDOC00	Active
Short Description	ODS Object ZMATDOC : Active Records	

Attributes Delivery and Maintenance Fields Entry help/check Currency/Quantity Fields

Field	Key	Initial Values	Data element	Data Type	Length	Decimal Places	Short Description
MAT_DOC	☑	☑	/BI0/0IMAT_DOC	CHAR	10	0	Material Document
RECORDMODE	☐	☑	RODMUPDMOD	CHAR	1	0	BW Delta Process: Record Mode
MATERIAL	☐	☑	/BI0/0IMATERIAL	CHAR	18	0	Material
PLANT	☐	☑	/BI0/0IPLANT	CHAR	4	0	Plant
OI_BUDAT	☐	☑	/BI0/0IOI_BUDAT	DATS	8	0	Posting Date in the Document
OI_BWART	☐	☑	/BI0/0IOI_BWART	CHAR	3	0	Movement type (inventory management)
QUANTITY	☐	☑	/BI0/0IQUANTITY	QUAN	17	3	Quantity
UNIT	☐	☑	/BI0/0IUNIT	UNIT	3	0	Unit of Measure

Figure 4.15 View of the DSO Table in Transaction SE11

In an SAP BW system that uses Oracle as the primary database, the database table is implemented as shown in Figure 4.16. Here, you can view that the VARCHAR2 database type is used instead of CHAR for the MAT_DOC field.

Fld Name	Position	Data Type	Length	Decimals	Not null	Default
MAT_DOC	1	VARCHAR2	30		X	' '
RECORDMODE	2	VARCHAR2	3		X	' '
MATERIAL	3	VARCHAR2	54		X	' '
PLANT	4	VARCHAR2	12		X	' '
OI_BUDAT	5	VARCHAR2	24		X	'00000000'
OI_BWART	6	VARCHAR2	9		X	' '
QUANTITY	7	NUMBER	17	3	X	0
UNIT	8	VARCHAR2	9		X	' '

Figure 4.16 View of the DSO Table in Oracle

You can use Transaction SE14 to gather information about how a table is mapped in the respective database. Enter the name of the table first, and click EDIT. Navigate to EXTRAS • DATABASE OBJECT • DISPLAY. An SAP BW on SAP HANA system maps the same SAP table, as shown in Figure 4.17.

Fld Name	Position	Data Type	Length	Decimals	Not null	Default
MAT_DOC	1	NVARCHAR	10		X	''
RECORDMODE	2	NVARCHAR	1		X	''
MATERIAL	3	NVARCHAR	18		X	''
PLANT	4	NVARCHAR	4		X	''
OI_BUDAT	5	NVARCHAR	8		X	'00000000'
OI_BWART	6	NVARCHAR	3		X	''
QUANTITY	7	DECIMAL	17	3	X	0
UNIT	8	NVARCHAR	3		X	''

Figure 4.17 View of the DSO Table in SAP HANA

Modifying the initial value with SAP HANA

When looking at Figure 4.16 and Figure 4.17, you certainly notice the different data types and their lengths. Take a closer look at the DEFAULT column now, whose content defines the respective initial value. If you examine the first line, for example, you can see that these two values differ. For example, an SAP BW system with Oracle specifies the ' ' (space) initial value for VARCHAR2, and SAP HANA maps the same line to the NVARCHAR data type and the '' (empty set) initial value. If individual fields of a table are not initialized, the system outputs the initial value. If this value changes, you must be particularly careful with the export of tables.

With this simple DSO example in mind, let's now get back to the known problem. Here, a table was exported, processed, and finally imported to another database regularly using SQL commands before the migration to SAP BW on SAP HANA. After the migration, it was exported from the SAP HANA database. Further processing or, more precisely, the import of the file to another database led to numerous terminations. The reason was the change of the initial value. For all text fields that are not specified in the table, the new initial value is used. When the table is exported to a file, the consequently system writes "" (empty set) instead of " " (space) to the file for all text fields that are not maintained. When this file was imported to another database, the empty set was interpreted as a NULL value. However, because the text fields were created with a NOT NULL condition, the database system could not perform the import. In this project, the problem was solved by replacing the empty sets of the affected text fields with a space for postprocessing. Although the described project can probably not exactly be extrapolated to your situation, you hopefully now know which pitfalls may arise from the modification of initial values from the technical perspective. The "Character Strings with Trailing Spaces" box provides more information on the handling of character strings with trailing spaces under SAP HANA.

Consequences of the changed initial value

| Character Strings with Trailing Spaces | [*] |

The ABABVARCHARMODE parameter in SAP HANA controls how character strings with trailing spaces are handled. If the parameter is set to TRUE, the database removes the space at the end when inserting new data records. If it is set to FALSE, the character string is used without changes. You can use the following SQL command to check whether this parameter is currently set: SELECT SESSION_CONTEXT('ABAPVARCHARMODE') FROM DUMMY. For example, if you query the parameter from SAP HANA Studio, it is usually set to FALSE. If you call the SQL command directly via the SAP BW system—for example, using TRANSACTION DB02 • SQL EDITOR—the parameter is set to TRUE by default, as shown in Figure 4.18.

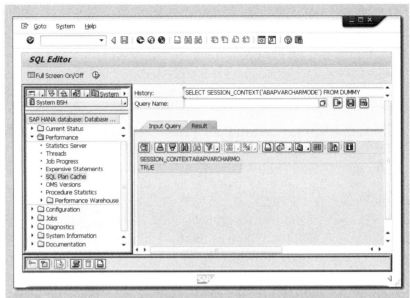

Figure 4.18 ABAPVARCHARMODE Set for SAP BW

Basically, you can set the parameter via SET 'ABAPVARCHARMODE' = 'TRUE' in SAP HANA Studio for testing purposes. If you now insert a data record with a trailing space, it is removed automatically. The following SQL code demonstrates this:

```
SET 'ABAPVARCHARMODE' = 'TRUE';
CREATE COLUMN TABLE TEST(ID INTEGER PRIMARY KEY,
STRING VARCHAR(20));
INSERT INTO "TEST" VALUES (1, ' ');
```

Execute the SQL code and then export Table TEST vian SAP HANA Studio. If you now view the content of the table (*data.csv* file), you will see that the trailing space has been replaced by the empty set 1,"".

For the SAP BW system, the modification of the ABABVARCHARMODE parameter, however, is neither provided nor recommended.

Queries based on MultiProviders

Finally, we'll look at a tip for optimizing the performance of BEx queries that are based on MultiProviders. Transaction RSRT (Query Monitor) enables you to define HANA-specific optimizations for BEx queries. Optimized access to SAP HANA is set by default (3 STANDARD; see Figure 4.19). However, if a MultiProvider is based on both SAP HANA-optimized InfoCubes and standard InfoCubes, this has a negative impact on the performance. In this case, SAP recommends that you either convert all InfoCubes into SAP HANA-optimized InfoCubes or change the entry for the respective query to 2 SINGLE ACCESS PER INFOPROVIDER in Transaction RSRT. If you deploy BEx queries that use exception aggregations, you may also specify 6 EXCEPTION AGGREGATION. In sample tests, the usage of this option resulted in a performance improvement of approximately 25%. But key figures with one of the following functions cannot calculate exception aggregations in the SAP HANA database:

▸ Non-cumulative key figures

▸ Key figures with elimination of internal business volume

▸ Virtual key figures

▸ Quantity conversion

▸ Formula calculation before aggregation

In addition, the BEx query must not contain virtual characteristics or use functions for the determination of time-dependent hierarchies. And the MultiProvider must not be based on compounded characteristics that are used in a BEx query as reference characteristics (see SAP Note 1009987).

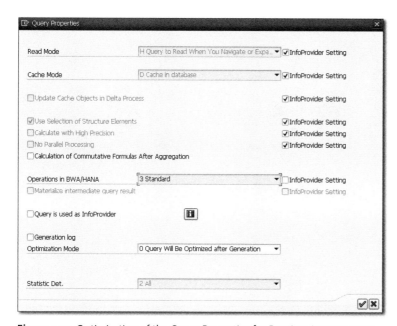

Figure 4.19 Optimization of the Query Properties for Runtime Improvement

Summary   The tips and tricks provided in this chapter are based on comprehensive experience and therefore enable you to avoid some pitfalls. Despite this knowledge, you won't be able to sidestep all problems, as new SAP BW on SAP HANA versions will probably also hold some surprises for you. Gathering experience with the latest versions before migrating to SAP BW on SAP HANA is the key to success.

This chapter presents the optimized concepts and new features of data modeling for SAP BW on SAP HANA and illustrates how to use or deploy them meaningfully.

5   Data Modeling in SAP BW on SAP HANA

Chapter 3 provided a comprehensive description of how to migrate an existing SAP BW system to SAP HANA. On this basis, Chapter 4 imparted tips and tricks from real life to facilitate the implementation of an SAP BW on SAP HANA migration. This chapter now presents the innovations that are available for SAP BW on SAP HANA from the modeling perspective. The reporting topic is discussed separately in Chapter 7.

You'll first obtain a sound overview of the essential changes for SAP BW data modeling with SAP BW on SAP HANA (see Section 5.1). You'll then get to know the *SAP BW modeling tools* with which you can now model and manage specific SAP BW object directly in Eclipse (Section 5.2). Specific SAP BW objects can be managed only via this modeling environment. For this reason, we assume that the SAP BW modeling tools will play a more important role in the future. Section 5.3 then discusses SAP HANA-optimized InfoCubes. Process chains can be handled more easily thanks to the more efficient data retention in SAP HANA. These changes and the resulting speed benefits are then described in Section 5.4. The deployment of SAP BW on SAP HANA and the more efficient data retention also impact SAP BW modeling with regard to the structuring of data along the *Layered Scalable architecture* (LSA).

Structure of this chapter

Under SAP BW on SAP HANA, it is now possible to overcome the disadvantages of the classic LSA approach and obtain a leaner layer structure. Section 5.5 is dedicated to this topic. Data retention in SAP BW is also discussed in Section 5.6, where you'll learn why it may be beneficial not to retain all SAP BW data in the main memory of SAP HANA. In this context, we'll also discuss the relevant options for optimizing the default system behavior. As was already mentioned in Chapter 1, Section 1.1.2, SAP HANA provides new features that allow for specific reporting and analysis tasks also without SAP BW. Section 5.7 describes how you can use these features (SAP HANA views) in the SAP BW system and which benefits result. At the end of this chapter, we'll outline SAP BW IP-based planning and show you how to accelerate, for example, planning functions with SAP BW on SAP HANA (see Section 5.8).

5.1 Special Characteristics in Data Modeling for SAP BW on SAP HANA

This section presents the optimized concepts, new features, and their impact on ABAP development in SAP BW, specifically for SAP BW on SAP HANA.

5.1.1 Optimized Concepts for SAP BW on SAP HANA

Previous meaning of InfoCubes

The deployment of SAP BW used to be required to retain data in an Info-Cube to accelerate analyses and reports. The data of an InfoCube was stored internally in a de-normalized *star schema*, in which a fact table (for key figures) and several dimension tables (for characteristics) have a star-like structure. This layout allowed for a high-performance and dimension-independent evaluation of key figures.

InfoCubes dispensable under SAP BW on SAP HANA

In SAP BW on SAP HANA, it is no longer necessary to use InfoCubes just for performance purposes. Reports and analyses that are based on a DSO are usually executed as fast as if they were based on an InfoCube, so it is generally useful after an SAP BW on SAP HANA migration to check whether you can spare InfoCubes. If you created your queries primarily on MultiProviders, you can replace the relevant InfoCube with the corresponding DSO of the data propagation layer without much effort, in the ideal case. When building new data models, you can generally do without InfoCubes. This also impacts the LSA architecture, which we'll discuss separately in Section 5.5.

Doing without InfoCubes pays off for several reasons. First, redundant data retention can be reduced if identical data has been retained in both DSOs and InfoCubes so far. If you can spare several large InfoCubes, this often results in major saving potential with regards to the data volume. Accordingly, the database's used memory requirement decreases, which, in turn, can cut down or simplify maintenance tasks. For example, this shortens the execution time when creating a database backup, and the costs for storing this backup decrease thanks to the reduced size. At the same time, you can also considerably reduce the execution times of process chains because the steps for loading data from the DSO to the InfoCubes can be skipped. Because virtually all data is retained in the main memory under SAP BW on SAP HANA, large data volumes in SAP BW can sometimes cause peak utilization of the main memory. In this case, the hardware capacities must be ramped up, or possibly, the data must be reorganized or archived (for example, using an NLS system; see Chapter 8). In this context, sparing InfoCubes can help you reach an effective usage of the main memory again. The capacities that thus become available can then be used to master future data growth.

Benefits of sparing InfoCubes

However, there are also reasons to still deploy InfoCubes under SAP BW on SAP HANA. Motives include the following, for example (see *http://www.saphana.com/videos/1443*):

Reasons for using InfoCubes under SAP BW on SAP HANA

- Significant efforts that speak against switching from InfoCubes to DSOs

- Transformations that contain a logic for supplying InfoCubes and that modify or enrich data when loading data into an InfoCube

- Usage of *non-cumulative key figures*, for example, with regard to inventories

- Usage of *real-time capable InfoCubes* for SAP BW-Integrated Planning (SAP BW-IP)

- Usage of the RSDRI interface for accessing InfoCubes

- Usage of virtual InfoProviders that don't retain data physically

- More than 16 key fields are required (a maximum of 16 key fields can be created for a DSO)

Converting InfoCubes

Provided that you want to keep InfoCubes or depend on them for these reasons, it is worthwhile to convert them to SAP HANA-optimized Info-Cubes. Section 5.3 describes how they differ from standard InfoCubes and how you can convert them.

New Composite-Provider as the basis for BEx queries

So far, the general rule applied for developing data flows in SAP BW is that BEx queries should never be based directly on InfoCubes or DSOs. Instead, SAP recommended that you always use a MultiProvider for this purpose. The primary purpose of MultiProviders is to combine data from different InfoProviders. Nevertheless, it can be useful to build a query directly on a MultiProvider, even if it retrieves the data from only a single InfoProvider. The advantage of this approach is that such data models can be extended more easily, for example, if the data of another InfoProvider is to be integrated with existing reports in the future. Additionally, you don't need to adapt any authorizations because they are based on the MultiProvider. SAP now backs away from this recommendation for SAP BW on SAP HANA systems, as of version 7.4 SPS 05. In the future, the new HANA CompositeProvider, which we'll discuss in detail in Section 5.1.2, will assume the task of the MultiProvider and is expected to also replace InfoSets, TransientProviders, and VirtualProviders in the long term.

Merging SAP BW data and data from SAP HANA views

SAP BW on SAP HANA also enables the merging of data from SAP BW and SAP HANA views. Section 1.1.2 already mentioned that you can evaluate operational enterprise data also without an SAP BW system. Tools like SAP Lumira and SAP BusinessObjects Design Studio are deployed here and can access the SAP HANA database directly. For this purpose, special data models must be created in the SAP HANA database via SAP HANA views. Past experience has shown that you can combine the benefits of SAP HANA views and SAP BW on SAP HANA skillfully. For example, in a scenario when data is loaded from an SAP HANA view to SAP BW, this data can be enriched with master data. This process of merging the data is outlined in Section 5.7.

Delta merge and DTPs

In SAP HANA, data changes are initially stored in a delta storage that is optimized for write access. The changes recorded in the delta storage are then transferred (asynchronously) to the main storage as part of a delta merge process (see Chapter 1, Section 1.4.3). After activation, the SAP BW system automatically checks for every DSO whether a delta merge can be carried out. This is different for InfoCubes. For standard and SAP HANA-optimized InfoCubes, you can use the Trigger Database Merge option in the corresponding DTP to control whether a delta merge is supposed to be triggered after the data load process (see Figure 5.1). This option is automatically preset when you create a DTP, but you can deselect it manually at any time, if required. This can be useful, for example, if data is loaded from various sources to one InfoCube and a delta merge is supposed to be run at the end of the entire load process.

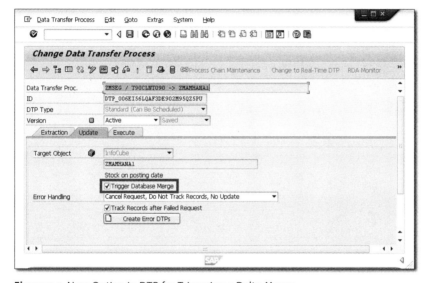

Figure 5.1 New Option in DTP for Triggering a Delta Merge

Several new features are available to you in SAP BW when you use SAP BW on SAP HANA. They are partially implemented via new InfoProviders and thus extend the options for data modeling. The following section discusses the most critical new features.

5.1.2 New Features in SAP BW on SAP HANA

With the release of SPS 05 for SAP BW on SAP HANA 7.4, various new features were introduced in SAP BW that both provide new options for data modeling and accelerate specific processes. Figure 5.2 shows which features are available for which SAP BW version. They include Smart

New features

Data Access, Open ODS views, the HANA CompositeProvider, Operational Data Provisioning, code push-down, and the generation of SAP HANA views from InfoProviders. Note that, in this context, Smart Data Access is not an SAP BW-specific feature. This feature is already available for using the SAP HANA database for various SAP solutions. However, using it under SAP BW on SAP HANA can be particularly worthwhile, which we'll discuss here in more detail. Operational Data Provisioning (ODP) is a new feature for data replication that doesn't necessarily require SAP HANA. ODP can be deployed as of version SAP BW 7.3 SPS 08 with restrictions (only as consumer) and is available with its full extent as of SAP BW 7.4 SPS 05. The combination of ODP and SAP BW on SAP HANA results in additional modeling options, which are also described later.

New Features	Available for SAP BW on SAP HANA 7.3	Available for SAP BW on SAP HANA 7.4
1. Smart Data Access	✔ *	✔ *
2. Open ODS View	✘	✔ **
3. HANA CompositeProvider	✘	✔ **
4. Operational Data Provisioning (ODP)	≥ BW 7.3 SPS 08 only consuming	✔ **
5. "Code Push-Down" in Transformations	✘	✔ **
6. Generation of HANA views form InfoProviders	✘	✔ **
* Available at SAP HANA Database SPS 06 ** Available at SAP BW 7.4 SPS 05		

Figure 5.2 New Features in SAP BW on SAP HANA

Smart Data Access

Integrating tables virtually With the availability of SPS 06 for the SAP HANA database, it is now possible to virtually integrate database tables from other databases with SAP HANA. This method is referred to as Smart Data Access. Once the virtual tables are created in the SAP HANA database, they can be used as data sources for SAP BW. This enables SAP BW on SAP HANA to access data from remote systems without having to store the source data locally. SAP-internal databases like SAP IQ or SAP HANA are supported for using Smart Data Access. In addition, you can integrate tables from third-party database systems, such as Oracle, Teradata, Microsoft SQL, IBM DB2, IBM Netezza, and Hadoop via Smart Data Access. Figure 5.3 provides an overview of the available options.

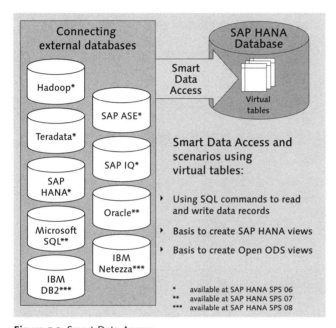

Figure 5.3 Smart Data Access

Compared to the access of default tables, some restrictions may apply in SAP HANA—for example, when you're creating database triggers. However, the read and write access using SQL commands usually works without any problems. Once you've created the required SQL commands, you can use the Smart Data Access-based tables as the basis for SAP HANA views or Open ODS views.

Open ODS View

SAP BW allows for complex analyses and quick reporting. However, this requires comprehensive and time-intensive modeling activities. You must perform numerous steps and activities in the SAP BW system, ranging from extracting data from the source systems to creating key figures and characteristics and creating multi-dimensional data structures.

Reducing the SAP BW modeling effort

Open ODS views can be a time-saving alternative in this respect. These involve *lean* InfoProviders that can access a database table or an SAP HANA view. InfoObjects are not required here. Calculations are run directly on the SAP HANA database using code push-down to accelerate the process (see Chapter 1, Section 1.4.5, Push-Down Principle). Moreover, you can define regular BEx queries on these InfoProviders.

Creating an Open ODS view

You create an Open ODS view either via the SAP BW modeling tools (see Section 5.2) or directly in SAP BW. To do so, right-click an InfoArea in Transaction RSA1 (InfoProvider View) and choose CREATE OPEN ODS VIEW. This opens an input mask, as shown in Figure 5.4.

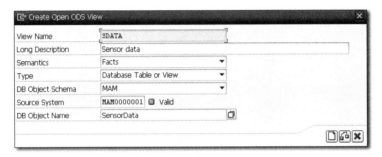

Figure 5.4 Creating an Open ODS View

First, enter a technical name and a description. Under SEMANTICS, you can define whether the data source involves texts, master data, or facts. You can then select whether the Open ODS view is supposed to be based on an SAP BW DataSource, a database table/view, or a virtual table (connected via SAP HANA Smart Data Access). We use sensor data in our example, which is available in a separate SAP HANA schema (MAM) in Table SENSORDATA. This data involves sensor data of mobile devices whose battery charge levels are recorded continuously. If all information of the input screen is correct, you can create the Open ODS view by clicking the 🗋 button.

Copying source fields

Next, you must define which sources files are to be copied for display in SAP BW (see Figure 5.5). With a right-click, you can assign a field of the category CHARACTERISTICS (KEY), CHARACTERISTICS, KEY FIGURES, CURRENCY, UNIT, CLIENT, or UTC TIMESTAMP. Optionally, you can assign the copied fields to an InfoObject. For example, we assigned the OCALDAY

InfoObject to the DATE field. If you don't make such assignments, the SAP BW system creates its own InfoObjects internally that are used by the Open ODS view. In our example, the 2FSDATA-DEVICEID InfoObject is used internally for the DEVICEID field.

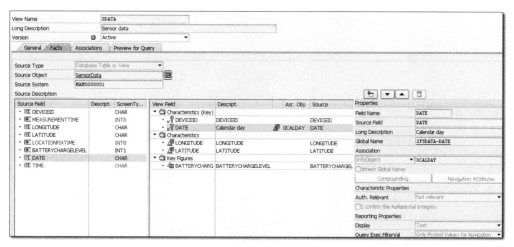

Figure 5.5 Open ODS View—Copying Source Fields

If you have problems activating the Open ODS view even though your specifications are complete and correct, you should try to exit the input screen. In our tests, we also received error messages during activation. In such a case, save the object and then restart Transaction RSA1. We observed that no further error message was output when you close and re-open the relevant Open ODS view.

Activating the Open ODS view

Once the object is active, you can display the data. To do so, right-click the active Open ODS view in the InfoProvider view and choose DISPLAY DATA. You can then view a data output that is similar to other InfoProviders (see Figure 5.6). In our example, you can see that the battery charge level is 100% for a mobile device.

Figure 5.6 Open ODS View—Displaying Data

Open ODS views and Smart Data Access

You can accelerate the data modeling in SAP considerably by combining Open ODS views and Smart Data Access. This allows you to integrate database tables of remote systems with SAP HANA. You can then create Open ODS views on these virtual tables. The benefit of this approach is that you can model scenarios very quickly because you don't have to load data to the SAP BW system and can save large parts of the usual SAP BW modeling effort using Open ODS views. Without the assignment of InfoObjects, however, you can't implement overly complex scenarios. But the deployment of Open ODS views in combination with Smart Data Access is definitely sufficient to quickly create prototypes.

The HANA CompositeProvider (HCPR)

CompositeProvider

SAP introduced the HANA *CompositeProvider* specifically for SAP BW on SAP HANA (see *https://scn.sap.com/docs/DOC-52329*). This Composite-Provider can be used only in combination with an SAP HANA database. The creation of a new CompositeProvider is not supported directly in SAP BW. Instead, you must use the Eclipse-based *SAP BW modeling tools*. Section 5.2 describes how to create a CompositeProvider of the new type yourself. If the creation of a new CompositeProvider is successful, it is displayed as usual in the InfoProvider view of Transaction RSA1. If you try to edit this CompositeProvider directly in SAP BW via the context menu, you receive a corresponding error message (see Figure 5.7).

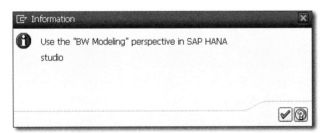

Figure 5.7 Error Message When Trying to Change a HANA CompositeProvider in RSA1

Usage

By means of the HANA CompositeProvider, you can merge data from different InfoProviders in SAP BW via union and join with particularly high performance. Moreover, you can connect data from SAP HANA views and join it with data from SAP BW InfoProviders. The new CompositeProvider is expected to be the central object of the virtual data mart layer in the future (see Section 5.5.3). According to SAP's plans, the HANA CompositeProvider is to replace the old CompositeProvider and the MultiProvider in the medium term. However, under SAP BW on SAP HANA, you can still create or edit an old CompositeProvider via Transaction RSLIMOBW. In another step, the HANA CompositeProvider is to supersede the InfoSet and replace both TransientProviders and VirtualProviders, at least for accessing SAP HANA views.

If only links via union are created within the new CompositeProvider, you can utilize the following SAP BW InfoProviders: InfoCubes, DSOs, semantically partitioned objects, Open ODS views, InfoObjects, VirtualProviders, InfoSets, and aggregation levels. If you want to use a join link, however, you can integrate the following InfoProviders: InfoCubes, DSOs, semantically partitioned objects (one per CompositeProvider only), and InfoObjects. It may sometimes be necessary to use both union and join links in a new CompositeProvider. In this case, you can integrate the following InfoProviders: InfoCubes, DSO (with generation of SID values), and InfoObjects. You can also use SAP HANA views (*analytic* and *calculation views*) for both link types, but you should note that the HANA CompositeProvider can be transported only if it is built exclusively on InfoProviders.

Integrating SAP BW InfoProviders and SAP HANA views

Today, the HANA CompositeProvider can be transported normally. The corresponding transport object is HCPR, which is the abbreviation of the term *SAP HANA CompositeProvider*. When you execute the export step, it is checked whether all dependent components of the relevant (new) CompositeProvider can be transported. In this context, it is not checked whether these objects are also contained in the same transport request. As a result, it is possible to transport the CompositeProvider only, without the InfoProviders used, so it is your responsibility to make sure that the required SAP BW objects are also available in the target system. For this purpose, you can use the transport connection in Transaction RSA1 to collect the dependent SAP BW objects and add them to a transport request. Note, in this context, that no checks are run for dependent SAP HANA views and that these must be transferred manually to the target system.

Transport of the HANA CompositeProvider

If you deploy an SAP BW on SAP HANA system, you should observe the SAP recommendations on how to use the new CompositeProvider (see *http://help.sap.com/saphelp_nw74/helpdata/en/5a/18066a61f34585af492 e7a95ac86d7/frameset.htm*):

▸ Create a CompositeProvider instead of a MultiProvider for new objects (see Section 5.1.1).

▸ Use a CompositeProvider instead of an InfoSet. Only if you want to define a time dependency or a key date for the join must you continue using an InfoSet.

▸ If possible, use an inner join because it can be processed particularly well.

▸ If the referential integrity is ensured, you should set the corresponding flag for the field on the OUTPUT tab. This improves performance further.

▸ You can use navigation attributes only if you select the DIRECT USAGE OF ASSOCIATED OBJECT BY NAME option. In this case, the name of the InfoObject, instead of a generated name, is displayed in the query.

Operational Data Provisioning (ODP)

Also with regard to *data provisioning*, new options arise when you use SAP BW 7.4 as of SPS 05. You can replicate data from different sources to SAP BW using the Operational Data Provisioning Framework (ODP). In this method, the data is not stored temporarily in the *Persistent Staging Area* (PSA) as usual. Instead, the data for extraction is picked directly in the source system. In this process, the ODP framework also supports the delta procedure for transferring data changes. The data is retained in the source systems in the Operational Delta Queue (ODQ). Compared to the classic replication procedure using PSA, it is now possible to connect more consumers to a common data source (see the "Data Provisioning with the Classic Replication Procedure" box). One advantage of the new ODQ approach, therefore, is that the data changes don't need to be retained redundantly in the source system. The retention of data in an ODQ also allows for higher data compression. Thus, according to SAP, a data compression of up to 90% is possible.

Data Provisioning with the Classic Replication Procedure [+]

In the classic replication procedure using PSA, multiple consumers (for example, various SAP BW systems) cannot obtain data changes from a common delta queue. Instead, a separate delta queue must be provided in the source system for each consumer. When you create an SAP BW system copy, this can result in problems if the created system copy is to be operated in parallel to the original system for a specific amount of time. This can be necessary, for example, if the original SAP BW system is still used in production after an SAP BW on SAP HANA migration until the new SAP BW on SAP HANA system has been tested extensively and is finally released. Because the delta data records can be called only once in the classic replication procedure, you cannot provide both SAP BW systems with the data changes. However, you can bypass this problem by cloning the delta queues in the original system before you start the SAP BW on SAP HANA migration. The Post Copy Automation (PCA) migration option is a suitable method here (see Chapter 3, Section 3.1.3).

Figure 5.8 provides a schematic overview of the replication using the ODP framework. This example shows how data of an SAP ERP system can be replicated to two SAP BW systems.

Replication

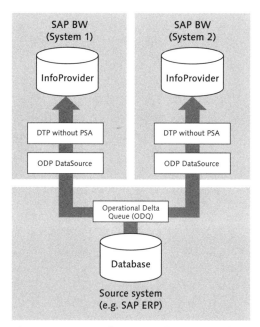

Figure 5.8 Data Replication via the ODP Interface

Here, the delta data records are retained centrally in the operational delta queue in the SAP ERP system. The two SAP BW systems or the respective InfoProviders (DSO) directly access the remote data of the SAP ERP system via an ODP DataSource during the data load process. In this process, data is not stored temporarily in the PSA.

Creating an ODP source system

If you want to use the ODP framework in your SAP BW on SAP HANA system, you must first create an ODP source system. To do so, call the source system view in Transaction RSA1. Here, you can view the following ODP-specific folders, which are still empty:

▸ ODP – SAP BW

▸ ODP – SAP (Extractors)

▸ ODP – SAP HANA Information Views

▸ ODP – SLT Queue

▸ ODP – SAP Business ByDesign

▸ ODP – Other Contexts

For each of these folders, you can create one or more ODP source systems. If you want to replicate, for example, data from an SAP HANA view to SAP BW via the ODP interface, you must create an ODP source system in the ODP – SAP HANA Information View folder. For this purpose, right-click the ODP folder and choose Create. Then, define a logical system name and the name of the source system. Subsequently, you must maintain the RFC connection parameters for the source system on a separate screen. Then, the ODP source system should be displayed in the corresponding folder structure (see Figure 5.9).

Source Systems	Tech. Name	Execute Function	Object Information
▸ ☐ BW	BW	Create…	
▸ ☐ SAP	SAP	Create…	
▸ ☐ ODP - BW	ODP_BW	Create…	
· ☐ ODP - SAP (Extractors)	ODP_SAP	Create…	
▾ ☐ ODP - SAP HANA Information Views	ODP_HANA	Create…	
· ☐ ODP Source System	ODS▮▮001	Display DataSource Tree	HANA
· ☐ ODP - SLT Queue	ODP_SLT	Create…	
· ☐ ODP - SAP Business ByDesign	ODP_BYD	Create…	
· ☐ ODP - Other Contexts	ODP	Create…	
· ☐ Data Services	BOBJDS	Create…	
· ☐ External System	PARTNERS	Create…	
▸ ☐ File	FILE	Create…	
▸ ☐ DB Connect	DB	Create…	
· ☐ UD Connect	UDC	Create…	
· ☐ Web Service	WEB	Create…	

Figure 5.9 Creating an ODP Source System

After you've successfully set up the ODP source system, you can create a DataSource for this system. To demonstrate this process, we'll use the example of sensor data, which is available in SAP HANA Table SENSOR-DATA in the MAM schema. Double-click the previously created ODP source system to go to the DataSource view in Transaction RSA1. You open the input screen by right-clicking any application component and selecting CREATE DATASOURCE (see Figure 5.10). Select the OPERATIONAL DATA PROVIDER (in our case, Table SENSORDATA in the MAM schema) and specify whether it involves master data, transaction data, or texts. Define the technical name of the DataSource before you confirm your entries.

Creating a Data-Source

Figure 5.10 Creating a DataSource for the ODP Source System

An input screen wherein you can set the DataSource configuration opens (see Figure 5.11). If supported by the selected source, you can choose the delta procedure, for example. Finally, you must activate your ODP DataSource. Then you can access the data source (the SAP HANA table, in this case) via this DataSource.

Subsequently, you can load the data to an InfoProvider using a data transfer process (DTP) without having to store the data in the PSA. In DTP, you can choose the corresponding option DO NOT EXTRACT FROM PSA, BUT DIRECT ACCESS TO DATA SOURCE if the source of the DTP is a DataSource that is based on an ODP source system. If errors occur on the SAP BW side during data processing, the data must be extracted again from the source system because it is not stored temporarily in the PSA. For delta-capable DTPs, you should also note that the data can be deleted in the source system's delta queue after a specific retention period. This occurs, for example, if the data was posted successfully in SAP BW and measures for delta queue reorganization are carried out in the source system. This can have particular impacts if you delete data packages in InfoProviders and then want to re-load the data. The source system data may no longer be retrieved. In this case, you can only delete all delta requests of the same DTP from the InfoProvider and then run another extraction with delta initialization.

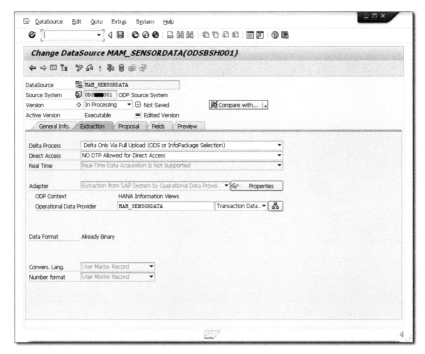

Figure 5.11 Configuration of the ODP DataSource

ODP DataSource and Open ODS view

Provided that you deploy SAP BW on SAP HANA, you can skillfully combine an ODP DataSource with the previously presented Open ODS views because, if you create an Open ODS view for an ODP DataSource (see Figure 5.12), all source data is stored neither in the PSA nor in an InfoProvider. If you create a BEx query for the Open ODS view and execute it, the data is loaded directly from the source system. This negatively impacts the performance of the source systems. But if you use an SAP HANA database as the source system, such a scenario could pay off. This way, you always have access to the current data of the source systems in SAP BW. Additionally, you can combine such an Open ODS view with the new CompositeProvider. In this case, you can enrich the data from the source system with master data, for example. You can monitor the data extraction and the replication processes of the delta queues in the source systems via Transaction ODQMON.

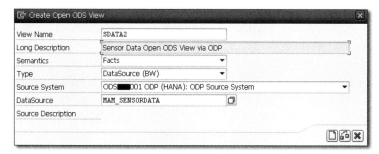

Figure 5.12 Creating an Open ODS View Based on the ODP DataSource

Prerequisites for Using ODP

You can fully utilize the ODP framework in SAP BW 7.4 with SPS 05 from the technical point of view. If the SAP BW system is supposed to retrieve data via the ODP framework as a consumer, this is possible with restrictions as of SAP BW 7.3 SPS 08. Refer to SAP Note 1848320 for this case. It provides important ODP corrections for this system version. For using OPD, it is generally not necessary to operate the SAP BW system with SAP HANA. However, SAP BW on SAP HANA provides more options, as was illustrated in the example of combining an ODP Data-Source with an Open ODS view. You can also deploy ODP DataSources in parallel to the classic data replication, but you don't have to migrate to existing extractors. In general, however, you should consider using new ODP DataSources when creating new data flows.

Code Push-Down in Transformations

As we already described in Chapter 1, the full performance potential of SAP HANA cannot be reached until the respective applications are optimized for SAP HANA (see Chapter 1, Section 1.4.5). For SAP BW on SAP HANA, performance-intensive processes—for example, for activating DSO requests—were moved from the SAP BW application server to the SAP HANA database in accordance with the push-down principle. Thanks to the in-memory technology and massive parallelization, such processes can now be executed considerably faster. Moreover, you don't need to exchange large amounts of data between the database and the application layer in this case because the required calculations are run directly on the SAP HANA database.

Benefits The principle of code push-down was implemented also for transformations in SAP BW on SAP HANA as of version 7.4 SPS 05. A transformation allows you to transfer data between a source and a target. During the load process, the data passes through at least one transformation rule that maps any number of fields of the source to at least one field of the target via a specific operation. The source and target are SAP BW-specific objects that store their data in database tables. For this very reason, the code push-down is particularly worthwhile for transformations because the source data table and the target data table are both located directly on the SAP HANA database. So far, the SAP BW application server has assumed the task of transferring data from the source to the target. For this purpose, all source data was loaded as packages from the database to the application server, where the data was processed and then returned to the database (target). The bypass via the SAP BW application server is now no longer required when you use code push-down. The data can all be processed internally in SAP HANA, which entails a major speed advantage and relieves the SAP BW application server.

Requirements In SAP BW on SAP HANA 7.4 SPS 05, you cannot yet execute all transformations on SAP HANA. Whether this will be possible basically depends on the operations used. At the moment, the following operations are already supported for code push-down:

▶ Simple mapping

▶ Conversions (times, units, currencies)

▶ Formulas

▶ Reading of master data from a DSO

▶ Expert routines, if SAP HANA SQLScript is used

If you want to use the code push-down for transformations, the sources must be of the type PSA, DSO, InfoCube, SPO, CompositeProvider, or MultiProvider. Only the DSO is currently supported as a target object. If you meet the requirements described, you can select the SAP HANA EXECUTION processing mode in DTP on the EXECUTE tab (see Figure 5.13). The data transfer is then carried out directly to SAP HANA at runtime. If you want to check for your SAP BW on SAP HANA system which transformations can be executed on the SAP HANA database, you can deploy the SAP BW Transformation Finder for this purpose. This tool was described in Chapter 3, Section 3.3.5.

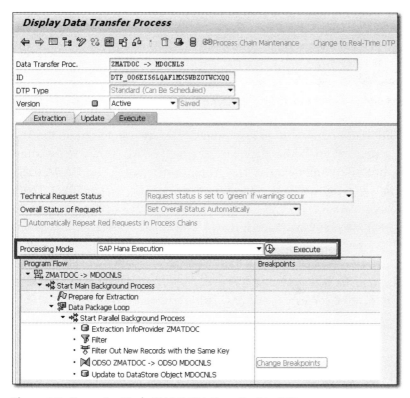

Figure 5.13 Processing Mode "SAP HANA Execution" in DTP

Generating SAP HANA Views from InfoProviders

You can now generate SAP HANA views directly from InfoProviders as another new feature of SAP BW on SAP HANA 7.4 SPS 05. Via these SAP HANA views, you can access data of the InfoProvider using external tools. For example, you can directly access data of a DSO and evaluate it using SAP Lumira or applications that have been created with SAP BusinessObjects Design Studio. To generate an SAP HANA view for an InfoProvider, open it in change mode. In the InfoProvider settings, set the checkmark for the EXTERNAL SAP HANA VIEW option so that the text

Generating
SAP HANA views

EXTERNAL SAP HANA VIEW FOR REPORTING is displayed, as shown in Figure 5.14. Then, reactivate the InfoProvider so that the corresponding view is generated in the background.

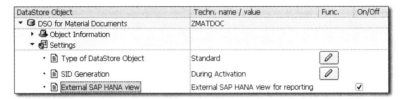

Figure 5.14 Generating an SAP HANA View for a DSO

Accessing the SAP HANA view

An SAP HANA view that was generated this way is not used by the SAP BW system, but it can be deployed as a native SAP HANA access interface for SAP BW models and data. You can specify the SAP HANA package in which the SAP HANA view is created in Transaction SPRO. To do so, choose SAP NETWEAVER • BUSINESS WAREHOUSE • GENERAL SETTINGS • SETTINGS FOR GENERATING SAP HANA VIEWS FOR INFOPROVIDER. In our SAP BW on SAP HANA system, for example, we defined the package `system-local.SAP BW.bw2hana` here. You can access the SAP HANA view of the *analytic view* type that was generated from a DSO via SAP HANA Studio and the corresponding navigation path (see Figure 5.15).

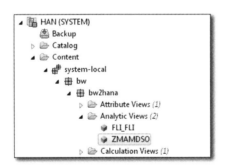

Figure 5.15 Generated SAP HANA View in the Content Directory

In addition to the generated SAP HANA view, the required SAP HANA authorizations are also derived from the SAP BW authorizations and automatically assigned to the SAP HANA database user via a role. In general, you can create SAP HANA views for the following InfoProviders:

- HANA CompositeProvider

- DSO, provided that SID generation is not turned off

- InfoCube, provided that its subtype is SAP HANA-optimized

- InfoObject, provided that it involves a characteristic

We won't discuss the general limitations with regard to the generation of SAP HANA views from InfoProviders at this point. The application helps provide detailed information on this topic, for example, for supporting navigation attributes of InfoObjects. To open the relevant help page, click the EXTERNAL SAP HANA VIEW option in the InfoProvider settings (as described previously) and then press the F1 key.

Restriction to 60 Characters No Longer Applicable in SAP BW 7.4   [+]

The deployment of SAP BW 7.4 has another advantage: in previous SAP BW versions, the characteristic values had a maximum length of 60 characters, and as of SAP BW 7.4, the maximum length is now 250 characters. The RSCHAVL domain was internally changed from CHAR60 to SSTRING for this purpose. For characteristics with text, the long text can be marked as *extra-long* and include up to 1,333 characters. For more information, refer to SAP Notes 1879618 and 1823174.

5.1.3 Impact of SAP BW on SAP HANA on ABAP Development

ABAP coding is often used within SAP BW data flows, for example, to modify or enrich data. If you use SAP BW on SAP HANA, you should follow some rules from the performance point of view so that your developments can fully utilize the performance potential of SAP HANA. Otherwise, it could happen that, after an SAP BW on SAP HANA migration, the data flows are not accelerated or are executed with less speed in some cases. The SAP document "Considerations for Custom ABAP Code when migrating to SAP HANA" provides a great introduction to this topic (see *http://www.saphana.com/docs/DOC-4120*). The most critical performance recommendations for a database access from ABAP to SAP HANA can be summarized in five rules:

Five performance rules

1. Keep the result set as small as possible.

2. Minimize the amount of data to be transferred.

3. Minimize the total number of data transfers.

4. Minimize the search effort.

5. Avoid unnecessary load on the database.

The following details some typical ABAP examples to illustrate the problems and optimization options.

Avoiding SELECT *

One of the most important recommendations is to no longer work with the * operator in a Select statement. This applies particularly if you access column-based tables. With a SELECT *, you request the fields of the entire row. However, if the data is retained in columns, the effort for reading the fields of each column is very high, so you should enter the exact columns in the SELECT statement that you require for subsequent processing. You should also avoid using SELECT SINGLE, and utilize internal tables in your source code instead.

Using the WHERE condition

When you process mass data or access large tables, you should also use a WHERE condition for the database query. This allows you to keep the result set as small as possible and minimize the access time on SAP HANA.

Using SAP HANA procedures

To optimize performance, it can be useful to create your own SAP HANA procedures. In this case, the SQL statements are not defined in the ABAP source code, but a relevant procedure called from ABAP. The application logic is defined through SQLScript. SAP HANA procedures include input and output parameters and can thus be deployed like ABAP methods. However, for a multilevel SAP BW system landscape database procedures cannot be transported via the SAP BW transport method. For more information on the SAP HANA procedures, refer to the following document: *http://scn.sap.com/docs/DOC-41604*.

Using standard functions

Particularly in SAP BW, with regard to SAP HANA, it is important that you use the appropriate standard functions within transformations. In the past, it was sometimes necessary to program your own solutions in ABAP for performance reasons. But now, the push-down principle in SAP HANA accelerates many standard functions (see Chapter 1, Section

1.4.5). For example, you should choose the READ MASTER DATA function for reading master data in the corresponding transformation rule and READ FROM DATASTORE for accessing a DSO. In SAP HANA, reading master data is usually more efficient than using navigation attributes. If you must access an InfoCube or an InfoSet in a transformation, you should use the corresponding standard API (RSDRI_INFOPROV_READ). Generally, you should define your own development in the start or end routine, if possible, and omit ABAP in the characteristic routines. If you want to use the option for code push-down of the entire transformation, utilize formulas instead of ABAP source code (see the Section "Code Push-Down in Transformations" in Section 5.1.2).

The *ABAP Routine Analyzer* was created specifically for SAP BW on SAP HANA. With this tool, you can automatically analyze individual data flows, process chains, and transformations. This tool is described in Chapter 3, Section 3.3.5, within the context of preparation steps for an SAP BW on SAP HANA migration. There, you'll also learn how to install and use this tool.

ABAP Routine Analyzer

5.2 Developing and Modeling Environments in SAP HANA Studio

This section deals with the tools in SAP HANA Studio that enable reporting on SAP HANA data. Within the scope of this book, we can provide an overview of only the most critical components of the tools. Chapter 6 describes the structure of SAP HANA Studio and its components. If you are not familiar with Eclipse, you should first read that chapter.

5.2.1 SAP BW Modeling Tools

The SAP BW modeling tools are an extension of SAP HANA Studio to be used in the context of SAP BW on SAP HANA. They continue the SAP trend of Eclipse-based applications. This very young tool is an alternative to the aged modeling interface of SAP GUI. You can use these tools to create and modify InfoProviders. The structure and functioning is similar to the InfoProvider area of Transaction RSA1.

Display of new InfoProviders

A separate, clear management interface is available in Eclipse for the Open ODS view and the HANA CompositeProvider (see Figure 5.16). The HANA CompositeProvider can also be created exclusively with SAP BW modeling tools.

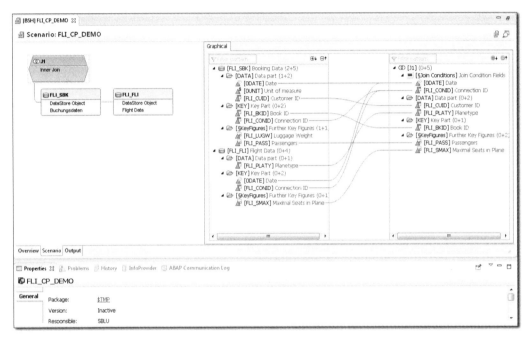

Figure 5.16 The HANA CompositeProvider in SAP BW Modeling Tools

Display of other InfoProviders

No native Eclipse interface is currently available for the other InfoProviders. If these InfoProviders are edited with the SAP BW modeling tools, a view opens with the SAP GUI interface (see Figure 5.17).

Installation

If you use SAP BW on SAP HANA, it is advisable to also engage with SAP BW modeling tools because SAP will increasingly rely on modeling in Eclipse in the future. Because they are not part of SAP HANA Studio, you must install them first. The necessary steps and requirements change with every version, so we want to refer you to the instructions at *http:// help.sap.com/download/netweaver/bwmt/SAP_SAPBW_Modeling_Tools_ Installation_Guide_en.pdf*.

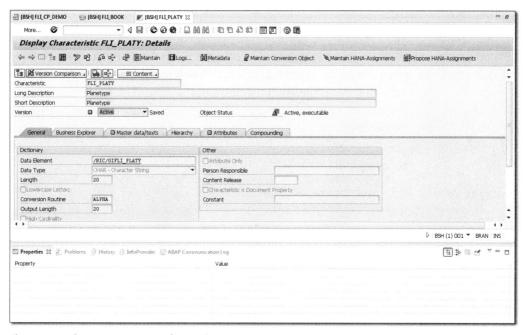

Figure 5.17 Characteristic as an InfoProvider in SAP BW Modeling Tools

Note that each update of SAP HANA Studio can also impact SAP BW modeling tools. If you want to continue to use the SAP BW modeling tools, we recommend installing an update on a copy of SAP HANA Studio. For this purpose, simply create a copy of SAP HANA Studio. It is usually located in the folder *C:\Program Files\sap*. The copy is also executable. In this copy, you can test whether the SAP BW modeling tools work as usual after the update. This allows you to save the trouble of a time-consuming reinstallation in case of an error.

Installing updates with caution

SP08 and SAP BW Modeling Tools

[!]

To ensure proper operation of the SAP BW modeling tools, SAP recommends that you import the notes that are available specifically for the SAP BW modeling tools into the SAP BW system. But if you follow this recommendation, problems could arise in a subsequent SAP BW update. SAP Note 2091812 points out that you should not upgrade to SP08 if you've already imported the notes for SAP BW modeling tools into your SAP BW system.

Login

Project Explorer

After installation, the new SAP BW MODELING perspective should be available in SAP HANA Studio. When you open this perspective, you can see a view for the connection to SAP BW systems that is analogous to the SYSTEMS VIEW in the administration perspective. The SAP BW Modeling perspective view uses Project Explorer for this purpose. If you've already developed in SAP HANA Studio, the development packages are also displayed. However, they are irrelevant for deploying SAP BW modeling tools.

Creating an SAP BW project

Right-click an empty space in the Project Explorer and choose NEW • OTHER and SAP BW PROJECT in the subsequent dialog box, and the window shown in Figure 5.18 opens. Select your SAP BW system by clicking BROWSE. You can select only SAP BW on SAP HANA systems that are entered in your SAP GUI (on the same system). The information available in SAP GUI is sufficient for the SAP BW modeling tools. Log on to the system with your SAP BW user name. You can now utilize the SAP BW modeling tools for this system.

Figure 5.18 Selecting an SAP BW System

Navigation

In PROJECT EXPLORER, the InfoProviders are sorted by InfoAreas and InfoProvider type. As you can see in Figure 5.19, the technical names of objects are displayed with a bolder font than their description. This can be confusing if you are used to Transaction RSA1, in which you can only view descriptions. A double-click takes you to the administration of the InfoProvider. As already mentioned, you either navigate to the SAP GUI directly or to a native Eclipse display. However, the SAP BW modeling tools currently focus on the creation of new CompositeProviders or Open ODS views. These are the only objects that can be created with the SAP BW modeling tools at the moment.

Figure 5.19 Project Explorer with InfoAreas of an SAP BW on SAP HANA System

Open ODS Views

Introduction

Section 5.1.2 already discussed Open ODS views. Let's summarize the most essential facts again for better understanding.

Modeling data objects in SAP BW allows for complex analysis and quick reporting, but it also requires a lot of time. A lot of modeling tasks are required, ranging from extraction of data from source systems, to the multidimensional data structure, to individual key figures and characteristics. Open ODS views can be a time-saving alternative. They have been introduced with SAP BW version 7.40 SP 05 and are available for SAP BW on SAP HANA systems only. The rather easy configuration doesn't permit any complex scenarios, but data can be integrated quickly with SAP BW.

Creating an Open ODS view

To create an Open ODS view, right-click the desired InfoArea and choose NEW • OPEN ODS VIEW. A window opens that provides details for creation (see Figure 5.20).

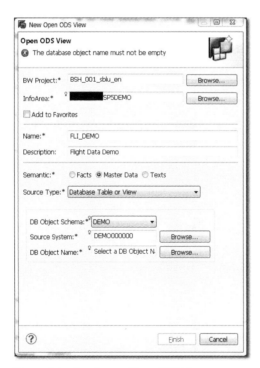

Figure 5.20 Creating an Open ODS View

First, select a data source. You can choose a DataSource, a DSO, or a database table. You can also link tables of other databases via *Smart Data Access*. More information on this variant is available in SAP Note 1868702 (SAP HANA Smart Data Access: Remote DataSource Driver).

If you select a database table as the source, the source system in SAP BW is created automatically as SAP HANA version 70 once you select the corresponding schema.

After you've entered a name and a description for your Open ODS view, the system opens an overview in an Eclipse view (see Figure 5.21).

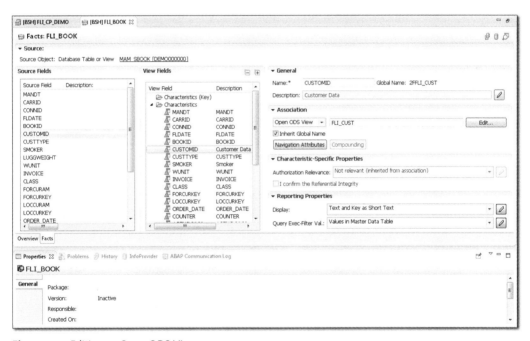

Figure 5.21 Editing an Open ODS View

In this view, you assign the columns of the used data source to the categories of an Open ODS view. This procedure is similar to the procedure for DS objects in SAP BW. Assign the primary keys, key figures, and characteristics. Different form the other InfoProviders, it is not required to model the corresponding InfoObjects. They are created automatically in the background. A proposal for assignment was already created when you generated the view. For each data field, you can also define further

Configuring the ODS view

237

details on the right-hand side. This enables you to, for example, reference fields with other Open ODS views, InfoObjects, or DSOs for reporting. As a result, you can provide additional information about a customer ID, for example, in a report, which is very similar to modeling. You can also specify the name to be displayed and define the type of aggregation for key figures. After you are done with the modeling of your Open ODS view, you can activate it via the ⚙ button. You can also start a check using the ✓ button. Your Open ODS view is now available for usage in reporting.

HANA CompositeProvider

Introduction of HANA CompositeProviders

Section 5.1.2 also already discussed the HANA (new) CompositeProviders. Let's summarize the most essential facts for this SAP BW object.

The HANA CompositeProvider was introduced for SAP BW on SAP HANA systems in SAP BW version 7.40 SP 05. The HANA CompositeProvider is supposed to replace the InfoProviders MultiProvider, InfoSet, VirtualProvider, and TransientProvider in the long term. However, it can be only used in an SAP BW on SAP HANA system at the moment and exists in parallel to the previous CompositeProvider. By means of the HANA CompositeProvider, unions and joins of InfoProviders and SAP HANA views can be implemented with a high performance. So far, these functions have been implemented separately by the other virtual InfoProviders. Since the introduction of the HANA CompositeProvider in SAP BW 7.4 SP5, SAP even recommends executing reports on CompositeProviders rather than on MultiProviders. The old CompositeProvider is also available in parallel on these systems, but it must be created explicitly using Transaction RSLIMO. Its new equivalent, by contrast, can be created and changed only via the SAP BW modeling tools.

Creating CompositeProviders

To create a HANA CompositeProvider, right-click the desired InfoArea and choose NEW • OPEN ODS VIEW. Like for the Open ODS view, a window opens that provides details for creation (see Figure 5.22).

Figure 5.22 Creating a New CompositeProvider

The HANA (new) CompositeProvider controls *unions*, *inner joins*, or *left outer joins*. Choose one of the variants and a name, and confirm with NEXT. You are now prompted to select the tables that participate in the union or join. Only then can you confirm with FINISH.

Figure 5.23 shows the editing view for the CompositeProvider. Establish the mapping between the data fields of your data sources and the output of the CompositeProvider on the right-hand side of the screen. More tabs are available in the lower area. The OVERVIEW tab is particularly interesting. Here, you can define details for execution, for example, the possible access to data from nearline storage.

Configuring CompositeProviders

After you've completed the modeling of your CompositeProvider, you can activate it with the ▢ button. You can also start a check using the ▢ button. Your CompositeProvider is now available for usage in reporting.

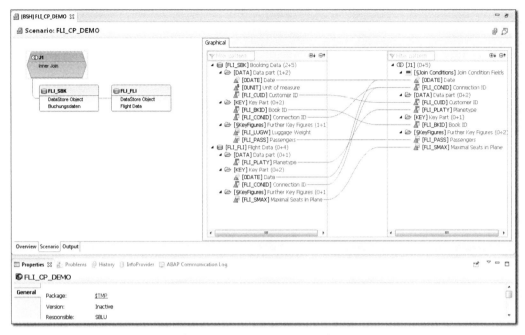

Figure 5.23 Editing a HANA CompositeProvider

Summary

The SAP BW modeling tools have only limited functionality at the moment, but the development trend is toward Eclipse-based tools. SAP HANA Studio itself, SAP BusinessObjects Design Studio, and ABAP for Eclipse are examples for this trend. If you want to utilize the benefits of the new InfoProviders, there is no way around using SAP BW modeling tools. The new CompositeProvider can be created only with these tools, and the Open ODS view also provides fewer functions, such as automatic assignment of data fields in the SAP GUI.

5.2.2   Modeling SAP HANA Views in SAP HANA Studio

Let's now discuss the modeling perspective. It is already part of the SAP HANA Studio installation, where it is referred to as *SAP HANA Modeler*. The modeling perspective is used for creating SAP HANA views.

In SAP HANA views, you can edit data from the database for a high-performance evaluation in BusinessObjects tools. They assume the task of SAP BW InfoProviders. In contrast to most InfoProviders, SAP HANA views are *non-materialized views*: that is, they access database tables directly and do not store them in another format. Unions, joins, calculated columns, and statements in SQLScript can be implemented in SAP HANA views. All necessary calculations are executed directly upon access. Here, a sound performance is possible because all source data is already available in the memory, and sufficient CPU resources are provided.

SAP HANA views

When you open the SAP HANA modeling perspective in SAP HANA Studio, the system opens an Eclipse view with an overview of all available activities (see Figure 5.24). All functions are described in summary and provided with additional links. If you still have problems finding your way around, this initial screen can be a good starting point. The available actions are described in the following.

SAP HANA modeling perspective

Figure 5.24 Initial Screen of the SAP HANA Modeling Perspective

Actions in the Modeling Perspective

Types of SAP HANA views
You can create three different types of SAP HANA views in the modeling perspective:

▶ Attribute views

▶ Analytic views

▶ Calculation views

They differ in their dimensions and the underlying engine for calculations (see Chapter 2, Section 2.3.2):

▶ **Attribute views**
Attribute views are two-dimensional, similar to a table. With these views, you can model master data objects and merge master data with the associated texts from different tables, for example (*join*). You can also carry out the initial steps for data editing and create calculated columns. However, an attribute view is not used directly in reporting; rather, it is used as the basis for building analytic views or calculation views.

▶ **Analytic views**
Analytic views are the SAP HANA counterpart of an SAP BW Info-Cube. They are multidimensional objects; that is, they can consist of several attribute views or database tables. For this reason, only a single-level join is supported in an analytic view. You can additionally set up calculated columns, filters, and input parameters in analytic views.

▶ **Calculation views**
Calculation views are more flexible but also more complex than the other two SAP HANA views. They can be created graphically or through SQLScript. Attribute views, analytic views, or database tables can be used as the data source. The range of available actions makes a calculation view more flexible than an analytic view. It can map multi-level unions or joins. If the calculation view is defined through SQLScript, you can choose the executing engine for some actions. This increases the performance considerably.

Other actions in the modeling perspective
Besides the modeling of SAP HANA views, you can also create other objects in the SAP HANA modeling perspective. We won't discuss these objects further, but we still want to briefly clarify their meaning:

▶ **Analytic privileges**
Analytic privileges control the access rights to SAP HANA views. They are created through filters that are customized to users or user groups. You can also use procedures for defining the filters. This allows for the provision of access rights that are flexible at runtime.

▶ **Packages**
Packages are the SAP HANA counterpart to SAP BW InfoAreas. They are used to classify SAP HANA views in a folder structure. The access authorizations can then be applied to various SAP HANA views via the package. Files of the XS development are also stored in packages. Packages can be found in the SYSTEMS view under the CONTENT folder.

▶ **Procedures**
Procedures contain program coding in SQLScript or R, a programming language for statistics functions. Procedures can be called in the SAP BW system using ABAP code. This is useful, for example, for complex transformations. If the transformations utilize ABAP code, which in turn calls an SAP HANA procedure, all necessary calculations can be performed directly at the database level. This corresponds to the push-down principle (see Chapter 1, Section 1.4.5).

▶ **Decision tables**
Decision tables map operational decisions, for example, classifications. They are designed to permit development without in-depth technical knowledge. After they have been defined, a column view is created via the generated SQLScript code, which displays the results. This view, in turn, can then be used in SAP HANA views.

Creating an SAP HANA View

Before you begin with the modeling of an SAP HANA view, you should ensure that your database user has the necessary authorizations (see Chapter 6, Section 6.2.2). For example, your database user must have the `Select` authorization for all tables that are supposed to be used in the SAP HANA view.

Requirements

The SAP HANA modeling perspective displays the SYSTEMS view on the right side, with all connected SAP HANA systems. Select your system with the desired user, and open the CONTENT folder. Navigate through the packages until you find the desired storage location for your view. Now, right-click the corresponding package, and choose NEW. Note that there are two NEW entries at this point due to the usage of Eclipse. Only one entry contains the desired objects; the other one should be grayed out. The objects that were discussed in the previous section should now be available for selection. Initially, the creation of an SAP HANA view is identical for all types.

After you've selected an attribute view, analytic view, or calculation view, a window opens with the details. The example in Figure 5.25 shows a calculation view. Enter a technical name and the description. You can also choose between the graphical creation and the SQLScript variant for the calculation view. Note that you can no longer switch between the two variants after you've created the view. Click FINISH after you've filled all necessary fields.

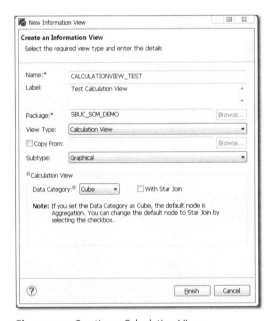

Figure 5.25 Creating a Calculation View

We cannot detail the SQLScript variant of the calculation view within the scope of this book because this would require a more comprehensive description of a view's functioning and the individual commands.

So, the following deals with the graphically created SAP HANA views only.

Structure of the view's overview

The graphical presentation of views that open after creation is similar for each view type. Figure 5.26 show the structure based on an analytic view example.

On the left side, under SCENARIO, you can view the structure of the view with all participating data sources, unions, joins, and other intermediate layers. The data target is an element bearing the name SEMANTICS. The individual elements are described in more detail in the following.

The lower area provides Eclipse views with details on the SAP HANA view and displays for any errors that occurred, as well as process information for activations and checks.

The top-right section provides DETAILS. Different information is displayed here depending on the element selected in the SCENARIO area. In Figure 5.26, you can view the information for the SEMANTICS element.

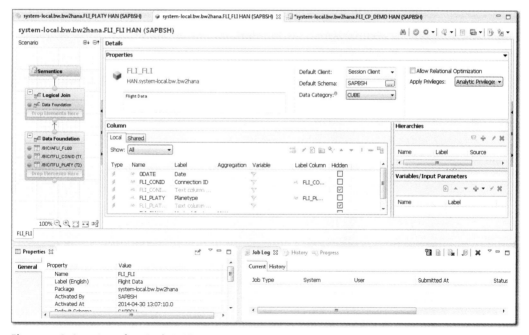

Figure 5.26 Overview of an Analytic View

Modeling and Activating an SAP HANA View

Overview For modeling, a maximum of three different graphical elements is available under SEMANTICS:

1. The database tables are loaded to the SAP HANA view in the DATA FOUNDATION. In calculation views, this is also possible at various layers using the elements AGGREGATION and PROJECTION.

2. Data is linked with attribute views or tables under UNIONS or JOINS. Here, as well, various layers can be available in calculation views.

3. Metadata of data fields is defined at the SEMANTICS layer.

The elements are used to carry out the modeling. This is done in four steps that are discussed in detail here:

1. First, you must add all data sources, like database tables or other SAP HANA views. Joins or unions are created in this step, if required.

2. Then, you edit the data through calculated columns, input parameters, or filters.

3. In the third step, you subdivide the output fields into characteristics and key figures, add descriptions, and define the aggregation function of key figures, if necessary.

4. Finally, you check the SAP HANA view for errors and then activate it.

Step 1: Select the data sources The selection of possible data sources depends on the type of view. Attribute views can access only database tables or database views. Analytic views can additionally utilize attribute views. Calculation views also deploy analytic views.

The general rule applies that database objects must be added to the DATA FOUNDATION view element. If various objects are used, a join is performed already at the data foundation level (see Figure 5.27). SAP HANA views are added via a union or join of the DATA FOUNDATION that may already exist. An analytic view always contains exactly one join object. In a calculation view, however, you can add several unions or joins using the toolbar on the right side.

You must first define data fields that are to be copied to the next level in the data foundation and in the unions or joins. To do so, click the gray dot on the left side of the data field. The color changes from gray to orange. This means that it will also be available at the next modeling level.

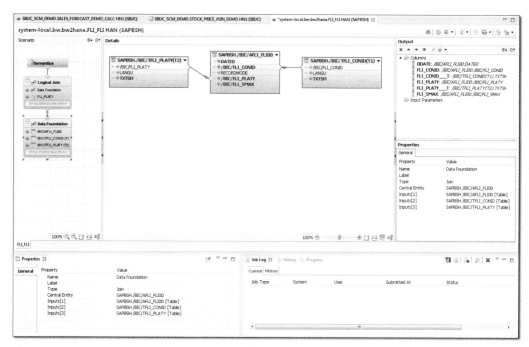

Figure 5.27 Data Foundation of an Analytic View with Joins

In the data foundation or in unions or joins, you can now view the list of columns in a folder in the top-right corner of the Eclipse view. You can prepare the data in other folders. Three objects are available for this purpose:

Step 2: Edit data

▶ **Calculated columns**

Calculated columns allow you to calculate values within a row. Text operations and mathematical calculations are possible here. Try to run as many calculations as possible at this level because, otherwise, they are carried out at the SAP BW server or BusinessObjects level for the SAP HANA view reporting. The performance is usually lower in this case.

▶ **Input parameters**
Input parameters provide the SAP HANA view with information at the time of execution. This enables you, for example, to load current currency conversion rates from a table so that the correct values are available at the time of reporting.

▶ **Restricted columns**
Restricted columns are filters. You can specify a value or value range for each column that is relevant for further usage.

Step 3: Generate semantic information

After you have edited the data according to your requirements, you must enrich it with semantic information. Use the SEMANTICS area for this purpose. Use the left mouse button to open an overview of data fields that are available for evaluation (see Figure 5.28).

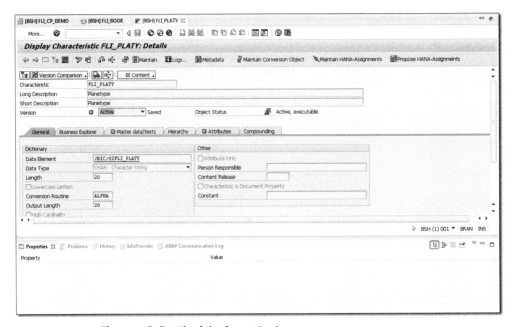

Figure 5.28 Details of the Semantics Area

If you used database tables as the data source, you must now decide whether they are key figures or characteristics. Keep in mind that only key figures have aggregations. If you choose key figures, you must also consider that they are already defined for calculated columns during creation.

Because many data fields do not have meaningful technical names, you should add a description in the LABEL column. If required, you can also hide individual data fields for reporting (HIDDEN column). This is useful, for example, if you have used a field for only one calculated column. The fewer data fields are available during report creation, the easier it is to keep an overview.

The administration of hierarchies and input parameters is not discussed in this section due to its complexity. The SAP HANA Modeling Guide (see *http://help.sap.com/hana_platform*) is a very good source of information if you are interested in these topics.

After you've completed the modeling of your SAP HANA view, you can activate it with the ⊕ button. You can also start a check using the ⊗ button. You can now use the activated SAP HANA view for modeling other SAP HANA views, open it with the analysis tools of the SAP BusinessObjects product portfolio, and use it for evaluation. It is also possible to use it as a data source in the SAP BW system (see Chapter 5, Section 5.7).

Step 4: Activation

Summary

SAP HANA views are an efficient option editing the data of an SAP HANA database for further usage in reporting. This provides added value, particularly for transactional systems, because you now use database means to analyze operational data with a high performance in real time. Moreover, SAP HANA views can also be consumed in SAP BW and expand SAP BW data models accordingly. For this reason, you should not consider SAP HANA views as a replacement of classic data retention in SAP BW. Rather, you should evaluate for individual situations if it makes sense to use them selectively, possibly in combination with SAP BW.

5.3   SAP HANA-Optimized InfoCubes

As described in Section 5.1, under SAP BW on SAP HANA you can build your reporting directly on DSOs instead of InfoCubes, considering performance aspects. If you still want to use InfoCubes because, for example, you don't yet want to modify the data model after an SAP BW on

SAP HANA migration, we recommend that you convert the existing InfoCubes to SAP HANA-optimized InfoCubes. SAP HANA-optimized InfoCubes are standard InfoCubes that have a simplified table structure and therefore accelerate the data load processes in SAP HANA. You can still use non-converted InfoCubes, as well, under SAP BW on SAP HANA. In this case, however, you do not benefit from the considerable acceleration of load processes. Additionally, all newly created InfoCubes are automatically created as SAP HANA-optimized InfoCubes after an SAP BW on SAP HANA migration.

Standard InfoCubes vs. SAP HANA–optimized InfoCubes The main difference between a standard InfoCube and an SAP HANA–optimized InfoCube is the underlying data model. For this reason, Figure 5.29 compares the two approaches. On the left side, you can view the advanced star schema of SAP BW, in which the two fact tables (E and F table) are linked via separate dimension tables.

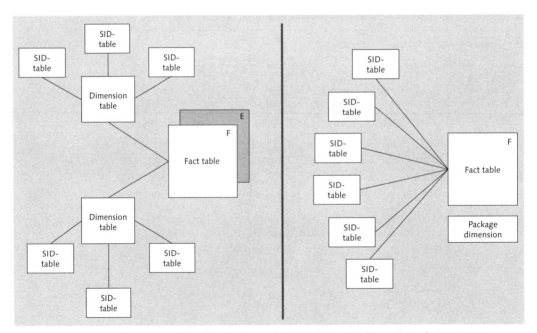

Figure 5.29 Data Model of an InfoCube (Classic Model on the Left, SAP HANA–Optimized Model on the Right)

The dimension tables refer to master data ID (SID) tables, via which you can establish a connection to the master data (attributes, texts, and hierarchies). The right side illustrates the SAP HANA-optimized data model. Here, the dimensions are no longer implemented as independent tables in the database. Instead, fact tables are linked directly with the SID tables. The structure is comparable to the previous option for creating a line-item dimension. The only exception in this context is the package dimension that is still provided as a separate table for performance reasons.

With regard to data loading, the major disadvantage of an InfoCube's classic data model is that the characteristics are not directly linked with the two fact tables. As a result, the data must be distributed to several tables for loading. SAP BW has used a complex logic to create the dimension entries with the corresponding primary and foreign key relationships in all tables required. The goal of this approach was to ensure high-performance reporting. However, particularly for large InfoCubes, it is often necessary to compress the data of the F fact table on a regular basis. In this process, the data is moved from the F fact table to the read-optimized E fact table, where it is aggregated. This entails another disadvantage: the request-based deletion is no longer available for compressed data packages.

Disadvantages of non-optimized InfoCubes

Thanks to the major speed advantages of SAP HANA, distributed data retention in InfoCubes is no longer necessary to accelerate reporting. The data load processes can be sped up considerably through the use of SAP HANA-optimized InfoCubes and elimination of dimension tables. You can still create different dimensions when modeling InfoCubes. However, they are used only for grouping InfoObjects from the semantic perspective (analogous to the usage in the MultiProvider) and have no impact on the data model in the database. Consequently, it is no longer required to occasionally remodel InfoCubes if dimension tables grow too fast. Only the package dimension remains as a separate table because this allows for effective deletion of data from an InfoCube on request. Reporting is also sped up considerably in SAP BW on SAP HANA because data retention is based on main memory, and the data of InfoProviders is now retained in column-based tables.

SAP HANA-optimized InfoCubes

Compression and
partitions

The function for compressing InfoCube requests is also available for SAP HANA-optimized InfoCubes. However, the data is no longer moved to another fact table here. Instead, from the database perspective, the F fact table of an SAP HANA-optimized InfoCube comprises the following four partitions (see SAP Note 1548125 and Chapter 1, Section 1.4.4):

1. Compressed deltas

2. Initialization data records

3. Historic transactions

4. Non-compressed requests

For compression, the contents of several requests are aggregated and moved from partition 4 to partition 1. Under SAP BW on SAP HANA, however, this has only little impact on the performance in reporting. For very large InfoCubes, this can result in shorter data load times, and it may help to reduce the utilization of the main memory. The compression is carried out via a database procedure directly in SAP HANA according to the push-down principle (see Chapter 1, Section 1.4.5) for acceleration. According to SAP, from the performance point of view, you don't need to run a compression for small- to medium-sized Info-Cubes (with approximately 10–50 million entries; see the SAP document "Aspects of the HANA-optimized InfoCube," *http://www.saphana.com/docs/DOC-1363*).

Restrictions and
additional
information

Note that the same SAP BW-specific restrictions apply for SAP HANA-optimized InfoCubes, as mentioned previously. Consequently, an Info-Cube may include a maximum of 233 key figures, 16 dimensions, and 248 characteristics. Additional technical information with regard to SAP HANA-optimized InfoCubes is available in the SAP document "Aspects of the HANA-optimized InfoCube" (see *http://www.saphana.com/docs/DOC-1363*).

Converting
InfoCubes

To be able to convert an InfoCube, call Transaction RSMIGRHANADB, or select the appropriate menu option in the InfoProvider view (GOTO • CONVERSION TO SAP HANA-OPTIMIZED).

Enter the technical name of the InfoCube (or a semantically partitioned object) in the dialog (see Figure 5.30). Note that the conversion of DSO is obsolete and no longer working (see the box "SAP HANA-Optimized DSOs Obsolete"). In the dialog box, which you can open by pressing F4, you can also select several InfoCubes at the same time and convert them jointly. If the InfoCubes to be converted are integrated with process chains, you don't need to adapt the process chains specifically. Even if the table structure of an InfoCube changes during conversion, the existing data is kept completely. Additional steps are usually not required. An exception could arise if you use FactViews in the custom programming logic because they are obsolete under SAP BW on SAP HANA (see Chapter 4, Section 4.3).

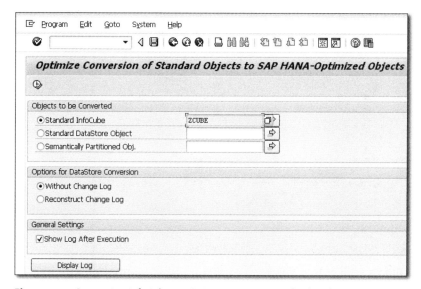

Figure 5.30 Converting InfoCubes to SAP HANA-Optimized InfoCubes

InfoCubes with Non-Cumulative Key Figures [+]

In Transaction RSMIGRHANADB, you can also convert existing InfoCubes with non-cumulative key figures to SAP HANA-optimized InfoCubes. In this context, you should familiarize yourself with the basic changes of the concepts for SAP BW on SAP HANA. For example, the logic of the data point update for SAP HANA was moved to the DTPs. A corresponding compression of the non-cumulative InfoCube is therefore no longer required. Detailed information on this topic is available in the document "First Guidance SAP BW 7.30 on HANA—Inventory InfoCubes," which you can open via the

following URL: *http://scn.sap.com/docs/DOC-28525*. SAP Note 1548125 provides additional, interesting facts on non-cumulative InfoCubes and using
SAP HANA.

Example In the following, we want to use an example to illustrate the background
of InfoCube conversion. In Figure 5.31, the InfoCube view shows the
typical structure of dimensions and the associated InfoObjects. The Info-
Cube has not been converted to an SAP HANA-optimized InfoCube yet.

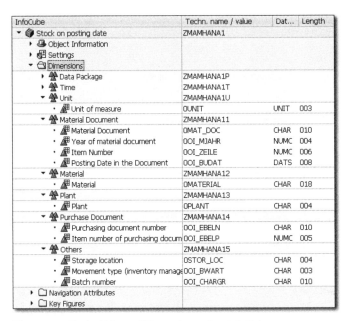

Figure 5.31 Typical View of Dimensions of an InfoCube

InfoCube You should carefully check the relation between dimensions and the
information database tables in the SAP BW system. For this purpose, click the information icon **i** in the InfoCube view or press Ctrl + F5 to obtain further information on the selected InfoCube. A new window opens (INFO
SELECTION; see Figure 5.32), in which you should click the DICTIONARY/
DB STATUS button in the DICTIONARY/DATABASE category.

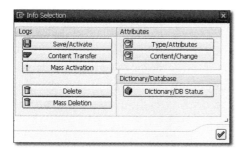

Figure 5.32 Calling the Info Selection for an InfoCube

Then, a window opens that shows the status information for the selected InfoCube (see Figure 5.33). The existing database tables are displayed for the InfoCube that has not yet been converted. The first two tables (/BIC/F<CubeName> and /BIC/E<CubeName>) correspond to the E and F fact tables. All other tables are dimensions. A table that ends with P is a package dimension. The ending T indicates the time dimension, and U indicates the unit dimension. The tables that end with a figure refer to the custom dimensions created by the user.

Tables of a non-converted InfoCube

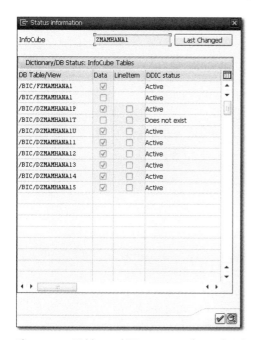

Figure 5.33 Tables and Dimensions of an InfoCube Not Optimized for SAP HANA

Tables of an SAP
HANA-optimized
InfoCube

The InfoCube of this example was converted to an SAP HANA-optimized InfoCube using Transaction RSMIGRHANADB. The conversion changes the defined data model of the InfoCube, and the tables are migrated to the SAP HANA database accordingly. Now, call the window with the status information for the selected InfoCube, as described previously. This time, however, only two tables are displayed: the F fact table and the table of the package dimension (see Figure 5.34).

Figure 5.34 Tables and Dimensions in SAP BW on SAP HANA

Summary

If you still want to use InfoCubes under SAP BW on SAP HANA, you should convert them to SAP HANA-optimized InfoCubes. This can be done easily using the transaction described previously. The full performance potential will be available also for data loading after you've completed the conversion. SAP HANA-optimized DS objects, however, have become obsolete in the meantime and should no longer be used (see the "SAP HANA–Optimized DSOs Obsolete" box).

SAP HANA-Optimized DSOs Obsolete [*]

In the context of SAP HANA-optimized InfoCubes, you should note that the usage of *SAP HANA-optimized DataStore objects* has become obsolete in the meantime. For this reason, it is no longer possible to convert DSOs to SAP HANA-optimized DSOs. If you've converted DSOs, SAP strongly advises you to revert this conversion. In this case, proceed as follows:

1. Use the InfoProvider settings to check whether it is an SAP HANA-optimized DSO. If so, the OPTIMIZED FOR SAP HANA entry should be available (Figure 5.35).

2. To revert the conversion to SAP HANA-optimized DSO in the past, use Transaction SE38 to start the `RSDRI_RECONVERT_DATASTORE` report (Figure 5.36). First, enter the technical name of the converted DSOs, and then click EXECUTE (F8).

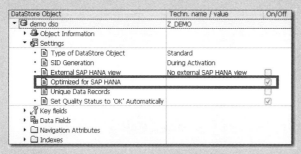

Figure 5.35 SAP HANA-Optimized DSO Obsolete

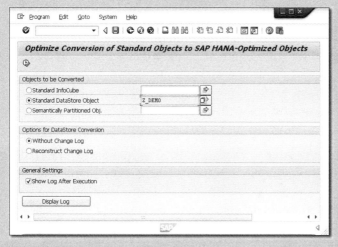

Figure 5.36 Reverting the DSO Conversion

3. Call the InfoProvider settings of the relevant DSO again. The OPTIMIZED FOR SAP HANA entry should no longer be available (see Figure 5.37).

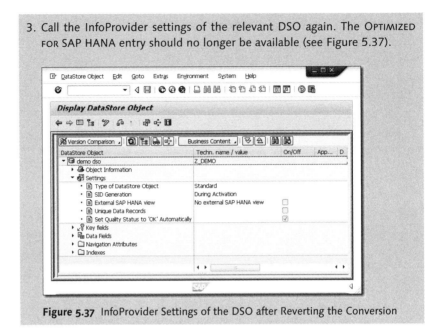

Figure 5.37 InfoProvider Settings of the DSO after Reverting the Conversion

5.4   Simplification in Process Chains

You can specifically control load and processing processes in SAP BW using process chains. A process chain is executed in the background and comprises several process steps. These process steps have a specific process type and control, among other things, the load processes, the post-processing in SAP BW, and the data target administration. Process chains in SAP BW with and without SAP HANA have different structures. To better illustrate these differences, we'll first discuss the typical structure of a process chain in SAP BW.

Typical process chain in SAP BW   A process chain in SAP BW includes a start process, the loading of data from the source systems, the transfer of data from the PSA to a DSO, and the subsequent update in an InfoCube. We are aware that this description of a process chain structure is closer to a textbook description than a real-world example, but the structure and usage of process chains differ considerably due to the versatile requirements. For example, some enterprises align it with the LSA architecture and load the data across applications from one layer to the next-higher level using one common process chain. Other customers, in turn, choose a domain-based approach in which related data is loaded from the PSA to an InfoCube of the reporting layer within one process chain. Still other customers intensively use events to appropriately link different process chains of different layers. Because we can't discuss all of these options within the scope of this book, we'll illustrate the differences of SAP BW and SAP BW on SAP HANA using a textbook SAP BW process chain.

The structure of such a process chain is illustrated in Figure 5.38 (on the left side). — Structure of a typical process chain

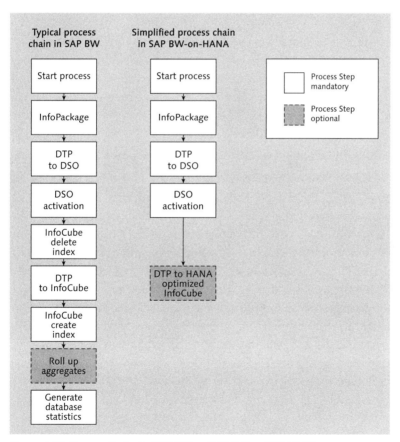

Figure 5.38 Process Chains in SAP BW vs. SAP BW on SAP HANA

After the start process, you load the data to the PSA by executing an InfoPackage. Then, the PSA writes this data to a DSO via a DTP. The data is then activated in the DSO. Before you can update the data from the DSO to an InfoCube, you should delete the index of the InfoCube. Otherwise, SAP BW must update the index each time a new data record is inserted, which involves a lot of work in the case of large amounts of data. After the index has been deleted, the data is loaded to the InfoCube using DTP, and a new index is created. In the next step, the data can additionally be loaded to an aggregate to speed reporting. Finally, you should update the database statistics.

Typical process chain under SAP BW on SAP HANA

Using SAP BW on SAP HANA entails many simplifications for handling process chains. They primarily arise from the special properties and enormous speed benefits of SAP HANA. For example, you can now build analyses and reports on non-aggregated mass data under SAP BW on SAP HANA. It is no longer necessary to aggregate data in advance or load data in aggregates for accelerating reporting. The simplified process chain under SAP BW on SAP HANA was derived from the typical process chain for SAP BW (as described previously). It is illustrated on the right-hand side of Figure 5.38.

Building a process chain in SAP BW on SAP HANA

After the start process, you again load the data to the PSA by executing an InfoPackage. If you deploy SAP BW 7.4 and data provisioning is carried out via Operational Data Provisioning Framework (ODP; see Section 5.1.2), you can skip this step and load the data directly from the DataSource to an InfoProvider. If you use an InfoPackage for loading data to the PSA, it is loaded to a DSO using a DTP. This DSO is then activated directly in SAP HANA, which results in considerable acceleration. All other process steps are not required under SAP BW on SAP HANA from the technical point of view. However, the concepts of the EDW approach and the LSA++ architecture usually require loading additional InfoProviders (see Section 5.5). From a performance point of view, you can build the reporting directly on a DSO and don't need to load the data to an InfoCube first. Possible reasons for holding on to InfoCubes were listed in Section 5.1. If you want to continue using your InfoCubes after an SAP BW on SAP HANA migration, we advise you to convert them to SAP HANA-optimized InfoCubes (see Section 5.3). You no longer need to use an index under SAP BW on SAP HANA, irrespective of the type of InfoCube you use, so deletion or reconstruction is not required. Updating aggregates and renewing the database statistics are also obsolete. Because these process steps are omitted, the execution of process chains is accelerated considerably under SAP BW on SAP HANA.

Obsolete Process Types When Using the SAP HANA Database   [*]

The following process types are not required when you use the SAP HANA database for SAP BW:

▶ Initial filling of new aggregates

▶ Update of explorer properties of SAP BW objects

▶ Roll up of filled aggregates/BWA indexes

▶ Adapting time-dependent aggregates

▶ Establishing database statistics

▶ Building an index

▶ Deleting an index

If you use SAP BW on SAP HANA, the optional process types (see "Obsolete Process Types When Using the SAP HANA Database" box) are no longer provided for process chain maintenance. If you migrated an SAP BW system to SAP BW on SAP HANA, your process chains usually still contain obsolete process types. A manual adaptation of such process chains is not required, however. Obsolete process types are simply skipped in SAP BW on SAP HANA and don't cause any errors.

Impact on existing process chains

Besides the simplification of SAP BW on SAP HANA process chains, we also want to take a look at their acceleration. Figure 5.39 provides another illustration of the typical sequence of a process chain.

Acceleration of SAP BW on SAP HANA process chains

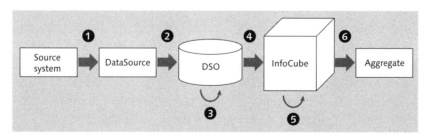

Figure 5.39 Acceleration of SAP BW on SAP HANA Process Chains

Initially, the data must be loaded from the source systems to the SAP BW system ❶. This process doesn't yet accelerate the operation of the SAP BW system under SAP HANA because the source system normally represents the *bottleneck*. Once the data is available in the SAP BW on SAP HANA system, all subsequent operations are accelerated. You can observe this already when transferring data from the PSA to the DSO ❷. The improvement is particularly striking in transformations during the code push-down (see Section 5.1.2). The activation of data in a DSO is also considerably faster under SAP BW on SAP HANA ❸. Here, the corresponding logic was moved to the SAP HANA database level, which results in a special performance boost (see Chapter 1, Section 1.4.5). If data is to be loaded from a DSO to an InfoCube ❹, this results in further acceleration during data loading, thanks to the modified data model for SAP HANA-optimized InfoCubes (see Section 5.3). Other common process steps, such as updating index ❺ or updating data to aggregates ❻, are omitted, as was described previously.

Summary Some process types that have been used so far become obsolete with the utilization of SAP BW on SAP HANA. If they are still included in process chains, they are skipped without any errors during execution. Thanks to their omission and other SAP BW on SAP HANA-specific improvements (code push-down during data activation, change of the data model for SAP HANA-optimized InfoProviders), the process chains are further accelerated under SAP HANA so that more time slots are again available for scheduling new process chains.

5.5 Layered Scalable Architecture ++ (LSA++)

To provide a consistent Enterprise Data Warehouse architecture and thus a consistent Business Intelligence and reporting solution, SAP proposed the Layered Scalable Architecture (LSA) in 2007. Structuring data on different layers supports a clear layout of the Enterprise Data Warehouse. The data is stored in different aggregation levels on the various layers. Figure 5.40 shows the classic structure of the LSA.

The data is stored persistently on most of the layers. In other words, parts of the data are stored redundantly. Any changes to the data are made between the layers using transformations, for example, between the data propagation layer and the business transformation layer.

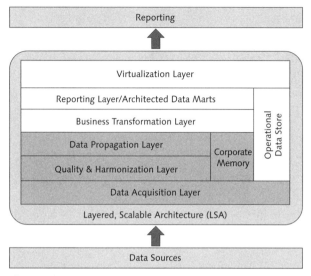

Figure 5.40 LSA Overview

The following briefly describes the individual layers to provide you with an overview of the LSA:

- On the data acquisition layer, data is stored as in the source system after the data has been extracted using the relevant SAP BW extractors on SAP Data Services (mainly for non-SAP data).

Layers of the classic LSA architecture

Note on SAP Data Services as an Extraction Tool　　　　**[+]**

SAP Data Services as an extraction tool can update data one-to-one from a source system to SAP BW. Because SAP Data Services are not limited to this extraction, the data can also be changed by SAP Data Services, and the transformation options contained therein.

- Then, the following tasks are performed at the quality and harmonization layer:
  - Harmonization of data
  - Quality assurance of the loaded data
  - Plausibility check of data

▶ The data propagation layer prepares and provides data with a quality level suited for reporting by integrating and merging the data. Data from different SAP ECC modules or SAP data sources, for example, are merged here to obtain a full overview of a subject area in reporting.

▶ The corporate memory is retained in parallel to these two layers—data propagation and quality and harmonization layer. It contains a one-to-one copy of the data from the data acquisition layer to preserve the data in the long term and in full. This way, you can revert to historic data even if it is no longer available in the source systems of SAP BW.

▶ The business logic is applied to the data between the data propagation layer and the business transformation layer to adapt it to the requirements of your user departments. The data adapted here is then stored in the business transformation layer.

▶ The reporting layer/architected data mart includes the data required for reporting. Here, too, transformations are applied to further summarize data for reporting.

▶ The operational data store comprises the data that is to be inserted in reporting virtually, in real time.

▶ The virtualization layer forms the basis for reporting. It consists of MultiProviders in the classic LSA. The SAP BW queries access data in SAP BW via these MultiProviders. The usage of MultiProviders allows you to add further data for reporting without having to adapt the SAP BW queries.

The previously described layers are partially combined in two groups for better differentiation. Traditionally, a distinction is made between the enterprise data warehouse layer and the BI applications:

Enterprise data warehouse layer

▶ The enterprise data warehouse layer comprises the following layers:

  ▶ Data acquisition layer

  ▶ Quality and harmonization layer

  ▶ Data propagation layer

  ▶ Corporate memory

It provides the single point of truth for all data and contains the data in a reusable historic view.

<table>
<tr><td>

Single Point of Truth

A single point of truth usually means that there's no redundant dataset, but only one dataset that contains the data to be used. So there's a central data retention to be used for reporting.

</td><td>

[*]

</td></tr>
</table>

▶ The BI applications, also referred to as architected data mart layer, include the following layers:

> Architected data mart layer

  ▶ Business transformation layer

  ▶ Reporting layer

  ▶ Virtualization layer

  ▶ Operational data store

The BI applications are the basis for reporting, which can be carried out with BEx tools as well as SAP BusinessObjects client tools. The individual layers must be structured individually for your enterprise.

Based on this reference architecture, you must define the customer-specific structure of your LSA and store it in an LSA standard guide. The BI projects that are planned and running in your enterprise should be based on this LSA standard guide to ensure that the LSA architecture is implemented in your SAP BW when projects are implemented. If you proceed consistently here, the LSA is applied in your SAP BW through changes to the existing developments or new developments within the scope of projects.

If the LSA is implemented in your SAP BW, the utilization of the LSA can result in the following benefits:

> Benefits

▶ It is a data model that contains various layers to cover different information requirements.

▶ The LSA can be used as an (enterprise) data warehouse.

▶ The LSA enables the integration and harmonization of all data.

▶ A single point of truth for all data is provided via the LSA.

▶ The LSA allows you to flexibly respond to new requirements (scalability).

- An improved total cost of ownership (TCO) can be expected by means of the LSA.

- The LSA supports the provision of data within the scope of a high-availability concept.

- Using this architecture ensures robustness of operation.

- The LSA is independent of a specific organization and can thus be customized for any kind of enterprise.

- The concept increases the scalability of your SAP BW system.

- Additionally, it increases the maintainability of your SAP BW system.

[⊕] | **Additional Information on LSA**

SAP BW: SAP BW Layered Scalable Architecture (LSA)/Blog Series:
http://scn.sap.com/people/juergen.haupt/blog/2009/05/16/sap-netweaver-
SAP BW-SAP BW-layered-scalable-architecture-lsa-blog-series

Data flow templates Since SAP BW 7.3, the usage of LSA is supported by data flow templates and semantically partitioned object templates. For a concrete implementation, you can thus ensure in your SAP BW system that the LSA is used consistently because the LSA standard guide is supported. This guide specifies standards and guidelines in an LSA architecture environment. This simplifies and accelerates the implementation of an LSA architecture in your enterprise. In particular, the support of semantically partitioned objects through predefined templates enables the usage of large amounts of data without impairing the reporting performance. Data flow templates allow you to implement a complete data flow in SAP BW that is based on templates for InfoObjects, InfoProviders, transformations, and so on that are provided by SAP.

[⊕] | **Additional Information on Automating the Creation of LSA Models**

Automated LSA with EDW Scalability Modeler—SPO Partition Templates & SPO BAdI:
http://www.sdn.sap.com/irj/sdn/go/portal/prtroot/docs/library/uuid/
a0ea9282-f44b-2e10-1e8a-d0241b466f56?QuickLink=index&overridelay-
out=true&50783693524512

All in all, the LSA is an SAP BW framework to be used in enterprises for reliably managing data and metadata in their life cycles. This is ensured by supporting the following elements:

▸ Data extraction and Real-Time Data Acquisition (RDA)

▸ Data modeling (by using InfoObjects)

▸ Authorizations

▸ Fast provision of "products" through the usage of transports

A disadvantage of the classic LSA is that it is cost intensive because many objects are required and a high number of data is "moved." The persistence of data at the various layers of the LSA also results in many redundancies. Moreover, the LSA is not flexible enough if new business requirements must be implemented because a great number of persistent InfoProviders are used. Particularly the use of InfoCubes in the reporting layer, which usually contain a one-to-one copy of data from the business transformation layer, is a point of criticism of the LSA. So, the deployment of the classic LSA is useful only if it involves an enterprise data warehouse.

To overcome these disadvantages of the classic LSA and utilize the new options of the SAP BW on SAP HANA scenario at the same time, LSA++ was presented as a further development of the LSA in 2012. Here, the priority is to slim down the classic LSA approach that is now referred to as the consistent core of an EDW. The consistent core comprises the layers of the LSA and contains consistent data because this data is secured by the LSA. The consistent core is enhanced by a virtual data mart layer and the Open Operational Data Store layer (Open ODS layer).

Figure 5.41 provides an overview of the individual layers that have both the consistent core and the new enhancements of the LSA architecture.

The Open ODS layer enables the data acquisition layer to also use data in SAP BW that is not modeled on the basis of InfoObjects. This data can be provided, for example, as SAP HANA tables, which are not supposed to be stored in SAP BW additionally. The virtual data mart layer allows you to combine classic EDW data and data from the Open ODS layer in order to provide reporting for this data.

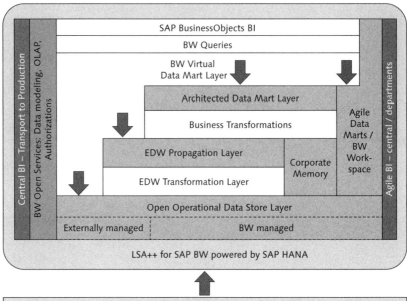

Figure 5.41 LSA++ Overview

With LSA++, you can therefore implement different variants of Business Intelligence based on your requirements. Within LSA++, data is modeled depending on the intended purpose or context. A distinction is made among the following three variants:

1. LSA++ operational enhancement: The context of the source data is preserved.

2. LSA++ flexible, consistent core: Classic LSA architecture

3. LSA++ agile enhancements: Agile/ad-hoc data

The LSA++ enhances the classic EDW core for operational reporting and agile applications of Business Intelligence.

The following characteristics must be defined depending on the variant you've selected in your SAP BW system:

▸ **Data model**
How do you model the data in your SAP BW system at the different layers of the LSA++ architecture?

▶ **Data processing**
Which transformations are necessary to be able to use the data for reporting?

▶ **Ownership**
Who is the owner of the data (source system or target system)?

▶ **Consistency**
How do you ensure the consistency of data across the various data sources?

▶ **Stability and robustness toward changes**
What happens, for example, if data is deleted or modified in the source system? Is it possible to use delta procedures?

▶ **Stability of the query results**
Depends on the stability and robustness toward changes.

▶ **Options for data revision**
Can you check historic data, for example?

The subsequent sections provide a detailed overview of the new elements of the LSA++ concept, starting with the changes in the consistent EDW core. You'll then learn about the Open Operational Data Store layer and the SAP BW virtual data mart layer.

5.5.1 Consistent EDW Core of an LSA++

The consistent core of the LSA++, which involves the classic concept of the enterprise data warehouse, comprises the following layers (see Figure 5.42):

Consistent EDW core

▶ **EDW transformation layer**
Connection between the source data and the EDW model; initial transformation of data.

▶ **Corporate memory**
Historization of source data; the source data is also available if it was deleted from the source system.

▶ **EDW propagation layer**
Persistence of source data after the initial transformation at the EDW transformation layer.

▸ **Business transformations**
Connection between the EDW model and the data marts; second transformation of data.

▸ **Architected data mart layer**
Persistence of data after the second transformation in business transformations; provision of data as data marts.

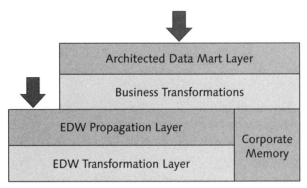

Figure 5.42 Consistent EDW Core in the LSA++

The consistent EDW core therefore comprises the data acquisition layer, virtualization layer, corporate memory, and all layers of the classic LSA architecture, which partially have a new or changed name.

Advantages of the consistent EDW core

Using the consistent EDW core and structuring in five layers provides you with the following options:

▸ **Transparency and addressability of different quality levels for data**
The data is aggregated/transformed on the individual layers. Reporting on data is already possible at the EDW propagation layer, although business transformations have not yet been applied.

▸ **Harmonization of data from different user departments**
You can summarize data from the SAP ERP components FI and CO, for example, to obtain a comprehensive picture of the development in your enterprise.

▸ **Increased maintainability through transparent standards**
Like in the classic LSA architecture, using the individual layers results in the deployment of a clear framework for the SAP BW system.

▶ **Robustness of the architecture through standards**
The selected definition of the LSA++ architecture can be used for different application areas and adapted to meet new requirements.

▶ **Auditability and reproducibility of the behavior or of data**
The usage of layers in the LSA++ ensures that, for example, the data can be reproduced from the corporate memory even if it is deleted from the source system (applicable to all data in the EDW).

▶ **Consistency and flexibility of data**
The data basis is identical for all subsequent data marts—data is extracted once and can then be used multiple times. Moreover, reusable metadata (e.g., InfoObjects or InfoProviders) are deployed to provide higher consistency and improved flexibility of data.

▶ **Increase of query performance**
This can be done by avoiding redundant calculations and transformations using architected data marts

The redundant storage of identical data has always been quoted as a weak point of the classic LSA architecture. Therefore, the LSA++ development focused on the reduction of persisting layers to obtain higher flexibility and lower total cost of ownership (TCO). Additionally, the design and implementation of persisting InfoProviders was adapted (for example, SAP HANA-optimized InfoCubes, new DSO types, and new InfoProvider types). You can increase the availability of data by using DSOs instead of InfoCubes and improving the DSO load and activation performance in the SAP BW on SAP HANA scenario.

Focus of the LSA++ development

The typical problem that the night is too short to run all process chains has been improved considerably. Furthermore, the modeling flexibility increases thanks to a lower number of InfoProviders used because data is not stored on all LSA++ layers. Data volume considerations don't play a major role in the individual InfoProviders any longer (domains/semantic partitioning) because you can process large amounts of data more easily by using SAP HANA as the database for SAP BW.

For most of the application cases that were discussed here, it was sufficient to store the data persistently in the EDW propagation layer. But if another persistent layer, usually the architected data mart layer, is required in addition to the EDW propagation layer, you should use either DSOs or SAP HANA-optimized InfoCubes in this persistent layer. Already, the usage of SAP HANA-optimized InfoCubes considerably increases the load performance because dimension tables are no longer required. Multidimensional modeling know-how is therefore no longer required when modeling these InfoCubes.

DSOs as a replacement for InfoCubes

SAP does not generally recommend using InfoCubes, because reporting can also be carried out with high-performance on the basis of DSOs. Therefore, it is usually recommended that you use DSOs also in the architected data marts layer. Because the SID generation was activated in DSOs and the optimizations were made in DSOs, the query performance based on a DSO is comparable with the query performance based on an InfoCube. In particular, the loading of data in a DSO has been increased considerably so that the activation of data can almost be neglected from the performance point of view, for example. As a result, DSOs are almost as good as in-memory-optimized InfoCubes in terms of load and query performance.

As described previously, a one-to-one transfer of data takes place between the DSOs in the business transformations and the InfoCubes in the architected data marts in a classic LSA architecture. You can skip this step if you use DSOs because the execution of queries, also based on DSOs, ensures high performance.

Eliminating Info-Cubes from data flows

You should check when it makes sense to eliminate InfoCubes from existing data flows considering the following aspects:

▸ The InfoCube can be removed if it contains the same data as a DSO.

▸ The InfoCube was not enriched with data that is not contained in the DSO (for example, reading of master data).

▸ No additional consistency checks are carried out in the load process from the DSO to the InfoCube.

▸ The BEx queries use a MultiProvider above the InfoCube as the data source. Thus, you can exchange the InfoCube for the DSO without having to adapt the BEx queries.

▸ Before you delete the identified InfoCube, you should check the query performance in Transaction RSRT. The measured performance should be compared with the performance that is available if only the DSO is used in the MultiProvider.

Another advantage of the LSA++ and the SAP BW on SAP HANA scenario is that you can also report directly on DSOs in the EDW propagation layer. Here, the performance is similar to the performance when using InfoCubes for reporting. Transformations that are used in the business transformations layer are not available here.

Reporting based on the EDW propagation layer

These advanced options for using DSOs or reducing the layers allow you, in the extreme case, to reduce the LSA++ concept to the EDW propagation layer and the EDW transformation layer together with the corporate memory. This, in turn, results in an improved total cost of ownership because only a few InfoProviders are required. It also increases the flexibility for using data, particularly with regard to new reporting requirements. Changes to the existing data model require so few adaptations that the time for implementing new reporting requirements is decreased considerably. This is also supported by the integrated functions in SAP HANA for running joins and transformations on the basis of SAP HANA instead of the SAP BW application server. Joins allow you to link data of several tables in a database, for example, to connect customers with the order data. New InfoProvider types (for example, the CompositeProviders and VirtualProviders presented in the following sections) allow you to run these joins and transformations directly on the basis of SAP HANA functions at a query's runtime without having to store this data in an LSA++ layer.

In the LSA++, virtual joins of data from the virtual data mart layer are carried out on the basis of CompositeProviders and MultiProviders. Virtual transformations are then run in the BEx queries (see Figure 5.43).

Virtual data mart layer as a supplement to the consistent EDW core

For the reporting of data, you often require a join for several DSOs, for example, to merge order and customer data. So far, it has been possible to carry out this join in transformations only through successive update of data or using InfoSets. The result of these transformations and thus the result of the join were stored in an InfoProvider (DSO or InfoCube).

A virtual join within a MultiProvider is not possible so far. You can implement a union only via a MultiProvider, which is usually not sufficient for the concrete reporting requirements, however. Virtual merging is therefore not possible.

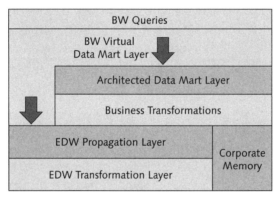

Figure 5.43 Consistent EDW Core, Supplemented with SAP BW Virtual Data Mart Layer and BEx Queries

CompositeProvider In comparison with the MultiProvider, the new CompositeProvider permits the modeling of a virtual join across several InfoProviders. The following join types are supported:

▶ **Inner join**
An inner join links several tables if at least one field of a data record is identical in two tables. Only the data records are copied to the results that occur in both tables.

▶ **Left outer join**
This join type returns all data records of the "left" table. The data records of the "right" table are copied to the result only if they match as specified in the join condition.

▶ **Union join**
The superset from the source tables is established analogous to the MultiProvider.

Local vs. enterprise-wide master data Because you can use different join types, you can utilize the CompositeProvider in different application areas. You can use the CompositeProvider, for example, if you must link enterprise data and local/department master data. Compared with the previous approaches, the

advantage of this approach is that you can also include frequently changing master data in reporting. If you create several CompositeProviders,
depending, for example, on the department master data to be supplemented, you can compile evaluations for different user departments that
each summarizes the corresponding master data additionally. Figure
5.44 shows an example wherein the data is supplemented with additional master data attributes at the enterprise level, depending on the
departments in Germany and Switzerland. This allows for department-
dependent reporting without you having to change the master data that
is valid throughout the enterprise. The local master data can be changed
more frequently without you having to rebuild the enterprise-wide master data.

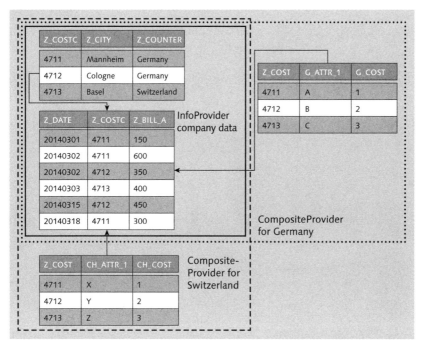

Figure 5.44 CompositeProvider as a Supplement of Local Master Data

You can deploy the CompositeProvider to reduce the number of Info-
Provider used. For all activities that reduce the number of InfoProviders
used, however, you must consider that not all OLAP functions of the
SAP BW OLAP engine have been moved to SAP HANA yet. Although

more and more functions are moved to SAP HANA with every update of SAP HANA and SAP BW, you must still observe that both the OLAP functions and the SAP BW OLAP engine are used on SAP HANA until the function transfer is complete. This can mean that the elimination of InfoProviders may have a negative impact on the query performance.

To achieve the goal of a complete virtualization of the architected data marts, you must determine when it makes sense to delete the Info-Providers. You can classify the InfoProviders used based on the criteria *granularity/cardinality* and *transformation/join logic*. The data mart can be eliminated if a lower granularity/cardinality of data exists in the architected data mart and no or only a few transformations/join logics must be run. The other extreme—that is, high granularity/cardinality and complex transformations/join logic—suggests that you should keep the data mart. Figure 5.45 shows all four possible quadrants of this decision matrix and the activities to be carried out.

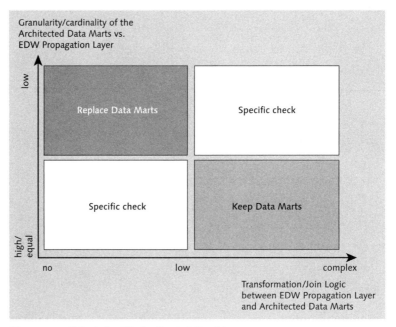

Figure 5.45 Criteria for Eliminating InfoProviders

If an InfoProvider falls within the *specific check* quadrant, you must carefully check the pros and cons of virtualizing data marts and thus Info-

Cubes or DSOs not to affect the existing reporting performance negatively, for example.

5.5.2 Open Operational Data Store Layer

The Open Operational Data Store layer (Open ODS layer), the second new layer in the LSA++ architecture, enables you to link an EDW with the approach of an operational BI. In other words, besides the data that is managed in SAP BW, you can also include data from other data sources in reporting without loading the data to SAP BW (see Figure 5.46, *externally managed*). Based on this data, you can establish a direct reporting without loading the data to SAP BW. This allows you to cover new report requirements quickly and easily without major development work and expenditure of time. Provided that these new report requirements can be planned in the long term, you can integrate the necessary data with EDW incrementally over time. The first step can be, for example, to integrate this data with an existing EDW data flow. The last step of the incremental integration with the consistent EDW core is probably to transfer the data to the SAP BW-managed part of the Open ODS layer.

Open Operational Data Store layer

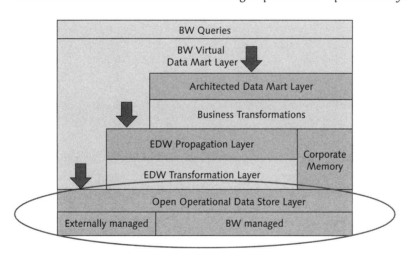

Figure 5.46 Open Operation Data Store Layer in the LSA++

The goal of the Open ODS layer is to provide services and technologies to ensure a holistic approach for Business Intelligence. The focus is not only on classic data sources (for instance, SAP ERP or SAP CRM), but also on other relational data sources whose connection to SAP BW has not been possible at all or required major effort.

The Open ODS layer as the replacement of the data acquisition layer of the LSA architecture forms the new entry layer for the LSA++. Source data can be utilized in different ways in SAP BW thanks to the distinction between SAP BW-managed and externally managed data. SAP BW-managed data is stored in InfoObjects as usual. Externally managed data, however, can be stored on a field basis. In other words, the structures of the source tables or views are also used in SAP BW. This is possible through the new transient InfoObjects that exist only at runtime—for example, when you execute a BEx query—to enable standard OLAP functions of SAP BW. Data that exists directly in tables of SAP HANA is an example here. Either this data can be loaded in SAP BW (SAP BW managed), or the HANA models can be used directly in SAP BW as InfoProviders via new InfoProvider types (for example, VirtualProvider; externally managed). Both application areas have their pros and cons, which you have to consider when implementing a project or modeling a data flow.

You require three central services to provide the necessary functions within the scope of the Open ODS layer for using these two data storage types. These services are described in more detail in the following sections:

▸ **SAP BW integration services**

   ▸ The SAP BW integration services allow you to consume SAP HANA models directly in SAP BW.

   ▸ Vice versa, you can also use SAP BW InfoObjects directly in SAP HANA models because you have the option to generate views based on InfoObjects.

   ▸ The SAP BW integration services also support an incremental change from externally managed SAP HANA models to SAP BW-managed scenarios, and vice versa.

▸ **SAP BW operational data services**

   ▸ The SAP BW operational data services supplement the support for real-time replication of data in SAP BW (SAP system landscape transformation services).

▸ Additionally, these services enable direct reporting based on all data sources. As a result, they also support the reporting based on SAP HANA models, which are integrated with SAP BW as externally managed data using the SAP BW integration services.

▸ Besides direct reporting, they also supplement the data modeling on the basis of field-based InfoProviders in the Open ODS layer.

▸ **SAP BW EDW services**

▸ The SAP BW EDW services within the scope of the Open ODS layer are the source for persistent EDW InfoProviders (InfoObject-based) and provide the following functions:

  – Consistency management (delta management)

  – Transfer of data between the layers

  – Transformation services for the EDW

▸ The InfoProviders of the Open ODS layer are the virtual part of the EDW and provide the following benefits:

  – Reduction of redundancy in data models

  – Increased availability of data because data doesn't need to be loaded to SAP BW first

Overall, the Open ODS layer is the link between two worlds—SAP BW and SAP HANA—where data can be managed by SAP BW or the data source. Both worlds have their advantages and disadvantages, which you should utilize depending on the concrete application case. The subsequent sections provide a detailed overview of the application areas and functions of the three services that were mentioned previously.

Open ODS layer— link between two worlds

SAP BW Integration Services

The SAP BW integration services provide functions for both application areas (SAP BW-managed and externally managed data; see Section 5.7). Here's a short definition proposal to better distinguish the two approaches:

SAP BW-managed and modeled data is usually available within an EDW and integrated with the LSA. They are model driven and have a regulated governance, and the authorizations are clearly defined.

SAP BW-managed data

279

Externally managed data Externally managed data (for example, SAP HANA) is usually available within a data mart. The data mart contains a wide variety of views or tables that are supposed to be provided for reporting. They offer high flexibility and performance, specifically if the data is located in SAP HANA. The data is stored in SQL tables/views from the technical point of view.

Based on these definition proposals, the question arises regarding how data can be used in SAP BW.

Using SAP HANA models directly in SAP BW To be able to use SAP HANA models as InfoProviders in SAP BW, they are integrated with TransientProviders or VirtualProviders. Moreover, SAP HANA data can also be loaded to SAP BW via data transfer processes (DTPs).

To integrate this data or the SAP HANA models with EDW, you can select different levels of modeling integration. These are illustrated in Figure 5.47.

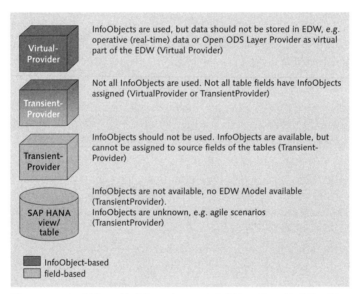

Figure 5.47 Field-Based InfoProviders vs. InfoObject-Based InfoProviders

Depending on the InfoProvider you select, the data is available in SAP BW as a reference only, or it was integrated completely with SAP BW. On the basis of the TransientProvider or VirtualProvider, modeling can also be made directly based on the table fields or InfoObjects. The following briefly describes the two InfoProviders that can be used.

For you to use the *VirtualProvider* in SAP HANA models, it was supplemented with the new type *based on HANA model*. Modeling is analogous to the VirtualProvider types that you already know. The "standard" properties of a VirtualProvider can also be used for a VirtualProvider of the based on SAP HANA model type:

VirtualProviders

▸ Usage in a MultiProvider or CompositeProvider

▸ Direct query execution

▸ Authorizations are also available for the VirtualProvider that is based on an SAP HANA model

Moreover, you can also link InfoObject-based master data (hierarchies, navigation attributes, authorizations, and so on) with the SAP HANA model in a VirtualProvider using a join.

Compared with the InfoObject-based VirtualProvider, the TransientProvider also enables modeling on a field basis. This is made possible using transient InfoObjects that exist only at runtime, for example, when executing a BEx query. Figure 5.48 shows the modeling of a TransientProvider based on an SAP HANA model.

TransientProviders

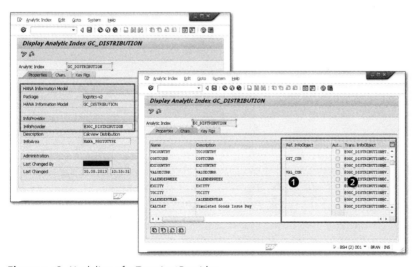

Figure 5.48 Modeling of a TransientProvider

281

On one hand, you have the option to assign InfoObjects to the individual table fields as references when modeling the TransientProvider ❶. On the other hand, this allows you to use SAP HANA models directly in SAP BW without having to assign InfoObjects ❷.

Based on the data source's metadata, a TransientProvider generates an SAP BW InfoProvider with the relevant metadata via the corresponding field when a BEx query is executed. This process does not create any InfoObjects in the classical sense with a persistent storage of data in SAP BW. The TransientProvider can be used like other InfoProviders for direct reporting via Multidimensional Expressions (MDX) and BI Consumer Services (BICS). Moreover, you can use all analytical options in BEx queries. These include the following:

▸ Restricted key figures

▸ Calculated key figures

▸ Exceptions

Because you have the option to reference *physical* InfoObjects, you can use the master data of these InfoObjects also in reporting based on an SAP HANA model with a BEx query. These include the following:

▸ Texts

▸ Display properties

▸ Display attributes

▸ Hierarchies

You can also use the authorizations you assigned to these physical Info-Objects for the authorization of data in the selected SAP HANA model.

SAP BW Operational Data Services

Extraction vs. replication Besides the integration of data in SAP BW, the Open ODS layer covers the data provisioning in SAP BW. Here, it is important whether the data is loaded to SAP BW via SAP-internal or customer-specific extractors. You also have the option to replicate data to SAP BW via the System Landscape Transformation (SLT). In most cases, the replication is better than the extraction of data because replication can be carried out virtually, in real time. However, you should consider the following criteria if you compare replication and extraction of data:

▸ **Application scenario and necessary up-to-date of data**
Operational BI scenarios require real-time and/or stable snapshots (planned vs. on demand). Direct replication from the source system can provide the required up-to-dateness of data.

▸ **Application scenario and consistency of data**
Data must be available in a stable state so that it can be used as a source for persistent EDW layers. Changes to data lead to corruption of the EDW. If you utilize replication, the changed data is also changed in SAP BW, and the history of data may no longer be replicable.

▸ **Application scenario and reproducibility**
Data must be available in a stable state so that it can be used as a source for persistent EDW layers. Deletion of data leads to corruption of the EDW. If you utilize replication, the deleted data is also deleted from SAP BW, or you would have to implement appropriate delta mechanisms for replication.

The following two sections provide an overview of the application areas for replication and extraction.

Real-Time Data Replication in SAP BW

You can replicate data from an SAP system (also non-SAP systems) to SAP BW using the SAP LT Replication Server. This enables real-time provisioning of data in the Persistent Staging Area (PSA) of SAP BW via a WebService DataSource. From the PSA, the data is updated within SAP BW using Real-Time Data Acquisition (RDA). Data can be updated directly in a DSO or in master data tables. Figure 5.49 provides an overview of the process for replicating data in SAP BW.

SAP LT Replication Server (SLT)

Starting from the application table, a logging table is filled in the source system using a trigger. This table serves as the data source for the SAP LT Replication Server. In the SAP LT Replication Server, the data is read from the logging table using the read module and prepared in structure mappings and transformations so that it can be updated in SAP BW via the write module.

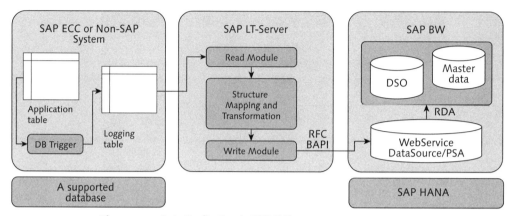

Figure 5.49 Data Replication in SAP BW

In SAP BW, the data is then transferred to the EDW layer via a WebService DataSource, as was described previously.

[⊕] **Additional Information on SLT Replication in SAP BW**

The following provide further information on SLT replication in SAP BW:

▶ Real-time Data Warehousing with SAP LT Replication Server (SLT) for SAP BW: *http://scn.sap.com/docs/DOC-40250*

▶ SAP LT Replication Server for SAP BW (PSA): SAP Note 1826585.

Using Extractors for Loading Data to SAP BW

SAP standard extractors

Compared to the replication of data, the extraction of data always involves a certain delay because the extraction takes places at scheduled intervals. This delay can be a disadvantage in specific scenarios, so you should consider the use of extractors, at least for new implementations.

Particularly in cases when standard extractors already exist in the BI content of SAP BW, you should carefully consider the possible added value of data replication. You must evaluate in detail the added value of replication compared to extraction for scenarios with complex logic in an extractor because the logic used must be reproduced in replication. This may involve a lot of time and work, which you can spare when using SAP standard extractors. You must also check the consistency for delta load processes, which exist for most standard extractors. In the case of replication, you must reproduce the necessary delta logic in SAP BW using transformations/BEx queries or via the SAP HANA Modeler in SQLScript/calculation views.

Advantages and Disadvantages of Extraction and Replication

Compared to replication, extraction has many advantages because it supports the classic principles of a data warehouse, as follows:

Comparison of extraction and replication

▶ Historization of loaded data: In principle, the original data is available prior to any change in the source system. Master data can be used time-dependently.

▶ Each data record has a unique stamp (e.g., request, package, or data record ID) that enables a generic delta for further processing of the data record in SAP BW—the logic for delta load processes must be reproduced in a complex process, as was described previously.

Data that is replicated directly from other data sources doesn't always follow these principles. Let's illustrate this using data from SAP HANA as an example: SAP HANA is a database above all. Every new data record that is to be stored in a table of SAP HANA initially triggers a database operation. All necessary or desired data records must be handled by replication (SAP LT Replication Server) or the extraction tool (for example, SAP DataServices). Examples are enriching or changing the data record's content and providing a criterion for the delta processing.

As an SAP BW user, you should consider the following criteria when you need to decide between data replication and data extraction:

Decision criteria

▶ In cases when replication makes sense, you should use replication in SAP BW

▶ SAP BW replication and SAP BW extractors enable the same functions:

  ▶ Direct reporting on data

  ▶ Generic delta for subsequent data record generation within SAP BW

  ▶ Transformation of data in SAP BW

Therefore, the decision between replication and extraction is made based on the data's content and the required up-to-dateness of data.

So, which SAP extractors should be replaced? Generic tables/view extractors are candidates here because they don't offer any added value compared to replication, and they often have technical shortcomings. These technical shortcomings include the following:

► Generic extractors that can load only the full extent of data:

   ► These extractors don't identify the deletion of data so that the usage is more difficult in the EDW and LSA++ architecture.

   ► These extractors cannot distinguish whether the data was changed, so they always load all data (for example, master data).

► Generic delta extractors require a security interval between two load processes, which prevents load processes in real time.

If one of the previously described extractors were used in your concrete application case or if the usage of such an extractor is planned, you should consider the replication of data. In these cases, all data is loaded anyway, or the replication enables the loading of data without the security interval, which allows you to implement new application areas in SAP BW.

Data Modeling Using Field-Based InfoProviders

The previous sections compared extraction and replication. The following now takes a look at the field-based InfoProviders, which have been mentioned briefly in the description of TransientProviders.

The Open ODS view is another new InfoProvider that was introduced with SAP BW 7.40 SP05, in addition to the TransientProvider. It enables the direct integration of tables or views in SAP BW without saving the data in SAP BW.

The modeling of the Open ODS view involves several steps (see Figure 5.50). The first step includes preparatory activities based on a table or view to create a model that is based on star schema components. That is, you analyze which master and transaction data is split or whether the transaction data can be stored in dimensions (see the left-hand side of the figure).

This is carried out in SAP HANA Studio. Then, you create an *SAP BW on SAP HANA field-based multi-dimensional model based on a star schema* in SAP BW. The new, Eclipse-based SAP BW Studio is used for this purpose. In the second step, you analyze the used tables in detail and model the necessary SQL views (see the right-hand side of the figure). In SAP BW, the modeling of the Open ODS view is based on the predefined SAP HANA semantic. This enables the modeling of BEx queries that permit all standard functions of BEx queries, for example, calculated/restricted key figures. Here, again, the modeling takes place in SAP HANA Studio or SAP BW Studio.

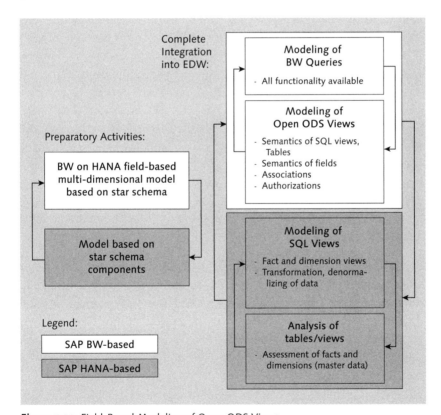

Figure 5.50 Field-Based Modeling of Open ODS Views

On this basis, you can also run a multi-dimensional analysis using relational data.

Additional Information on the Open ODS View InfoProvider
SAP First Guidance—SAP NetWeaver SAP BW 7.40 SP5 powered by HANA— Open ODS View: *http://www.sdn.sap.com/irj/scn/go/portal/prtroot/docs/library/uuid/ 40f377fd-194d-3110-469b-82a4131689cf?QuickLink=index&overridelay- out=true&59180354393386*

Replication of Master Data

Replication of master data using SLT

Besides the processing of transaction data, which was described previously, you can process master data using the SAP BW EDW services. This means that the loading of master data InfoObjects is made possible. The loading of master data is often very difficult due to the high number of data records. Examples include master data for materials, vendors, and customers. Because this data has to be loaded almost entirely in full loads, with only little changes occuring in the data records, many data records are transferred unnecessarily. This results in long load runs, which impede the loading of transaction data. Particularly if you use SAP BW on a global basis, the loading of master data becomes problematic because there's never a point in time when the master data is "stable". Users in different time zones can always make changes to the master data. The post-processing activities, such as the change run, have also resulted in long runtimes for loading data.

Real-time update of master data

By using SAP BW on SAP HANA, you can now update master data analogous to the transaction data directly via SLT. This enables an update of master data almost in real time. You no longer need to define a load time, and updated master data is always available for reporting. Users in different time zones can change the master data at any time and find these changes directly in reporting. However, analogous to the replication of transaction data, you must consider that joins across several tables are required for some master data (for example, material). Here, you must carefully check the usage of master data replication. Figure 5.51 gives an overview of the two options for loading master data with data.

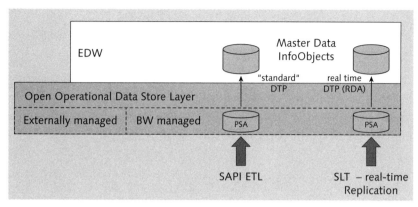

Figure 5.51 SLT—Real-Time Replication for Master Data

If a replication is useable or desired, the advantage of the master data replication is that synchronization problems no longer occur between the master and transaction data. It is no longer possible that transaction data is loaded to SAP BW and the load process is incomplete because the master data has not been updated.

Additionally, the administration and usage of master data is simplified. Projects can also be realized more easily; as a result, you achieve higher flexibility when using master data.

Benefits

The problem of master data consistency that exists in many enterprises is relieved as well. Many enterprises invest in their SAP ERP systems to achieve consistent master data and processes. SAP BW should therefore use the SAP ERP system as a reference system for all master data that is used in SAP BW. All other systems from which data is loaded to SAP BW should use this master data or adapt the master data that exists in these systems.

SAP BW EDW Services

The SAP BW EDW services ensure the connection from the Open ODS layer to the consistent EDW core. As was already described, the Open ODS layer serves as the source for the EDW InfoProviders. SAP BW EDW services include the following:

Services for creating and using EDW

289

▸ Provision of a consistent, generic delta for data transfer

▸ Option to carry out initial data transformations in the Open ODS layer based on the InfoProviders (within the scope of further processing of data in the consistent EDW core)

▸ Provision of source table field mappings to the EDW data model that already exists or is being developed through optional assignment of InfoObjects (particularly when using TransientProviders)

Summary Overview of the Open ODS Layer

The implementation of an LSA++ architecture in your SAP BW system can be made incrementally, thanks to the advanced options that virtual InfoProviders offer for LSA++. In particular, the use of the Open ODS layer ensures the independence of the data source. You can still use data from the Open ODS layer in SAP BW, whether in an EDW data model or through direct reporting, independent of the data source.

Benefits of the Open ODS layer

All in all, the new Open ODS layer provides the following benefits:

▸ LSA++ inbound layer as a central layer for subsequent use of data—the subsequent use of data is decoupled from the data source. The hybrid functionality of the Open ODS layer allows you to map both data acquisition functions for the EDW layer and perform a direct reporting on this data.

▸ A uniform framework is created for all types of sources.

▸ The integration of SAP BW-managed and externally managed (primarily SAP HANA) source data is provided.

▸ The field-based data can be used on a field basis in SAP BW; direct reporting for this data is also possible.

▸ Many SAP BW services can be applied to externally managed data, including, for example, the following:

  ▸ OLAP functions

  ▸ Master data services

  ▸ Authorizations

▶ The data can be loaded to SAP BW via SAP extraction (SAPI), SAP BusinessObjects data services for non-SAP data sources, and SLT for real-time replication.

5.5.3 SAP BW Virtual Data Mart Layer

The SAP BW virtual data mart layer is not a new layer from the LSA architecture's point of view. However, its application area has increased. This section discusses these changes (see Figure 5.52).

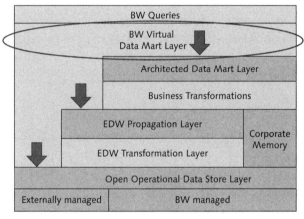

Figure 5.52 SAP BW Virtual Data Mart Layer

The virtual data mart layer uses BEx queries to provide data from different layers to reporting (see Figure 5.53).

Virtual data mart layer as the basis for reporting

Based on the architected data marts, MultiProviders are supplemented in the virtual data mart layer for the SAP BW-managed data. This is possible as long as EDW data is used. MultiProviders provide a certain degree of flexibility toward the changes in the underlying InfoProviders. Furthermore, you can add new InfoProviders without having to modify the BEx queries.

Field-based InfoProviders like VirtualProviders/TransientProviders/Open ODS views cannot be used in a MultiProvider (see Figure 5.53). Direct reporting, however, is also possible based on these InfoProviders. If data from these InfoProviders is combined with data from the EDW, you must use the HANA CompositeProvider, which allows you to combine Virtual-

MultiProvider vs. CompositeProvider

Providers/TransientProviders with, for example, MultiProviders, so that a superset of data emerges that is available for reporting. (Remember: a MultiProvider permits a union of only the underlying InfoProviders). The CompositeProvider is then available as a source data provider in the BEx queries (see Section 5.7). Moreover, SAP introduced the HANA CompositeProvider for the SAP BW on SAP HANA scenario, which merges data from different InfoProviders via unions and joins (see Section 5.1.2 and Section 5.2.1). The SAP BW virtual data mart layer thus provides a flexible option to combine data from different data sources. This basically also increases the flexibility in reporting because the SAP BW virtual data mart layer allows you to quickly respond to new reporting requirements, for example, by combining TransientProviders and MultiProviders in a CompositeProvider.

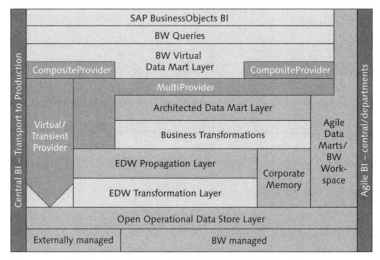

Figure 5.53 InfoProviders for the SAP BW Virtual Data Mart Layer

5.5.4 Benefits of the LSA++ Architecture

Combining SAP BW on SAP HANA with the LSA++ architecture provides the following benefits or options:

► It is possible to iteratively/incrementally use a multi-dimensional modeling approach based on an EDW approach that additionally utilizes Open ODS views. This is available for SAP BW-managed and non-SAP BW-managed data.

- LSA++ offers stability for the used framework, which is defined by the LSA++ layers and the EDW dimensions that are determined by the core InfoObjects.

- You can also use field-based InfoProviders to open your system for external data sources. You can thus attain a higher level of integration for modeling, particularly for non-SAP data because this data can be integrated with the consistent EDW core.

- The TCO is reduced because a cost-effective solution design can be approached (consuming instead of loading data), which focuses on business requirements. Then, further development can be carried out in an integrated EDW or an EDW-like solution.

The original LSA architecture focused on EDW scenarios. LSA++ can now be used for both BWs, which are primarily focused on EDW scenarios, and scenarios that are based on field-based data because this is now supported by the new Open ODS layer and the new InfoProviders (see Figure 5.54).

LSA++ for EDW-based or field-based scenarios

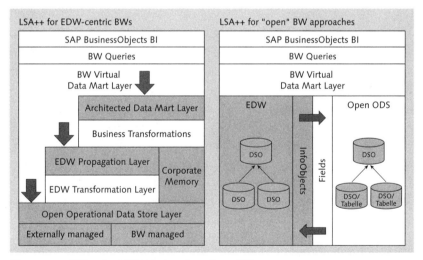

Figure 5.54 LSA++ for EDW-Centered vs. Open BWs

You can develop any mixed form between the two extremes of an EDW-centered SAP BW and an open SAP BW to optimally meet the requirements of your user departments and processes.

> **Additional Information on LSA++**
>
> The following provide additional information on LSA++:
>
> ▶ LSA++ for SAP BW on SAP HANA:
> *http://www.sdn.sap.com/irj/scn/go/portal/prtroot/docs/library/uuid/7076b1f6-e942-3010-d1b9-ecd1416458a5?QuickLink=index&override-layout=true&57909044127356*
>
> ▶ SAP HANA as Driver for EDW Evolution: LSA++ for SAP BW-on-HANA:
> *http://www.sdn.sap.com/irj/scn/go/portal/prtroot/docs/library/uuid/809b78e4-55cf-2f10-fdb4-86865b81cdeb?QuickLink=index&overridelay-out=true&56375740733224*
>
> ▶ A Holistic BI Architecture with SAP Business Warehouse and SAP HANA—RDP 301:
> *http://www.saphana.com/community/blogs/blog/2013/11/26/teched-recap-SAP BW-740*

5.6 The Concept of Non-Active Data (Hot/Warm/Cold)

Non-active data In an SAP BW on SAP HANA system, virtually all data is retained in the main memory to accelerate the processing of data. But, because the available main memory is restricted in size, the growing amount of data can force you in the medium or long term to take reorganization activities or expand the main memory's capacity. On the other hand, an SAP BW system usually contains a high amount of data that is hardly ever or no longer used in reporting or for analysis. Such data is referred to as non-active data in the following. It must still be retained in the system because this is required by internal or legal specifications, and occasional usage of data cannot be excluded. However, you are not required to permanently retain this data in the main memory.

The concept of non-active data For this reason, the *concept of non-active data* was introduced for SAP BW on SAP HANA as of version 7.3 SPS 08. Broadly speaking, it allows you to swap data of specially marked tables from the main memory. If the available main memory runs short at a specific point in runtime, the data of this table can be displaced from the main memory. A bottleneck usually occurs if a main memory requirement of a database process exceeds a specific threshold value. If you need to access the displaced data later on, it is automatically loaded from the secondary memory to the main memory in the background. This initially requires longer load times, which results in longer processing times. But because you should only mark tables with non-active data, this delay is usually acceptable. There are no further restrictions, or even function limitations, for tables with non-active data. You can mark not only tables, but also individual table partitions, to optimize memory management. As a result, a partitioned table can include table partitions with both active and non-active data.

The concept of non-active data is implemented in SAP BW on SAP HANA using the UNLOAD_PRIORITY attribute, which can be set to a specific value ranging between 0 and 9 in each table. The value 0 means that the table is not supposed to be displaced from the memory in general. The higher the value, the more likely it is that the data of the relevant table is swapped in the case of a main memory bottleneck. In an SAP BW on SAP HANA system, however, only the values 0, 5, and 7 are currently used. SAP BW-specific tables have the value 5 by default. PSA tables and the tables of write-optimized DSOs, by contrast, have the default value 7, which means that the content of these SAP BW objects can be displaced from the main memory more quickly. The value of the UNLOAD_PRIORITY attribute can be modified for a specific table using the SQL statement ALTER TABLE <Table> UNLOAD_PRIORITY <VALUE>;.

UNLOAD_PRIORITY

This section also presents a monitor tool in SAP BW with which you can change the value of the attribute for selected SAP BW objects or their database tables. However, you should only make such changes if you are fully aware of their effects. For example, fact tables of InfoCubes or DSO tables are usually not suited to increase the value of the UNLOAD_PRIORITY attribute because, if you displace data of such tables from the main memory, this results in major performance losses. This can be the case if you subsequently run SAP BW reports that call the data from these tables or if data load processes access the tables. For this reason, you should not set the UNLOAD_PRIORITY values of all SAP BW tables to 7 just because you want to save money for the main memory equipment.

Displaying the
UNLOAD_PRIORITY
value

You can display the UNLOAD_PRIORITY parameter for a specific table in the SAP BW on SAP HANA system. For this purpose, call Transaction SE14, and choose GOTO • STORAGE PARAMETERS (see Figure 5.55). Note that a change of this table property is not transferred via the transport system and is supported by only the SAP HANA database.

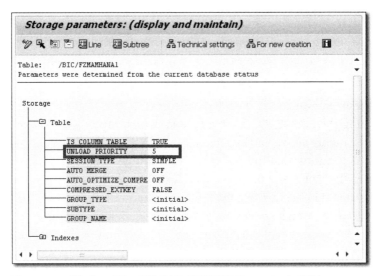

Figure 5.55 Display of the UNLOAD_PRIORITY Parameter in SE14

Automatic displace-
ment of data

During the post-processing work for an SAP BW on SAP HANA migration, you can set the UNLOAD_PRIORITY for specific SAP BW tables and partitions using the RS_SAP BW_POST_MIGRATION report (see step 4 in Chapter 3, Section 3.5.1). By default, all PSA and change log tables, as well as the tables of write-optimized DSOs, are marked accordingly. The data of these objects is displaced first from the main memory prior to the data of other SAP BW objects, such as InfoCubes or standard DSOs. If you must access a specific table column after the displacement of data from the main memory, only the data of the relevant columns is loaded to the main memory. This can be the case, for example, if you selected specific table columns only during a transformation for reloading specific fields. All other columns remain in the secondary memory in this case. In addition, SAP BW on SAP HANA is optimized to load only specific partitions of the PSA, change logs, or write-optimized DSOs to the main memory as needed. SAP recommends in this context that you avoid regular accesses to such tables using own programs or table processing (Transaction SE16). Otherwise, the entire table could be loaded to the main memory unintentionally. More details are available in SAP Note 1741844, Monitoring for the Concept of Non-Active Data.

The monitor tool for non-active data (Transaction RSHDBMON) allows you to monitor the handling of non-active data in SAP BW and modify the existing settings as required. For this purpose, you can set the *early unload* option for selected SAP BW objects. The `UNLOAD_PRIORITY` parameter is then set in the background to value 7 for one or more tables, as required. Figure 5.56 shows the initial screen of the monitor tool, which provides some information on the properties and the current state of the SAP HANA database. To monitor SAP BW objects, click the detail icon in the top-left corner.

Monitor tool for non-active data

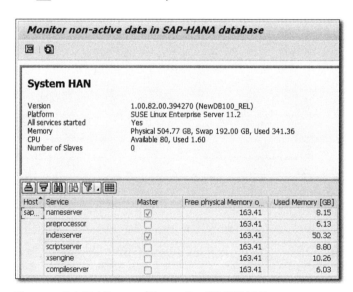

Figure 5.56 Initial Screen of Transaction RSHDBMON

The tool takes you to the detail selection (see Figure 5.57), where you can choose specific SAP BW objects (InfoAreas, InfoProviders, or DataSources). Note that the * operator currently cannot be used as usual in the search field.

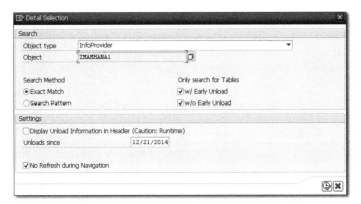

Figure 5.57 Detail Selection in Transaction RSHDBMON

Properties of the InfoCube

If you select an InfoCube, its properties are now displayed (see Figure 5.58). The TABLE column provides the name of the relevant fact table, and the PARTITIONS column shows the number of table partitions. The checkmark for the EARLY UNLOAD field is set if the option is active for the given table. This is not the case for the ZMAMHANA1 InfoCube because, as shown previously, the UNLOAD_PRIORITY value is 5 for the fact table (refer back to Figure 5.55).

InfoArea	InfoProvider	TLOGO	Sub...	Table	Partitions	Early Unload	Unloads	Loaded to Memory?
SAP_HANA_STOCK_SCENARIO	ZMAMHANA1	🔷	F	/BIC/FZMAMHANA1	4	☐	0	PARTIALLY

Figure 5.58 Properties of the Selected InfoCube

You can execute various functions for the SAP BW object in question using the LOAD/UNLOAD icon [icon]. For example, you can explicitly remove the data of the associated table from the main memory or load it to the main memory. You can also control the early unload option with this icon (see Figure 5.59). SAP generally advises against activating the early unload option for InfoCubes and DSOs (see SAP Note 1767880) because, if you do, all data of the relevant InfoProvider would always be displaced from the main memory. If such an InfoProvider is integrated with a periodic load process, however, this can be a major disadvantage. For example, if the data of an InfoProvider is loaded to the main memory on a daily basis due to a load process and the data is displaced again later on, this considerably extends the execution of the associated process chain. The option for early unload could be useful for InfoProviders with historic data that is used only rarely in reporting. In this case, however, it usually makes more sense to use an NLS system for archiving the data (see Chapter 8).

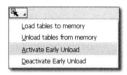

Figure 5.59 Early Unload for Selected InfoCube

If you select the ACTIVATE EARLY UNLOAD option, it is active for the rele- **Activate Early** vant SAP BW object or its used database table as of this point in time (see **Unload** Figure 5.60). In case of a main memory bottleneck, the data of this SAP BW object is displaced earlier from the main memory than others.

InfoArea	InfoProvider	TLOGO	SubType	Table	Partitions	Early Unload	Unloads	Loaded to Memory?
SAP_HANA_STOCK_SCENARIO	ZMAMHANA1		F	/BIC/FZMAMHANA1	4	☑	0	PARTIALLY

Figure 5.60 Early Unload Active for Selected InfoCube

If you call the corresponding database table in Transaction SE14 again and navigate to GOTO • STORAGE PARAMETERS after you've activated the early unload option, you will see that the value of the UNLOAD_PRIORITY parameter of the table in question has changed from 5 to 7 (see Figure 5.61).

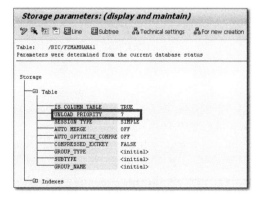

Figure 5.61 Value of the UNLOAD_PRIORITY Parameter Has Changed

Besides the distinction of active and non-active data, data is also often classified by its access frequency. Here, the data is classified in three categories: *hot*, *warm*, and *cold* (see Figure 5.62). All data of the hot category is accessed very often, for example, via reports in reporting (BEx queries on InfoCubes or DSOs) or data load processes, such as reading of data in transformations. This type of data has been referred to as active data so far. Data of the warm category is accessed only infrequently. This includes, for example, data in write-optimized DSOs of the acquisition layer or data of the PSA that has already been posted. Thus, this data broadly corresponds to non-active data. Data of the cold category, by contrast, is required only sporadically and is usually no longer modified. This data includes, for example, historic data of previous years that needs to be accessed by reporting in exceptional cases only.

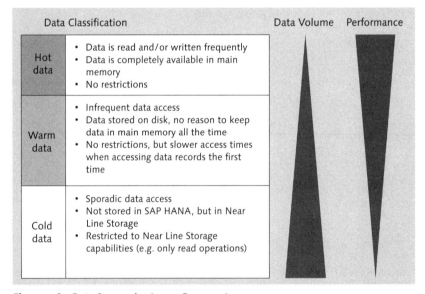

Figure 5.62 Data Storage by Access Frequencies

The purpose of the hot, warm, cold classification in SAP BW on SAP HANA is to utilize the main memory optimally in order to decrease the *total cost of ownership*. Data of the hot category must always be retained in the main memory due to its frequent use. Data of the warm category, however, doesn't need to be available in the main memory permanently. It can be loaded from the secondary memory (file system) to the main memory, if required. The early unload option, which was discussed previously, is used for this purpose, and the value of the UNLOAD_ PRIORITY parameter is set to 7 for the corresponding tables. It is advisable for data of the cold category to be swapped permanently from the SAP BW on SAP HANA system. Frequently, it is considerably more cost-effective to retain this data in a nearline storage than keeping it in the SAP HANA database. Using the SAP IQ database as an NLS solution enables you to directly access this swapped data from reporting without having to reload it to the SAP BW system first. Chapter 8 details this process and how you must configure the SAP BW on SAP HANA system for this purpose.

Today, you can optimize the memory management in SAP BW on SAP HANA using the distinction of active and non-active data, as well as the classification of data retention with the hot, warm, and cold categories. You can optimally utilize the main memory in SAP BW on SAP HANA with the introduction of the early unload option for database tables. You can also reduce the total cost of ownership if you additionally deploy an NLS system. Depending on the structure and usage of the SAP BW system, you can achieve major or minor main memory savings. An SAP BW on SAP HANA system that comprises a large corporate memory and utilizes many write-optimized DSOs accordingly, for example, will benefit considerably from the new data retention concept. On the other hand, the reduction of the main memory requirement in an SAP BW system that primarily provides InfoCubes in the reporting layer is considerably lower. It is generally important to be familiar with the concepts described here so that you can correctly judge the system behavior of SAP BW on SAP HANA. You now have the option to control the load and unload processes as required.

Summary

5.7   Consuming SAP HANA Models in SAP BW

Version 7.4 SPS 05 for SAP BW on SAP HANA introduced many new functions that further improved the interoperability between the SAP BW system and other systems. These include, among others, the integration of virtual tables via Smart Data Access, the data provision for multiple consumers using Operational Data Provisioning, and the direct usage of SAP

Interoperability

HANA views in SAP BW using the HANA CompositeProvider (see Section 5.1.2). Particularly this last item is discussed in detail in this section. But before you learn about the options for consuming SAP HANA data models in SAP BW on SAP HANA, we'll give you some technical basics.

SAP BW database schema

In an SAP BW on SAP HANA system, all SAP BW-specific data is available in the corresponding database tables in the SAP HANA database. These tables are all part of a common database schema that you can visualize as some kind of container for various database objects. It usually bears the name SAP<SID>, where *SID* stands for the system ID of your SAP BW system. If the SID of your SAP BW system is BW1, for example, all SAP BW data is usually available in a database schema bearing the technical name SAPBW1. However, the administrator can also select a different name during the installation of an SAP BW on SAP HANA system. You can determine the database schema that was specified for your SAP BW on SAP HANA system when you select SYSTEM • STATUS in the SAP menu and navigate to the OWNER field in the DATABASE DATA category. Don't get confused by the term *owner*. By default, SAP HANA creates an identically named database user for a new database schema. So for the previously described example, not only the SAPBW1 schema exists in the SAP HANA database, but also an SAPBW1 database user that has full access rights to the schema.

Additional SAP HANA database schemas

More schemas are available in an SAP HANA database besides the SAP BW database schema. This is useful, for example, to strictly separate SAP BW database objects from objects in other applications. Because every database schema usually belongs to a separate database user, you can implement simple and effective authorization concepts with this approach. Figure 5.63 illustrates the context between the SAP BW database schema and other schemas of the SAP HANA database. The connected source systems are used to load transaction data to the PSA in the SAP BW system. In this process, all imported data is stored in tables that belong to the SAP BW schema. If the data is updated in SAP BW and written from the PSA to a DSO, this data is again stored in tables of the SAP BW schema. The situation is different if you replicate data to the SAP HANA database for building an operational analytics approach (see Chapter 1, Section 1.1.2). For evaluating operational enterprise data, it is possible here to implement simple reporting and analysis tasks directly using SAP HANA without an SAP BW system. This operational enterprise data is then retained in tables of a separate database schema. Based on these tables, you can then create SAP HANA database models (SAP HANA *calculation* and *analytic views*), which you can access using different tools (for example, SAP Lumira or SAP Predictive Analysis, edition for office) to evaluate the data.

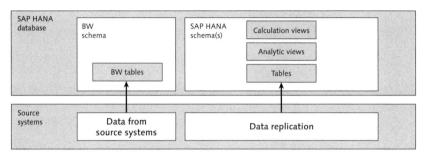

Figure 5.63 SAP BW and Other Database Schemas in SAP HANA

If you want to link the data of various database schemas, you basically have two options. On one hand, you can copy the data of one schema to another to permit common evaluation. However, this approach requires a redundant data retention, which occupies additional memory space in the database and possibly in the main memory. On the other hand, you can expand the access rights of a database user so that this user can access the data of the other schema. You could, for example, grant the database user of the SAP BW database schema the additional authorization to read operational enterprise data. This is the approach that forms the basis for consuming SAP HANA models in SAP BW.

Merging various database schemas

If the SAP BW database user has the necessary rights, the data from SAP HANA views can now be consumed under SAP BW on SAP HANA. Figure 5.64 illustrates the most critical options. Note that this diagram does not claim to be exhaustive and presents only those paths that we considered useful for consuming SAP HANA data models. The database access to any database schema is possible using the three InfoProviders: TransientProvider, VirtualProvider, and the HANA CompositeProvider. These InfoProviders, however, cannot access tables directly. But, they can access data outside of SAP BW using SAP HANA data models. The data is not stored additionally in SAP BW. Instead, it is called via SAP HANA

Consuming SAP HANA data models

views (calculation or analytic views) at runtime. You can then use the TransientProvider, VirtualProvider, or the HANA CompositeProvider to link or enrich the connected data with SAP BW data. With the HANA CompositeProvider, you can also connect data from a VirtualProvider or TransientProvider with data from SAP BW. The MultiProvider also permits such a merging of data indirectly via a VirtualProvider.

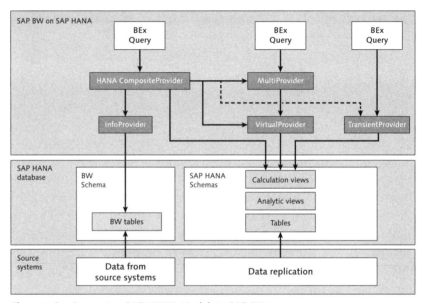

Figure 5.64 Consuming SAP HANA Models in SAP BW

Sample scenario

We'll consider a sample scenario to detail the benefits of consuming SAP HANA data models in SAP BW. We've created an SAP HANA view (analytic view) on an SAP BW external table (MMDOC, see Figure 5.65). It comprises various characteristics, a key figure, and the material number. This data can now be consumed, for example, using a HANA Composite-Provider in SAP BW. In this process, the original data of the SAP HANA view can be extended with the SAP BW material master data. Via the assignment of material numbers, you can thus supplement the report output with material text and other material properties, for example. Because this is done at runtime, you don't need to temporarily store the enriched data in SAP BW. You can create SAP BW reports on foreign data and without additional SAP BW data load processes, which can be enriched with SAP BW master and transaction data. The following now describes how to implement this scenario. The original data of our example originates from a flat database table (MMDOCS) that contains fictional data, for example, material documents and material number (see Figure 5.65).

	Name	SQL Data Type	Dimension	Column Store Data Type	Comment
1	MBLNR	VARCHAR	10	STRING	Number of Material Document
2	MATNR	VARCHAR	18	STRING	Material Number
3	WERKS	VARCHAR	4	STRING	Plant
4	BUDAT	DATE		DAYDATE	Posting Date in the Document
5	BWART	VARCHAR	3	STRING	Movement Type (Inventory Mana...
6	MENGE	INTEGER		INT	Quantity

Figure 5.65 Database Table with Demo Data

Based on this table, we created an analytic view in SAP HANA Studio that outputs this data without any changes. Section 5.2 already described how to create an analytic view. We illustrated the data output of the SAP HANA view in Figure 5.66 for better understanding.

Analytic view

BUDAT	MENGE	MBLNR	MATNR	WERKS	BWART
May 7, 2012	307	9183030	00000000010009000	DE01	501
Dec 21, 2011	211	9184211	00000000010009000	DE01	501
Dec 26, 2011	246	9185009	00000000010009000	DE01	501
May 7, 2012	110	9185044	00000000010009000	DE01	501
Dec 21, 2011	281	9185220	00000000010009000	DE01	501
May 7, 2012	235	9185437	00000000010009000	DE01	501
Dec 5, 2011	211	9185921	00000000010009000	DE01	501
Dec 21, 2011	699	9188203	00000000010009000	DE01	501
May 7, 2012	148	9188717	00000000010009000	DE01	501
Apr 6, 2012	309	9189025	00000000010009000	DE01	501
May 7, 2012	182	9189417	00000000010009000	DE01	501
Dec 21, 2011	315	9189602	00000000010009000	DE01	501
May 7, 2012	223	9190034	00000000010009000	DE01	501
May 7, 2012	947	9191180	00000000010009000	DE01	501
May 7, 2012	264	9192806	00000000010009000	DE01	501
Dec 21, 2011	418	9193713	00000000010009000	DE01	501
May 7, 2012	307	9195034	00000000010009000	DE01	501
May 7, 2012	196	9195118	00000000010009000	DE01	501
Dec 21, 2011	956	9195514	00000000010009000	DE01	501
May 7, 2012	173	9196524	00000000010009000	DE01	501
May 7, 2012	471	9197619	00000000010009000	DE01	501
Dec 5, 2011	960	9198109	00000000010009000	DE01	501
May 7, 2012	279	9199021	00000000010009000	DE01	501
Dec 21, 2011	189	9199508	00000000010009000	DE01	501

Figure 5.66 Sample Data of an SAP HANA Analytic View

Creating a HANA
CompositeProvider

In the next step, we'll create a HANA CompositeProvider. Section 5.1.2 already presented this InfoProvider type, which is available for SAP BW on SAP HANA systems only. You can use this InfoProvider to merge data from different InfoProviders and/or SAP HANA views via union or join. You can create a HANA CompositeProvider only via the Eclipse-based SAP BW modeling tools (see Section 5.2). To do so, create a new SAP BW project in SAP HANA Studio. In this process, specify the connection to your SAP BW on SAP HANA system, and log on to the correct client (usually 001) using your SAP BW user name and password. Now, go to the Project Explorer, and open the INFOPROVIDER folder. Navigate to an appropriate InfoArea and right-click it. Now, select NEW • COMPOSITE-PROVIDER. A dialog window opens in which you can enter information on the CompositeProvider to be created (see Figure 5.67).

Figure 5.67 Creating a HANA CompositeProvider via SAP HANA Studio

Adding data sources

Once the HANA CompositeProvider is created, you can add your data sources on the SCENARIO tab. To do so, right-click and choose ADD. In the window that opens, you must first select whether you want to connect an InfoProvider from the SAP BW system or an SAP HANA view of any database schema. For our sample scenario, we want to merge the data from the previously created analytic view with the material master data. For this reason, we first add the corresponding SAP HANA view (HANAVIEW; see the left side of Figure 5.68). The master data for the material is encapsulated in the 0MATERIAL InfoObject, which we'll add to the CompositeProvider in the next step (see the right-hand side of Figure 5.68). If your desired SAP HANA view is not displayed in the selection, you may not have the necessary authorizations. You must check whether the SAP BW database user of the SAP HANA database has access to the relevant database schema. Chapter 6, Section 6.2 discusses how to assign authorizations to SAP HANA users.

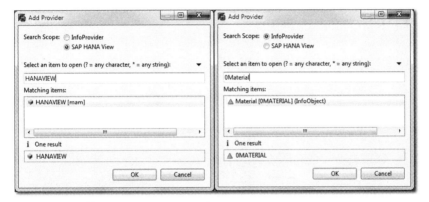

Figure 5.68 Adding Data Sources

You must now link the two data sources with one another. In our case, we opted for the union operation because this merges all values. In general, you also have the option to create a join link (either *inner join* or *left outer join*). As shown in Figure 5.69, we established a connection between the two data sources via the MATNR field of the SAP HANA view and the key of the InfoObject for 0MATERIAL. Additionally, we copied all fields of the SAP HANA views to the output but excluded the fields for 0Material. Finally, click the ACTIVATE icon. Any error messages are displayed in the PROBLEMS window.

Linking data

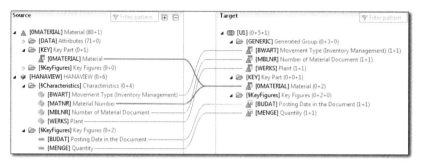

Figure 5.69 Link of 0MATERIAL and SAP HANA Analytic View in the HANA CompositeProvider

Creating a BEx query

Next, we'll create a BEx query for the HANA CompositeProvider using BEx Query Designer. As you can see in Figure 5.70, we classify the key figures of the SAP HANA view in the columns. In the rows, we add the material document number, as well as 0Material, including the length, width, and height attributes.

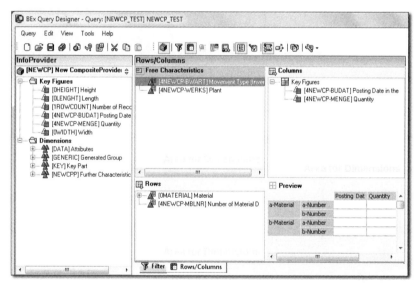

Figure 5.70 BEx Query for the Created HANA CompositeProvider

Executing the query

In the last step, we now execute the BEx query. The result is shown in Figure 5.71. As you can see in the graphic, the data of the SAP HANA view is now enriched with the material master data, as intended. For this reason, the report can now output the material number, material text, and associated attributes of the material (length, width, and height). The scenario presented in this section is rather simple to ensure better understanding. Nevertheless, it already illustrates the distinct strengths of the approach to consume SAP HANA views in SAP BW on SAP HANA. It enables you to enrich external data with virtually any master and transaction data from SAP BW without having to store the external data in SAP BW additionally. As a result, the most current data is always available for reporting.

You can further extend this approach by integrating tables from other databases in SAP HANA using Smart Data Access. Then, you can create an SAP HANA view on the virtual table and consume its data directly in SAP BW. In this scenario, however, high performance of the external database and a fast connection to SAP BW on SAP HANA are important prerequisites for an efficient reporting.

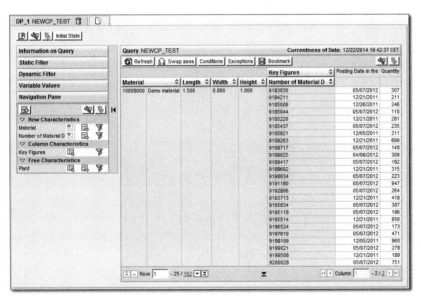

Figure 5.71 Output in the BEx Query

Besides consuming SAP HANA views via the HANA CompositeProvider, you can use a VirtualProvider or TransientProvider in SAP BW on SAP HANA (see Figure 5.64). However, SAP recommends that you use the

InfoProviders for consuming SAP HANA views in SAP BW

HANA CompositeProvider if possible because its functions are particularly accelerated via a code push-down (see Chapter 1, Section 1.4.5). If you still consider the use of the other two InfoProviders—for example, because you don't have access to the SAP BW modeling tools—you should know their advantages and disadvantages, which we'll discuss now.

TransientProvider

The TransientProvider was developed as an InfoProvider specifically for accessing SAP HANA views. It is intended for creating ad hoc scenarios and permits modeling without InfoObjects. For this reason, this InfoProvider type is particularly well-suited if you want to create demo scenarios in an SAP BW system on a short-term basis and require data access to SAP HANA views for this purpose. Optionally, you can also assign InfoObjects to the fields of an SAP HANA view. In both cases, you can build BEx queries on the TransientProvider. This TransientProvider, however, can be added to the new CompositeProvider, but not to a MultiProvider. The integration with SAP BW master data is limited because navigation attributes are not supported. The transport of a TransientProvider is not intended, either. The authorization check is run only for assigned InfoObjects.

Creating a TransientProvider

You cannot create a TransientProvider directly in Transaction RSA1. Instead, you must use Transaction RSDD_HM_PUBLISH to create an analytic index (see Figure 5.72). To do so, first select a PACKAGE and an SAP HANA data model (HANA INFORMATION MODEL), and click CREATE. In the next window, you can define an assignment of the analytic index for an InfoArea and assign it to InfoObjects that correspond to the characteristics and key figures. After you've completed your configuration, the TransientProvider is available in the BEx Query Designer. You can access it using the technical name `@3<name of analytic index>`. Note, however, that this InfoProvider is not displayed in the InfoProvider view of Transaction RSA1 and cannot be transported for this reason. The VirtualProvider is usually the better option if you want to establish a permanent and consistent solution without using the HANA CompositeProvider.

Publish SAP HANA Model

HANA Model

Package	mam
HANA Information Model	HANAVIEW

Edit Publication (Analytic Index)

🖑 Display	✎ Change	🗋 Create	🗑 Delete

Figure 5.72 Creating an Analytic Index for the TransientProvider

The VirtualProvider was introduced prior to SAP HANA. As a result, it not only supports access to SAP HANA views, but also retrieves data from function modules or BAPIs. During modeling, it is mandatory to assign InfoObjects. Consequently, the SAP BW authorization concepts take full effect. The VirtualProvider can be added to a new CompositeProvider or MultiProvider to combine data from SAP BW with other InfoProviders. But, before you follow such an approach, you should first check whether the use of the HANA CompositeProvider would also be possible.

VirtualProvider

To create a VirtualProvider, select the InfoProvider view in Transaction RSA1. You can create a VirtualProvider by opening the context menu with a right-click. In the input screen, select the InfoProvider type VIRTUALPROVIDER, BASED ON A SAP HANA MODEL. Then, click DETAILS, as shown in Figure 5.73.

Creating a VirtualProvider

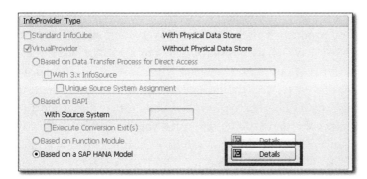

InfoProvider Type

☐ Standard InfoCube   With Physical Data Store
☑ VirtualProvider   Without Physical Data Store
  ○ Based on Data Transfer Process for Direct Access
    ☐ With 3.x InfoSource
      ☐ Unique Source System Assignment
  ○ Based on BAPI
    With Source System
      ☐ Execute Conversion Exit(s)
  ○ Based on Function Module   Details
  ◉ Based on a SAP HANA Model   Details

Figure 5.73 Creating a VirtualProvider Based on an SAP HANA Data Model

This takes you to another window in which you can select the appropriate package and the SAP HANA view. The system takes you to the regular modeling view, which is also used for InfoCubes. Add your characteristics and key figures. To make the assignments between the InfoObjects of the VirtualProvider and the SAP HANA view, right-click the corresponding InfoObject and choose PROVIDER-SPECIFIC PROPERTIES. In the ATTRIBUTE NAME (HANA) field in the subsequent dialog window, you can assign the field of the SAP HANA view to the selected InfoObject using the ⎡F4⎤ help. When you activate the VirtualProvider, you can use it in RSA1, as well as BEx Query Designer.

[⊕]   **Information Material**

If you want to obtain more detailed information on the topic of consuming SAP HANA data models in SAP BW, refer to the "Step-by-Step Guide of Modeling HANA Views into SAP BW in SAP BW 7.4 on HANA" (*http://scn.sap.com/docs/DOC-53352*). It is also worthwhile to view the two SAP presentations "SAP BW/SAP HANA Mixed Scenarios—News, Added Value, and Customer Examples" (*http://scn.sap.com/docs/DOC-46093*) and "Modeling SAP BW and SAP HANA Mixed Scenarios" (*http://scn.sap.com/docs/DOC-33716*). However, you still cannot avoid testing the various InfoProvider types yourself to judge their strengths and weakness comprehensively.

Summary   You can consume the data of SAP HANA models in SAP BW on SAP HANA using the three InfoProvider types: TransientProvider, VirtualProvider, and the HANA CompositeProvider. Provided that the SAP BW modeling tools are available to you, you should discuss the HANA CompositeProvider because its features are optimally supported in SAP HANA, and it is rumored to replace the other InfoProvider types in the long term. For productive use, your SAP BW system should have at least version SAP BW 7.4 with SPS 07. You can also start with lower versions of SAP BW. In this case, however, you must import numerous SAP Notes. Additionally, you should use the latest version of the SAP BW modeling tools because experience has shown that the support of SAP HANA views for the HANA CompositeProvider works flawlessly and comprehensively as of version 1.3.2 only. Also note that the InfoProviders in SAP BW and the connected SAP HANA views cannot be transported together. We also want to point out that data consumption is also possible in the opposite direction. SAP HANA views can be generated automatically for SAP BW InfoProviders at the touch of a button. These views can then be accessed from external tools (see the section "Generating HANA Views from InfoProviders" in Section 5.1.2). In general, you should keep the complexity low. Specify for a scenario whether you implement a complex calculation logic in either the SAP HANA view or the BEx query. You should avoid, for example, using a calculated key figure in the SAP HANA view together with an exception aggregation in the BEx query. You can achieve a higher performance and clearer solution if you only merge data in SAP HANA views and implement the other logics in SAP BW on SAP HANA using a BEx query.

5.8   Planning Application Kit

The *Planning Application Kit* (PAK) is an optional component that permits the accelerated execution of planning applications in SAP BW Integrated Planning (BW-IP). An SAP BW on SAP HANA migration already speeds up the planning applications compared with an SAP BW system without SAP HANA. This results primarily from main memory-based and column-based data retention under SAP HANA. Performance can be increased even further if you execute the used function types or the planning functions that are used in BW-IP directly on the SAP HANA database, rather than on the SAP BW application server. In compliance with the push-down principle, many planning function types were reimplemented on the SAP HANA database and can be deployed as of SAP BW on SAP HANA version 7.3 SPS 05 (see Chapter 1, Section 1.4.5). For this purpose, the PAK must be activated via a Customizing entry. Only then can you use the new SAP HANA-specific planning functions. As illustrated in Figure 5.74, the Planning Application Kit permits the direct execution of planning functions in the *planning engine* of the SAP HANA appliance. However, the usage of PAK requires the license *SAP Business Planning and Consolidation* (SAP BPC), *version for SAP NetWeaver*. Without this license, you may not use the Planning Application Kit in production, and the planning functions can be executed only in the SAP BW

SAP BW Integrated Planning

application server. Because no technical dependencies exist between SAP BPC and BW-IP, you don't need to install SAP BPC for using PAK.

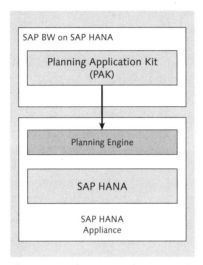

Figure 5.74 Planning Application Kit (PAK)

Benefits of the PAK   The PAK can provide considerable speed boosts, particularly for medium-sized and large planning scenarios in which more than 10,000 data records are selected for executing a planning function. Thanks to the considerable acceleration, you can build planning on a larger data basis and perform planning runs more frequently. For example, if you can perform planning runs several times a day and also include data with a higher granularity in the planning process, this usually results in higher planning accuracy. Let's use the example of disaggregation in the context of budget planning to illustrate where the speed benefits of PAK come from.

Budget planning example   The BW-IP based planning application is supposed to be used to adapt an already existing budget planning (2016) for a sales organization. Subsequently, the figures should be broken down to the material group and month level. We assume that the originally planned budget of sales organization 2400 is to be increased from 4,250,000 USD to 4,500,000 USD (see Figure 5.75). We further assume that we must consider 20 sales offices, five sales channels, and 50 material groups along the hierarchy.

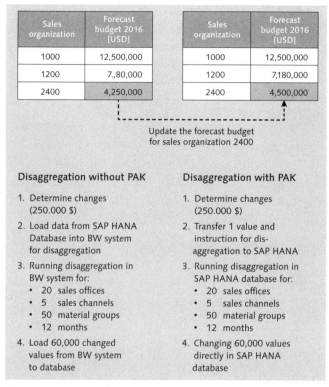

Sales organization	Forecast budget 2016 [USD]
1000	12,500,000
1200	7.,80,000
2400	4,250,000

Sales organization	Forecast budget 2016 [USD]
1000	12,500,000
1200	7,180,000
2400	4,500,000

Update the forecast budget
for sales organization 2400

Disaggregation without PAK

1. Determine changes
   (250.000 $)
2. Load data from SAP HANA
   Database into BW system
   for disaggregation
3. Running disaggregation in
   BW system for:
   • 20 sales offices
   • 5 sales channels
   • 50 material groups
   • 12 months
4. Load 60,000 changed
   values from BW system
   to database

Disaggregation with PAK

1. Determine changes
   (250.000 $)
2. Transfer 1 value and
   instruction for dis-
   aggregation to SAP HANA
3. Running disaggregation in
   SAP HANA database for:
   • 20 sales offices
   • 5 sales channels
   • 50 material groups
   • 12 months
4. Changing 60,000 values
   directly in SAP HANA
   database

Figure 5.75 Example for Disaggregation—Budget Planning

If you change the planning budget as described without using the PAK, the value change is determined in step 1 (250,000 USD). In the second step, all necessary data is transferred from the database to the SAP BW server. The disaggregation then takes place on the SAP BW server (step 3), and a total of 60,000 values is changed (20 sales offices × 5 sales channels × 50 material groups × 12 months). Finally, all 60,000 changes are transferred from the SAP BW server to the database in step 4. In particular, the transfer of data from the database to the SAP BW server and back causes a high time overhead.

Disaggregation without using PAK

When you use PAK, the change of the planning budget for sales organization triggers the following process: In the first step, the value change is determined (250,000 USD). In the second step, this value is transferred to the SAP HANA database. Here, the database receives instructions from the SAP BW server to which objects this value is to be broken

Disaggregation using PAK

down. SAP HANA then performs the disaggregation as defined in the instruction (step 3) and finally saves the changes (step 4). Here, the major benefit is that the data doesn't need to be transferred to the SAP BW server for calculation and then returned individually to the database. The same principle applies to the execution of other SAP BW-IP planning functions, for example, copying of data.

Currently, about 90% of the available planning function types are supported by the PAK for direct execution on the SAP HANA database. The detailed overview of Table 5.1 shows which planning function types you can use with which SAP BW on SAP HANA version when you deploy PAK. Further information on the support of additional functions in SAP HANA—for example, data slices—is available in SAP Note 1637199.

Planning Function Types	Description	Available as of
0RSPL_COPY	Copy	7.3 SPS 05
0RSPL_CREATE_CR	Create combinations	7.3 SPS 05
0RSPL_CURR_CONV	Currency translation	7.4 SPS 08 (workaround possible via FOX formulas and CURC)
0RSPL_DELETE	Delete	7.3 SPS 05
0RSPL_DELETE_CR	Delete invalid combinations	7.30 SPS 09/ 7.31 SPS 07 or SAP Note 1778939
0RSPL_DISTR_KEY	Distribution by keys	7.30 SPS 10/ 7.31 SPS 09 or SAP Note 1821899
0RSPL_DISTR_REFDATA	Distribution by reference data	7.3 SPS 05
0RSPL_FORMULA	Formula	7.3 SPS 05
0RSPL_REPOST	Reposting	7.3 SPS 05
0RSPL_REPOST_CR	Repost due to characteristic relationships	7.30 SPS 10/ 7.31 SPS 09 or SAP Note 1855154
0RSPL_REVALUATION	Revaluation	7.3 SPS 05

Table 5.1 Supported Planning Functions with PAK

Planning Function Types	Description	Available as of
ORSPL_SET_VALUES	Set key figure values	7.3 SPS 05
ORSPL_UNIT_CONV	Unit conversion	7.4 SPS 08

Table 5.1 Supported Planning Functions with PAK (Cont.)

Provided that you have the necessary SAP BPC license, you may activate PAK on your SAP BW on SAP HANA system using a Customizing setting. Proceed as specified in SAP Note 1637199, and open the maintenance dialog for Table RSPLS_HDB_ACT in Transaction SM30 (see Figure 5.76). Select DEEP HANA INTEGRATION ACTIVE, and save your changes. As of SAP BW on SAP HANA version 7.4 SPS 06, the SAP HANA execution of the planning functions is activated for all InfoProviders by default (see SAP Note 1930335). In earlier SAP BW versions, you still had to release the InfoProviders individually via Table RSPLS_HDB_ACT_IP in Transaction SM30 to utilize the PAK optimization. You can use ABAP report RSPLS_PLANNING_ON_HDB_ANALYSIS in Transaction SE38 to check whether the PAK activation was successful in your system and the planning functions are now executed on the SAP HANA database. Note that you must first import SAP Note 1637148 for SAP BW on SAP HANA systems whose version is lower than SAP BW 7.4 SPS 05 before you can activate PAK using the appropriate Customizing setting.

Activating PAK

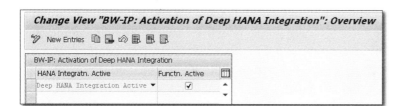

Figure 5.76 PAK Activation using Transaction SM30

Additional Information

Please refer to the following sources to obtain more in-depth information on the *Planning Application Kit* topic and the optimization of planning applications using SAP HANA:

▶ SAP Presentation "Planning Applications Kit—In memory planning in action": *http://scn.sap.com/docs/DOC-36441*

- ▶ SAP Presentation "How to Use SQLScript for Planning Functions in PAK": *https://scn.sap.com/docs/DOC-53800*
- ▶ Espresso webinar: "In Memory Planning with SAP HANA and the Planning Application Kit": *http://www.sdn.sap.com/irj/sdn/go/portal/prtroot/docs/library/uuid/ 700bccf5-645f-3010-678b-80069f8eda1d?QuickLink=index&overridelay- out=true&58029303198551*

[!] | **Problems with Open Planning Requests**

Under SAP BW on SAP HANA and BW-IP, problems may occur when you close open planning requests in the context of using real-time InfoProviders. If you close such a request with the RSAPO_CLOSE_TRANS_REQUEST function module and then trigger a DTP for data loading, this can result in a termination. This is because SAP HANA is accelerated quickly and some SAP BW-internal processes are not yet complete (Qualok status), although you want to close the request. In this case, the DTP is triggered a bit too early. According to SAP, this problem was solved in the meantime with SAP Notes 1842311 and 1968396. If you still encounter comparable problems in your system, you can simply integrate a short delay after the execution of the previously mentioned function module as an ad hoc measure.

Summary and outlook
Using the Planning Application Kit accelerates the execution of the planning functions in BW-IP significantly if you select large amounts of data and execute the relevant planning function types directly in the SAP HANA database. This allows you to use a larger data basis and execute planning runs more frequently, which usually results in higher planning accuracy. However, the use of the PAK requires an SAP BPC software license, which is a rather significant investment for most customers. In the future, planning with SAP BPC and BW-IP is supposed to be merged in one uniform product (*SAP Business Planning and Consolidation 10.1, version for SAP NetWeaver*, also provisionally referred to as *Unified Model*). In SAP BPC, for example, it will then be possible to execute SAP BW-IP planning functions and thus utilize the SAP BW on SAP HANA-optimization for PAK. More information is available in SAP Note 1919631 and at *http://help.sap.com/bopac*.

SAP HANA Studio is a central tool for administration, monitoring, development, and modeling tasks in SAP HANA. This chapter introduces you to this powerful tool.

6   Administration with SAP HANA Studio

SAP HANA is not just a database: it also provides functions for developing programs and modeling data. You can also integrate and manage content from other data sources here. SAP HANA Studio plays an important role as a common interface for all of these functions. This chapter is intended to impart the functional scope of SAP HANA Studio and describe its usage based on some examples.

SAP HANA Studio is based on an open-source Eclipse project and thus assumes the structure of the user interface, referred to as a *workbench*. To help you find your way around in SAP HANA Studio, we'll first explain the terms, workbench, perspective, and view.

The term *workbench* refers to the interface of Eclipse. In Figure 6.1, you can view the different parts of this interface. Besides the usual menu bars and toolbars, it consists of a perspective that in turn combines various views ❶.

Workbench

Perspectives ❷ are containers for views and menus. They are preset for a specific purpose and can be adapted individually. Various perspectives are available for selection under the menu bar ❸ and toolbar ❹. They use views in a defined structure and may possibly contain new menu items. By default, Eclipse comprises several perspectives for Java development, as well as a debugging perspective.

Perspective

Figure 6.1 Structure of the SAP HANA Studio Interface Administration Console

Some perspectives were added in SAP HANA Studio:

▶ **SAP HANA Development perspective**
The SAP HANA Development perspective is used to develop applications on HANA (XS applications). The XS applications run on SAP HANA-specific application server and can be accessed via a web server. The default Eclipse perspective can be used for debugging.

▶ **SAP HANA Modeler perspective**
The SAP HANA Modeler perspective is used to create analytical data models, the *information views*. Chapter 7 discusses these in more detail.

▶ **SAP HANA PlanViz**
The SAP HANA Plan Visualizer is a tool for analyzing the performance of queries in a graphical form. It is described more comprehensively in Section 6.3.

▶ **Lifecycle Management**
Lifecycle Management performs complex administration tasks. These

include the implementation and administration of a cluster, as well as the renaming and updating of the system.

▸ **Administration Console**
The administration perspective is a central interface for numerous administration and monitoring tasks. It is discussed in Section 6.1.

Further perspectives become available if you install the SAP BW modeling tools. These are detailed in Chapter 5, Section 5.2.

Showing Hidden Perspectives	[+]
Some of the mentioned perspectives are not displayed as shown in Figure 6.1 when you start SAP HANA Studio for the first time. You can call them via the menu path WINDOW • OPEN PERSPECTIVE • OTHER. They are then displayed under the toolbar.	

Views (❶, see Figure 6.1) are structured as windows and can be moved and realigned via drag-and-drop. Similar to the handling of a Windows desktop, you can close, minimize, or maximize them using the icons in the top-right corner. New views are inserted via the menu path WINDOW • SHOW VIEW.

Views

SAP HANA Studio can be downloaded from the SAP Software Download Center. However, it is also possible to download Eclipse directly from the project website (*https://www.eclipse.org/downloads*). For using Eclipse in SAP HANA Studio, you require the Eclipse IDE for Java EE Developers variant. Note that the latest version of Eclipse is often not supported by the SAP HANA Studio plug-ins. The corresponding information is available at *tools.hana.ondemand.com*. There, you can also learn how to manually install SAP HANA Studio and other tools using the standard Eclipse tools.

Install

The next sections describe how SAP BW database administrators can implement their tasks in SAP HANA Studio. Also refer to the comprehensive SAP documentation. The current version is available under *https://help.sap.com/hana_appliance*. The SAP HANA Administration Guide is of particular importance for the tasks mentioned here. The user and authorization administration is discussed in the SAP HANA Security Guide.

6.1   Administration Perspective

Figure 6.1 provided initial insight into the administration perspective. On the left side, you can view the SYSTEMS view, including the managed systems. The right side provides a large view with nine tabs. These tabs contain numerous tools and information for configuring and monitoring the database. Before we discuss these tasks, let's first have an overview of the perspective's interface.

6.1.1   Systems View

The view on the left side of the ADMINISTRATION CONSOLE is empty when you start SAP HANA Studio for the first time. Here, you can add SAP HANA database servers that you want to manage in the future.

Adding a system   For this purpose, right-click the view, and choose ADD SYSTEM. Enter the host name and the number of the SAP HANA instance. Entering a description is optional. Define the database user and the password in the next dialog step. This should be a user that was created specifically for your task. We advise against using the SYSTEM user, which is created during installation, permanently. For more information, see Section 6.2.

Depending on the database configuration, you must activate the logon via SSL or HTTPS. You can also store the logon details via STORE USER-NAME AND PASSWORD IN SECURE STORAGE. Then, you don't need to enter the logon data again when you restart SAP HANA Studio.

[+]   **Logon with sidadm**

If the server is available and the logon via the database user fails, you can use the operating system user of the database for logon. In this case, you are automatically prompted to enter the data. The user consists of a three-digit system ID and "adm." You can now view the status of the SAP HANA processes and access the diagnosis files to examine the cause of the problem.

You can log on to systems in your SYSTEMS view in this diagnosis mode by clicking the [⣿ ▼] icon.

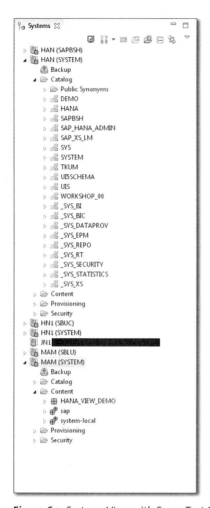

Figure 6.2 Systems View with Some Test Systems

If the system is added and online, you can expand the entry as a tree (see Figure 6.2). It contains the following entries:

▶ BACKUP
Here, you can schedule and manually execute backups, as well as monitor previous backups.

▶ CATALOG
The CATALOG lists the schemas of the database and its full content (tables, procedures, views, and so on) in a tree structure.

▶ CONTENT

The CONTENT comprises the packages of applications that are available in the development perspective.

▶ PROVISIONING

Data provisioning entails the configuration of data accesses to external systems.

▶ SECURITY

You maintain roles and users, as well as encryption and password settings, in the SECURITY area.

With a right-click, you can quickly reach the various SAP HANA Studio functions already mentioned. Double-click the previously created system to open the system's Administration Editor on the right-side of the screen.

6.1.2   Administration Editor

The Administration Editor of the selected system is displayed (Figure 6.3). It contains nine tabs with detailed information on the respective system.

Figure 6.3 Administration Editor of SAP HANA Studio

The following sections discuss all tabs in detail, so we'll summarize the functions only briefly now:

▸ **Overview**
The OVERVIEW tab displays version information and the utilization of CPU, main memory, and hard disk resources. It also summarizes alert messages.

▸ **Landscape**
The LANDSCAPE tab provides information on the running SAP HANA processes. In case of a cluster scenario, further information on individual servers and their interaction is available here.

▸ **Alerts**
The ALERTS tab provides administrators with system messages that are classified by their importance. Under this tab, the system prompts you to perform a new backup or warns against main memory shortage.

▸ **Performance**
The PERFORMANCE tab indicates the utilization of the system resources and provides performance information for processes and queries.

▸ **Volumes**
The database's data is backed up on hard disks on a regular basis. Data operations are entered in logs between the save points and also stored on hard disks. You can monitor the speed and size of these transfers with the VOLUMES tab.

▸ **Configuration**
The SAP HANA database has several configuration files. Under the CONFIGURATION tab and the appropriate user interface, they can be edited more conveniently than at the operating system level.

▸ **System Information**
The SYSTEM INFORMATION tab comprises additional information from SAP HANA system views on different topics.

▸ **Diagnosis Files**
With the DIAGNOSIS FILES tab, you can view files for error analysis. Each process creates a file for information and another file for serious errors or warnings. Traces and operation times are also stored in the appropriate files.

▸ **Trace Configuration**
To examine errors or performance data, you can run traces with the
Trace Configuration tab.

Since SAP HANA SPS 08, it is also possible to call this information via an
SAPUI5 menu. This dashboard (see Figure 6.4) displays the overview in
tiles and takes the users to the detail views when they click the relevant
elements. You can open the dashboard by right-clicking an added system under View Systems • Configuration and Monitoring • Dashboard.

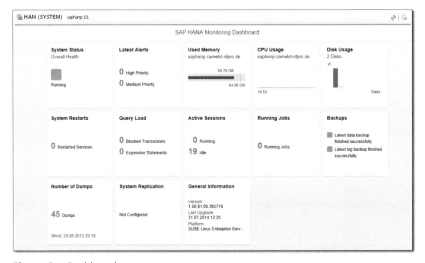

Figure 6.4 Dashboard

6.2 User and Authorization Administration

Independent of the authorizations in the SAP Business Warehouse application server, users and roles are also available in the database. They can
be managed with various SQL commands. SAP HANA Studio offers a
graphical user interface for this purpose.

This section first illustrates how to manage database users and roles in
SAP HANA Studio. Then, we'll summarize the most critical roles and
explain their meaning.

After the setup of SAP BW on SAP HANA, SAP HANA includes some standard users that are required by the system:

▸ SYS, _SYS_STATISTICS, _SYS_REPO, _SYS_DATAPROV, and _SYS_AFL are technical users that are deployed within the database. You cannot use them for logon. But in some cases, it is necessary to grant them additional access rights.

▸ The user of the SAP BW system, usually SAP<SID>, is created when you install the application server. It includes a database schema in which you store its contents.

▸ SYSTEM is a database user with comprehensive rights. It is used to create user accounts for administrators and any kind of users and to assign corresponding rights. In test and development systems, it is often used for different tasks of several persons. In such a case, every person who has access to this user can perform all tasks on the database and can cause incorrect configurations. For this reason, you should not utilize this user in production systems.

Alternatively, the user and role management can be performed completely with SQL commands. The syntax of the relevant commands, such as CREATE USER, GRANT, or REVOKE, are described in detail in the "SAP HANA SQL and System Views Reference," the current version of which is available at *help.sap.com/hana_platform*.

6.2.1 Creating and Managing Users

The tasks of all persons participating in the database are customized and may possibly require authorizations from different application areas (development, modeling, administration, and so on). For this reason, you should create a separate database user for every person, even if this initially means that several users have the same authorizations. For this case, you can create roles that combine several authorizations. They facilitate the search for tables and other database objects because only those elements are available that are relevant for them.

Upon creation, every user receives its own database schema with the same name. First, only the corresponding user itself holds the authorizations for this database schema. Even if you create the user with the

SYSTEM user, SYSTEM still has no authorizations for the schema of this user. If you want to grant access for additional users, you must do so with the created database user.

User Administration in SAP HANA Studio

Open the SECURITY folder in the SYSTEMS view. You can find all users under USERS. By double-clicking a user entry, you navigate to the respective administration view. In the lower section, you can see the authorizations of the user. This section is subdivided into seven tabs. Here, you can see only the authorizations that are issued to the user that you use in SAP HANA Studio:

▶ **Granted roles**
Here, you find all roles that are assigned to the user. Roles are discussed in Section 6.2.2.

▶ **System privileges**
System privileges enable the user to access system functions. These include the import or export of data, development of native applications, user and role management, monitoring, and many more.

▶ **Object privileges**
Object privileges control the access rights to database schemas and their contents.

▶ **Analytic privileges**
Analytic privileges define which data a user may access in an SAP HANA view. SAP HANA views without analytic privileges are fully available to all users who have access to the SAP HANA views themselves.

▶ **Package privileges**
Package privileges control access to the packages that you can find in the CONTENT folder of the SYSTEMS view in SAP HANA Studio. Applications and SAP HANA views are stored in packages.

▶ **Application privileges**
Application privileges are roles that are defined in XS applications. A newly installed SAP HANA system already contains some of these roles, which are required for XS development or monitoring, among

other things. Additionally, you can define new roles in your own applications.

▸ **Privileges on users**
Privileges on users allow other users to debug applications that are executed by the user directly.

Missing Authorizations

If you execute an action for which your database user doesn't have the necessary rights, you don't obtain any information about the authorization that is actually missing. In Figure 6.5 and Figure 6.6, you can view two examples of error messages indicating insufficient authorizations. Figure 6.5 shows an error message that appears when you execute an SQL command. Similar messages are output in diagnosis files or when you execute SQL code manually. It becomes clear in this example that the executing user would require the `Select` authorization on the `SPLFI` database table in the database schema `DEMO`.

```
Could not execute 'select * from DEMO.SPFLI' in 31 ms 749 µs
SAP DBTech JDBC: [258]: insufficient privilege: Not authorized
```

Figure 6.5 Access to a Table Fails Due to Insufficient Privileges

In the example in Figure 6.6, we tried to open the ADMINISTRATION EDITOR without the required privilege. Here, the error message doesn't contain an SQL command. For this reason, you cannot determine which privilege is missing. In this case, you should consult the SAP HANA Administration Guide (*help.sap.com/hana_platform*). For our example, this guide informs us that the `MONITORING` role is missing. Similar scenarios can occur, for example, when modeling SAP HANA views or creating XS applications.

Figure 6.6 Access to the Administration Editor Fails Due to Insufficient Privileges—Error Message

[+] **The SYSTEM User**

There are several restrictions for the assignment of rights. To prevent users from obtaining rights without permission, users are prohibited from assigning rights to themselves. Moreover, users can only assign authorizations for which they have the GRANTABLE option. The SYSTEM user is an exception. This user may also grant some authorizations that it doesn't have itself. This includes authorizations in monitoring and development. For this reason, it should only be used for creating database users and then be deactivated again. You require a user with the User Admin system privilege for this purpose. Right-click your system in the SYSTEMS view, and choose SQL CONSOLE. Now, enter the following SQL command and execute it by pressing [F8]:

```
ALTER USER SYSTEM DEACTIVATE USER NOW
```

In case of emergency, you can reactivate the SYSTEM user with the same authorization:

```
ALTER USER SYSTEM ACTIVATE USER NOW
```

If you haven't done so and can't remember the password of the SYSTEM user, the usage of SAP HANA is now possible only to a limited extent. In this case, log on to the operating system of the SAP HANA server as the <SID>adm server. Shut down the SAP HANA instance with the following command-line command:

```
/usr/sap/hostctrl/exe/sapcontrol -nr <instance number>
-function StopSystem HDB
```

Now start parts of SAP HANA manually. To do this, first activate the name and compile server in the background:

```
/usr/sap/<SID>/HDB<instance number>/hdbenv.sh
/usr/sap/<SID>/HDB<instance number>/exe/hdbnameserver &
/usr/sap/<SID>/HDB<instance number>/exe/hdbcompileserver &
```

Then start the index server in the foreground:

```
/usr/sap/<SID>/HDB<instance>/exe/hdbindexserver -console
```

After you've successfully started the index server, you can change the password:

```
ALTER USER SYSTEM password <your new password>
```

Now terminate the index, compile, and name server. To do this, you must first find out the process IDs:

```
ps ax | grep hdb
```

Then terminate the processes with the following command:

`kill <process ID>`

You can now start SAP HANA as usual from SAP HANA Studio. From now on, your new password is applicable for the `SYSTEM` user.

6.2.2 Creating and Managing Roles

To simplify authorization administration, you can define a role with all necessary rights, which you can then assign to multiple users. In the SYS-TEMS view of SAP HANA Studio, you can find the roles in the SECURITY folder under ROLES. Roles contain the same authorization types as users. A more detailed description is available in Section 6.2.1.

Some roles were already created during the installation of SAP HANA. In the following, we'd like to discuss the most critical application areas:

▶ **User and authorization administration**
Because the `SYSTEM` user should not be used for the administration of the database, you first need to create a new database user for assigning authorizations. The system privileges `ROLE ADMIN` und `USER ADMIN` are suitable for this purpose.

Which roles for which task?

▶ **Development**
The `DEVELOPMENT` role is used for developing native applications on SAP HANA. However, this privilege allows only development itself. Additionally, you also require the package privileges `REPO.READ`, `REPO_EDIT_NATIVE_OBJECTS`, `REPO.ACTIVATE_NATIVE_OBJECTS`, `REPO.MAINTAIN_NATIVE_OBJECTS` in the package of the SAP HANA repository in which you want to develop.

For using the web-based development interface, the user requires the `sap.hana.xs.ide.roles::Developer` role. Some more functions are made available to the user through the roles in the packages `sap.hana.xs.ide.roles` and `sap.hana.xs.admin.roles`.

▶ **SAP HANA view modeling**
SAP HANA views are also stored in the packages of the repository. For this purpose, you require the package privilege `REPO.MAINTAIN_NATIVE_OBJECTS` for the package `root`, as well as `REPO.READ`, `REPO_`

EDIT_NATIVE_OBJECTS, and REPO.ACTIVATE_NATIVE_OBJECTS for the storage location of your SAP HANA views. To enable you to create packages yourself, you additionally require the authorization REPO.MAINTAIN_DELIVERY_UNITS.

Moreover, you require the basic authorization for accessing SAP HANA view, the analytical privilege _SYS_BI_CP_ALL. This privilege permits global access to SAP HANA views and shouldn't be assigned to end users by any means.

The _SYS_REPO system user requires the authorization for SELECT on all schemas from which you want to use tables for SAP HANA views.

▶ **Monitoring**
For monitoring the system, you should create your own user that can access all relevant tools.

The MONITORING role is sufficient to access the Administration Editor. The sap.hana.admin.roles::Monitoring role is required for accessing resource utilization, memory overview, and system dashboard. The TRACE ADMIN system privilege grants access to the diagnosis files, as well as the configuration of traces.

▶ **Backups**
You require the BACKUP ADMIN and CATALOG READ system privileges for creating and managing backups.

[!]	**The sap.hana.xs.admin.roles::SQLCCAdministrator Role**
	The sap.hana.xs.admin.roles::SQLCCAdministrator role allows developers to set up database access without authentication in native SAP HANA applications. In this context, any activated database user can be used—and so can SYSTEM and other users with extensive rights. No password needs to be assigned for this. If the user also has developer rights, the user can execute any SQL code now without having the appropriate rights. The authorization for updating the _SYS_XS.SQL_CONNECTIONS table can also be used for this purpose.
	Accordingly, you should use caution when assigning these authorizations. They are only relevant for XS developers and should be assigned only to users that are created specifically for this purpose.

6.3   Monitoring

A core task of SAP HANA Studio is to provide detailed data on the current database status. A database administrator is responsible for providing sufficient hard disk memory space, main memory, and CPU resources. The administrator is also responsible for analyzing errors and removing them. Section 6.1 already introduced you to the structure and administration of SAP HANA Studio. This section therefore deals with the monitoring process from these points of view.

6.3.1   Main Memory and CPU

The fact that all data is saves in the main memory distinguishes SAP HANA from many other databases. This is the primary reason for the major speed benefits compared with other databases. The main memory stores tables, program code, query data, statistics, and all temporary data that is generated at runtime. SAP HANA is therefore referred to as an *in-memory database*. Accordingly, the main memory requirement is high.

Main memory in SAP HANA

Like with other operating systems, this is the reason Linux extends its physical main memory by a SWAP memory. This involves a file or partition on a hard disk that expands the size of the main memory. The resulting total memory is referred to as virtual main memory. If a process requires too much main memory, parts of the memory are swapped to the SWAP area. The speed benefit of the main memory is lost in this process. For the operation of SAP HANA, it is therefore essential to prevent this from happening in SAP HANA processes. For this purpose, the following guidelines apply to the database:

▶ All SAP HANA processes can allocate a specific part of the whole main memory that is physically available. A maximum of 90% of the initial 64GB and 97% of the remaining main memory can be used by SAP HANA. This is referred to as the *allocation limit*. The remaining main memory is available to other applications and the operating system. You can restrict this value downward in the SAP HANA configuration by changing the global allocation limit (see Section 6.4).

Guidelines for the database

▸ The main memory management is withdrawn from the operating system. SAP HANA occupies the required main memory and manages it in a separate memory pool. If parts of the memory are no longer required, they still remain in the memory pool and are not released for the operating system. The monitoring of the main memory utilization with operating system means doesn't provide any correct data.

▸ The minimum size of the required main memory is calculated in a size check report before installation or migration to SAP BW on SAP HANA.

▸ Usually, live SAP HANA installations may be operated only as dedicated installations; in other words, no other application software is operated on the server apart from SAP HANA. Multiple Components One Database (MCOD) installations are exceptions (see SAP Note 1661202).

▸ If the main memory still runs short, SAP HANA removes tables from the main memory that have not been used for a long time (see Chapter 5, Section 5.6). They are still available on the hard disk, but the speed benefit of the fast main memory is lost. This is not a swap because this process is run internally in SAP HANA and not by the operating system.

▸ Because a swap does not occur, SAP HANA processes are *memory resident*; that is, the operating system must not swap.

To pre-empt the unloading of data from the main memory and thus prevent loss in performance, you must quickly identify that the main memory is running short.

CPUs in SAP HANA The monitoring of the CPU usage is similarly important. If calculations must be made using database content, this results in a considerable speed boost if they are made at the database level. In current versions of SAP BW, more and more tasks are transferred from the application server to the database if it is an SAP HANA database.

When certifying the offers of server manufacturers for SAP HANA, attention is paid to a proper ratio between the size of the main memory and the CPU resources. The appliance principle should thus prevent unbalanced hardware equipment. High utilization of the CPUs is still

possible, for example, due to defective processes or particularly comput-
ing-intensive tasks, such as SAP BW migration to SAP HANA or updates
and upgrades.

The OVERVIEW tab of the administration perspective provides three bars
that inform about the status of the main memory and CPU usage (see
Figure 6.7).

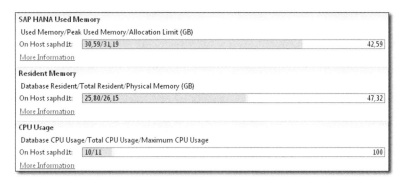

Figure 6.7 Used Memory and CPU Usage

Administration
Editor

The upper bar presents the actual usage of the main memory by SAP
HANA. At this point of, the memory reserved by SAP HANA is not used
to its full extent. Initially, an SAP HANA-internal memory pool is
formed that is available flexibly for various purposes. If main memory
becomes available again after use, it is not returned to the operating system, but instead remains in the memory pool. Information about the
operating system doesn't give much evidence about the actual usage of
the main memory. The bar represents the share of this used memory in
the allocation limit. Either this is calculated automatically through the
method mentioned, or the manually defined global allocation limit is
used (see Section 6.4.1). The maximum memory used since the last start
of the database is indicated in gray. In the long term, these values can be
used, for example, to document the growth of the memory usage for a
specific period of time or to identify memory shortage.

The bar in the middle refers to the resident physical main memory—that
is, the physical main memory that is permanently occupied. Swapped
parts of the main memory or data whose swapping is permitted are not

included in the calculation. What's left are processes of the database (dark green), as well as large parts of the operating system and applications for which fast access is required (light green). They are illustrated as part of the server's entire physical main memory.

Further processes Because SAP HANA can never occupy the entire main memory, the remaining part is available for other processes, of which large parts can also be swapped. Of the remaining contents, 6.4GB can be addressed on an SAP HANA appliance with a size of just 64GB. This is definitely sufficient in a production system with dedicated operation.

Nevertheless, this presentation is relevant for development and test systems, whose operation, in many cases, is not dedicated. As a result, a second SAP HANA database can be operated on the same server, for example. The monitoring of the resident memory plays a significant role in this case because you must prevent the memory from overflowing with non-swappable data. This could result in a database crash or even operating system failure.

The lower bar presents the general CPU utilization of the server in light green; the share of the database is marked in dark green.

[+] **Monitoring the Main Memory without SAP HANA Studio**

Only the main memory reserved by the processes and its general reservation are transparent for the operating system. Neither the composition nor the actual usage of reserved memory can be analyzed comprehensively. Thus, the information content of commands like top or ps is low.

It makes more sense to determine the internal system views via SQL queries to the SAP HANA database. They are documented in the "SAP HANA SQL and System Views Reference." Views like M_MEMORY provide detailed information and are used for presentation in SAP HANA Studio, among other things.

Checking processes in the Landscape tab To obtain detailed information on the resource usage, you can use the LANDSCAPE tab of the administration perspective (Figure 6.8). Under SERVICES, you can view a list of SAP HANA processes with the associated main memory values and the CPU statistics. You can supplement it with further columns using the 🔩 button.

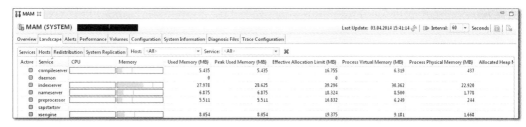

Figure 6.8 Processes in the Landscape Tab

The presentation can also be used if an SAP HANA cluster is deployed, and it can evaluate the processes of each host individually in this case. To understand the information in the list, you must be familiar with some terms:

▶ **(Peak) used memory**
Used memory is the process's main memory that is currently being used.

▶ **Effective allocation limit**
As already mentioned, the global allocation limit can be set manually or calculated automatically. This results in an effective allocation limit for each process. This limit implies how much main memory is available to the process if the current consumption of all other processes remains stable.

▶ **Virtual memory**
Virtual memory refers to the size of the allocated main memory. This is granted by the operating system but not fully reserved during implementation. By means of appropriate algorithms of the operating system, it can reserve more main memory than is actually available in the physical or swapped space.

▶ **Physical memory**
Physical memory is the main memory that is reserved by the operating system for the process. It is larger than the used memory because the internal memory pool of SAP HANA doesn't release any memory that is no longer required.

▶ **Heap memory**
Heap memory is part of the physical memory that was allocated dynamically. This is done in the SAP HANA code using special allocation

Different main memory types

techniques. The value is only important for users if it becomes exceptionally high.

▸ **Shared memory**
Shared memory is a shared area for exchanging data among different processes.

[*]
Monitoring Cluster Systems

The LANDSCAPE tab provides further monitoring options for SAP HANA systems that consist of various servers. The HOSTS area contains an overview of servers, REDISTRIBUTION informs about the distribution of tables among servers, and SYSTEM REPLICATION shows any replication servers that are set up.

The SERVICES area also distinguishes the processes by the server on which they run.

Memory Overview
A new function, MEMORY OVERVIEW, is available since SAP HANA SPS 7 if you want to analyze the utilization of the main memory by content type. If you use SAP HANA Studio as of revision 70, you can open the MEMORY OVERVIEW when you right-click a system in the SYSTEMS view.

[+]
Authorization for the Memory Overview

A new role is provided with SAP HANA SPS 07: `sap.hana.admin.roles:: Monitoring`.

The database user that uses the MEMORY OVERVIEW must have this authorization. The `SYSTEM` user, which is often used for administration purposes, doesn't have this role by default.

Users that don't have this authorization receive a corresponding error message when trying to access the overview. For more information on the rights management of database users, see Section 6.2.

This note also applies to the RESOURCE UTILIZATION view, which is discussed in Section 6.3.4.

The memory view overview is displayed with four pie charts. You can click on any section of the charts. A dialog window indicates the system views and calculation steps that led to the relevant value. The texts below the charts comprise supplementing key figures. For a cluster system, you can select the hosts to be analyzed in the upper area.

The charts in Figure 6.9 show the utilization of the physical main memory, composition of the USED MEMORY by usage, shared columns and row-based tables, and the usage of internal memory management. In this view, ideally, you can analyze problems with memory consumption.

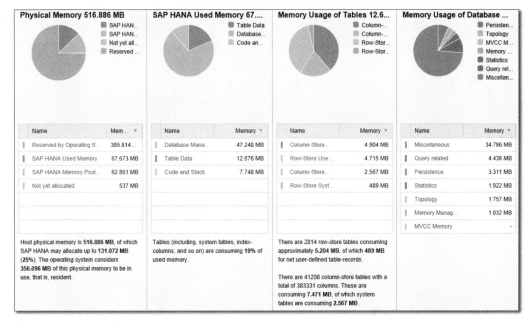

Figure 6.9 Memory Overview

6.3.2 Hard Disks

In SAP HANA, data is obtained from the main memory. The stored contents are available only as long as the power supply is uninterrupted. The data must also be available on a hard disk so that it is not lost if there is a power failure.

Write processes that are very quick in the main memory cannot be run with the same speed on the hard disk. Instead of synchronizing the data continuously, only the changes in the dataset are stored there. To prevent increasing memory requirements, old logs are moved to another location on a regular basis (log backup).

Logs, save points, backups

339

Moreover, a copy of the SAP HANA dataset is backed up to the hard disk at regular intervals (when *save points* are reached). Based on the last save point and the log entries that were made after this save point, you can restore the status before a crash. Because logs have a timestamp, point-in-time recovery is also possible. This enables you to define any point in time to which the status of the database is to be reset on the basis of the logs. Section 6.4.1 describes the configuration of log behavior.

Backups are used to enable data restore even after hard disk errors. You require neither logs nor save points for this process. But this involves loss of data for the period of time that is not covered. Backups can be restored if you want to undo an error in the database—for example, an update of the application server.

If an error occurs in one of these processes, this may lead to a loss of data. Accordingly, monitoring hard disk activities is very important in the SAP HANA in-memory database.

Memory space
In the Administration Editor, the bar chart on the right-hand side informs about the remaining free space in the storage location for logs, data (that is, save points), and trace files, which are discussed in Section 6.3.5 (see Figure 6.10). If no more space is available for log files, the SAP HANA database stops all activities.

To prevent space shortage, you can swap the storage location to another partition. Section 6.4.1 describes the necessary steps.

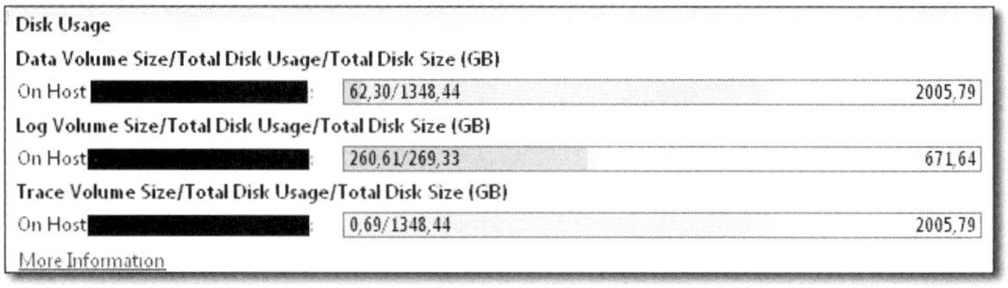

Figure 6.10 Space Overview

Hard disk performance
In the VOLUMES tab, you can find detailed hard disk statistics (see Figure 6.11). Here, you are provided with a summary of statistical data for read

and write accesses, which are divided by processes. Here, you can monitor the access times or their scope in case of problems with long load or storage times of save points and logs.

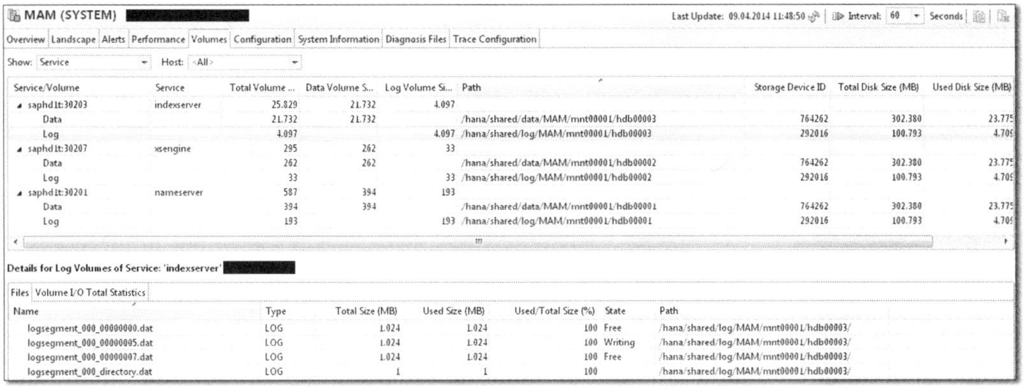

Figure 6.11 Volumes Tab

In the lower area of the tab, you can see the files used for storage and their reservation. Depending on the configured log mode, old entries are not deleted. The available log files can be occupied completely after some time. Section 6.4.1 discusses the log modes in more detail.

Trigger Read Ratio/Trigger Write Ratio   **[+]**

The trigger read or write ratios are key figures displayed in the VOLUMES tab. Their calculation is associated with the internal functioning of SAP HANA. SAP HANA accesses the hard disk with asynchronous operations. In doing so, a data request is sent to the hard disk, and further operations are carried out while the data is still transferred. This can considerably reduce the time during which database access is possible, for example, after a database restart.

The quotient of the time for request and the time for its fulfillment is calculated as a key figure for write and read operations, respectively. This involves trigger read ratio and trigger write ratio. Results between 0 and 1 are possible, whereas a low value is normal.

6.3.3 Database Performance

The analysis of currently running work processes on SAP HANA is important if the execution of data operations takes a very long time. In this case, the PERFORMANCE tab offers four display options:

▶ **Threads**
The THREADS area displays running operations of different types. These can be the execution of SQL queries, database-internal operations, or the execution of programs.

▶ **Sessions**
The SESSIONS area displays the sessions that are currently running. For each session, you can view key figures like the average runtime of queries or their number.

▶ **Blocked Transactions**
Some operations cannot be executed because tables or rows that must be accessed are blocked. They are listed with more detailed information under BLOCKED TRANSACTIONS.

▶ **Job Progress**
Operations like data compression can take longer. Their progress is shown in the JOB PROGRESS area.

6.3.4 Historic Performance Data

The performance and its resource consumption often need to be observed over a longer period of time. For this purpose, SAP HANA stores a variety of key figures at regular intervals.

Performance load   In the Administration Editor, the history of resource data is displayed for a specific period of time under LOAD on the PERFORMANCE tab (Figure 6.12).

For example, if the main memory runs short, you can identify the point in time when the utilization increased suddenly. When a system goes live, you can monitor the load during core hours and identify increasing memory utilization in the long term.

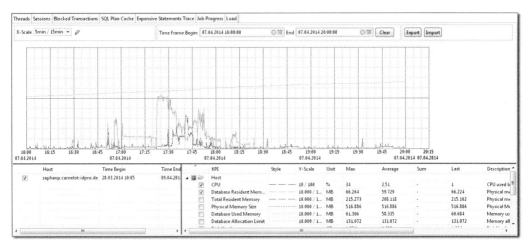

Figure 6.12 Performance Load—Timescale of an SAP BW Update

Another variant to analyze the resource utilization of a period of time is available in the RESOURCE UTILIZATION view. Like for the MEMORY OVERVIEW, you can open the view by right-clicking a system in the SYSTEMS view (Figure 6.13).

Resource Utilization

This display is similar to the previous one, but it provides some additional functions. If, for example, you click a point in the diagram, the exact value is indicated on the right of the corresponding key figure.

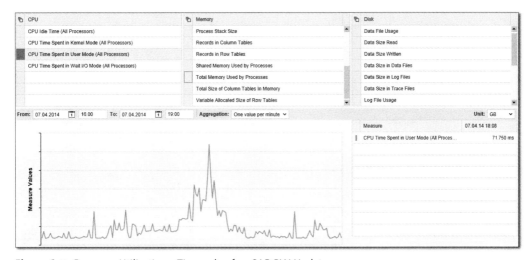

Figure 6.13 Resource Utilization—Timescale of an SAP BW Update

343

SQL Plan Cache

Data queries can be monitored in the SQL PLAN CACHE area. SQL commands that have been executed once or multiple times are collected here. Detailed performance data is available for these commands. This enables you to compare the runtimes of your programs' queries or determine SQL commands with long runtimes.

SAP HANA Plan Viz

SAP HANA PlanViz is suitable for a more detailed performance analysis. Click an SQL entry in the table and choose VISUALIZE PLAN. An SQL view with the selected command opens initially. Then, you can view a graphical display of the operations performed, like unions and joins, in boxes (Figure 6.14).

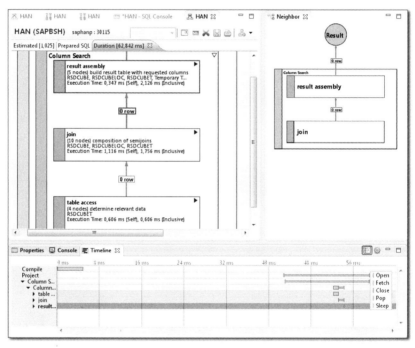

Figure 6.14 Performance Measurement in PlanViz

Each box show an estimated value for this part's share in the total runtime. You can also determine this yourself. To do so, right-click the boxes, and choose EXECUTE. Now, a performance measurement takes place for the appropriate part. You obtain an overview of the runtime and the time share for sorting, reading of data, unions, or joins. A new view, TIMELINE, opens below this display. This view displays the timeline graphically.

You can edit the SQL command manually in the SQL view and display it again by right-clicking VISUALIZE PLAN. You can also check newly developed SQL codes with this method.

> **Error Message "Invalid table name"** [!]
>
> In the SQL PLAN CACHE, all SQL commands are stored as they are received. A command of a database user is automatically executed in its associated database schema if no schema name was specified. If you want to execute or display these commands with another user, this results in the error message "Invalid table name." In this case, you should manually supplement the schema before the tables. Also ensure that your user has the rights required for the SQL code.

If the runtime of queries exceeds a preconfigured limit, it is displayed in the EXPENSIVE SQL STATEMENTS TRACE area of the PERFORMANCE tab. The trace must be activated by clicking the [🖉 Configure...] button.

Expensive SQL Statements Trace

6.3.5 Troubleshooting

Typical error sources for SAP HANA include updates, high resource utilization, hardware errors, and incorrect configuration.

It's not always immediately clear where the error can be found or how to solve it. The following three options are available for troubleshooting in SAP HANA Studio.

Alerts

SAP HANA checks various key figures at regular intervals. If a preset threshold value is reached, the system creates an alert, which is displayed in the ALERTS tab (Figure 6.15). There are five classification levels: INFORMATION, LOW, MEDIUM, HIGH, and ERROR. With these alerts, you can be warned against imminent main memory shortage, errors, or incorrect configuration. With the [🖉 Configure...] button, you can set up automatic email notification. The threshold values can be adapted for all alerts.

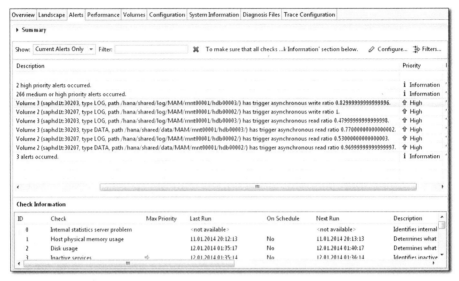

Figure 6.15 Alerts in a Test System

To obtain further information on an alert, double-click the corresponding entry. A dialog window opens that contains, among other things, recommended actions.

[Ex] **Asynchronous Read Ratio Alert**

In Figure 6.15, you can view various alerts with high priority. They refer to the asynchronous hard disk communication of SAP HANA that is mentioned in Section 6.3.2. In revision 70, the display is faulty because it reports very low values with high priority. This can be remedied by importing SAP Note 1965379.

Only if the displayed values are permanently high (more than 0.5) and you notice poor performance for hard disk accesses—for example, when creating save points—should you consider using the solution approach of SAP Note 1930979, which is recommended by the alert.

Diagnosis Files

If a problem exists, you should first examine the diagnosis files under the DIAGNOSIS FILES tab (Figure 6.16). Even if the database can no longer be started, you can still access the files via the diagnosis mode (see Section 6.1.1).

346

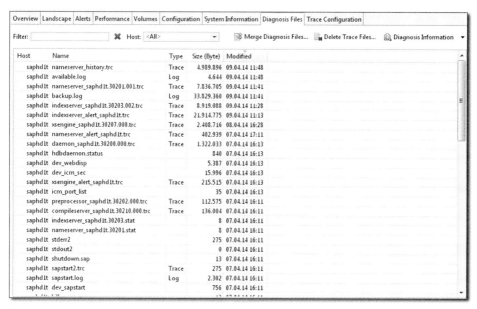

Host	Name	Type	Size (Byte)	Modified
saphdlt	nameserver_history.trc	Trace	4.989.896	09.04.14 11:48
saphdlt	available.log	Log	4.644	09.04.14 11:48
saphdlt	nameserver_saphdlt.30201.001.trc	Trace	7.836.705	09.04.14 11:41
saphdlt	backup.log	Log	33.829.360	09.04.14 11:41
saphdlt	indexserver_saphdlt.30203.002.trc	Trace	8.919.088	09.04.14 11:28
saphdlt	indexserver_alert_saphdlt.trc	Trace	21.914.775	09.04.14 11:13
saphdlt	xsengine_saphdlt.30207.000.trc	Trace	2.408.716	08.04.14 16:28
saphdlt	nameserver_alert_saphdlt.trc	Trace	402.939	07.04.14 17:11
saphdlt	daemon_saphdlt.30200.000.trc	Trace	1.322.033	07.04.14 16:13
saphdlt	hdbdaemon.status		840	07.04.14 16:13
saphdlt	dev_webdisp		5.387	07.04.14 16:13
saphdlt	dev_icm_sec		15.996	07.04.14 16:13
saphdlt	xsengine_alert_saphdlt.trc	Trace	215.515	07.04.14 16:13
saphdlt	icm_port_list		35	07.04.14 16:13
saphdlt	preprocessor_saphdlt.30202.000.trc	Trace	112.575	07.04.14 16:11
saphdlt	compileserver_saphdlt.30210.000.trc	Trace	136.004	07.04.14 16:11
saphdlt	indexserver_saphdlt.30203.stat		8	07.04.14 16:11
saphdlt	nameserver_saphdlt.30201.stat		8	07.04.14 16:11
saphdlt	stderr2		275	07.04.14 16:11
saphdlt	stdout2		0	07.04.14 16:11
saphdlt	shutdown.sap		13	07.04.14 16:11
saphdlt	sapstart2.trc	Trace	275	07.04.14 16:11
saphdlt	sapstart.log	Log	2.302	07.04.14 16:11
saphdlt	dev_sapstart		756	07.04.14 16:11

Figure 6.16 List of Diagnosis Files on the Diagnosis Files Tab

A separate diagnosis file exists for each database process. If applicable, there may also be a file with severe errors, like files with dumps after crashes. Their file names include the term "alert" or "dump." We'll discuss some of the other log files in the following:

Which diagnosis files are available?

▶ `available.log`
A background process runs on the database server, even if SAP HANA is shut down. It creates a log file that logs the times and dates when SAP HANA is available (or not available). If the server itself is shut down or fails, this period of time is not covered in the file. This file is also available for SAP application servers.

▶ `backup.log`
Information on the progress and success are stored in this file during a backup operation.

▶ `dev_webdisp.log`
The web dispatcher is used by the SAP HANA XS Engine. It involves a process similar to a web server.

▶ `icm_dev_sec`
This is the security log of the web dispatcher. It is important, for

example, if problems occur when you attempt to log on to an XS application.

▶ hdbsetup

This is the log file of the SAP HANA installation. Many of the system messages that are logged in this file are not displayed to the user during the installation process. If problems arise during or after installation, this is a very good focal point.

▶ hdbupd

This is the log file of a database update. The same statements as for hdbsetup apply to this log file.

Figure 6.17 shows the indexserver_alert file as an example. This file is used for severe errors of the index server.

Figure 6.17 Diagnosis File Example

Finding information   The files often contain text with a volume of several MB. It is therefore advisable to use the search function of Eclipse, Ctrl + F. Search terms could be "error," "failed," or the relevant time. Also note that only the last 1,000 lines of the file are displayed by default. For Figure 6.17, we had to display 10,000 lines to find the relevant section.

If you enter another value, you must click the REFRESH button in the top-right corner to reload the data. Only then does the system search for your terms in older entries. You may also download the files.

Main Memory Shortage   [Ex]

The log file displayed in Figure 6.17 contains several entries of the type "Failed to allocate [...] OUT OF MEMORY."

Loading a table to the main memory was not possible due to insufficient memory space. The database's reaction is to unload some tables that are then available only on the hard disk. SAP HANA databases that have not reached the main memory limit yet start these actions at a very early stage. Due to loss of performance, you should quickly take action in this case, for example, by cleansing temporary tables of your application server.

Traces

A trace generates very detailed information on the actions entered by the user and stores it in a file. Because of the high volume of information, the generated files quickly become very large. For this reason, you should restrict the trace's content and keep it active only during the required period. The SAP HANA traces are stored together with the other diagnosis files and are available on the DIAGNOSIS FILES tab.

On the TRACE CONFIGURATION tab, you are provided with seven trace types:

Trace types

▶ **SQL Trace**

All incoming SQL commands are stored in an SQL TRACE. You should filter at least by database user and the required statement type (see Figure 6.18). The SQL TRACE is particularly useful if you want to trace the data operations of the BW system without a debugger.

▶ **Database Trace**

The DATABASE TRACE is active by default. The diagnosis files for all SAP HANA processes, which were discussed in the previous section, are created here. Not all available data is stored for all information areas. Depending on their severity, they are classified as DEBUG, INFO, WARNING, ERROR, and FATAL. You can configure which trace content is to be written to the files. Again, you must consider the scope of the trace here.

349

▸ **User-Specific Trace**

The USER-SPECIFIC TRACE is similar to the DATABASE TRACE, but it only logs the activities of a user. This can be, for example, the user of a BW application server. This way, you can safely decrease the logging level without generating an excessive amount of data.

▸ **Performance Trace**

The PERFORMANCE TRACE is intended for developers. It stores information on the database-internal processing steps of a query.

▸ **Expensive Statements Trace**

The EXPENSIVE STATEMENTS TRACE stores its data on the PERFORMANCE tab in the EXPENSIVE SQL STATEMENTS TRACE area (see Section 6.3.4).

▸ **End-to-End Traces**

END-TO-END TRACES log for external applications like SAP Solution Manager. It is active by default.

▸ **Kernel Profiler**

The KERNEL PROFILER is not visible in some cases because the scroll bar is too short. It is intended for developers and logs internal program runs.

A window with additional settings opens for each trace. Make use of all available options to keep the trace's scope as low as possible. This way, you can find the relevant part more easily, and the database requires less computing power and memory.

Trace settings   In Figure 6.18, you can view the settings for an SQL trace. You can restrict them by logging the activities of only a specific database user or limiting the monitoring to a table, for example.

[Ex] **Table Accesses**

If you want to access database tables for your own applications or SAP BW objects, traces can be very useful. For example, if the creation of an SAP BW DataSource on a database table fails, you can use the SQL trace to check whether the system accesses the table correctly. For this purpose, you can deploy the database user of the application server and table name, as well as the restriction to DDL (SQL) commands (see Figure 6.18).

Figure 6.18 SQL Trace Setup

6.4 Database Configuration

SAP HANA utilizes several configuration files for managing settings. One file is assigned to each SAP HANA process, respectively. Further information on the processes and their task areas is available in Chapter 2, Section 2.3.

In SAP HANA Studio, the configuration files are available in the administration perspective under CONFIGURATION. Each configuration file is subdivided into various sections, which in turn contain several parameters. By means of filters, you can search for a specific parameter without knowing its position in the files. They are distinguished by several values: DEFAULT is the default value of the respective parameter and active after installation. SYSTEM is a manually set value that applies to the entire

Configuration in
SAP HANA Studio

SAP HANA landscape. This value concerns all instances in a distributed database. A HOST column is also available for each instance. In this column, you can assign individual values. The example for Figure 6.19 has only one instance. The green icons in the SYSTEM column identify active values that overwrite default settings.

Normally, SAP HANA immediately identifies any changes to the configuration, so it is usually not necessary to restart SAP HANA after a change is made.

After a new installation, the files don't yet contain all possible sections or parameters, and they must be added manually with a right-click, as required.

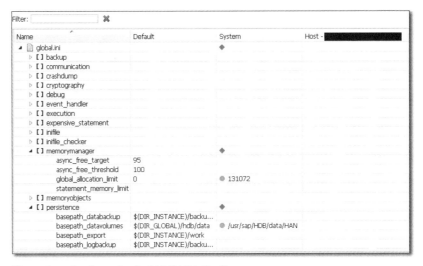

Figure 6.19 Configuration in SAP HANA Studio

Changing Configuration Files via the Operating System

You can find the storage location of the configuration files in the SAP HANA installation folder under *global/hdb/custom/config*. In some cases, it can be useful to change the SAP HANA configuration by manually editing the respective files. This is the case if you don't have the required authorizations on the database or want to change the configuration while SAP HANA is shut down.

All files have the same structure. Sections are defined in square brackets, followed by a list of parameters and their values. The files record modifications only. The default values are not included.

The following section details the most critical parameters and their usage. When editing sections and parameters, ensure that SAP HANA is case sensitive.

6.4.1 global.ini

The *global.ini* configuration file contains parameters that are valid across all SAP HANA processes.

Global Allocation Limit

Live SAP HANA instances work on a dedicated server; that is, no other applications may be operated in parallel. This restriction doesn't apply to development or quality assurance systems.

To save resources, you can operate these two systems in parallel on these systems. In this case, you install two database instances on the same physical server. In the default configuration, both instances will try to occupy the majority of the main memory (see Chapter 2, Section 2.1). The main memory can thus reach its capacity limits, so the volume of the main memory usage must be restricted.

Restricting the main memory usage

This is also necessary if SAP HANA is run on a system whose main memory capacity is higher than defined by the license.

You can adapt the main memory that can be occupied at maximum via the `global_allocation_limit` parameter in the `memorymanager` section. The relevant unit is megabyte.

Basepath

The data and log files of the SAP HANA processes and their backups are stored in files on the hard disk. Among other things, they are used to restore the dataset in the main memory after a restart or an unexpected crash. Accordingly, you should provide sufficient space for these files.

If the memory space nevertheless runs short or the hard disk needs to be exchanged, it may be necessary to change the storage path.

For this purpose, the `persistence` section comprises various parameters with the name `basepath_<service>`. You can use them to change the storage location of the data and log files. We advise you to shut down the database first and then implement the changes in the operating system as described in the box of Section 6.4. Before starting SAP HANA again, you should move the files accordingly. In doing so, ensure that the original Linux access authorizations are retained.

Make sure that sufficient memory is available for each service. The `basepath_logbackup` parameter should refer to a different partition from `basepath_log` so that sufficient memory is always provided for the log files. The following section details this process.

Log_mode

The redo logs document every change to the data and its structure in SAP HANA. They are required for a restore after a system crash to repeat the changes that were made since the last data backup (save point, see Section 6.3.2).

Redo log Redo logs are usually also retained after save points to enable point-in-time recovery. This method enables you to roll the database back to a status at any point in time. This is done independently of the time of the last save point and can be defined for a period before or after the last save point.

The memory requirement continuously grows through permanent saving of logs. For this reason, old logs are moved to another memory (log backup).

This process can be influenced through the configuration in *global.ini*. In the `persistence` sections, the parameters `enable_auto_log_backup` `Log_backup_timeout_s` ,, and `log_mode` are available for this purpose. `enable_auto_log_backup` activates the automatic log backup and is active by default. `Log_backup_timeout_s` specifies the time interval at which the log backup is started. If no memory is available for logs during this period of time, a log backup is done anyway. You can influence the log behavior via `log_mode`. The default value `normal` results in the previously described behavior for normal operation. The `overwrite` value terminates automatic log backup and overwrites old log files periodically. If you use `legacy`, no log backup is performed. Old logs are not overwritten, but deleted as soon as a database backup is complete. This option should no longer be used since SAP HANA SPS 2.

For the configuration, you must bear in mind that SAP HANA will consume all memory of the corresponding partition for logs if no log backup is scheduled. As soon as there's no free memory available any longer, the database will stop working.

6.4.2 indexserver.ini

The *indexserver.ini* configuration file comprises numerous parameters for controlling the database management in SAP HANA.

reload_tables

After a restart, SAP HANA will reload all tables to the main memory that had been loaded before the restart. This is not usually necessary for development and test systems. By preventing this behavior, you can accelerate the restart to some extent. To do so, in the `sql` section, set the `reload_tables` parameter to `false`.

Influencing the loading of tables

Activating R

R is a programming language that is used for statistics functions. In SAP HANA, you can use R code in database procedures, which is then available to the BW system. For this purpose, however, your R server must be activated in SAP HANA.

After you've set up the R server, you can make it known to the index server. To do so, the `cer_rserve_addresses` parameter is provided in the `calcEngine` section. Here, you can specify the address of several R servers using the format "Hostname1:Port1; Hostname2:Port2."

R server

6.4.3   statisticsserver.ini and nameserver.ini

The statistics server is a specific SAP HANA process used for entering and analyzing database statistics. Without this server, no historic performance data could be displayed in SAP HANA Studio. To spare the overhead of a separate process, SAP has extended the name server. As of SAP HANA SPS 07, it can also assume the tasks of the statistics server. For this purpose, you must disable the old statistics server manually and start the name server.

Disabling the Statistics Server

In the *statisticsserver.ini* file in the `statisticsserver_general` section, set the ACTIVE value to FALSE for this purpose. Then activate the new statistics server by setting the ACTIVE value to TRUE in the *nameserver.ini* file under STATISTICSSERVER.

Now, the database automatically migrates the statistics server. Once the migration is complete, statistics server processes will no longer occur.

6.4.4   xsengine.ini

The *xsengine.ini* configuration file contains settings for the development and operation of native SAP HANA applications.

XS Debugger

Eclipse   If you develop native SAP HANA applications (XS applications), you usually use Eclipse as the development environment. Because your code is executed in the database and the development takes place on the client, additional communication is required between these two for debugging.

To activate debugging, change the ENABLED value to TRUE in the DEBUGGER section.

XS Jobs

XS jobs are native SAP HANA applications that run in the background at regular intervals. To enable the scheduling of XS jobs, you must set the ENABLED parameter to TRUE in the SCHEDULER section.

6.4.5 filter.ini

Similar to Windows Explorer, there are hidden elements in SAP HANA. Tables that end with an underscore ("_") are not displayed in the default version of SAP HANA Studio. To also display hidden tables, you must set the INCLUDE HIDDEN parameter to TRUE in the FILTER section of the *filter.ini* file.

Showing hidden tables

6.4.6 Creating and Restoring Backups

You can ensure a database restore for any point in time by deploying savepoints and redo logs. However, you should also run regular backups. If savepoints or logs are lost due to hard disk errors, only backups allow a complete recovery. Backups are usually created before and after major operations like migrations, database updates, or similar. Note that configuration files are not backed up, and any changes that are contained in these files may still be valid after a restore.

Remember to do backups

Creating Backups

You can create backups by right-clicking a system under SYSTEMS • BACKUP AND RECOVERY • BACK UP SYSTEM…. In the dialog box that opens (see Figure 6.20), you can specify the target folder and the backup prefix.

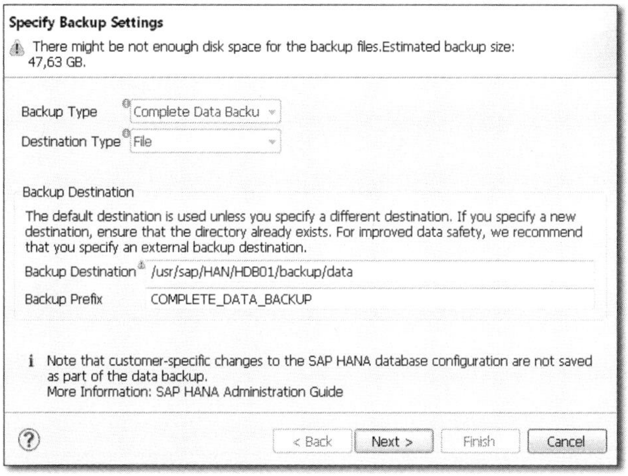

Figure 6.20 Creating a Backup

To prevent the collective loss of logs, save points, and backups, you should choose another hard disk for backups.

Restoring Backups

You must shut down your system for restoring the dataset. You can start recovery by right-clicking a system under SYSTEMS • BACKUP AND RECOVERY • RECOVER SYSTEM. The dialog box shown in Figure 6.21 provides you with three methods:

Recovery methods

▸ RECOVER THE DATABASE TO ITS MOST RECENT STATE
This option uses the save point and redo logs for recovering the current dataset.

▸ RECOVER THE DATABASE TO THE FOLLOWING POINT IN TIME
Only if the log backups are activated (see Section 6.4.1) can you run a *point-in-time recovery*. Here, you can select any point in time to which the database's dataset is to be restored.

▸ RECOVER DATABASE TO A SPECIFIC DATA BACKUP
The third option allows you to restore the backups that you've created yourself. This is the fastest method because changes to the dataset based on redo logs don't need to be reconstructed elaborately here.

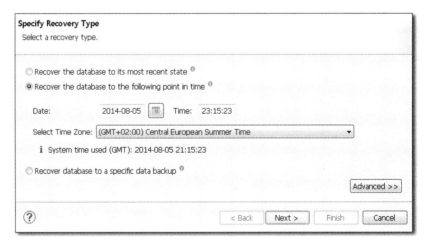

Figure 6.21 Restoring the Database

This chapter presents the trends and reporting options that are available to you after the migration to SAP BW on SAP HANA. You'll also learn how to integrate BEx queries and SAP HANA views with the reporting tools.

7 Reporting with SAP BW on SAP HANA

After you've completed the migration of your SAP BW to the SAP HANA database, you can turn your attention to the actual task of SAP BW again: reporting. This chapter discusses the latest developments in reporting and the specific changes in reporting on SAP HANA. You'll get to know the most critical server components, like the BI Launch Pad and the Central Management Console, as well as client tools.

7.1 Reporting Trends

In reporting, a distinction is often made among three purposes:

Purposes for reporting

1. Data analysis in operational systems

2. Data warehouse-based analyses

3. Department-specific analyses

For these three purposes, you must take into account the disadvantages and advantages listed in Table 7.1.

An SAP BW on SAP HANA system belongs to the data warehouse-based analyses. The department-specific analyses are covered by the reporting tools of the self-service category, which we'll discuss next. Data analyses in operational systems can be covered by the side-by-side approach or through integrated approaches (see Chapter 1, Section 1.1). Because this book focuses on SAP BW on SAP HANA, we won't discuss these approaches further in this chapter.

Purpose	Advantages	Disadvantages
Data analysis in operational systems	▶ Presentation of the most current transactional data ▶ High granularity of available data	▶ Mainly low performance in analyses ▶ Potential deceleration of the operational system ▶ Data is available from only one system. ▶ No complex reports possible
Data warehouse-based analyses	▶ Integration, harmonization, and consolidation of data from different systems is possible. ▶ Data is not volatile or time-dependent. ▶ Consistent and stable analysis results are available. ▶ Fast response times	▶ Latency of data, partially outdated dataset ▶ High costs for processing data and ensuring quality ▶ Low agility ▶ High maintenance effort
Department-specific analyses	▶ High flexibility ▶ Fast developments ▶ Independence of IT resources	▶ Fragmentation in silos for data and definitions ▶ Heterogeneous BI solutions, hidden costs

Table 7.1 Advantages and Disadvantages of the Various Purposes for Reporting

Reporting trends

Besides these three purposes, there are additional trends that speak in favor of reporting based on SAP BW on SAP HANA because they require a new technology:

▶ **Analysis of large amounts of data (big data)**
Enterprises want to analyze large amounts of structured and unstructured data.

▶ **Real-time analysis**
To be able to immediately respond to changes in the enterprise environment, reporting requires the most current transactional data.

▶ **Integration of flexible data analysis and an enterprise-wide data warehouse**
To avoid silos of data in different user departments, you must create a BI solution in your enterprise that combines the two requirements of flexible data analysis and enterprise-wide data warehouse.

▶ **Provision of advanced analysis techniques**
Simulation and forecasting of future developments continuously gain in importance and must therefore be supported by a BI solution.

▶ **Simple and mobile usability of reports**
Mobile end devices have become more and more widespread, which also increases the expectations that reports can be utilized on these devices.

To be able to cover the trends described, you require a data warehouse platform (backend) and a reporting platform (frontend). SAP provides the SAP BusinessObjects Business Intelligence platform as the frontend for the SAP BW on SAP HANA scenario (see Figure 7.1).

SAP Business-Objects BI platform

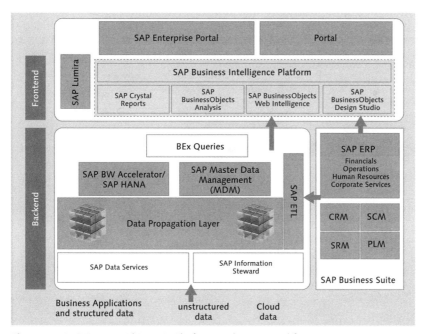

Figure 7.1 SAP BusinessObjects BI Platform as the Frontend for SAP BW on SAP HANA

Client tool categories

In line with the previously mentioned trends, client tools, which you can use for creating reports, are classified in three categories (see Figure 7.2):

▶ Self-service

▶ Dashboards and apps

▶ Reporting

The client tools of the self-service category comprise tools that primarily allow for department-specific analyses. Particularly with SAP Lumira, user departments support the creation and distribution of appealing analyses.

The dashboards and apps category considers client tools that can be used for the creation of complex as well as mobile analyses and dashboards. In this context, the user departments are users rather than developers.

For formatted reporting—for example, for monthly and quarterly reports—you can deploy the client tools from the reporting category.

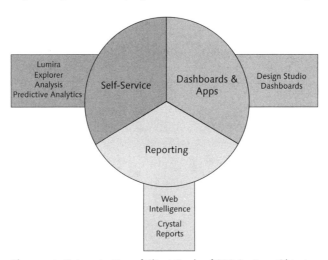

Figure 7.2 Categorization of Client Tools of SAP BusinessObjects

Support of advanced analysis techniques

You can use SAP Predictive Analytics for simulation and forecasting to also provide advanced analysis techniques. In the SAP BW on SAP HANA scenario, you can accelerate the simulation and forecasting by utilizing the statistical language R in combination with SAP HANA. This enables the analysis of large amounts of data.

Mobile usage of created reports is possible in all client tools except for Analysis, edition for Office because this tool is restricted to Microsoft Excel or PowerPoint.

Using SAP HANA as a database for SAP BW doesn't initially result in any changes to the presentation options for the reporting tools. You still report on the basis of BEx queries, which are now based on DataStore Objects (DSOs) or CompositeProviders instead of InfoCubes. You can now also report directly on data in the SAP HANA database via SAP HANA views.

7.2 SAP BusinessObjects Business Intelligence as a Reporting Platform

SAP BusinessObjects Business Intelligence (BI) 4.1 is the premium alternative to tools of the BEx suite, which are delivered in SAP BW by default. The SAP BusinessObjects Business Intelligence platform (BI platform) consists of two parts: the server installation forms the basis and provides several functions (for example, central administration and central administration of data sources) and central storage of documents. In addition, it includes numerous client tools for designing and displaying documents, for example, SAP Crystal Reports and SAP BusinessObjects Design Studio.

SAP Business-Objects BI 4.1

7.2.1 Server Components

The following sections describe server components that are frequently used: *BI Launch Pad* is the central entry point for all users that run documents or reports via a web interface. The *Central Management Console* is the administration interface that system administrators can use, for example, to restrict access to documents or reports and to reach all management functions of a server.

BI Launch Pad

The SAP BusinessObjects BI platform is the platform for reporting using SAP BusinessObjects products. All client tools store the created documents

Server component— BI Launch Pad

in the *BI Launch Pad*. Similar to a Microsoft SharePoint Server, the BI Launch Pad can be used as a central storage for documents, in this case documents that were created using SAP BusinessObjects client tools. The central storage of documents provides the following advantages:

▸ Simplified access to documents

▸ Secured access to all documents and client tools

▸ Simplified entry point for users, thanks to an intuitive design

Logon
You access the BI Launch Pad via the URL *http://<server name>:<Port>/ BOE/BI*. After you've called the URL, the logon screen shown in Figure 7.3 is displayed. You log on to the system by entering the corresponding system in the format *<server name>:<port>* and the associated user name/password combination.

Figure 7.3 Logon to BI Launch Pad

BI Launch Pad—Initial Screen

Initial screen of the BI Launch Pad
The initial screen is displayed after logon (see Figure 7.4). Users can arrange this screen according to their requirements. The default version is divided into five areas:

▸ The MY RECENTLY VIEWED DOCUMENTS area displays the last ten documents that the user called in the BI Launch Pad. These can include, for example, Crystal Reports documents, BEx web applications, Web Intelligence reports, documents of the OLAP edition of SAP BusinessObjects Analysis, Excel spreadsheets of SAP BusinessObjects Analysis' Microsoft Office edition, Design Studio apps, or BI workspaces.

▸ The inbox and thus the UNREAD MESSAGES IN "MY INBOX" area contains the last ten messages, for example, Crystal Reports documents that were generated as PDF documents using the scheduling or publication function of the SAP BusinessObjects BI platform and stored in your personal inbox.

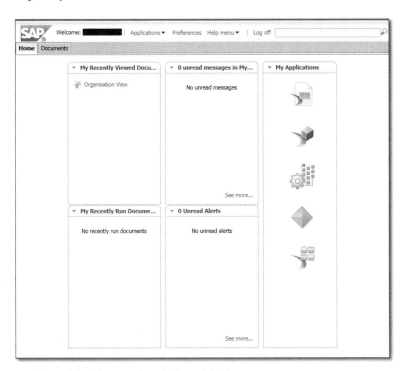

Figure 7.4 Initial Screen of the BI Launch Pad

▸ The MY RECENTLY RUN DOCUMENTS area shows the last ten jobs that were run by scheduling or the creation of a publication. Jobs are scheduled updates of Crystal Reports documents or publications based on Web Intelligence documents.

▸ The UNREAD ALERTS area displays alerts that the user subscribed and that occurred. Alerts can be subscribed in the individual documents using functions that are provided by the platform. For example, you can define exceptions in a Web Intelligence document that trigger an alert if they occur.

- ▶ By clicking an icon in the MY APPLICATIONS area, you open a new tab in the BI Launch Pad, and the selected application (for example, SAP BusinessObjects Web Intelligence or BEx Web Application) is started.

Documents

Documents in the BI Launch Pad

Initially, the user is provided with the HOME and DOCUMENTS tabs (see Figure 7.5). The latter tab displays the documents that exist in the BI platform, provided that the user has the appropriate authorizations.

Figure 7.5 Documents in the BI Launch Pad

The documents are stored in different folder structures depending on the user's selection. These folder structures are subdivided into the following:

- ▶ MY DOCUMENTS
- ▶ FOLDERS
- ▶ CATEGORIES
- ▶ SEARCH

MY DOCUMENTS displays the documents that the user has stored in his personal folder:

- ▶ MY FAVORITES
- ▶ INBOX
- ▶ MY ALERTS

▸ SUBSCRIBED ALERTS

▸ PERSONAL CATEGORIES

Similar to the initial screen, this section displays not only the last ten documents, but all documents that were created by the user. Users can create their personal folder structure in the MY FAVORITES folder, for example, Web Intelligence documents that they require for their personal reporting requirements. The INBOX folder contains all messages that were sent to this specific user. These particularly include documents that were created along with publications or when scheduling report generation.

The two folders, MY ALERTS and SUBSCRIBED ALERTS, classify the alerts that were created by the users themselves or that the users were subscribed to, respectively.

Alerts

Additionally, users can create their own categories in their personal folders to further structure their documents.

Documents can be stored in personal folders and in public folders. The latter are created under FOLDERS. Depending on the user's authorizations, this section displays the public folders and the documents contained therein (see Figure 7.6).

Figure 7.6 Documents in Public Folders

You can use the SEARCH entry to search for documents and content of documents (see Figure 7.7). The search permits fast access to documents that include a specific search term. Administrators can restrict the access to the individual areas of the DOCUMENTS tab using the Central Management Console.

Figure 7.7 Searching for Documents

BI Workspace

The *BI workspace* replaces the *Dashboard Builder* functionality to create appealing applications in the BI Launch Pad that may contain various documents, such as dashboards, Web Intelligence reports, or Crystal Reports documents. The idea of the BI workspace is to provide information and applications that are required for daily work in a central location. This also supports the approach of department-specific reporting. To achieve this goal, users can adapt the various options for displaying information according to their requirements. This should also ensure higher productivity of users in their daily work.

Creating a BI workspace

Users can create BI workspaces independently by reusing existing documents. This is supported by a tab-based navigation structure that provides a wide variety of layout options. Figure 7.8 shows an empty BI workspace that you can fill with content using drag-and-drop.

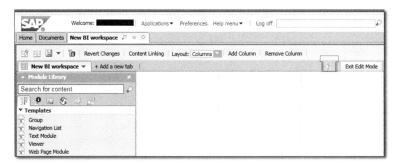

Figure 7.8 BI Workspace—Module Library

By means of the MODULE LIBRARY on the left-side of Figure 7.8, you can drag existing templates, documents, and so on to the layout area (see Figure 7.9).

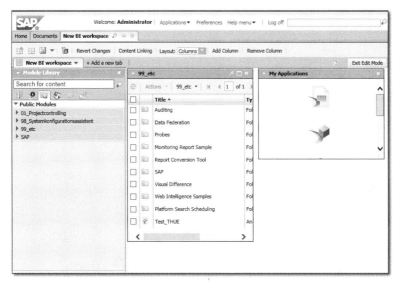

Figure 7.9 BI Workspace—Example

The following modules are available:

Modules in the BI workspace

- ▶ Templates
- ▶ Modules of the BI Launch Pad (for example, MY INBOX)
- ▶ Public modules
- ▶ Personal modules
- ▶ BI workspaces
- ▶ Document Explorer

You can create the BI workspaces based on these elements. This allows you, for example, to combine a dashboard with a Web Intelligence document. Additionally, depending on the users' requirements, they can also insert links to external websites. If you select an element and drag it to the layout area, the element is inserted in the BI workspace. Once the layout area includes all elements that are required for creating the BI workspace, you can add content linkings. This allows you to exchange parameters between two different elements.

When you click the CONTENT LINKING button, a dialog window opens to link contents (see Figure 7.10).

Content linking within a BI workspace

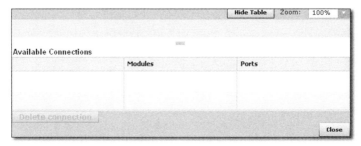

Figure 7.10 Content Linking

The following scenario could be an example for a possible content linking. A dashboard provides the option to run a selection for calendar year/month. This selection is also copied to all other elements in the BI workspace. Via content linking, you can link the characteristics in the individual elements that correspond to the calendar year/month. If the user of the BI workspace changes the selection in the dashboard, all other elements are updated with the new selection. This allows you to create powerful BI workspaces that link the contents of the inserted elements. If the configuration of the BI workspace is complete or you want to view the result during layout creation, click the EXIT EDIT MODE button. The BI workspace is then displayed as it will be presented to the user (see Figure 7.11).

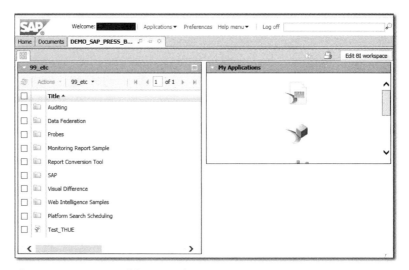

Figure 7.11 User View of the BI Workspace

Central Management Console

The *Central Management Console (CMC)* is the second server component of the BI platform besides the BI Launch Pad. You manage the BI server via the CMC. You access it via the URL *http://<server name>:<port>/BOE/CMC*. Port 8080 is used by default. Log on with a user name/password combination to navigate to the home page (see Figure 7.12).

CMC

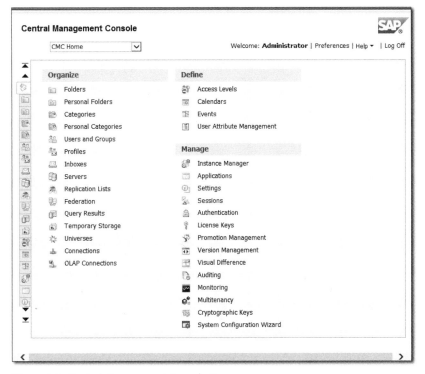

Figure 7.12 Central Management Console Home

Access Authorizations

Note that you must assign explicit rights to users for accessing the CMC. A user that views and updates documents and creates new BI workspaces usually doesn't have any access to the CMC. A user who creates documents using SAP BusinessObjects Web Intelligence, for example, may require access to the OLAP connections.

Assigning authorizations

To be able to assign these authorizations to users or user groups, you must set the access authorizations (see Figure 7.13). For this purpose, select the ACCESS LEVELS entry from the dropdown menu or click the corresponding entry in the CMC home page.

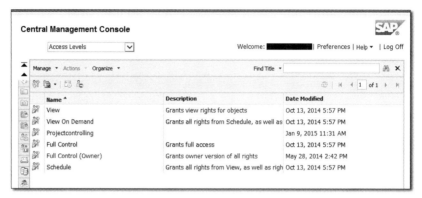

Figure 7.13 Access Levels

Depending on the settings selected here, the users have access to individual tools, documents, BI workspaces, and so on. To change the settings, click a group of access levels, and the PROPERTIES of the access levels are then displayed (see Figure 7.14).

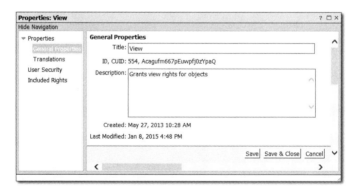

Figure 7.14 Properties of Access Levels

You can display and change the authorizations that are currently included via the INCLUDED RIGHTS menu entry (see Figure 7.15). The authorizations are divided into the following areas:

- GENERAL
- CONTENTS
- APPLICATION
- SYSTEM

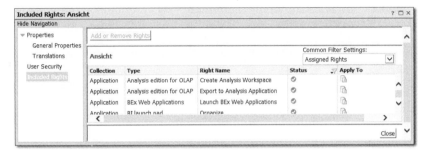

Figure 7.15 Selecting the Access Levels for a Group

Select the authorizations for an access level group. They can then be assigned to individual users or a group of users.

Access level group

OLAP Connections

To be able to access connections to OLAP data sources in the various client tools, you must first create them. To do so, select the OLAP CONNECTIONS menu item from the CMC home page (see Figure 7.12). The OLAP connections enable you, for example, to access SAP BW via the *BI Consumer Services interface* (BICS) or SAP HANA views.

OLAP connections

You must first create a new OLAP connection for accessing a BEx query or SAP HANA view. An OLAP connection has a name, an optional description, and a provider, respectively (see Figure 7.16).

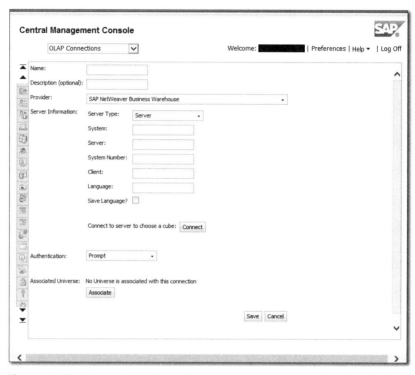

Figure 7.16 Creating an OLAP Connection

Providers for OLAP
connections

The following providers are available:

▸ SAP BW

▸ SAP HANA

▸ SAP Profitability and Cost Management 7.5 and 10.0

▸ SAP Business Planning and Consolidation 7.5 and 10.0 for SAP Net-
Weaver and the Microsoft platform

▸ Advanced analysis functions in SAP Financial Consolidation 7.5 and 10.0

▸ Microsoft Analysis Services 2008 and 2012

▸ Teradata

Select the appropriate field settings under of the SERVER INFORMATION area, for example, for an SAP BW server or SAP HANA. This information can be established via the SAP Logon Pad in SAP GUI or via SAP HANA Studio. By means of the CONNECT button, you can test the connection and select an InfoCube or a DataStore object as the data source for an SAP BW OLAP connection.

Three procedures are available for authentication:

Authentication of an OLAP connection

▸ PROMPT
The user is prompted to enter the user name and password when calling a document that uses this OLAP connection.

▸ SSO
Single sign-on is used for accessing this OLAP connection. It must be set up in advance between the BI server and SAP BW/SAP HANA.

▸ PREDEFINED
A user name/password combination is defined in the OLAP connection. Every user that calls a document using such an OLAP connection can view the data in the document for which the defined user is authorized in the OLAP connection. Any user can thus access data; for this reason, you should use this authentication type for test purposes only.

Click the SAVE button to display the created OLAP connection in the corresponding folder of the CMC (see Figure 7.17).

You can then access the created OLAP connection—for example, using the OLAP edition of SAP BusinessObjects Analysis—and analyze the selected data on this basis (see Figure 7.18). After you've selected the system, you can choose the query or SAP HANA view to be used. You still require BEx queries to create documents using SAP BusinessObjects BI client tools that are based on SAP BW data. You can also integrate SAP HANA views.

OLAP connection for SAP Business-Objects Analysis

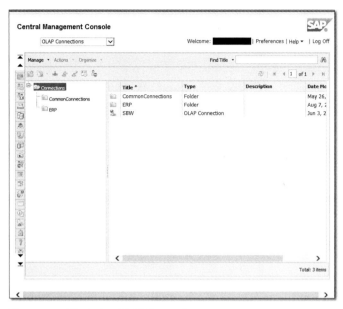

Figure 7.17 Displaying OLAP Connections

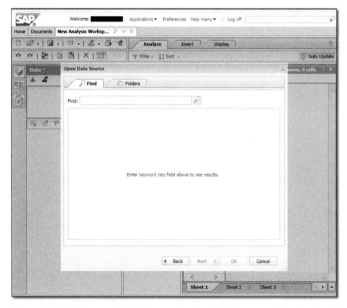

Figure 7.18 Using an OLAP Connection in SAP BusinessObjects Analysis, Edition for OLAP

After you've selected a system, you must log on to this selected system   **Logon**
if no standard user name/password was defined in the OLAP connection
or if SSO (single sign-on) is not used. After logon, you can search for a
BEx query; an InfoCube; or SAP HANA views, in the case of SAP HANA
(see Figure 7.19).

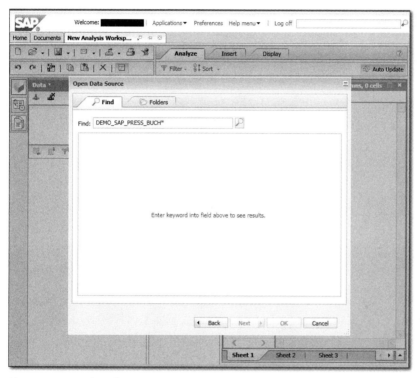

Figure 7.19 Searching for a BEx Query in SAP BusinessObjects Analysis, Edition
for OLAP

You can search for a BEx query using the technical name or description.   **Finding a BEx query**
BEx queries that correspond to the search criteria are returned as the
result. After you've selected a BEx query, the variable screen is displayed
if variables were used in the BEx query (see Figure 7.20).

After the variables have been filled as necessary, the BEx query result is
displayed in the OLAP edition of SAP BusinessObjects Analysis (see Figure 7.21). Then, the user can run the free OLAP analysis.

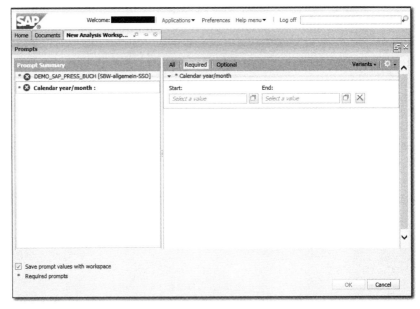

Figure 7.20 Variable Display in the BEx Query

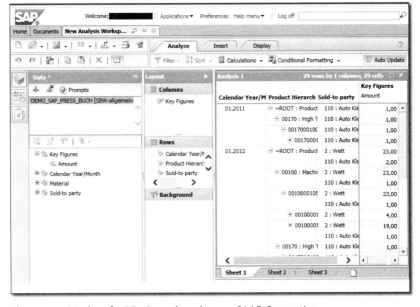

Figure 7.21 Display of a BEx Query based on an OLAP Connection

7.2.2   Client Tools

The following sections provide an overview of the client tools of SAP BusinessObjects BI 4.1. The tools that are provided with SAP BusinessObjects BI 4.1 depend on the license you purchased. The following client tools are provided in principle:

Client tools of SAP Business Objects BI 4.1

- Reporting
  - SAP Crystal Reports 2013
  - SAP Crystal Reports for Enterprise
  - SAP BusinessObjects Web Intelligence
- Dashboards and apps
  - SAP BusinessObjects Dashboards
  - SAP BusinessObjects Design Studio
- Self-service
  - SAP BusinessObjects Analysis, Edition for Microsoft Office
  - SAP BusinessObjects Analysis, Edition for OLAP
  - SAP BusinessObjects Explorer
  - SAP Predictive Analytics
  - SAP Lumira
- Tools for data access (third-party data sources)
  - SAP BusinessObjects Universe Design Tool
  - SAP BusinessObjects Information Design Tool

The tools for data access are not required for accessing data in SAP BW. SAP BW is accessed via the BICS interface. Different SAP BW versions are supported depending on the tool (see Table 7.2). SAP Note 1869560 informs you which BEx query elements are supported, respectively. You must also note that a higher SP level of the SAP BusinessObjects BI platform is required for certain SAP BW versions.

Required SAP BW version

Product	Connectivity	SAP BW 7.01 SPS 6 and higher	SAP BW 7.01 SPS 8 and higher	SAP BW 7.02 SPS 2 and higher	SAP BW 7.30 SPS 3 and higher	SAP BW 7.31 SPS 4 and higher	SAP BW 7.40 SPS 2 and higher
SAP Business-Objects Web Intelligence	BICS (dimensional transient universe)	✓	✓	✓	✓	✓	SP 1 and higher
SAP Crystal Reports for Enterprise		✓	✓	✓	✓	✓	SP 1 and higher
SAP Business-Objects Dashboards		✓	✓	✓	✓	✓	SP 1 and higher
SAP Business-Objects Web Intelligence	UNV OLAP	✓	✓	✓	✓	✓	SP 1 and higher
SAP Business-Objects Live Office		✓	✓	✓	✓	✓	SP 1 and higher
SAP Business-Objects Web Intelligence	Multi-source universe (relational)	✓	✓	✓	✓	✓	SP 1 and higher
SAP Crystal Reports for Enterprise		✓	✓	✓	✓	✓	SP 1 and higher
SAP Business-Objects Dashboards		✓	✓	✓	✓	✓	SP 1 and higher
SAP Business-Objects Explorer		✓	✓	✓	✓	✓	SP 1 and higher
SAP Business-Objects Analysis, Edition for OLAP[1]	BICS (directly to BEx)	✓	✓	✓	✓	✓	SP 1 and higher

Table 7.2 SAP BusinessObjects BI 4.1—SAP BW Access

Product	Connectivity	SAP BW 7.01 SPS 6 and higher	SAP BW 7.01 SPS 8 and higher	SAP BW 7.02 SPS 2 and higher	SAP BW 7.30 SPS 3 and higher	SAP BW 7.31 SPS 4 and higher	SAP BW 7.40 SPS 2 and higher
SAP Business-Objects Analysis, Edition for Microsoft Office[2]		[5]	[5]	[5]	[5]	[5]	[5]
SAP Business-Objects Dashboards	BICS (SAP BW Java stack)	✓	✓	✓	✓	✓	SP 1 and higher
SAP Business-Objects Explorer	SAP BWA[4]	✓	✓	✓	✓	✓	SP 1 and higher
SAP Crystal Reports for Enterprise	Direct to Data (D2D)	–	–	–	–	–	–
SAP Crystal Reports 2013	Direct connection to SAP BW data	✓	✓	✓	✓	✓	SP 1 and higher
BEx Web Applications of BEx Web Application Designer[3]	Integrated with BI 4.1	–	✓	✓	✓	✓	SP 1 and higher

[1] Analysis, Edition for OLAP supports SAP BW 7.0 SPS 23 and higher.

[2] Analysis, Edition for Microsoft Office supports SAP BW as of release 7.0 without the use of the BI platform.

[3] You can find further information in SAP Notes 1541365 and 1476156.

[4] SAP BusinessObjects Explorer supports SAP BWA 7.20, Revision 19 and higher.

[5] Further information is available in the product availability matrix for Analysis, Edition for Microsoft Office.

Table 7.2 SAP BusinessObjects BI 4.1—SAP BW Access (Cont.)

Access to SAP HANA views is supported in addition to the direct access to data in SAP BW, also in the SAP BW on SAP HANA scenario. The access to SAP HANA views also requires specific versions both for SAP

Required SAP HANA version

HANA and for the SAP BusinessObjects BI platform (see Table 7.3, the entry SP 1, for example, means that SP 1 of SAP BusinessObjects BI is required).

Product	Connectivity	SAP HANA SPS 5	SAP HANA SPS 6	SAP HANA SPS 7	SAP HANA SPS 8
SAP Business-Objects Web Intelligence	UNX (relational universe)	✓	SP 1 and higher	SP 2 and higher	SP 4 and higher
SAP Crystal Reports for Enterprise		✓	SP 1 and higher	SP 2 and higher	SP 4 and higher
SAP Business-Objects Dashboards		✓	SP1 and higher	SP 2 and higher	SP 4 and higher
SAP Business-Objects Analysis, edition for OLAP	Direct connection (BICS)	2	SP 1 and higher	SP 2 and higher	SP 4 and higher
SAP Business-Objects Analysis, Edition for Microsoft Office		1	1	1	1
SAP Business-Objects Explorer	Direct connection (JDBC) UNX (relational universe)	✓	SP 1 and higher	SP 2 and higher	SP 4 and higher
SAP Crystal Reports 2013	Direct connection	✓	SP 1 and higher	SP 2 and higher	SP 4 and higher
SAP Crystal Reports for Enterprise	Direct to Data	✓	SP 1 and higher	SP 2 and higher	SP 4 and higher

[1] Further information is available in the product availability matrix of SAP BusinessObjects for Analysis, Edition for Microsoft Office.

[2] Note that SAP HANA SPS 5 with SAP BusinessObjects Analysis, Edition for OLAP is compatible only up to SAP BusinessObjects BI 4.1 SP 2.

Table 7.3 SAP BusinessObjects BI 4.1—Access to SAP HANA

The following sections discuss the individual client tools, except for the tools for data access, which you'll need to use only in scenarios when you must create a universe. For this SAP BW on SAP HANA scenario, this is the case only if you want to report directly on HANA views and use SAP BusinessObjects Web Intelligence or SAP BusinessObjects Dashboards. Neither of these two client tools, however, is recommended for usage in SAP BW scenarios. The following therefore does not provide a detailed description of the tools for data access.

Reporting Category

According to their own statements, SAP provides two reporting client tools: *SAP Crystal Reports* is the classic reporting tool for creating perfectly formatted reports for a large group of users, and *SAP Business-Objects Web Intelligence* is a client tool for the interactive analysis of primarily relational data.

SAP Crystal Reports

Crystal Reports documents are created by IT and made available to users. Here, the documents are static with regard to formatting, and only the data can be updated. The static formatting of documents does not allow for free analysis.

SAP Crystal Reports

Two versions of SAP Crystal Reports are provided with SAP Business-Objects BI Platform 4.1: SAP Crystal Reports 2013 and SAP Crystal Reports for Enterprise. SAP Crystal Reports 2013 is a direct further development of SAP Crystal Reports 2008/2011. Hence, data in SAP BW is still accessed via an MDX driver with restrictions that already applied to SAP Crystal Reports 2008/2011. In comparison, SAP Crystal Reports for Enterprise is a completely new development that focuses primarily on improved user-friendliness.

In SAP Crystal Reports for Enterprise, you integrate BEx queries directly using the BICS interface. A BEx query is displayed with a universe icon in this context (see Figure 7.22).

SAP Crystal Reports for Enterprise

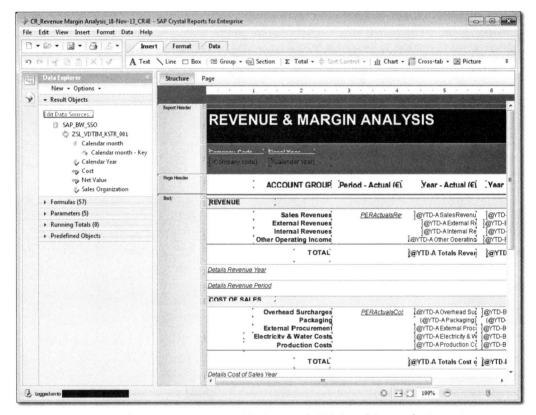

Figure 7.22 Integrating a BEx Query with SAP Crystal Reports for Enterprise

Only the actual data source—SAP BW SSO in Figure 7.22—indicates that this involves a BEx query.

Editing the BEx query
If you click EDIT DATA SOURCES, you can change the properties and the initial drill-down of the BEx query (see Figure 7.23).

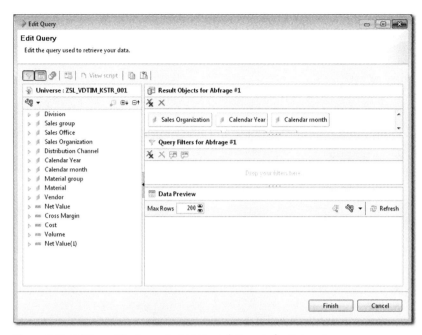

Figure 7.23 Editing a BEx Query in SAP Crystal Reports for Enterprise

The left part of the dialog window displays all properties and key figures of the BEx query. You can drag-and-drop the characteristics and key figures to the RESULT OBJECTS area to define the initial drill-down of the Crystal Reports document. You can also specify additional query filters for the characteristics that have not yet been defined as filters of the BEx query. Don't let the UNIVERSE: ZSL_VDTIM_KSTR_01 information confuse you. This is a BEx query and not a universe.

The access to SAP HANA views is identical to the access to BEx queries. First, you select an OLAP connection that is based on SAP HANA (see Figure 7.24). Then, you select the SAP HANA view that is to be used in your report from the displayed folder structure.

Defining the SAP
HANA access

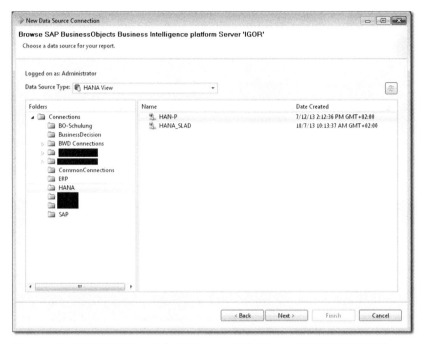

Figure 7.24 SAP Crystal Reports for Enterprise—Selecting an SAP HANA OLAP Connection

Defining result objects

Then, edit the RESULT OBJECTS like in a BEx query. You can also create new filter objects and get an initial overview of the result of your SAP HANA views (see Figure 7.25). Note the following: Here, too, the term *universe* is used, even though the query is based on an SAP HANA view. After you've completed the query, complete the editing by clicking FINISH. The report is then edited as usual with tables, graphics, and so on.

SAP Crystal Reports 2013

In SAP Crystal Reports 2013, BEx queries are displayed as database fields (see Figure 7.26, right-hand side—FIELD EXPLORER). You can arrange each database field individually or as a group in the DESIGN area.

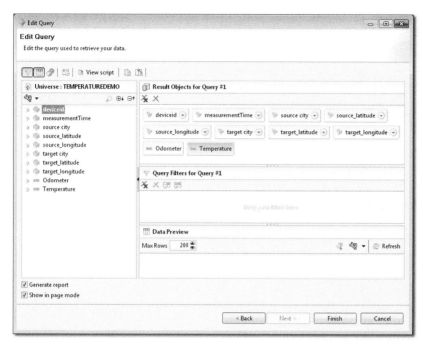

Figure 7.25 SAP Crystal Reports for Enterprise—Editing a Query in an SAP HANA View

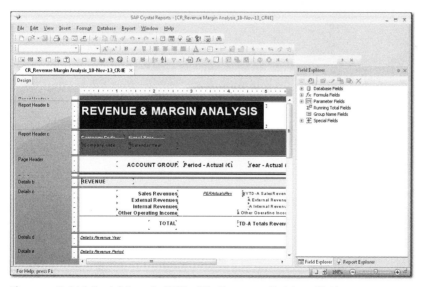

Figure 7.26 SAP Crystal Reports 2013—BEx Query as a Database Field

Connecting the
database

To connect a new database, for example, a BEx query, choose DATABASE
• DATABASE EXPERT. The DATABASE EXPERT is where you can select the
database, in this case an SAP BW system, and the associated BEx query
(see Figure 7.27). The characteristics and key figures of the BEx query
are then available as database fields. In SAP Crystal Reports 2013, you
cannot edit the initial drill-down of the BEx query flexibly as in SAP
Crystal Reports for Enterprise.

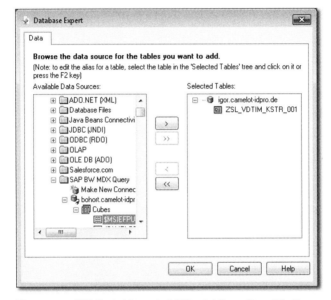

Figure 7.27 SAP Crystal Reports 2013—Adding a New BEx Query

In SAP Crystal Reports 2013, you can access SAP HANA views via ODBC
and thus SQL statements. For this purpose, you must first install the
ODBC driver for SAP HANA. You can then access the SAP HANA database via the ODBC (RDO) entry.

SAP BusinessObjects Web Intelligence

SAP Business-
Objects Web
Intelligence

SAP BusinessObjects Web Intelligence is a client tool for the interactive
analysis of primarily relational data. SAP BusinessObjects Web Intelligence is delivered in two variants: On one hand, a web variant is available that is fully integrated with the BI Launch Pad. You can use it to
generate documents online that are stored directly in the SAP Business-
Objects BI platform. On the other hand, you can use the client variant

SAP BusinessObjects Web Intelligence Rich Client. By means of this client variant, you can also utilize Microsoft Excel spreadsheets for interactive analysis, for example.

The typical user of SAP BusinessObjects Web Intelligence is a business analyst that creates analyses independently and, to a limited extent, the information consumer that uses the previously created analyses. You require little technical expertise to create interactive analyses based on different data sources. The analysis of data is supported by the existing functions of SAP BusinessObjects Web Intelligence so that inexperienced users can quickly create analyses of their data.

SAP BusinessObjects Web Intelligence 4.x can also access SAP BW as a data source. However, you must consider that SAP BusinessObjects Web Intelligence is not an OLAP tool for analyzing multi-dimensional data. Although hierarchical presentations of characteristics are also supported, the functions are still aligned with relational data.

BEx queries are accessed via the BICS interface. When you create a new Web Intelligence document, you can select a BEx query as the data source (see Figure 7.28).

Accessing BEx queries

Figure 7.28 SAP BusinessObjects Web Intelligence—BEx Query as the Data Source

After you've selected an OLAP connection, you can then choose the BEx query that is supposed to be used as the basis for the Web Intelligence document (see Figure 7.29).

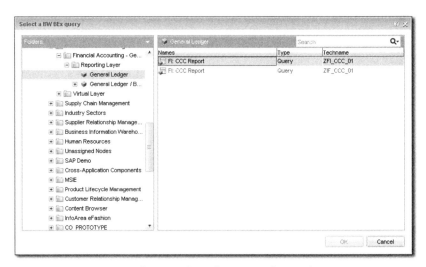

Figure 7.29 SAP BusinessObjects Web Intelligence—Selecting the BEx Query

Query Panel

Like for SAP Crystal Reports for Enterprise, the QUERY PANEL for editing the query is displayed after you've selected the BEx query (see Figure 7.30). Here, you define the characteristics and key figures from the BEx query that are supposed to be used for the query. Additionally, you can define further query filters. Click CLOSE • APPLY CHANGES AND CLOSE, the query is copied to the Web Intelligence document, and you can start designing the document using tables and diagrams.

Accessing SAP HANA views

Access to SAP HANA views is somewhat more difficult because no direct interface exists to SAP HANA; consequently, an OLAP connection of the SAP HANA type cannot be used. To access SAP HANA, you must make a detour via a universe. For this purpose, you must create a universe based on the SAP HANA view using the information design tool and integrate this universe with SAP BusinessObjects Web Intelligence. We won't discuss this procedure here because it requires an additional semantic layer (universe) and may also decrease the performance of SAP HANA due to the additional layer.

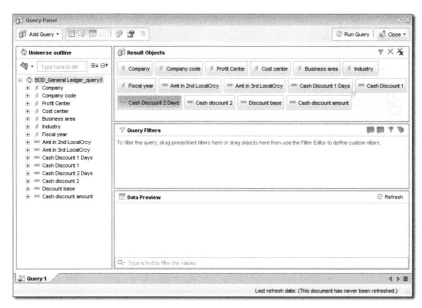

Figure 7.30 SAP BusinessObjects Web Intelligence—Editing the Query

Dashboards and Apps Category

SAP provides SAP BusinessObjects Design Studio and SAP Business-Objects Dashboards to support you in the creation of your own dashboards.

SAP BusinessObjects Design Studio

Within the SAP BusinessObjects BI suite, SAP BusinessObjects Design Studio is positioned as a tool with which you can create dashboards and BI applications. SAP BusinessObjects Design Studio applications are created using a client that you must install independently of the SAP BusinessObjects BI platform. The basis of the client is similar to that of SAP HANA Studio (see Chapter 6) and the SAP BW modeling tool in Eclipse (see Chapter 5, Section 5.2). The output format of an SAP BusinessObjects Design Studio application is HTML5; this ensures that the created application can be displayed without any problems on both the desktop and mobile devices, so you don't need to create applications for mobile devices and desktops separately.

SAP Business-Objects Design Studio

Besides SAP BW, SAP BusinessObjects Design Studio also supports the following additional data sources:

► SAP BW: InfoProvider, BEx queries, and BEx query views

► SAP HANA: calculation and analytic views

► UNX universes

Adding a data source
This also allows for applications that are based on both a BEx query and an SAP HANA analytics view. In SAP BusinessObjects Design Studio, you access a data source by adding it directly to the application (see Figure 7.31).

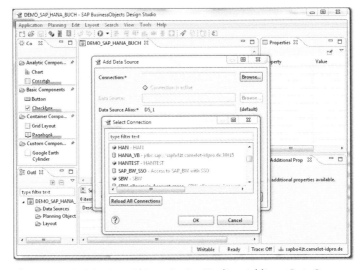

Figure 7.31 SAP BusinessObjects Design Studio—Adding a Data Source

In the SELECT CONNECTION screen, you can select both SAP BW and SAP HANA systems. After you've selected a connection and the associated BEx query or SAP HANA view, you can edit the initial view. SAP BusinessObjects Design Studio thus enables you to adapt the BEx query, SAP HANA view, or universe according to your requirements. You can define which characteristics/key figures are to be displayed in the COLUMNS or ROWS. You can also specify additional filters (BACKGROUND FILTER) or activate/deactivate hierarchies. Furthermore, under GLOBAL DATA SOURCE SETTINGS, you can adapt the settings for displaying negative values and zero values (see Figure 7.32 for the BEx query).

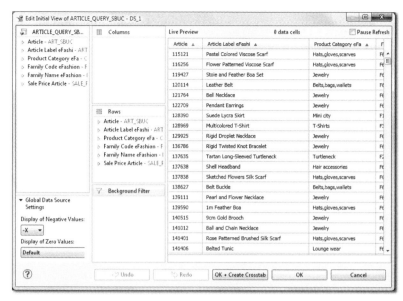

Figure 7.32 SAP BusinessObjects Design Studio—Editing Initial Views of a BEx Query

Figure 7.33 shows the setting options for an SAP HANA view.

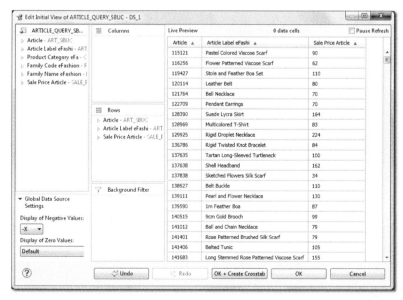

Figure 7.33 SAP BusinessObjects Design Studio—Editing Initial Views of an SAP HANA View

Components in
SAP BusinessObjects
Design Studio

After you've edited the data source, you can use the components in SAP BusinessObjects Design Studio to create an application (see Figure 7.34, left side). Components include, among other things, analytic components such as tables or charts. For you to provide these components with data, the components are connected with the data sources. For this purpose, select the corresponding DATA SOURCE under DATA BINDING in the PROPERTIES of the component (see Figure 7.34, right side). Once the connection is established, the system displays the result in the middle of the screen in the form of a table (see Figure 7.34, center). By double-clicking the ○ ▾ button, you can execute the created application locally or via the SAP BusinessObjects BI platform.

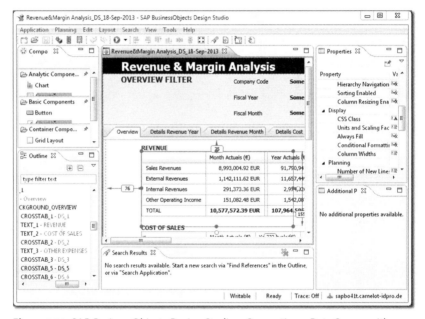

Figure 7.34 SAP BusinessObjects Design Studio—Connecting a Data Source with a Component

You can use SAP BusinessObjects Design Studio as an input option for BI-Integrated Planning. In SAP BusinessObjects Design Studio, you can integrate planning functions using the PLANNING menu item.

SAP BusinessObjects Dashboards

SAP BusinessObjects Dashboards is the new name for SAP Business-Objects Xcelsius. Typically consumers of dashboards include information consumers and managers who want to consume data in a plainly formatted and appealing form. Additionally, simple simulations like what-if analyses should be possible. Dashboards are created by the IT department or power users and provided to a large group of users.

SAP BusinessObjects Dashboards enables you to access BEx queries directly, and it was one of the first SAP BusinessObjects tools that used the BICS interface for this purpose. The major innovation of the latest version of SAP BusinessObjects Dashboards is a more direct integration with universes and BEx queries, which no longer requires the use of Excel spreadsheets, which has been a major criterion so far. This is made possible through the Query Browser that is similar to the initial view in SAP BusinessObjects Design Studio. Here you can select a BEx query or universe and model a query according to the dashboard's requirements (see Figure 7.35).

SAP Business-Objects Dashboards

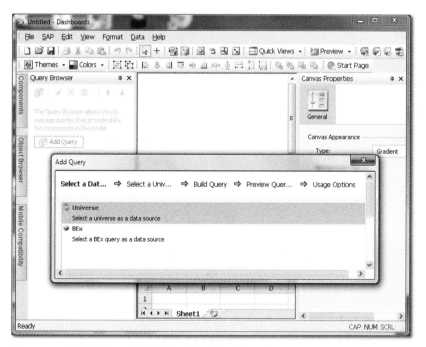

Figure 7.35 SAP BusinessObjects Dashboards—Query Browser

After you've selected a BEx query as the data source, you must initially choose the SAP BW system (see Figure 7.36). Because the SAP BW system is still the central system for access in an SAP BW on SAP HANA scenario, you can also use BEx queries that belong to an SAP BW on SAP HANA system. By contrast, you can utilize SAP HANA views via a universe only, analogous to SAP BusinessObjects Web Intelligence.

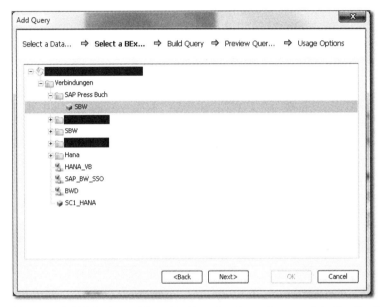

Figure 7.36 SAP BusinessObjects Dashboards—Query Browser: Selecting the System

After you've selected the system, choose the desired BEx query (see Figure 7.37).

Figure 7.37 SAP BusinessObjects Web Intelligence—Query Browser: Selecting the BEx Query

You can then adapt the query to the requirements in your dashboard (see Figure 7.38). However, you have fewer setting options than in SAP BusinessObjects Design Studio. Moreover, the displayed query is a flat table, rather than a multi-dimensional analysis as provided SAP BusinessObjects Design Studio.

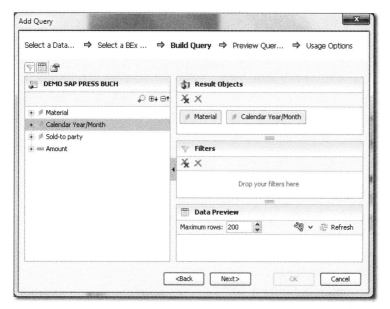

Figure 7.38 SAP BusinessObjects Dashboards—Creating the Query in the Query Browser

After you've successfully created the query, you can directly deploy it using the components of SAP BusinessObjects Dashboard, similarly to data binding in SAP BusinessObjects Design Studio. In a component's properties, you can choose the query that is to be used with this component. Select the query data as the data source for this purpose (see Figure 7.39).

After you've clicked QUERY DATA, you must select the query (in this example, QUERY 1) and the AMOUNT result objects that are to be displayed in the component (see Figure 7.40).

Selecting a query

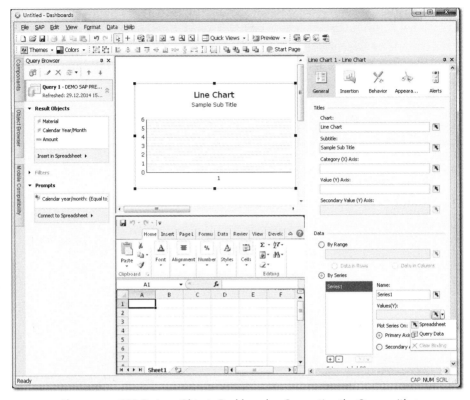

Figure 7.39 SAP BusinessObjects Dashboards—Connecting the Query with a Component

Figure 7.40 SAP BusinessObjects Dashboards—Selecting from the Query

When you click OK, the connection is established between the component and the query, and the data is displayed directly in the component (see Figure 7.41). In this example, the line chart displays the query values.

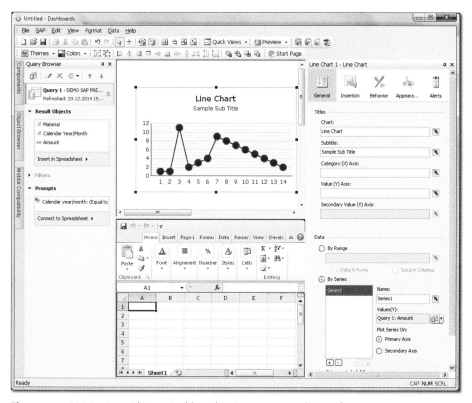

Figure 7.41 SAP BusinessObjects Dashboards—Component with Data from a Query

Self-Service Category

SAP provides various client tools in the self-service area, and we describe here how to set them up. We also discuss the advantages and disadvantages of these tools.

SAP BusinessObjects Analysis, Edition for Microsoft Office

SAP BusinessObjects Analysis, edition for Microsoft Office is the premium variant of the BEx Analyzer. Compared with the BEx Analyzer, the edition for Microsoft Office provides the following benefits:

- Native integration with Microsoft Excel as a ribbon
- Usage of Microsoft Excel functions for calculations
- Full integration with Microsoft Excel through, for example direct link to Microsoft Excel diagrams
- Support of Microsoft PowerPoint

Target group The target group of the Microsoft Office edition of SAP BusinessObjects Analysis includes primarily data analysts that want to perform an OLAP analysis on multi-dimensional data. Information consumers can also use the created Excel workbooks or PowerPoint presentations for ad hoc OLAP analysis. In particular, in Microsoft PowerPoint, you can create presentations on SAP BW and SAP HANA data that accesses live data.

With SAP BusinessObjects Analysis, edition for Microsoft Office, all functions of the BEx Analyzer are available. Additionally, the *Design Panel* was introduced as the most critical innovation that permits, like a query view, ad hoc change of the underlying query. Currently, you can use SAP BW and SAP HANA as the data source.

You can access a BEx query or SAP HANA view by clicking the 🏆 button. You must then select a data source—the SAP BW system or SAP HANA (see Figure 7.42).

Figure 7.42 SAP BusinessObjects Analysis, Edition for Microsoft Office—Selecting the Data Source

After you've selected the data source, you can choose the BEx query or SAP HANA view that should be displayed in Excel (see Figure 7.43).

Figure 7.43 SAP BusinessObjects Analysis, Edition for Office—
Selecting the Data Source: BEx Query

A BEx query is selected in Figure 7.43, but the same procedure also applies to SAP HANA views. After you've clicked OK, the BEx query or SAP HANA view is displayed in the Excel sheet (see Figure 7.44).

You can drag-and-drop in the Design Panel (see Figure 7.44, right side) to adapt the analysis flexibly to the user's requirements.

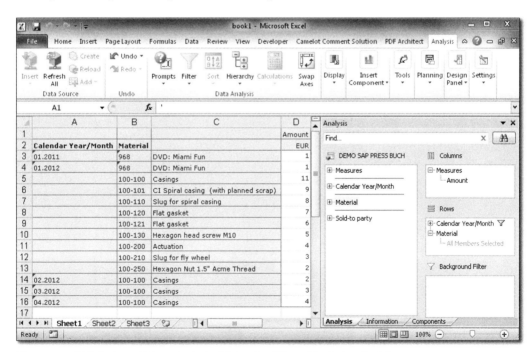

Figure 7.44 SAP BusinessObjects Analysis, Edition for Office—Displaying the BEx Query in Excel

BI-Integrated Planning   You can use SAP BusinessObjects Analysis as an input option for BI-Integrated Planning, as well. By means of integrated application programming interfaces, you can also use the SAP BusinessObjects Analysis functionality automatically via Visual Basic Script. This allows you to implement complex requirements in Microsoft Excel and Microsoft PowerPoint using the data from SAP BW or SAP HANA.

SAP BusinessObjects Analysis, Edition for OLAP

Target group of the edition for OLAP   The second product under the name SAP BusinessObjects Analysis is *SAP BusinessObjects Analysis, edition for OLAP*. The target group includes primarily business analysts that want to use an OLAP client to run complex analyses of data from an OLAP data source. You can create ad-hoc reports for analyzing data and browse the data using slice-and-dice. You have access to BEx queries and SAP HANA views, too, with SAP BusinessObjects Analysis for OLAP.

Selecting a data source   Immediately when you start the application, you must select a data source that is used as the basis of your analysis (see Figure 7.45).

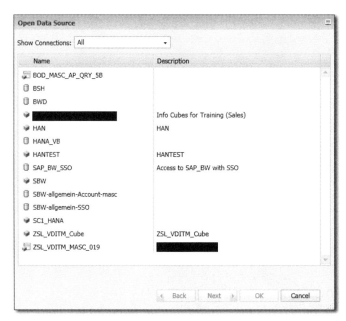

Figure 7.45 SAP BusinessObjects Analysis, Edition for OLAP—Selecting the Data Source

After you've selected the data source and the associated BEx query or SAP HANA view, you can run your analysis via drag-and-drop. In Figure 7.46, the analysis was created based on an SAP HANA view. The characteristics or key figures were dragged from the DATA area to the analysis area. The analysis result is updated according to your selection.

Creating an analysis

As shown here, SAP BusinessObjects Analysis, edition for OLAP is optimized for the interactive analysis using limited layout and formatting options. For this purpose, you are provided with options for creating exceptions and conditions; additionally, you can insert simple and dynamic calculations.

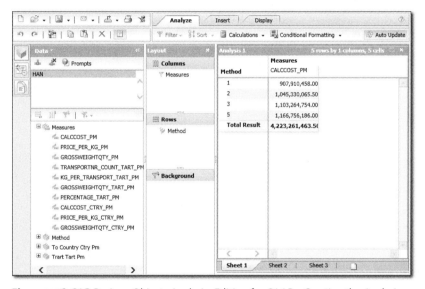

Figure 7.46 SAP BusinessObjects Analysis, Edition for OLAP—Creating the Analysis

If you insert a chart to the analysis of data, you can choose from the standard chart types of the SAP BusinessObjects BI platform. If a table and a chart are connected with the same data source, changing the drill-down in a table also changes the chart. If a lot of data is displayed in a chart, a miniature of the entire chart is displayed above the actual chart. The chart then shows parts of the analyzed data.

Charts

SAP BusinessObjects Explorer

SAP Business-
Objects Explorer

SAP BusinessObjects Explorer is a web-based solution to browse large amounts of data quickly and easily. This supports the decision-making process. SAP BusinessObjects Explorer is designed in such a way that users can utilize it without special training. For this reason, it provides a Google-like search. Thanks to this simplified handling, SAP Business-Objects Explorer is particularly suited for executive managers and information consumers.

SAP BusinessObjects Explorer provides a search mask as the entry point for analyzing data. Then, the navigation is identical to the navigation on a website. The following data sources can be used here:

▸ SAP BW via SAP BW Accelerator (BWA) indexes

▸ SAP HANA

Information space

SAP BusinessObjects Explorer offers information spaces for analysis. To create a new information space, select MANAGE SPACES and then the desired SAP HANA system or BWA index (see Figure 7.47).

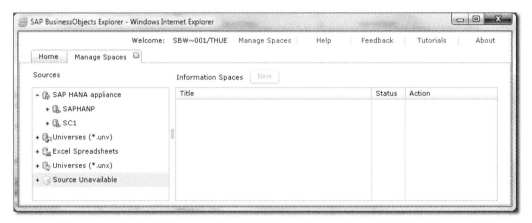

Figure 7.47 SAP BusinessObjects Explorer—Creating a New Information Space

After you've selected a data source and clicked the NEW button, you must enter additional information on the information space (see Figure 7.48).

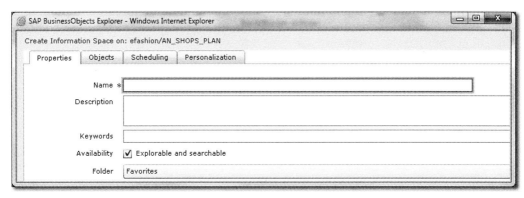

Figure 7.48 SAP BusinessObjects Explorer—Creating a New Information Space: Editing the Properties

You must specifically select the characteristics and key figures to be used (see Figure 7.49). Don't be confused: in SAP BusinessObjects Explorer terminology, characteristics are referred to as FACETS.

Selecting characteristics and key figures

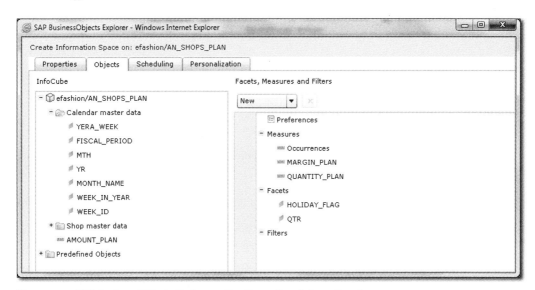

Figure 7.49 SAP BusinessObjects Explorer—Creating a New Information Space: Objects

After you've finished the creation of the information space, you must index the information space by clicking on the INDEX NOW button. You can then use the information space for analysis (see Figure 7.50).

Index and analysis

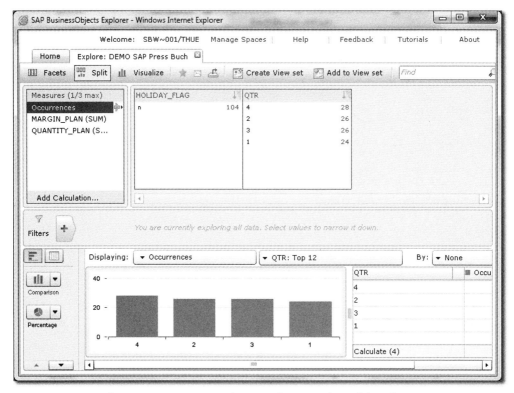

Figure 7.50 SAP BusinessObjects Explorer—Analysis of the Information Space

Besides the interactive analysis of data, you can also create *Exploration Views* for visualizing explored data. These views consist of several graphical and/or tabular elements.

SAP Lumira

SAP Lumira is the latest member of SAP tools for analyzing data. SAP Lumira was developed in response to tools like QlikView or Tableau and was initially used in combination with SAP HANA views only. Recently, SAP Lumira can also access BEx queries. SAP Lumira is particularly useful for occasional users who want to analyze their data easily and quickly. Integration of data sources is also very easy.

Selecting a data source

You create a new analysis via DATASETS • NEW DOCUMENT. Next, select the data source. Here, you can choose between SAP HANA views (online/offline) and BEx queries, among others (see Figure 7.51).

Figure 7.51 SAP Lumira—Creation of a New Document: Selecting the Data Source

The following example uses an SAP HANA view as the data source so that you must enter the information of the desired SAP HANA system after you've clicked CONNECT TO SAP HANA (see Figure 7.52). This information includes the server, port, and user/password combination.

Entering SAP HANA information

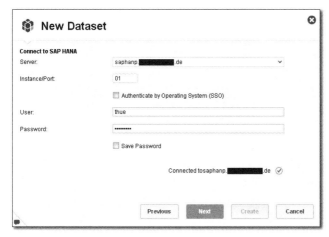

Figure 7.52 SAP Lumira—Creation of a New Document: Entering the Required Information of the Desired System

Click NEXT to go to the selection of the SAP HANA view (see Figure 7.53).

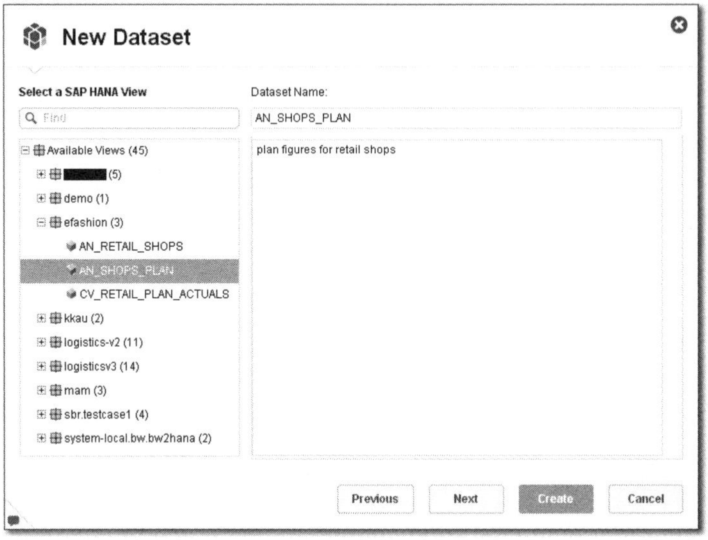

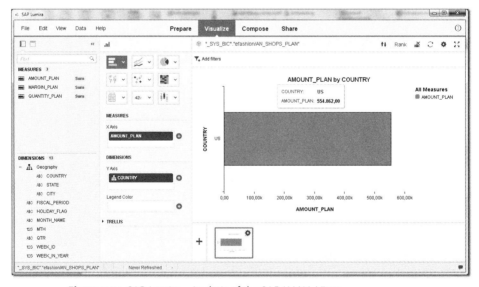

Figure 7.53 SAP Lumira—Creation of a New Document: Selecting the SAP HANA View

Creating an analysis   When you click CREATE, the data is loaded to SAP Lumira, and you can start the composition of your data analysis (see Figure 7.54).

Figure 7.54 SAP Lumira—Analysis of the SAP HANA View

As shown in Figure 7.54, you can create your analysis via drag-and-drop and also compose visualizations. When you go to the COMPOSE tab, you can create stories that combine various visualizations and other elements (for example, Microsoft PowerPoint slides; see Figure 7.55).

Creating a story

You can use the SHARE tab to store the created documents on the SAP Lumira server or in SAP Lumira cloud, for example. The SAP Lumira server and the SAP Lumira cloud are the counterparts to SAP Lumira Desktop, which is presented as the client installation here.

Figure 7.55 SAP Lumira—Creating Stories

SAP Predictive Analytics

To catch up with other providers in terms of statistical analysis of data, SAP has presented a new tool, SAP Predictive Analytics. From the technical point of view, this tool is based on SAP Lumira and thus provides the same visualization options as SAP Lumira. Additionally, statistical functions can be integrated on the basis of the R language. Because the presentation of options in SAP Predictive Analytics would go far beyond the scope of this book due to their complexity, it is not further discussed here. Please refer to the literature specializing in SAP Predictive Analytics (see John MacGregor, *Predictive Analysis with SAP: The Comprehensive Guide*, SAP PRESS, 2013).

7.2.3 Summary for Reporting Using SAP BW on SAP HANA

No changes in reporting caused by SAP BW on SAP HANA

As outlined in this chapter, reporting hasn't change with SAP BW on SAP HANA because BEx queries can still used as the data source in reporting tools. Only the execution time of BEx queries improves considerably when SAP BW on SAP HANA is used. Except for SAP HANA views, no new features are available in reporting.

However, if you also deploy scenarios in addition to SAP BW InfoProviders that also use SAP HANA views (calculation or analytic views), you can still utilize all reporting tools presented here. As discussed, most reporting tools can access SAP HANA directly—SAP Crystal Reports for Enterprise, SAP BusinessObjects Design Studio, SAP BusinessObjects Analysis (edition for Office and edition for OLAP), SAP BusinessObjects Explorer, SAP Lumira, and SAP Predictive Analytics. Other tools require "detours" via universes—SAP BusinessObjects Web Intelligence and SAP BusinessObjects Dashboards.

Focus on few tools required

From this perspective, all reporting tools can also be used in these scenarios, in principle. But, because you surely don't want to use all tools, you should focus on the tools that provide you with the best advantages for SAP BW on SAP HANA. Experience has shown that these tools include SAP Crystal Reports for Enterprise, SAP BusinessObjects Design Studio, and SAP BusinessObjects Analysis, edition for Office. SAP Lumira is useful only if you set great value on department-specific reporting that is to be created independently by the user departments. With these reporting tools, you are optimally geared for both worlds—SAP BW on SAP HANA and pure SAP HANA scenarios.

Nearline storage occurs for data archiving. For SAP BW, using nearline storage is particularly worthwhile because reporting also works for archived data records. In combination with SAP BW on SAP HANA, you can also optimize the memory utilization.

8   Nearline Storage for SAP BW on SAP HANA

Nearline storage (NLS) is used to archive data that is required only in very rare cases. For an SAP BW system, you can, for example, transfer selected data records of an InfoProvider to an archiving system in a targeted manner. If you use the SAP-specific archiving solution on the basis of the SAP IQ database (previously SAP Sybase IQ), the data is available online for reporting despite archiving. This is a significant advantage compared to classic archiving approaches in which archived data must be returned to the SAP BW system for evaluation. In the SAP BW system, you can thus also map archived and non-archived data jointly in one report. However, the data that was outsourced to an NLS system can no longer be modified. Figure 8.1 outlines the data retention of SAP BW on SAP HANA when using an NLS solution.

NLS system

The SAP BW system accesses non-archived data via the database interface (DBSL) directly on the SAP HANA database. In the case of archived data, the data is accessed via the NLS interface. Here, you must generally differentiate whether you want to deploy the SAP-specific NLS solution (SAP IQ) or a certified partner solution, for example, from PBS Software, SAND Technology, or FileTek.

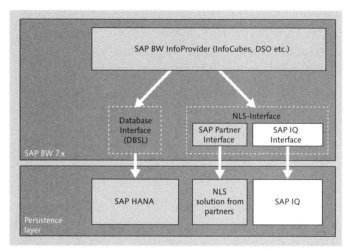

Figure 8.1 Data Retention in SAP BW on SAP HANA When Using an NLS Solution

Example

Let's consider a simple example. Specific key figures are retained in an Info-Cube for the years 2005 through 2015. Because older data up until 2010 is hardly ever used for evaluations, it is to be archived. In the SAP BW system, you only need to do a few mouse clicks to trigger an archiving process that transfers the data from the InfoCube to the NLS system. After the transfer is complete, the data from 2005 until 2010 is no longer present in the SAP BW system. BEx queries can still access the archived data. If you execute a query and select the period 2005 through 2015, the system reads the archived data from the NLS system and the non-archived data from the SAP BW system. The data is displayed jointly in one report, and the user cannot determine whether the data is retained in the NLS or SAP BW system. Only the access time will increase slightly when accessing archived data.

Benefits of an NLS system for SAP BW on SAP HANA Virtually all data is retained in the main memory under SAP BW on SAP HANA. If data is continuously growing, you must take appropriate countermeasures so that the available main memory is not fully utilized sooner or later. Periodic cleanup activities (see Chapter 3, Section 3.3.2) will not prevent this, but only delay it at best. Instead, you must deal with the extension of the system capacities (see Chapter 2, Section 2.1.3) or a data reorganization in the medium term. An effective possibility for mastering the increasing amount of data is to archive it using an NLS system. Archived data is no longer retained in the main memory. Because in the NLS system the data is stored in a column basis like in SAP HANA, it is possible to access this data quickly. However, you cannot reach the high access times of SAP HANA. Because you primarily archive data that is required for reporting very rarely, higher access times are acceptable in most cases. In reality, it is more important to have the data available for reporting immediately without having to import data archives back.

For a better overview, we have gathered the most important information material on NLS in the box below. In the following, we'll discuss how you can use the SAP-specific archiving solution based on the SAP IQ database for your SAP BW on SAP HANA system. For this purpose, we first describe how you can integrate an NLS system with your SAP BW system. We then outline the archiving of SAP BW data based on a holistic example.

Information material and structure of this chapter

Additional Information

For additional information, refer to the following sources:

▶ SAP First Guidance—SAP-NLS Solution with SAP IQ:
http://scn.sap.com/docs/DOC-39627

▶ Online help of SAP IQ 16.0 SP04:
http://infocenter.sybase.com/help/index.jsp • SAP Sʏʙᴀsᴇ IQ 16.0 SP04

▶ SAP Help Portal—Configuring SAP IQ as a nearline storage solution:
https://help.sap.com/saphelp_nw73/helpdata/en/e8/395401e46f4ed-ca50aefeead7f3a44/frameset.htm

▶ SAP Help Portal—Creating a data archiving process:
http://help.sap.com/saphelp_nw73ehp1/helpdata/en/4c/75184b167821d1e10000000a42189c/frameset.htm

▶ SAP IQ—Downloading a free evaluation version:
http://global.sap.com/campaign/ne/sybase/iq_16_free_trial_download/index.epx

▶ Documents for introducing SAP IQ:
http://global.sap.com/campaign/ne/sybase/iq_16_free_trial_download/iq_quick_start_guide.epx

▶ SCN overview page for SAP BW NLS with SAP IQ:
http://scn.sap.com/docs/DOC-39944

▶ SAP how-to guide "How to Archive Data from SAP NetWeaver BW to SAP IQ as Near line Storage":
http://scn.sap.com/docs/DOC-54510

8.1   Connecting the Nearline Storage System with SAP BW

Even though we cannot discuss the installation of an NLS system within the scope of this book, we want to briefly outline how you can connect an existing NLS system with your SAP BW or SAP BW on SAP HANA system. You can find information on how to install an NLS system in the document "SAP First Guidance—SAP-NLS Solution with IQ" (see the "Additional Information" box). This chapter describes the procedure based on an SAP BW on SAP HANA system with SAP BW 7.4 SPS06 and an SAP IQ database version 16.5, which is used as an NLS system.

Driver

Initially, archiving SAP BW data requires a driver that permits access from the SAP BW system to the SAP IQ database. For this reason, you should first check whether the *lib_dbsl for SAP IQ* is already installed on the application server of your SAP BW system. Take a look at the instance directory of your SAP BW application server where the executable files are located (for example, */usr/sap/<SID>/DVEBMGS00/exe*). Find out whether the file *dbsybslib.so* or *dbsybslib.dll* is available there. This should already be the case for current systems. Depending on the version used, an installation or update may be required. You can download the driver from the SAP Service Marketplace as part of the SAP kernel. SAP Note 1737415 provides more detailed information. Also note that you may need to restart the application server after you've installed the driver.

DBCO connection

Next, you must set up the *database connection* (*DBCO*) to be able to access the SAP IQ database from the SAP BW system. You set up the necessary DBCO connection using Transaction DBCO. In the input mask, which is shown in Figure 8.2, you must specify the database ID, user and password information, and additional connection parameters. The general format for entering this information is `Key-1=<Value-1> Key-2=<Value-2> ... Key-n=<Value-n>`. When you do this, you must enter the values for the `SYBASE_SERVER`, `SYBASE_PORT`, `SYBASE_IQ_ENGINE`, `SYBASE_DBNAME`, `SYBASE_CONTYPE` keys. The following list provides an overview of the key-value pairs we've used for successfully establishing the DBCO connection:

- ► `SYBASE_SERVER= <server>.<domain>.<extension>`

- ► `SYBASE_PORT=<port>`, for example, `2641`

- ► `SYBASE_IQ_ENGINE=<NLS server>`, for example, `SAPIQDB`

- ► `SYBASE_DBNAME=<database>`, for example, `SAPIQDB`

- ► `SYBASE_CONTYPE=IQ`

- ► `SYBASE_IQ_LOAD=1`

- ► `SYBASE_IQ_CESU-8=1`

- ► `SYBASE_IQ_BUFFER_SIZE=500000`

- ► `SYBASE_IQ_LOCKWAIT=600`

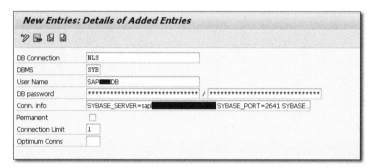

Figure 8.2 Creating a DBCO Connection

After you've saved the DBCO information, you should determine whether the connection can be established between the SAP BW application server and the NLS system. For this purpose, execute the `ADBC_TEST_CONNECTION` ABAP report using Transaction SE38. Enter the previously defined name in the DB CONNECTION NAME field (see Figure 8.3).

Testing the connection

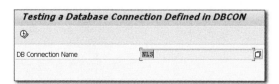

Figure 8.3 Testing the DBCO Connection

Figure 8.4 shows the report after the DBCO connection has been established successfully.

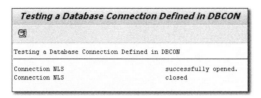

Figure 8.4 Result of the DBCON Connection Test

Activating archiving

Because the database access to the SAP IQ database works in principle, you must inform the SAP BW system that this connection is to be used for archiving SAP BW data. To do so, call Transaction RSDANLCON, where you can define the archiving based on the previously created DBCO connection. Figure 8.5 shows the input mask of this transaction. Specify a name for NEAR-LINE CONN. (in our example, SYB_NLS). Next, enter the technical name CL_RSDA_SYB_CONNECTION under NAME OF CLASS. Now select the DBCO connection that you've just created in the DB CONNECTION field. If you entered all information correctly, the STATUS under DIAGNOSIS is displayed as a green traffic light icon. The NLS system is now available for archiving your SAP BW data.

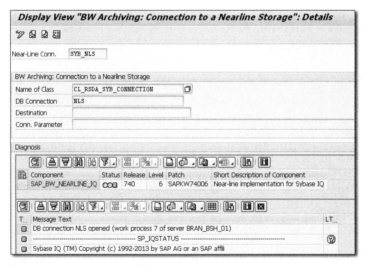

Figure 8.5 Setting Up the SAP BW Archiving

The next section teaches you how to archive data and how to access the outsourced data for reporting.

8.2   Data Archiving

To illustrate the subsequent procedure for data archiving, we'll use a   Example
holistic example in this section. For this purpose, we've loaded 10 million data records in a DSO (ZMATDOC2). The data refers to the years 2010,
2011, and 2012. For the sake of simplicity, the quantity is used as a key
figure only (0Quantity). We also created a BEx query to output the data
of the DSO in an aggregated form. The report is structured in such a way
that the quantity is listed in a separate column for each year. In the further course of this example, we'll then archive the data from the year
2010 and show you how this changes the output of the BEx query.
Finally, you'll learn what you can do to recover the original view.

Before you can archive data records, you must first create an archiving   Archiving process
process for the InfoProvider in question. To do so, select an InfoProvider in the INFOPROVIDER view of Transaction RSA1 and right-click it.
Then, choose START ARCHIVING PROCESS. This takes you to an input
mask, as shown in Figure 8.6. In this mask, do not activate ADK-BASED
ARCHIVING; choose the connection you've previously created under
NEAR-LINE CONNECTION (see Section 8.1).

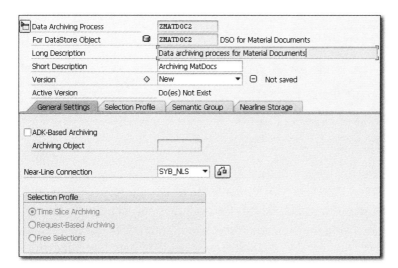

Figure 8.6 Creating an Archiving Process (Part 1)

Defining further properties

Next, go to the SELECTION PROFILE tab (see Figure 8.7). Here, you must select the characteristic for the time slice to define which InfoObject archiving uses for chronological orientation. In our DSO, only one time characteristic (InfoObject OOI_BUDAT) exists that corresponds to the posting date in the document. In principle, you can also define further partitioning objects in addition to the time characteristic, but we will omit them in this example. On the SEMANTIC GROUP tab, you can optionally define a semantic group. On the NEARLINE STORAGE tab, you also have the option to restrict the size of the data package and the maximum number of data objects. By clicking on the ⬚ button, you can test the NLS connection via this screen.

Figure 8.7 Creating an Archiving Process (Part 2)

Test query

Before we archive the first data records, we'd like to present our test query. Figure 8.8 shows the output of the test query. Note column 2010, which presents the quantities for the year 2010 sorted by plant. For testing the archiving function, you can create a simple BEx query using the BEx Query Designer. For the first test case, select an InfoProvider whose data you don't need in live operation. You can then run your test query using Transaction RSRT.

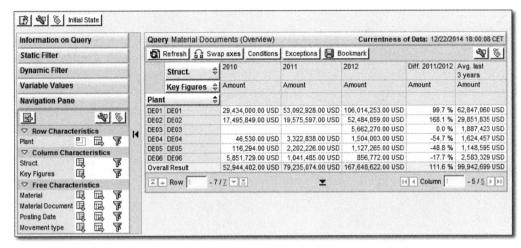

Figure 8.8 Running the Test Query Before Data Archiving

In the next step, you'll archive all data records of a DSO for the year 2010 and move them to the NLS system. For this purpose, you must create an activation request, as shown in Figure 8.9. A prerequisite for this step is that you've created an archiving process. You must define a selection condition in this screen. All data records that meet your selection are then archived. You can enter relative or absolute values. *Relative* means that the execution refers to the current date and collects all data records that are older than one year. For absolute values, by contrast, you define the selection specifically. We'll use exactly this option for our example. All data up to 12/31/2010 is to be archived later. We "generously" set the field of the start date to 01/01/1000. Because we only have data records from 2010 through 2012 in our DSO, 01/01/2010 would have been sufficient as the start date.

Creating an archiving request

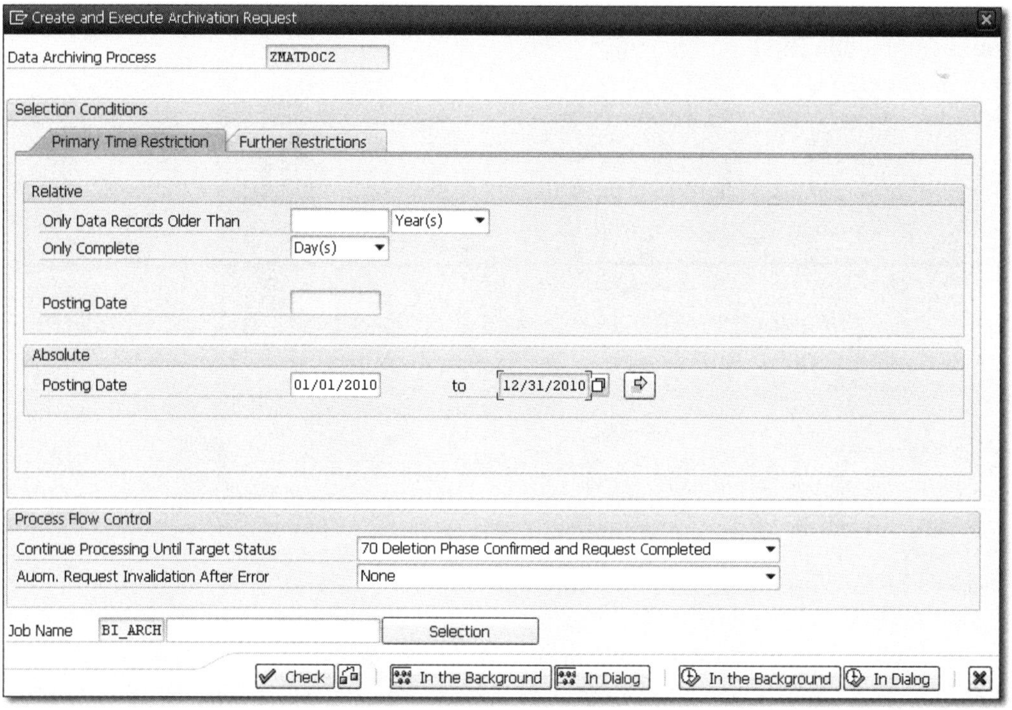

Figure 8.9 Create and Execute Archivation Request

Executing an archivation request — If you now click the IN THE BACKGROUND button, the system schedules and executes an appropriate background job. You can monitor this process using Transaction SM37, for example (see Figure 8.10).

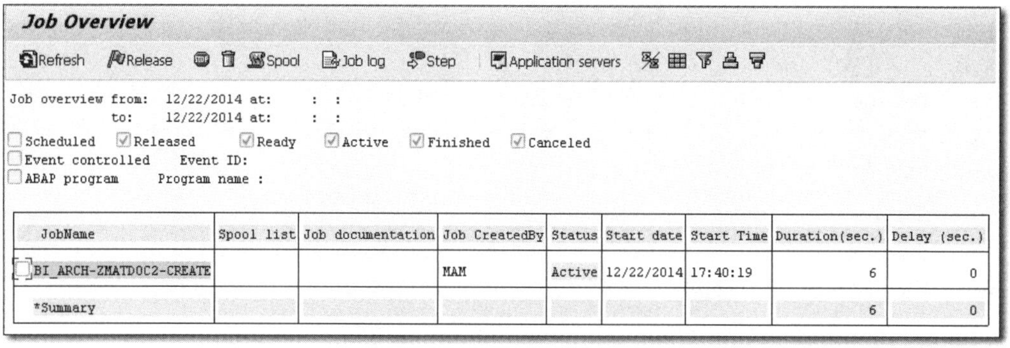

Figure 8.10 Archiving Process Running

If you want to ensure that SAP BW data is archived on a regular basis, you can extend existing process chains or create new ones. To do this, use the ARCHIVE DATA FROM AN INFOPROVIDER process step, which you can find in the DATA TARGET ADMINISTRATION. Ideally, data is archived in three different phases. First, the data is transferred to the NLS system, then the write operation is verified, and finally the data is removed from the SAP BW system. For more information, refer to the SAP How-To Guide (see "Additional Information" box).

Controlling the archiving via a process chain

Once the archiving process is complete, you should check which data is still in the InfoProvider or whether the output of the test query differs from the previous execution. For the execution of the test query presented here, you can see that the column 2010 remains empty (Figure 8.11). All data from 2010 was archived to the NLS system and therefore no longer appears in the report. However, it is possible to adapt the configuration in such a way that data from the archiving system is also considered in the output.

Executing the test query for the second time

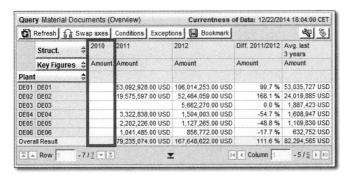

Figure 8.11 Execution of the Test Query: Column 2010 Is Empty

If you want archived data to be used for a query execution, you can define this in the properties of the InfoProvider. To do this, call the properties for the relevant InfoProvider (DSO in our example; see Figure 8.12). Select the X NEAR-LINE ACCESS SWITCHED ON option for the NLS USAGE field.

Displaying archived data

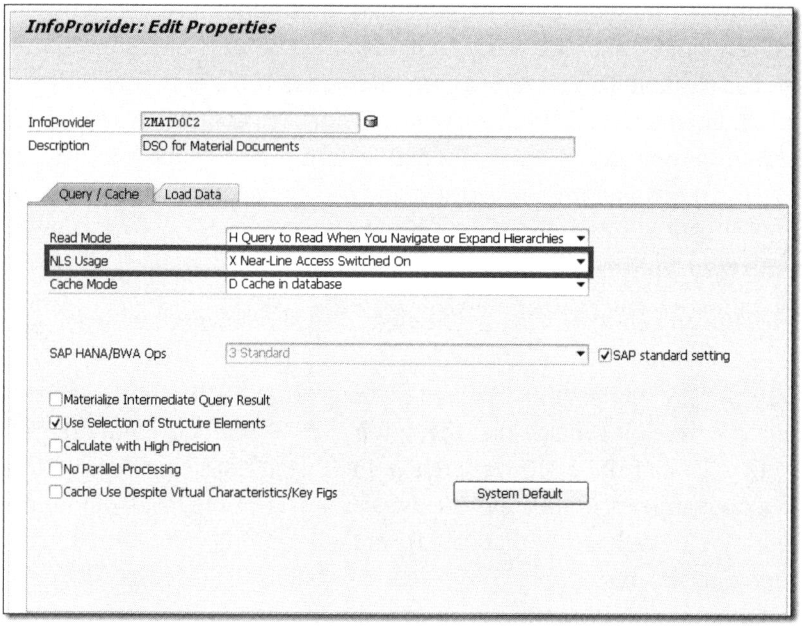

InfoProvider: Edit Properties

InfoProvider ZMATDOC2

Description   DSO for Material Documents

Query / Cache Load Data

Read Mode   H Query to Read When You Navigate or Expand Hierarchies ▼

NLS Usage   X Near-Line Access Switched On   ▼

Cache Mode   D Cache in database   ▼

SAP HANA/BWA Ops 3 Standard   ▼ ☑SAP standard setting

☐ Materialize Intermediate Query Result
☑ Use Selection of Structure Elements
☐ Calculate with High Precision
☐ No Parallel Processing
☐ Cache Use Despite Virtual Characteristics/Key Figs   System Default

Figure 8.12 Adapting the InfoProvider Properties for NLS Usage

Executing the test query for the third time Next, execute the test query once again. All data is displayed again (Figure 8.13). The system merges the data of the SAP BW and NLS system internally for this purpose. In some cases, errors may occur when you execute the query if you've changed the InfoProvider properties. You can usually remedy these errors by regenerating the relevant BEx query. To do this, call Transaction RSRT. Select your query and click GENERATE.

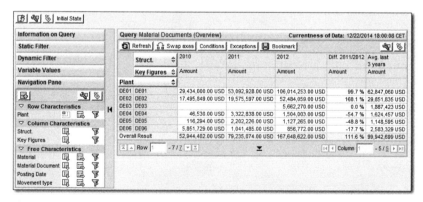

Figure 8.13 Running the Test Query after Adapting the InfoProvider Properties

To display InfoProvider data in Transaction RSA1, you also need to decide whether archived data is to be displayed. In the selection screen for data display, you can control this using the READ DATA FROM NEAR-LINE STORAGE option. In our example, we have not initially selected this option, and we have restricted the selection to the posting period from 01/01/2010 to 12/31/2010 (see Figure 8.14).

Displaying
InfoProvider data

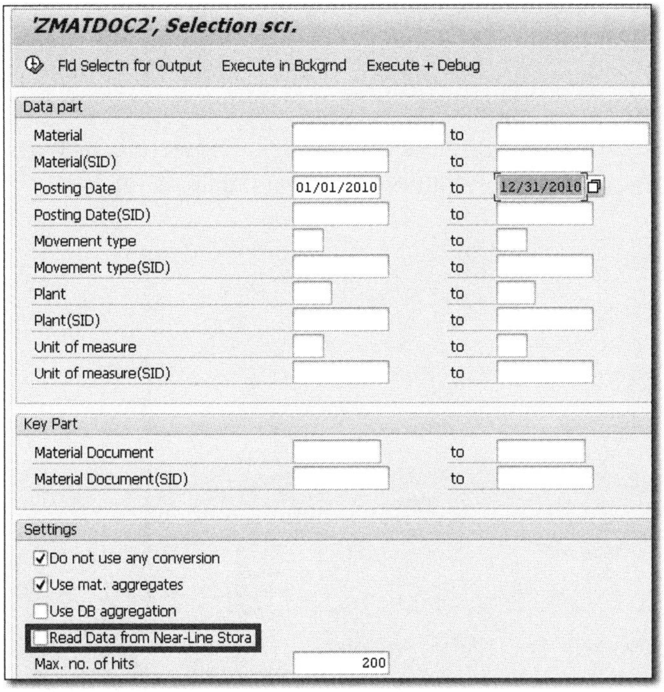

Figure 8.14 Data Display of the InfoProvider in RSA1

Because we have not selected the READ DATA FROM NEAR-LINE STORAGE option, the output remains empty (see Figure 8.15).

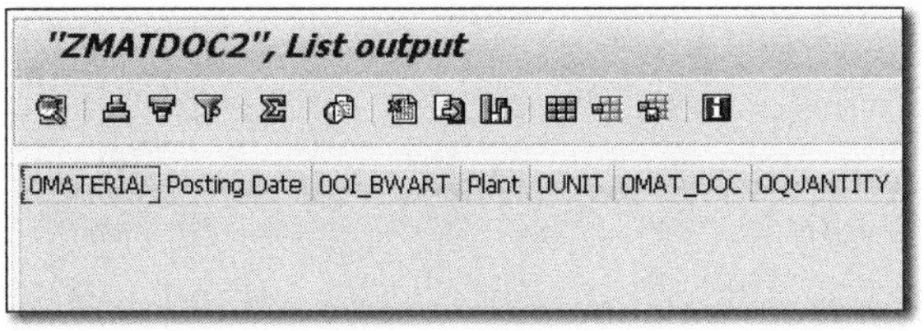

Figure 8.15 Output without Data

However, if you select this option in the selection screen (see Figure 8.16), the archived data is displayed in the output. Here again, the data from the SAP BW and NLS system is merged internally.

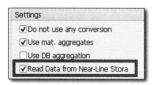

Figure 8.16 Data Selection with Read Data from Near-Line Storage

As a result, the system also displays the archived data records in Transaction RSA1 for the display of InfoProvider data (Figure 8.17).

OMATERIAL	Posting Date	OOI_BWART	OPLANT	OUNIT	OMAT_DOC	Quantity
"ZMATDOC2", List output						
000000000019370100	10/23/2010	501	DE01	ST	0017700004	18
000000000019370100	10/23/2010	501	DE01	ST	0017700009	18
000000000019370100	10/23/2010	501	DE01	ST	0017700014	18
000000000019370100	10/23/2010	501	DE01	ST	0017700019	18
000000000019370100	10/23/2010	501	DE01	ST	0017700024	18
000000000019370100	10/23/2010	501	DE01	ST	0017700029	18
000000000019370100	10/23/2010	501	DE01	ST	0017700034	18
000000000019370100	10/23/2010	501	DE01	ST	0017700039	18
000000000019370100	10/23/2010	501	DE01	ST	0017700044	18
000000000019370100	10/23/2010	501	DE01	ST	0017700049	18
000000000019370100	10/23/2010	501	DE01	ST	0017700054	18

Figure 8.17 Display of Archived Data of InfoProvider

Summary Based on our simple example, you should now understand the basic principle of data archiving with an NLS system. It should have become clear that it's up to you whether archived data is to be considered for reports and data display in Transaction RSA1. It depends on the application case whether this makes sense. Before you can archive data, you must first connect the NLS system with the SAP BW system once. You can then create an archiving process for each InfoProvider and execute one or more archivation requests. Specifically, when you use this method in combination with SAP BW on SAP HANA, deploying an NLS system is particularly useful. After all, virtually all data is retained in the main memory under SAP BW on SAP HANA. Due to the growing amount of data in SAP BW, the main memory will reach its capacity limits sooner or later if no manual intervention is taken. By archiving data that is no longer required, an NLS system can help you optimize the main memory utilization in the medium and long term. Archived data records don't occupy the main memory and are still available at any time for active reporting.

Now that we've presented the many benefits of SAP BW on SAP HANA, we'll take a look at the future of SAP BW reporting.

9 Outlook: The Future of SAP BW Reporting

For many years, enterprises have successfully deployed SAP BW for analyzing their business data. However, it has not been possible to always implement today's requirements when it comes to flexibility, real-time capability, and efficient handling of mass data in SAP BW. With the introduction of SAP BW on SAP HANA a major change was heralded in this context. Thanks to the new in-memory technology and the many other software- and hardware-specific innovations (see Chapter 1, Section 1.4), reporting scenarios can be implemented today that were inconceivable before.

For example, SAP BW on SAP HANA allows for high-performance reporting based on very detailed mass data without having to compress the data in advance. In contrast to BWA, virtually all data is retained in the main memory in SAP HANA, which accelerates all analyses and reports. Many improvements have arisen for building data flows. Chapter 5, Section 5.1 outlined that today, reporting can also be built based on DataStore objects (DSO) and that the usage of InfoCubes is optional from a performance viewpoint. The load times under SAP BW on SAP HANA are considerably faster, and many process steps in the process chains are obsolete today (see Chapter 5, Section 5.4). Ultimately, in SAP BW on SAP HANA, it has become easier to merge external data with master or transaction data in SAP BW and evaluate the data jointly. By consuming SAP HANA data models in SAP BW, you can not only combine current data with historic data of SAP BW, but also implement real-time scenarios. Additionally, experience from practical use has proven that the deployment of SAP BW on SAP HANA (if it is planed correctly

Changes triggered by SAP HANA

and migration is implemented carefully) is ideally suited for productive use today. Altogether, these are very good reasons that speak in favor of SAP BW on SAP HANA.

Strengths and weaknesses

Nevertheless, some critics won't stop talking about the fall of SAP BW. They already see the end of classic SAP BW reporting coming with the introduction of SAP HANA. An occasional position is that the deployment of an SAP BW system could become obsolete in light of the SAP HANA-specific reporting options. But because we as the authors don't hold this view, we'd like to illustrate the strengths and weaknesses of these SAP HANA-specific reporting options in more detail. Finally, this chapter outlines the reasons why the deployment of SAP BW is not only justified in future, but also mandatory for most enterprises.

9.1   SAP HANA Live for Operational Reporting

Operational analytics

Chapter 1, Section 1.1.2 briefly outlines the options of SAP HANA for implementing operational reporting approaches. The major benefit of this approach is that you don't require any SAP HANA system for creating reports and executing analyses. Instead, you create data models (SAP HANA views) in SAP HANA Studio via which specific analysis tools of the SAP BusinessObjects product portfolio—for example, SAP Lumira—have direct access to the data of the SAP HANA database. Chapter 7, Section 7.2 informs you which tools support the usage of SAP HANA views.

SAP HANA views

At the moment, you can create three different types of SAP HANA views in SAP HANA Studio: With an *attribute view*, you can model master data objects and merge master data with the associated texts from different tables, for example. In an *analytic view*, you can combine existing attribute views with a fact table, comparable with the data model of an SAP BW InfoCube. A *calculation view* is based on an analytic or another calculation view and enables you to extend it via a graphical interface or using a SQLScript. Chapter 5, Section 5.2 describes how to create such SAP HANA views yourself and how to model a calculation view. Additional information is available at *http://www.saphana.com/docs/DOC-3896*.

Analogous to *SAP BW content*, SAP HANA Live provides a *virtual data model* (VDM) that enterprises can use to implement their operational reporting (see Figure 9.1). The virtual data model consists primarily of calculation views that encapsulate the access to the underlying database tables. Users therefore don't need to know from which database tables and fields they can obtain specific information. Here, the views are assigned to different levels and partly build on one another. Predefined query views can then be used to run specific analyses.

SAP HANA Live

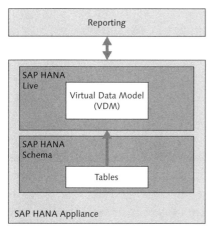

Figure 9.1 Overview of the SAP HANA Live Architecture

Depending on your license, you can also adapt or extend the SAP HANA views individually. SAP HANA Live is provided as a separate software package for various products and is available for SAP ERP on SAP HANA, SAP SCM on SAP HANA, or SAP CRM on SAP HANA, among others. Some technical objects or URLs still contain parts of the former product names *SAP HANA-Based Analytics* (HBA) or *SAP HANA Analytics Foundation* (SHAF), such as the SAP HANA Live website in the help portal, which ends with "hba" (*http://help.sap.com/hba*).

To increase the clarity of the virtual data model, SAP provides the *SAP HANA Live Browser*. This is an SAPUI5-based web application with which you can easily browse the virtual data model (see Figure 9.2). With the SAP HANA Live Browser, you can search the predefined views sorted by application components or packages.

SAP HANA Live Browser

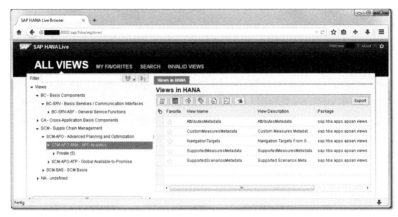

Figure 9.2 SAP HANA Live Browser—View Overview

When you click on the  icon, you can export the technical names of a view's tables that are used in the background of a text file. This is useful, for example, if you want to replicate the table contents from an SAP system to the SAP HANA database using the SAP Landscape Transformation Service (SAP LT) within the scope of a side-by-side implementation. Moreover, you can also use the SAP HANA Live Browser to graphically display dependent tables and views for a selected view (see Figure 9.3).

Figure 9.3 SAP HANA Live Browser—Graphical Display

The virtual data model of SAP HANA Live comprises numerous SAP HANA calculation views, which are assigned to different levels. The *private views* of the lowest level in the database model (see Figure 9.4) are not released for end-customer usage. Rather, these views implement the technical access to the relevant database tables. Private views form the basis of the *reuse views*, which involve reusable objects. They usually combine various private views to provide a holistic view of specific data. You can use them as the basis for creating your own query views (reports). However, it usually makes more sense to include another level with customer-specific extensions. This allows for customer-specific extension of the predefined reuse views and the addition of individual fields, for example. Based on this level, customers can then create their own query views. The query views should be the only views that are used by the analysis tools of the SAP BusinessObjects product portfolio.

Structure of the virtual data model

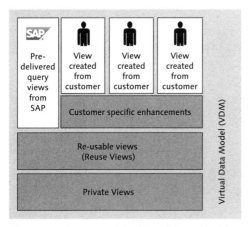

Figure 9.4 Structure of the Virtual Data Model

Two different scenarios are provided for implementing SAP HANA Live. On one hand, you can import SAP HANA Live directly into an existing SAP Business Suite system within the scope of an integrated scenario (see Figure 9.5, left-hand side). However, this requires an existing SAP ERP on SAP HANA system, for example. In this case, the components of SAP HANA Live are imported directly into the SAP HANA database of the SAP ERP on SAP HANA system. Using the analysis tools of the SAP BusinessObjects product portfolio, the virtual data model can then directly access the ERP data in the SAP HANA database. But, because not

Implementation scenarios

all customers operate their SAP Business Suite system on the basis of an SAP HANA database, a side-by-side approach is also possible (see Chapter 1, Section 1.1.1). In this case (see Figure 9.5, right-hand side), an independent SAP HANA database can be created along with an existing SAP ERP system, for example. In this case, the data of the SAP ERP system is transferred continuously to the SAP HANA database using a replication tool, such as SAP LT. Then, the SAP HANA Live components are not installed on the SAP ERP system, but on the side-by-side SAP HANA database. Reporting doesn't access the SAP ERP system, either, but this separate SAP HANA database.

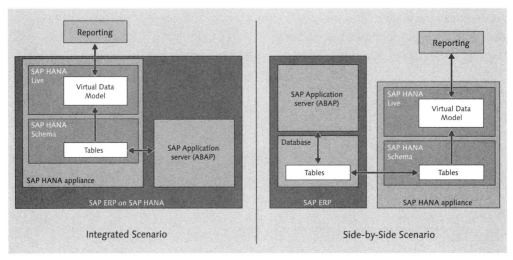

Figure 9.5 Two Implementation Scenarios for SAP HANA Live

Benefits of SAP HANA Live The primary benefit of SAP HANA Live is that you can evaluate transactional data, for example, from an SAP ERP system, in real time without requiring a data transfer to the SAP BW system. In this context, SAP HANA Live provides a comprehensive virtual data model that can easily be understood by the employees of the user departments. Predefined query views can be used immediately and extended easily (depending on the existing license). Besides the analysis tools of the SAP Business-Objects product portfolio, SAP HANA Live also supports the development of UI5 applications for mobile end devices. The usage of SAP HANA Live, without customer-specific extensions, is currently free of charge. The following sections discuss the various disadvantages of SAP HANA

Live, while also reflecting on the strengths of the SAP BW system at the same time. Further sources of information with regard to SAP HANA Live are compiled in the following box.

Information Material on SAP HANA Live
The following material provides further information on SAP HANA Live:
► SAP HANA Live FAQ: *http://www.saphana.com/docs/DOC-2923.*
► SAP HANA Live in the SAP Help Portal: *http://help.sap.com/hba*
► SAP how-to document "How to Utilize the View Browser Application Which Accompanies SAP HANA Live for SAP Business Suite": *https://scn.sap.com/docs/DOC-40300*

9.2 Reasons for SAP BW

For many years, SAP BW has formed the technological basis for building comprehensive and highly complex analysis and reporting scenarios. It comprises numerous tools and methods for merging structured and unstructured data from different sources of information. Moreover, integrated functions are available for data modeling, data retention, evaluation, planning, simulation, and monitoring. Thanks to these functions, SAP BW can be used to build cross-enterprise evaluations, analyze data of individual divisions, implement planning scenarios, and simulate envisaged decisions and business scenarios in advance. Information and knowledge can be derived in SAP BW from the data that is merged from different sources. This can form the basis for making profound business decisions. Enterprises can use SAP BW to efficiently visualize their strategies and goals. Furthermore, planned/actual deviations can be evaluated systematically, and initiated measures can be checked in terms of their effectiveness.

Benefits of SAP BW

Today, SAP BW on SAP HANA combines the comprehensive functions of SAP BW with the major speed benefits of SAP HANA. In contrast, SAP HANA Live doesn't provide comparable functions of an SAP BW system and is only used for covering operational reporting scenarios on the

SAP BW on SAP HANA vs. SAP HANA Live

433

basis of transactional data. Consequently, the differences between the two approaches are considerable. Before detailing them, let's first compare the architectural structure of the two approaches. On the right-hand side of Figure 9.6, you can see the structure of SAP HANA Live for the integrated scenario. In this approach, SAP HANA Live is imported directly into the SAP HANA database of the SAP ERP on SAP HANA system. The reporting is made via direct access from the corresponding analysis tools to the SAP HANA views (virtual data model) in the SAP HANA database. In comparison, SAP BW on SAP HANA is a separate system from which you can extract the data from different source systems, for example, SAP ERP or SAP SCM. SAP BW reports don't directly access the raw data, but formatted data via SAP BW modeling objects.

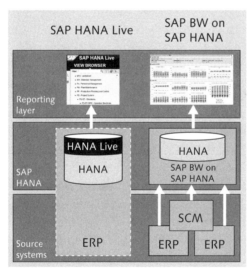

Figure 9.6 Architectural Differences of SAP HANA Live and SAP BW on SAP HANA

Data consolidation   The previously illustrated structure reveals that only SAP BW provides real data consolidation via different sources. From a technical point of view, other system data can be replicated to the SAP HANA database, for example, using SAP LT (see the SAP document "How to Realize Cross-System Reporting Using SAP HANA Live Content," via the URL *http://scn.sap.com/docs/DOC-42917*). A cross-enterprise reporting on the basis of harmonized, cleansed, and consolidated data, however, cannot be realized here. This is possible only if additional products, like SAP Data Services, are integrated with such a scenario. However, this results in complex and confusing solutions whose maintenance and extensibility is more complex than that of SAP BW.

Also, data preparation in SAP BW is outclassing the data preparation of SAP HANA Live. In SAP BW, you can unify the data of different source systems through partially complex computing operations, mapping tables, and transformations. Moreover, you can enrich raw data using meta information, such as data type, conversion procedure, description in various languages, time dependencies, and administration information. This allows for complex analyses with multi-language capability, as well as currency and unit conversion without major effort. When you use SAP HANA views within the scope of operational reporting, such comprehensive semantic concepts are missing, and a complex data preparation must be implemented, as well. Time- and version-dependent structures, such as time-dependent hierarchies, can't be implemented in SAP HANA Live. In SAP BW, by contrast, a query key date can be transferred when you execute reports. This key date uses the hierarchy version that is valid on this date. Finally, more complex logics can be realized in SAP BW by deploying user exits.

Data preparation

Detailed access rights can be managed for each SAP HANA Live model. But because no superordinate semantic level exists like SAP BW already provided, you must maintain these authorizations separately for each data model. If, for example, a user may view key figures for only a specific region, this restriction must be defined in the respective views. Currently, authorization variables or hierarchy-dependent authorizations cannot be implemented with SAP HANA Live.

Authorizations

If an SAP BW system is used (as recommended by SAP) for archiving operational enterprise data—for example, for implementing compliance regulations—you can create evaluations on chronological periods of time. Transactional systems, by contrast, archive operational data in periodic distances. Such data can no longer be evaluated using SAP HANA Live. Data that has been overwritten in the meantime is no longer available for reporting, either. In an SAP BW system, however, the history is usually available in its entirety for analysis.

Historical data

Planning   Very simple planning scenarios can be realized directly in the SAP HANA database via *stored procedures*. You can implement simple planning applications by combining query views with the OData interface (interface for data access in SAP HANA). The SAP BW system, on the other hand, provides Integrated Planning (SAP BW-IP) as a sophisticated solution for most complex planning procedures. This allows for planning based on historical data, for example. Chapter 5, Section 5.8 presented a performance-optimized extension for the accelerated execution of planning functions when you use SAP HANA.

Hybrid approach   Even though this section clearly illustrated the strengths of SAP BW, or SAP BW on SAP HANA, compared with the operational reporting approach based on SAP HANA Live, we'd like to encourage you to consider the usage of hybrid solutions. Chapter 5, Section 5.7 already described how to enrich external data with SAP BW master and transactional data and how to build comprehensive reporting. Deploying SAP BW on SAP HANA does not rule out the usage of SAP HANA Live. Both solutions have their own strengths, which must be combined skillfully. Figure 9.7 summarizes the recommendations for using SAP HANA Live and SAP BW on SAP HANA from the customer requirements' view.

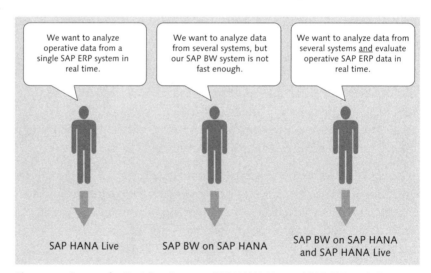

Figure 9.7 Support for Deciding Between SAP HANA Live and SAP BW on SAP HANA

With SAP HANA Live, it is not possible to build company-wide reporting on the basis of harmonized, cleansed, and consolidated data (*Single Point of Truth*) right now, nor will it be in the near future. If, however, only operational data of a single SAP Business Suite system is to be evaluated, the usage of SAP HANA is definitely an interesting option. Besides, the two approaches are not mutually exclusive. So, you should combine the various strengths of the solutions. The end of the SAP BW era is not foreseeable. Cards would only be reshuffled if SAP's vision becomes a reality in the remote future. This vision is that all SAP products of an enterprise use one SAP HANA database for data retention. Until then, we stick to our statement that the future use of SAP BW or SAP BW on SAP HANA is indispensable for company-wide reporting.

A   Appendix

This appendix provides some overviews that we hope will support you in your migration and subsequent work with SAP BW on SAP HANA.

A.1   List of Abbreviations

The following table gives an overview of abbreviations used in this book:

Abbreviation	Description
ABAP	Advanced Business Application Programming
AFL	Application Function Libraries
ALE	Application Link Enabling
ASCS	ABAP SAP Central Services
AWS	Amazon Web Services
BEx	Business Explorer
BFL	Business Function Library
BI	Business Intelligence
BICS	BI Consumer Services
BW	Business Warehouse
BWA	Business Warehouse Accelerator
BW-IP	BW Integrated Planning
CMC	Central Management Console
CO-PA	Profitability Analysis
D2D	Direct to Data
DB	Database
DBA	Database Administrator
DBCO or DBCON	Database Connection

Abbreviation	Description
DBSID	Database ID
DBSL	Database Shared Library
DBSL	Database Interface
DDIC	Data Dictionary
DMO	Database Migration Option
DNS	Domain Name System
DSO	DataStore Object
DTP	Data Transfer Process
EDI	Electronic Data Interchange
EP	SAP Enterprise Portal
ETL	Extract, Transform, Load
HBA	HANA-Based Analytics (former name of SAP HANA Live)
HEC	HANA Enterprise Cloud
HPI	Hasso Plattner Institute
IDocs	Intermediate Documents
ITaaS	Infrastructure as a Service
LSA	Layered Scalable Architecture
LT	Landscape Transformation
LVM	SAP Landscape Virtualization Management
MCOD	Multiple Components One Database
MDX	Multidimensional Expressions
MIGMON	Migration Monitor
NIST	National Institute of Standards and Technology
NLS	Nearline Storage
NUMA	Non-Uniform Memory Access
NW	NetWeaver

Abbreviation	Description
ODP	Operational Data Provisioning
ODQ	Operational Delta Queue
OLAP	Online Analytical Processing
OLTP	Online Transactional Processing
PaaS	Platform as a Service
PAK	Planning Application Kit
PAL	Predictive Analysis Library
PAM	Product Availability Matrix
PAS	Primary Application Server
PCA	Post Copy Automation
PoC	Proof of Concept
PSA	Persistent Staging Area
RDA	Real-Time Data Acquisition
RDS	Rapid Deployment Solutions
RFC	Remote Function Call
RHEL	Red Hat Enterprise Linux
SaaS	Software as a Service
SAP BPC	SAP Business Planning and Consolidation
SAP BWA	SAP Business Warehouse Accelerator
SCN	SAP Community Network
SHAF	SAP HANA Analytics Foundation (former name of SAP HANA Live)
SID	System ID
SLES	SUSE Linux Enterprise
SLT	System Landscape Transformation
SP	Support Package
SPS	Support Package Stack

Abbreviation	Description
SQL	Structured Query Language
SSO	Single Sign-On
SWPM	Software Provisioning Manager
TCO	Total Cost of Ownership
UAC	User Account Control
VDM	Virtual Data Model
VM	Virtual Machine
VMM	Virtual Machine Monitor
XS	Extended Application Server
XSJS	Extended Application Server JavaScript

A.2   SAP Notes Used

The following SAP Notes were referenced in this book:

SAP Note	Description
41300	Table DBTABPRT or DBTABLOG is very large
48400	Reorganization of TemSe and Spool
317096	Migration key generation for ABAP systems
430486	Overview/repair of F fact table of an BW InfoCube
434902	ALLOCATION: Many entries in Table DBTABLOG
449891	Temporary database objects in BW 3.x
505608	ALE: Reorganization IDOCREL
552464	What is Big Endian/Little Endian? What Endian do I have?
561961	Deactivating/activating usage of fact table view
590370	Too many uncompressed requests (f table partitions)

SAP Note	Description
666290	Deleting "orphaned" job logs
706478	Measures against fast growing basis tables
732470	Contract: Logging data changes
736976	RFKKCOPM/FP03F—dump for DATASET_REOPEN
752505	SAP system provisioning/installation problems
784969	Program RSBTCDEL2
789220	Support Package levels for SAP NetWeaver installations/upgrades
857081	Unicode Conversion: Estimated downtime
886102	Copy of the system landscape for SAP BW
937697	Using SAP NetWeaver BI Diagnostics & Support Desk Tool
966854	Reorganization—new report
1003894	RSBCS_REORG: Corrections
1009987	Compounding problem in MultiProviders
1031096	Installation of Package SAPHOSTAGENT
1067221	Composite note for heterogeneous installation
1139396	Temporary database objects in BW 7.x
1150724	Consolidated note on the check & repair reports for PSA
1310037	SUSE LINUX Enterprise Server 11: Installation Notes
1338943	Schedule Job BI_DELETE_OLD_MSG_PARM_DTP-TEMP – SAP&DEL_MSG
1370848	New master data deletion—information
1511501	P25: BATCH: Time selections for deleting old messages
1514966	SAP HANA 1.0: Sizing SAP in-memory database
1514967	SAP HANA: Central Note
1548125	Interesting facts about Inventory Cubes

SAP Note	Description
1572522	EDI/IDoc: Deleting and reorganizing IDocs with SARA
1589145	Task Manager for technical configuration
1592528	Delete authorization logs from BW table RSECLOG to gain memory space and improve performance
1594606	BW lock server and standalone enqueue server II
1600066	Available DBSL patches for NewDB
1600929	SAP BW powered by SAP HANA DB: Information
1614266	System Copy: Post Copy Automation 3.0/LVM 1.0
1626753	Activating Multiprovider hint on SAP HANA DB
1634681	DB Migration: Report for finding large row store tables
1637145	SAP BW on HANA: Sizing for SAP HANA
1637148	BW on HANA: Activating the Planning Application Kit
1637199	Using the Planning Application Kit
1644396	SMIGR: No data export of aggregate tables
1659383	RowStore list for SAP NetWeaver on SAP HANA database
1661202	Support for multiple applications on SAP HANA
1667731	Rapid database migration of SAP BW to SAP HANA
1695112	Activities in BW after migrating to the SAP HANA database
1695778	Partitioning BW tables in SAP HANA database
1702409	HANA-DB: Optimal number of scale out nodes for BW on HANA
1707321	BW System Copy: Automation of copy post-processing (BW PCA)
1729988	SAP BW, powered by SAP HANA—Checklist Tool
1736976	Sizing program for BW on HANA
1741844	Monitoring for the "non-active data" concept

SAP Note	Description
1766419	SYB: Usage of fact table view
1767880	"Non-active data" concept for BW on SAP HANA DB
1775293	Migration/system copy to HANA using the current SWPM 1.0
1778939	HANA planning functions: further developments
1797362	Dual-stack split for systems based on SAP NetWeaver
1808450	Homogeneous system landscape for SAP BW on SAP HANA
1813548	Database migration option (DMO) for Software Update Manager
1815547	Row/column store check without rowstorelist.txt
1821899	Distribution by keys in in-memory mode
1823174	BW 7.4 conversion and custom programs
1824819	SAP HANA database: Recommended operating system settings for SLES 11/SLES for SAP Applications 11 Support Package 2
1825774	SAP Business Suite powered by SAP HANA—multi-node support
1826585	SAP LT Replication Server for SAP BW (PSA)
1829728	Worklist for SAP BW Housekeeping
1846493	Important SAP Notes for SAP BW 7.3x, powered by SAP HANA
1847431	SAP BW: ABAP Routine Analyzer
1849151	SAP NetWeaver 7.4 Java on HANA release information
1855154	Planning functions DSO in-memory II
1869560	SAP BusinessObjects BI Support Matrix for SAP BW
1879618	Pre-upgrade measures for upgrade/update to 7.4
1887076	SAP BW Nearline Storage rapid-deployment solution

SAP Note	Description
1897236	HANA: Error "insufficient privilege: Not authorized" in SM21
1900822	Using the reorganization of the SAP HANA landscape from SWPM
1908367	SAP BW: transformation finder
1909597	SAP BW migration cockpit for SAP HANA
1913805	SAP Business Intelligence Adoption RDS V3.41
1914052	SAP NetWeaver 7.40 database dependencies
1921023	SMIGR_CREATE_DDL: corrections and enhancements for SAP HANA
1930178	ANALYZE_RSZ_TABLES: Selection split between local filters
1930335	BW-IP (PAK): default data processing option for Info-Providers
1930979	Alert: Sync/Async read ratio
1932459	BW DataSource: Loading data to multiple BW target systems not supported
1938158	How To: Clean up table RSBERRORLOG
1944799	SAP HANA guidelines for SLES operating system installation
1948334	SAP HANA database update paths for maintenance revisions
1949273	Important Notes for SAP BW 7.40, powered by SAP HANA
1951491	Minimal DB system platform requirements for SAP NetWeaver 7.4 SP08
1953429	SAP HANA and SAP NetWeaver AS ABAP on one server only
1953984	SHDB: Development of tool classes for NW 7.30 SP12
1965379	Correction of threshold values for alerts 60 and 61 in SAP HANA Revision 70 (Support Package Stack 7)

SAP Note	Description
2001528	Linux: SAP HANA Database SPS 08 revision 80 (or higher) on RHEL 6 or SLES 11
2009879	SAP HANA guidelines for Red Hat Enterprise Linux (RHEL)
2020199	SAP HANA database (SPS 08) Revision 80
2021789	SAP HANA revision and maintenance strategy
2022386	Migration to HANA. Software provisioning manager terminates when executing HdbSlLib: java.lang.OutOfMemoryError: Java heap space
2091812	BW update of Release 7.40 with SP05, SP06, or SP07 to SP08

A.3   ABAP Reports Used

The ABAP reports listed in the following table were discussed in this book and can be called using Transaction SE38:

ABAP Report	Description
/SDF/HANA_BW_SIZING	Determines the BW-relevant DB-size for HANA sizing
ADBC_TEST_CONNECTION	Tests a database connection defined in DBCON
BTCTRNS1	Transport system: Sets the "completed due to upgrade" status for jobs
RS_BW_POST_MIGRATION	Heterogeneous BW migration, invalidation of generated routines
RS_SYSTEM_SHUTDOWN	Stops and restarts BW processes
RSAR_PSA_NEWDS_MAPPING_CHECK	Checks the PSA tables under SAP HANA for inconsistencies
RSBATCH_DEL_MSG_PARM_DTPTEMP	Deletes old messages, parameters, and Temp.DTP data

ABAP Report	Description
RSDRI_RECONVERT_DATASTORE	Reconverts SAP HANA–optimized DSOs
RSDU_TABLE_CONSISTENCY	Checks tables for inconsistencies
RSPLS_PLANNING_ON_HDB_ANALY-SIS	Analysis: Do the planning functions run in the SAP HANA database?
RSR_MULTIPROV_CHECK	Deletes or rebuilds the metadata runtime (CL_RSD_MULTIPROV)
RSUPGRCHECK	Upgrade check
SAP_DROP_TMPTABLES	Removes temporary database objects
SAP_UPDATE_DBDIFF	SAP BW: Refreshes Table DBDIFF (inconsistencies DDIC-DB)
SMIGR_BIG_ROW_STORE_TABS	Determines the largest row-based tables
SMIGR_CREATE_DDL	Report SMIGR_CREATE_DDL: Generates DDL statements for migration
Z_SAP_NOTE_ANALYZER	Note analysis program
ZBW_ABAP_ANALYZER	SAP BW ABAP Routine Analyzer
ZBW_HANA_CHECKLIST	SAP BW Checklist for SAP HANA
ZBW_HANA_MIGRATION_-COCKPIT	SAP BW Migration Cockpit for SAP HANA
ZBW_TRANSFORM_FINDER	SAP BW Transformation Finder

A.4   Important Transactions

Here, we've compiled the most important transactions for SAP BW on SAP HANA:

Transaction	Description
AL11	Display SAP Directories
BDLS	Convert Logical System Names

Transaction	Description
DB02	Tables and Indexes Monitor
DB13	DBA Planning Calendar
DBACOCKPIT	Start DBA Cockpit
DBCO	Database Connection Maintenance
ODQMON	Monitor for Operational Delta Queue
RSA1	Modeling—BW Workbench
RSA7	BW Delta Queue Monitor
RSCUSTV23	BW Customizing—Authorization Concept
RSDANLCON	Set Up Near-Line Connections
RSDD_HM_PUBLISH	Publish HANA Model
RSECADMIN	Manage Analysis Authorizations
RSHDBMON	SAP HANA Database Monitoring
RSLIMOBW	Process (old) CompositeProviders
RSMIGRHANADB	Conversion of InfoCubes to SAP HANA-optimized
RSPC	Process Chain Maintenance
RSPLSE	BI Planning: Lock Management
RSRT	Start of the Report Monitor
RSSGPCLA	Maintain Program Class
RSZC	Copy BEx Queries
RZ04	Maintain SAP Instances
RZ10	Maintain Profile Parameters
RZ12	Maintain RFC Server Group Assignment
SARA	Archive Administration
SCU3	Table History
SE11	Maintain ABAP Dictionary
SE14	Utilities for Dictionary Tables
SE16	Data Browser

Transaction	Description
SE38	ABAP Editor
SECSTORE	Administration of Secure Storage
SICK	Installation Check
SLG1	Application Log: Display Logs
SLG2	Application Log: Delete Logs
SLICENSE	Manage SAP Licenses
SM04	User List
SM28	Installation Check
SM30	Call View Maintenance
SM37	Overview of Job Selection
SM58	Asynchronous RFC Error Log
SM59	RFC Destinations (Display and Maintenance)
SM63	Display/Maintain Operating Mode Sets
SM69	Maintain External OS Commands
SMLG	Maintain/Assign Logon Group to Instance
SMQR	Registration of the Inbound Queue
SNOTE	Note Assistant
SP12	TemSe Administration
SPAD	Spool Administration
SPRO	Customizing—Edit Project
STC01	Task Manager for Technical Configuration
STMS	Transport Management System
STRUST	Trust Manager
SU01	User Maintenance
SU10	Mass Maintenance User
WE20/WE21	Partner Agreements/Port Definition

A.5   Important Views

We've compiled some database views, which can be useful sources of information. They contain more detailed information than the corresponding overviews of SAP HANA Studio. The views are available in the database profile SYS, but you can use them via SQL as well, without specifying the profile.

View	Description
AFL_FUNCTIONS	List of all available functions of Advanced Function Libraries (AFLs)
M_HOST_INFORMATION	Hardware information on all database servers
M_HOST_RESSOURCE_UTILIZATION	General main memory information for each database server
M_SERVICE_MEMORY	Detailed main memory information for each process and database server
M_RS_TABLES	Table information for the rowstore (row-based tables)
M_CS_TABLES	Table information for the columnstore (column-based tables)
M_VOLUME_FILES	Overview of all data and log files on the hard disk
M_SHARED_MEMORY	Overview of the shared memory (main memory that is used by multiple processes at the same time)
M_SQL_PLAN_CACHE	Detailed evaluation of SQL statements
M_CS_UNLOADS	Tables unloaded from the memory
M_DELTA_MERGE_STATISTICS	Performance statistics on the delta merge process of tables
M_FEATURES	Version information for all HANA functions

A.6   SQL Statements

The following SQL statements for the main memory, housekeeping, and administration can be useful for your daily work in an SAP BW on SAP HANA system.

A.6.1   Main Memory

SQL Statement	Description
SELECT T1.HOST,T1.FREE_PHYSI-CAL_MEMORY, T1.USED_PHYSICAL_MEMORY+T2.SHARED_MEMORY_ALLO-CATED_SIZE, T2.PHYSICAL_MEMO-RY_SIZE,T1.FREE_PHYSICAL_MEM-ORY+T1.USED_PHYSICAL_MEMORY FROM M_HOST_RESOURCE_UTILIZATION AS T1 JOIN (SELECT M_SERVICE_MEMORY.HOST, SUM(M_SERVICE_MEMORY.PHYSICAL_MEMORY_SIZE) AS PHYSICAL_MEMORY_SIZE, SUM(M_SERVICE_MEM-ORY.SHARED_MEMORY_ALLOCATED_SIZE) AS SHARED_MEMORY_ALLO-CATED_SIZE FROM SYS.M_SER-VICE_MEMORY GROUP BY M_SER-VICE_MEMORY.HOST) AS T2 ON T2.HOST = T1.HOST	HANA Studio Overview: Calculate Database Resident/Total Resident/Physical Memory (in bytes)

SQL Statement	Description
SELECT M1.HOST AS HOST, M1.ALLOCATION_ LIMIT AS ALLOCATION_LIMIT, M1.INSTANCE_TOTAL_MEMORY_ USED_SIZE AS TOTAL_MEMORY_ USED_ SIZE, B1.PEAK+M1.INSTANCE_ CODE_SIZE+ M1.INSTANCE_ SHARED_MEMORY_ALLOCATED_ SIZE AS PEAK FROM SYS.M_ HOST_RESOURCE_UTILIZATION M1 JOIN (SELECT A2.HOST AS HOST, SUM(IFNULL (A1.INCLUSIVE_ PEAK_ALLOCATION_ SIZE, A2.HEAP_MEMORY_USED_ SIZE)) AS PEAK FROM SYS.M_ SERVICE_MEMORY A2 LEFT OUTER JOIN (SELECT HOST, PORT, INCLUSIVE_PEAK_ALLOCA- TION_SIZE FROM SYS.M_HEAP_ MEMORY_RESET WHERE DEPTH = 0) AS A1 ON A2.HOST = A1.HOST AND A2.PORT = A1.PORT GROUP BY A2.HOST) AS B1 ON M1.HOST = B1.HOST	HANA Studio Overview: Calculate Used Memory/Peak Used Memory/Allocation Limit (in bytes)

A.6.2   Housekeeping

SQL Statement	Description
SELECT COUNT(DNAME) FROM SAP< SID>.TST01 WHERE DNAME LIKE ' JOBLGX%'	Number of job logs in the system; according to SAP Note 48400, the number should not exceed 100,000 in a production system.

SQL Statement	Description
SELECT SCHEMA_ NAME AS "SCHEMA", ROUND(SUM(ALLOCATED_FIXED_ PART_SIZE + ALLOCATED_VARI- ABLE_PART_SIZE)/1024/ 1024) AS "SPEICHERPLATZ IN MB YTE", COUNT(TABLE_ NAME) AS "NUMBER OF TABLES" FROM M_RS_TABLES GROUP BY SCHEMA_NAME ORDER BY "MEMORY SPACE IN MBY TE" DESC	Memory space and number of all row-based tables, sorted by schema (in MB)
SELECT SCHEMA_ NAME AS "SCHEMA", ROUND(SUM(ALLOCATED_FIXED_ PART_SIZE + ALLOCATED_VARI- ABLE_PART_SIZE)/1024/ 1024) AS "MEMORY SPACE IN MBY TE", COUNT(TABLE_ NAME) AS "NUMBER OF TABLES" FROM M_RS_TABLES GROUP BY SCHEMA_NAME ORDER BY "MEMORY SPACE IN MBY TE" DESC	Memory space and number of all column-based tables, sorted by schema
SELECT (ALLOCATED_FIXED_PART_ SIZE + M_RS_TABLES.ALLOCATED_ VARIABLE_PART_SIZE) MEMORY_ SIZE_IN_TOTAL, TABLE_NAME FROM M_RS_TABLES WHERE SCHEMA_NAME = ' ' UNION ALL SELECT MEMORY_ SIZE_IN_TOTAL, TABLE_NAME FROM M_CS_TABLES WHERE SCHEMA_NAME = ' ' ORDER BY MEMORY_SIZE_IN_ TOTAL <SCHEMA> <SCHEMA> DESC	Union of row-based and column-based tables of the <SCHEMA> schema, sorted by size in descending order (in MB)

SQL Statement	Description
ALTER SYSTEM CLEAR TRACES('AL ERT', 'CLIENT', 'INDEXSERVER' , 'NAMESERVER', 'STATISTICSER VER','*');	Delete traces
SELECT SCHEMA_ NAME AS "SCHEMA", TABLE_ NAME AS "TABELLE", ROUND(MEM-ORY_SIZE_IN_TOTAL/1024/ 1024) AS "MEMORY SPACE IN MBY TE" FROM M_CS_TABLES ORDER BY "MEMORY SPACE IN MBY TE" DESC LIMIT 100	Memory requirement of the 100 largest column-based tables (in MB)
SELECT SCHEMA_ NAME AS "SCHEMA", TABLE_ NAME AS "TABELLE", ROUND((ALLOCATED_FIXED_PART_ SIZE + ALLOCATED_VARIABLE_ PART_SIZE)/1024/ 1024) AS "MEMORY SPACE IN MBY TE" FROM M_RS_TABLES ORDER BY "MEMORY SPACE IN MBY TE" DESC LIMIT 100	Memory requirement of the 100 largest row-based tables (in MB)

A.6.3 Administration

SQL Statement	Description
SELECT * FROM "SYS"."EFFECTIV E_ROLES" WHERE USER_NAME = '<USER>'	Output the role of the <USER> user
MERGE DELTA OF "<SCHEMA>"."<T ABLE>"	Execute delta merge for the "<SCHEMA>"."<TABLE>" table

SQL Statement	Description
SELECT SCHEMA_NAME, TABLE_ NAME, RAW_RECORD_COUNT_IN_ DELTA FROM "SYS"."M_CS_ TABLES" WHERE RAW_RECORD_ COUNT_IN_DELTA <> 0 ORDER BY RAW_RECORD_COUNT_IN_ DELTA DESC	Output number of delta store rows
SELECT * FROM M_SESSION_ CONTEXT WHERE CONNECTION_ID = CURRENT_CONNECTION	Display processes of own connection
SELECT SCHEMA_NAME, OBJECT_ NAME, OWNER_ NAME from OWNERSHIP	Displays the database objects (for example, tables, procedures, and so on) and their owners

B   The Authors

Dr. Matthias Merz holds a degree in information management and has worked in the SAP environment for more than 10 years. At Camelot ITLab GmbH, he leads the Center of Excellence for SAP HANA and provides consultation for enterprises, particularly in the area of SAP BW on SAP HANA. In addition to the implementation of customer projects, his work focuses on the evaluation of new software technologies and the publication of specialist articles. He was previously employed at a data center where he focused on high-performance computing and SAP Basis administration.

Steve Blum is a junior consultant at Camelot ITLab GmbH and works at the Center of Excellence for SAP HANA. His working fields in the SAP BW on SAP HANA environment include SAP HANA XS development, SAP HANA administration, nearline storage, and the evaluation of new functions. In the context of co-operative studies at SAP, he received his Bachelor of Science in information management. During this time, he worked in various departments in the SAP BW and SAP HANA environment, as well as in the field of process consultation.

Dr. Torben Hügens is head of Reporting and Performance Management at Camelot ITLab GmbH. He was previously employed at SAP Deutschland AG & Co. KG and worked as a consultant in the SAP BusinessObjects Business Intelligence/SAP Business Warehouse area. Initially, his work focused on the creation of reports using SAP BusinessObjects BI products and the design of data flows in SAP BW. Since then, his focus has shifted to the area of business transformation services. Here, his tasks include the design and optimization of enterprise-wide reporting solutions, as well as project management. In addition, he provides consultation regarding the design and implementation of holistic solutions for strategic management using SAP Strategy Management.

Index

▶ Get the basics on working with SAP BW

▶ Use step-by-step instructions to master data modeling, ETL, reporting, and more

▶ Learn about new developments in the 7.4 release

Palekar, Patel, Shiralkar

SAP BW 7.4—Practical Guide

Don't just read about SAP BW — get your hands dirty with this must-have guide. Tackle all of the common tasks you'll encounter when working with SAP BW, from creating objects to mastering the BEx tools. Keep your skills sharp with information new to this edition, including updates for SAP BW 7.4 and BW on SAP HANA. You'll also follow along with a comprehensive case study to cement your knowledge.

851 pages, 3rd edition, 2015, $69.95/€69.95
ISBN 978-1-4932-1191-3
www.sap-press.com/3733

Interested in reading more?

Please visit our website for all new
book and e-book releases from SAP PRESS.

www.sap-press.com